FUN & GAMES FOR A SMARTER DOG

FUN & GAMES FOR A SMARTER DOG

Sophie Collins

lumina
MEDIA

First published in the UK by
Ivy Press
Ovest House
58 West Street
Brighton
BN1 2RA
www.ivypress.co.uk

ISBN: 978-1-62187-120-0

This book was conceived, designed, and produced by
Ivy Press
Publisher: Susan Kelly
Creative Director: Michael Whitehead
Art Director: Wayne Blades
Editorial Director: Tom Kitch
Designer: Tania Gomes
Photographer: Neal Grundy
Dog Handler: Michelle Garvey
Agility Course Designer: Janet L. Gauntt
Agility Course Illustrator: John Woodcock
Editorial Assistant: Jenny Campbell

LUMINA MEDIA™
Chairman: David Fry
Chief Executive Officer: Keith Walter
Chief Financial Officer: David Katzoff
Chief Digital Officer: Jennifer Black-Glover
Vice President Content: Joyce Bautista-Ferrari
Vice President Marketing & PR: Cameron Triebwasser
Managing Director, Books: Christopher Reggio
Art Director, Books: Mary Ann Kahn
Senior Editor, Books: Amy Deputato
Production Director: Laurie Panaggio
Production Manager: Jessica Jaensch

The Library of Congress Catalog-in-Publication Data has been applied for.

Lumina Media
2030 Main Street, Suite 1400
Irvine, CA 92614
www.facebook.com/luminamediabooks
www.luminamedia.com

Printed and bound in China
19 18 17 16   2 4 6 8 10 9 7 5 3 1

Front Cover Photo: Antonio Gravante/Shutterstock

CONTENTS

INTRODUCTION

When it comes to teaching your dog, one thing is certain: you won't be short of advice. Whether you have a new puppy, have just adopted a rescue dog, or have decided that the affable but not-so-obedient family pet that you've had for some years needs a behavioral tune-up, there are a lot of dog-training experts around. Many will simply tell you, unasked, on the street or at the park, that you're doing something wrong, while others will offer alternatives; some will insist that your dog won't respect you unless you dominate him (in particular, ignore these ones), others will tell you about the perfect pet professional who turned their problem pet around. And, of course, this book, too, is one of many, plenty of which offer conflicting advice. All this can create a lot of confusion. So how can you teach your dog in a way that will build your relationship, make sure you have fun together, and incorporate lessons that will help him to get along in our human-managed society? And can it be done in a way that will keep—or get—you both fit, too, and generally make you both happy?

It's a lot to ask, but you do have one true expert on hand, and that's your dog himself. Among all the information people will offer you, something is often overlooked—that we can learn as much, or more, from dogs as they can learn from us. After all, they live in a world that is made for people, following people's rules. Generally, they manage this successfully; far more so than most people would if the situation were reversed and they were transplanted into a world of dogs.

Domestic dogs are, as a species, extraordinary adaptable and tolerant. They are highly social animals that collect huge amounts of information from us, often learning more from our body language than from what we tell them verbally (more on that later). Their senses are more developed than ours. With noses around a thousand times more sensitive, they naturally rely on smell for a lot of their daily news and make up the balance largely with minute observation of what's going on around them. True, they can't talk, but they both watch and listen intently. They're also remarkably forgiving. Even after you've messed up the job of teaching them something simple, confusing your signals, sending conflicting body language, and raising your voice instead of concentrating on what you're saying, your dog will usually still be hanging in there, looking to you for amended instructions and remaining willing to try to understand, however confusing you're being.

These are all good reasons for you to take the trouble to learn to teach your dog properly and patiently, with a consciousness of what usually works and what may not, and with an awareness that your dog is a dog, not a small and sympathetic person in a furry coat. The chapters that follow take account of all these factors.

Working with your dog should continue throughout his life as part of your owner/pet relationship. At some point, you will probably feel that he is trained—when he knows what's considered acceptable, both at home and out and about, and sticks to the rules most of the time. But if you stop there, as many people do, you'll be missing a trick (sometimes literally). Because a mix of training and playing is fun, and a short session—ten minutes is enough—over and above the walking and playtime that dog owners build into every day will bring rewards out of proportion to how long it takes. Mix things you want him to know with things he loves doing, keep it fresh by interweaving elements of routine with challenges and surprises, and you'll have a pet who stays young for his years and who'll always welcome the chance to spend more time with you.

And what about the "smarter" part of the equation? Can you really train your dog to be smarter? It may not be the case that you can actually raise his canine IQ, but with short, regular, consistent playing-and-training sessions, you can build on his strengths, get rid of most day-to-day difficulties, broaden his horizons, and be sure he's an all-around good canine citizen with plenty of personality and a healthy respect for the rules. All of which adds up to a smart dog.

PLAYING SAFE

There are almost endless possibilities when it comes to games and activities you can play with your dog. Before you start, however, it is essential that you make sure you will be playing safe.

AGE AND FITNESS

Almost every dog can play some games, learn some tricks, and enjoy doing both. If you're teaching a particularly young or old dog, however, be careful that you don't push him too far. Dogs that are still at the growing and developing stage (under a year and up to two years in some breeds) shouldn't do any jumping and shouldn't be allowed to overtire themselves, so use your common sense if your dog seems to be wearing himself out—a young dog won't always know when he's had enough. At the other end of the age scale, don't push an elderly dog beyond his comfort zone; the stamina of a ten-year-old probably won't be as high as that of a dog in his prime of fitness, and older or arthritic pets shouldn't be overexcited so much that they hurt themselves.

Jumping, standing or "walking" on their back legs, or turning awkwardly can all cause injuries that may recur or lead to long-term strain or weakness in young, old, overweight, or unfit dogs, so use your common sense when judging what's suitable for your particular pet. Additionally, brachycephalic breeds (those with flat faces, such as Bulldogs) should not be allowed to overexert themselves. In the following chapters, we've included a note in cases where the occasional trick or game isn't the best choice for a puppy, an older dog, or a less fit dog, plus suggestions on how to modify it, if necessary.

KNOW YOUR DOG

If you're playing with your own dog, you are probably the person who knows best what he will enjoy, and you can play to his strengths. If you're with a dog that isn't yours, check his preferences with his owner and be careful and observant during play. You need to know about a dog's behavioral tendencies before you start. For example, if a dog tends to get be guarded about favorite toys, it's best to get him familiar with the idea of leaving (see pages 56–57) or swapping (see pages 86–87) before you introduce a toy-based game; dogs who tend to engage in one-upmanship need to be introduced carefully and in a controlled way to competitive games, such as tug. If your pet isn't enthused by a particular activity, don't keep pushing it at him—instead, try a different one. There are plenty of choices, and he'll learn much more easily if you focus on his strengths, whether he turns out to be an athlete, a thinker, or even a clown who loves to play to an audience.

CHILDREN AND DOGS

Children and their pets can have great play relationships, but they should always be carefully managed. Never leave a young child alone with a dog. If excitement ramps up too far, the high-pitched shouting of children can agitate dogs, and play can turn snappy. Younger children need to be taught how to play appropriately without manhandling or scaring a dog. Prolonged eye contact—in particular, when it's at the dog's own eye level, as a toddler often will be—must be avoided. Dogs aren't generally comfortable being stared at, and if a child is at face level with a dog, he or she is also at jaw level if the dog feels threatened—this is why children often get bitten. Make sure you supervise play between children of any age and your dog, don't allow small children to pull him around, and either discourage chase games or police them extremely carefully (a dog is more probable to jump up and nip in excitement when he "catches" the child). Engage children in teaching exercises from the start. Training your dog through all the stages of an easy exercise with a child's help is an excellent way for them to learn how to get along together in an enjoyable way.

BE OBSERVANT

Problems in dog/person play often arise because one species is misunderstanding the body language of the other. Learn to watch your dog carefully as you teach. Getting into the habit of being observant around him will familiarize you with his norm, and thus make you aware of when a game isn't as much fun for him as it is for you, as well as of any dislikes or sensitivities that need to be managed.

Remember, too, that every dog is an individual and will have different enthusiasms and limits. An enjoyable game of finding a treat for one dog may overstimulate another; a natural retriever may love games that teach him to carry different items, while another dog may not see the point of carrying things at all. Make informed choices, and your games will be fun for both of you.

CHAPTER 1

PLAY AND TRAINING

UNDERSTANDING HOW DOGS THINK ABOUT PLAY

Not all species love to play, but both humans and dogs belong in the category that do. If you've lived around dogs, you'll have found that a lot of interaction comes naturally—throwing a ball, playing a game of chase, or coaxing certain behavior using treats are probably all activities you've enjoyed with your pet without even thinking about them. However, if you want to use play in a broader way, to train your dog or encourage his initiative, it's worth learning a little more about how play develops in dogs and how you can take advantage of a dog's natural behaviors.

NATURAL PLAY

Play comes naturally to dogs, and puppies are usually actively exploring their surroundings from the time they are three weeks old, using their paws and mouths and tumbling with their littermates. By four weeks, any time not spent feeding or sleeping will generally be taken up by an indistinguishable mixture of playing and exploration.

GAME OR PRACTICE?

Small puppies spend a little time playing with their mother (and the dam will use the "games" to start teaching them polite canine behavior—for example, holding down with a paw a puppy who nips too hard), but they spend far more time, as they grow, with their siblings. If you watch one-month-old puppies, you'll see recognizable games. They will play rudimentary chase and rollover games with another puppy, and they will play solo, too, rolling a ball and running after it, and exploring other objects with their teeth.

So far, so familiar: Many playful exercises could have originated as practice for the life of an adult dog in the wild—a dog that has to catch or scavenge for its own food. And to some extent, puppies' games mirror the behavior seen in plenty of other young mammal species that also enjoy playing when they're immature but lose their enthusiasm for play as they transition into the serious business of adulthood.

A TRAIT IN COMMON

Although not all species take their playfulness beyond adolescence into maturity, both dogs and humans do. Dogs appear to understand play for the sake of it much as people do, purely for the pleasure of the moment, either in the enjoyment of a toy or in the interaction with other dogs or with people. Most dogs can be encouraged into one form of play or other, and if they see the impulse in others, they recognize it. Dog to dog, they've developed a fluent body language that other playful dogs read and respond to, from the play bow that acts as an invitation, to the wide-open mouth that marks play nipping as not being serious. It's worth learning by watching dogs play together, so that you, too, become familiar with the signs that behavior is only play or something more serious. You will then know whether or not to move in and interrupt play that's getting too intense and learn to recognize when the dogs are just having fun together.

WHAT IF YOUR DOG DOESN'T LIKE TO PLAY?

Just like people, some dogs are more playful than others. Some are natural clowns, others have more reserve, and still others see a game as a job to do—this last group tends to be particularly easy to teach to perform tricks, because they like to have an aim with a treat and praise as the end result. In the rare case that a dog really doesn't want to engage in play, you'll find ideas in the following chapters for how to encourage him.

WHEN PLAY = TRAINING

Too often in the past, training your dog and playing with your dog have been treated as different activities. Training is the hard work, the thinking goes, while playing is the reward you both enjoy when the work is over. But there's no reason you can't teach your dog by playing with him. Games can strengthen your bond, encourage your pet to be more attentive to your signals, and make your relationship more enjoyable all-around.

DOES YOUR DOG KNOW THE DIFFERENCE?

Can your dog tell whether he's learning a lesson or playing a game? The short answer is no. Studies show that dogs' distanced awareness (the degree that they are able to see themselves in a situation as if by a third party looking on) probably doesn't extend far. If you're playing a hunt-out-the-treat game, for instance, your pet probably won't be wondering whether you're teaching him a lesson or not. He'll be aware that he's interacting with you, that the interaction is positive, and that he can't wait to find the next treat. His high concentration level will help him to think hard (as the treats are hidden in increasingly tough-to-nose-out places), and he will look to you for your cooperation (hints for where he'll find the next treat) in continuing an activity he's enjoying. It's a win/win situation.

WHERE DOES THE TRAINING COME INTO IT?

Every time your dog engages with you, he's learning to read your signals better. If you play with him with specific goals, you can use play to channel his concentration, which, in turn, will help to build the bond between you. In the process, you'll be sending increasingly clear signals about what you want him to do—and showing him that doing what you want has a positive outcome. He gets something he enjoys by behaving in the way you want. It's operant conditioning at its simplest, and it works.

DO DOGS LEARN IN DIFFERENT WAYS?

To some extent, every dog will learn in the same way, but, like people, dogs have different personalities, and some are naturally smarter than others (just as some are more affectionate, or more energetic), so it makes sense to engage with your dog in a way that suits his strengths. The chapters that follow cover all kinds of games and activities, but they also offer suggestions for tailoring them to your own dog's preferences.

For example, if you have a dog that goes from zero to fifty miles per hour on the excitement scale when you show him a squeaky toy, but what you really want is for him to be less hyper when he engages with you, pay particular to the Brain Games chapter (see pages 88–113), which offers ways for you to help your pet focus without tipping him into overexcitement. He'll still think he's playing when you offer these games, but he'll be playing toward the goal you want.

WHICH DOG
BREEDS AND PLAY

A couple of hundred years ago, it would have been taken for granted that every dog had a job to do, whether it was killing rats or herding sheep. Today, every dog has a working heritage, whatever his breed or breed mix. Does the breed of your dog genetically affect the way he plays? Although there isn't a solid yes-or-no answer to the question, most professional trainers would say that it does to some extent, and your dog's breed origins may offer clues to some of his behavioral tendencies.

SHOW CATEGORIES

Most national kennel clubs divide dogs into breed categories that depend on the functions that the breeds originally served. While these categories vary a little both in naming and in the ways in which they are divided—for example, the Herding Group recognized by the American Kennel Club (AKC) is broadly equivalent to the Pastoral categorization in the UK—they make it easy to place a label on a dog's heritage and the probable hardwiring of his personality. The AKC's categories are Toy, Terrier, Herding, Sporting, Hound, Working, and Non-Sporting (the mixed bag of the selection); the UK's are Toy, Terrier, Pastoral, Gundog, Hound, Working, and Utility (the closest equivalent to the AKC's Non-Sporting). Categorizing dogs by their class can be a blunt instrument and may also lead to stereotyping of the "of course, all terriers love digging" kind, but it usually gives some idea of what to expect of their personality and play style. It's worth thinking about your pet's breed when you're looking at the issues of training and teaching him.

TYPICAL OF HIS BREED?

If you have a purebred dog, you'll have been told often what his characteristics are supposed to be. Along with training advice, there's nothing that other dog owners like to share so much, and you will find that it's an area where everyone tends to be an expert. The owners of toy dogs laugh about their pets' Napoleon complexes, while terrier lovers will agree that their dogs are tenacious, stubborn, energetic, and often noisy. Spaniels are known to follow their noses ("ideal for tracking"), while Border Collies are incredibly clever but can become obsessive if they don't have enough exercise and mental stimulation. Every dog has his own definition, and your own example of the breed may conform to it to a greater or lesser degree. Do not let the labels blind you to your dog's personal preferences or stop you from experimenting. There are plenty of exceptions in every class, and the best way to keep any dog enthused with tricks and games is to alternate the old favorites with something fresh and surprising.

WHAT THE GROUPS MEAN: A SHORT GUIDE

You can take the definitions with a pinch of salt, but this is the official view of the main dog groups as defined within the American and UK Kennel Clubs. Other kennel clubs vary in the breeds included within different groups but generally follow these categories with some variations.

 TOY

Small dogs originally bred as companions. Within this group, however, toys are a general class, because the group includes miniatures of dogs of other types; for example, a toy terrier might share typical terrier characteristics, while a diminutive Italian Greyhound may behave more like a Greyhound, its large sighthound brother.

TERRIER

Breeds created to hunt small prey or vermin, such as rats or rabbits. Terriers are considered to be willful, determined, energetic, and sometimes stubborn.

HERDING/PASTORAL

Bred for herding (and sometimes guarding) livestock. As you might expect from a broad group encompassing the Corgis, the Border Collie, and the Maremma, characteristics are varied, with some breeds coming hardwired with stronger herding instincts than others.

SPORTING/GUNDOG

Generally bred to assist with either sighting and flushing game or retrieving game after it has been shot. Includes spaniels, pointers, and retrievers, plus some less familiar breeds. Usually labeled "trainable" and often with strong sight or scent bias.

HOUND

Bred to hunt and divided into two types, depending on the way they were traditionally used: scenthounds and sighthounds. The former, originally used for tracking, have exceptionally sensitive noses (even by canine standards), while the latter, originally used in the chase, have exceptional speed.

WORKING

A group that, in most kennel clubs, encompasses large breeds that work, but in a non-sporting context, often intelligent and responsive guarding or search-and-rescue dogs, including breeds such as the Doberman Pinscher, the Newfoundland, and the St. Bernard.

NON-SPORTING/UTILITY

The catchall group, covering most breeds that, while bred for a purpose, don't fit into any of the other categories, usually because that purpose is specific. No class that covers Poodles, Dalmatians, or French Bulldogs can have even the broadest generalizations made about its members, who must be "read" by individual breed instead of as a group.

THE OBSESSIVE

Less an aspect of personality than a type of behavior, obsession can crop up when you're teaching your dog. It may emerge over a toy or a particular kind of play; for example, a ball-obsessive dog will want to play with a particular ball, and it will prove hard to move his focus onto any other activity. If you find that your dog has this tendency, you need to respond by keeping play activities lively and play objects varied so that his focus shifts to you and away from the subject of his obsession. There's more on coping with a toy-obsessed dog on pages 30–31.

WHICH DOG
PERSONALITY AND PLAY

Whether or not your dog conforms to his breed standard, first and foremost he is an individual. He may be a typical terrier or spaniel, but, just as important, he has his own personality. As his owner, it's unlikely that anyone knows him better than you, and you can probably tell how he will adapt to new ideas even before you begin to introduce them.

Every breeder knows that personality tends to come over and above breed. A litter of, say, Golden Retrievers, a breed known for its skills with people and its great trainability, will still have its rogue, its clown, its shy guy, and its genius. And while it's simplistic to reduce individual personalities to types, certain traits will affect how your dog learns, whoever it is that's teaching him.

"YES DOG" OR FREE THINKER?

Dog trainers joke that when an owner boasts about how smart their pet is, the correct rejoinder is "bad luck." Of course, there's nothing wrong with an inherently smart dog, but if he's able to think around what you want him to do, he may decide he'd prefer to do something else. To some extent, independent thinking may be decided by breed. Dogs that have been bred for generations to guard sheep sensibly may have the genes that dictate that they are mostly self-motivated rather than ones that are directed by the desire to please. However, independent dogs crop up in every breed, and they can present more challenges than an easygoing dog who just wants to have fun and who naturally looks to you for guidance.

SHY OR FEARFUL?

The other canine personality that may need some extra thought when you're training is the shy or fearful dog. The timidity may be the result of an under-socialized puppyhood, during which your pet wasn't given the opportunity of getting familiar with all the experiences the world has to offer, or it may come naturally with a dog that simply prefers the quiet life and is apprehensive about new challenges. If it seems to you that your dog belongs in this category, take things slowly and never try to coerce him into anything he clearly doesn't want to do. A slow-and-steady approach generously scattered with rewards should eventually persuade even a shy dog that some things are worth learning.

THE TEAM PLAYER

The team-player dog is usually the most straightforward to teach. He's confident without being too self-reliant. He's eager to interact with you, and he generally thinks that something new will probably be something that's fun. If you have a team player at home, teaching him tricks and games to develop his skills shouldn't provide too many problems.

ABOUT YOU
WHAT *YOU* NEED TO DO

When you're teaching a dog something new and problems crop up, it can seem natural to blame the dog for being slow or just not getting it. There are occasional "About You" pages in the chapters that follow. These are there to encourage you to check what you're doing yourself. Are you confusing your dog or sending him mixed messages by the way you're behaving? There is a range of common mistakes we make with dogs that arise from basic differences in canine/human body language.

BODY LANGUAGE—THE EXPERTS

Most dogs are able to read our body language faster and in more detail than another human can, and often it leads them to draw the wrong conclusion—or at least not the conclusion we want them to draw. From the human side, we can be extraordinarily dense when it comes to understanding that our dogs don't speak English. Pay more attention than usual to how you're standing and what you're doing with your hands, and be aware of whether or not you're moving around. Get someone to watch you to see whether you're sending unconscious signals.

WHAT DID YOU SAY?

Dogs can learn to do many things, but our verbal instructions are only a small part of the picture. And it's hard for us to limit ourselves to short instructions, said once. Unless we get an instant result, we tend immediately to repeat and—worse still—to elaborate: "Come here, Rex, come boy, here, HERE, to me," and so on. No wonder that dogs end up looking for clues in our body language to figure out what it is we want them to do.

WHEN YOUR VOICE AND BODY DON'T MATCH

A well-known behaviorist tells a story about a dog that was brought to her because, although he seemed bright enough, his owner couldn't seem to teach him anything apart from "Sit," and the dog was becoming increasingly tense in training sessions.

The behaviorist watched them together and noticed that the owner always gave a brief, unconscious nod when she gave her dog a direction, whatever the direction was, and the dog had clearly decided that the nod was his signal. He knew his owner wanted him to do something, and because the first thing she'd taught him to do was "Sit"—using a nod as the signal, or so he thought—he sat. Every time.

It was only when the behaviorist watched the "unteachable" dog that the problem was diagnosed. As soon as the owner knew what the issue was, she stopped nodding, and the dog quickly began to widen his repertoire. It illustrates how carefully we have to watch exactly what we're doing with our own faces and bodies, as well as voices, when we set out to teach our pets.

IF YOUR DOG DOESN'T LIKE STRANGE NOISES

If you know that your dog has a tendency to be frightened of unfamiliar noises, buy a quiet or adjustable clicker (the level and type of noise clickers make varies; test different kinds in the store before you buy), and when you use it, hold it behind your back instead of pointing it toward your dog.

CLICKER TRAINING

Using a clicker helps you to get your timing exactly right when you're teaching your dog. A clicker is a small boxlike gadget enclosing a flat strip of metal that produces a distinctive "click" sound when you press it with your thumb—a clear, clean noise that a dog can pick up and respond to easily. You can use it to reinforce your dog's actions. Having accustomed him to the way it works, you click it just as he is doing what you want him to do, whether that's sitting, fetching, or anything else.

The principle is to use the clicker as an event marker for your dog. The click happens immediately when the dog behaves in the way you want and signals that a reward will follow. It's particularly useful if you find it difficult to keep your requests short, or if you tend to do too much talking as you teach.

WHAT ARE YOU GOING TO DO?
Teach your dog what a clicker means—and that is that a reward is coming.

1. Wait for a moment when your dog isn't engaged by anything, and have a pocketful of small but high-value treats (such as tiny pieces of cheese or sausage) on hand. Click the clicker and give your dog a treat. Now the clicker will become an object of interest.
2. Click it again, and again give him a treat. (If he looks up and moves toward you, that's great, but at this point the treat is unconditional—he's learning that click equals treat.)
3. Spend a few days practicing with a short session every day without adding any new elements, until your dog clearly associates the click with the treat he's going to get and the clicker is getting his attention instantly.

4. Now you can move on to things your dog already knows how to do and incorporate the clicker. For example, if you're telling him to sit, say "Sit." And at the moment he's in the act of sitting, click the clicker and follow up—immediately—with a treat.

The click happens as your pet does what you want him to do and sends a clear message that it's the right thing to do. It's a noise that isn't easily confused with anything else and, provided you can master the split-second timing needed to click just when your dog is doing the thing you've asked rather than before he starts or after he's finished, the clicker is a successful way to train.

WHAT HE LEARNS
Your dog will learn that the click means a treat, and he will quickly figure out the specific behavior that earns the treat.

WHY IT'S USEFUL
Once your dog is accustomed to a clicker, you can use it out and about as well as at home and in circumstances in which he might otherwise be distracted. It's also a useful tool when you start to teach tricks or games that happen in several stages.

USING TOYS

For many of the games and exercises in the following chapters, you'll need some toys, preferably ones that your dog is already interested in. Whether he already has a box full of toys with plenty of favorites or prefers a found toy, such as an empty plastic bottle, most play and many training exercises need props. Knowing what your dog will choose as his favorite over any other can also give you clues about the games and activities he will probably be smartest at.

SAFE TOYS

Make sure that your dog's toys are safe for him to play with. This isn't always as simple as buying a toy that's labeled as suitable for dogs, because there are plenty that are sold as being appropriate that aren't made well or strong enough. You know how your dog plays and will have a good idea of how much he chews and how strong his jaws are, so judge for yourself whether a specific toy is sturdy enough.

DIFFERENT KINDS OF TOY

Invest in a few different toy types, and think about what your dog likes best. "Take It" and "Fetch" games will be much easier to teach if you already have a toy that your dog is happy to pick up. Some dogs get excited by a toy that squeaks, so you can consider one or two of those, too, and use it both to dial up excitement levels as you play and to manage that excitement and teach your dog self-control by making access to the toy conditional on particular behaviors.

Almost every dog enjoys a tennis ball, a basketball, or a soccer ball. Pick an appropriate ball for your pet. If you have a large dog, a tennis ball may be too small to play with (it can get stuck in the dog's throat if grabbed too enthusiastically), so

use your common sense. If your pet prefers a basketball, keep it well inflated or he'll puncture it in a game. In a lively game of catch or chase, the ball can be good punctuation in a training session where you've been asking your pet to think hard.

If you want your pet to entertain himself when you're out or going to be busy for an hour or two, the safest pick is probably a tough, hollow rubber Kong-type toy you can fill it with food so your dog can take his time figuring out how to extract it. If you have a strong chewer, it may be best not to leave him with toys at all; some dogs can destroy even "indestructible" toys, so use your common sense.

TOYS AS REWARDS

If your pet isn't particularly greedy, food may not always be enough of an incentive to get him to concentrate. If so, use a favorite toy in training sessions instead. Make sure that he knows that you have it on hand; if it's not actually incorporated into the game or exercise you're working on, place it in view and glance at it significantly when you're asking your dog to work on something. Then, when he manages to do what you're asking, grab the toy and offer it to him.

DON'T PLAY WITH WOODEN STICKS

If your dog loves to play with a stick, buy one of the rubber sticks available instead of letting him take them straight from nature. Why? Veterinarians will tell you that stick injuries (normally from splinters or swallowing the stick) are common. It is better to be safe than sorry.

DO

- Do make sure your dog is getting plenty of exercise. Obsessions tend to arise when he's got too much mental energy to spare. Take him for extra-long walks or play an energetic game that doesn't involve the toy he's obsessed with.
- If his focus is on a specific toy, wait until he's distracted and remove it. You're not being unkind. The toy isn't making him happy, and he may actually be relieved that you've taken the responsibility away from him.
- If his obsession is on an activity—playing "Fetch," for example—include it in your routine, but for a set, short time and after some energetic exercise doing something else.

DON'T

- Don't challenge him directly over a toy he has become guarded around. Wait until he leaves it (at some point he will, although you may have to wait) and substitute it for something new and exciting that you can play with together.
- Don't encourage his excitement when you're trying to limit access to an activity he's obsessed with—behave as if "Fetch," or whatever the game is, is something you're prepared to engage in but find slightly dull.
- Don't narrow down his choice of toys and games. Instead, provide plenty of alternatives and introduce some new ones; this tactic may help to refocus his attention.

DEALING WITH A TOY-OBSESSED DOG

Sometimes a dog will become completely focused on a particular item, usually a toy. This isn't the same as having a favorite toy that he enjoys carrying around and perhaps taking to bed with him, or being excited by a game of "Fetch" or football. Instead, it's an extreme, intense, uncomfortable focus that means that he can't relax around a specific item or in a situation in which he has access to it.

HOW CAN YOU TELL IF HE'S GETTING OBSESSIVE?

Dogs that become obsessive tend to be those who, in a working life, might be herding or hunting breeds, with personalities in which concentration and intelligence are combined. And obsession isn't always limited to toys—dogs can become overly focused on activities, too. Some may dig obsessively, while occasionally a dog may even become completely engrossed in chasing or stalking light and shadow patterns as they move around the room. You can tell that your dog has moved beyond play, because the object or activity won't seem to bring him pleasure anymore; it will make him anxious and he may become guarded around it. If it's a toy, he won't want you to pick it up or interact with him when he has it, and if it's an activity, he may growl and be bad-tempered if he's interrupted in the course of it.

WHAT TO DO

If you've spotted signs that your dog's developing an obsession, you need to deal with it—it probably won't solve itself. Behaviorists offer a variety of possible solutions, depending on what the focus of the obsession is and how strongly it's taken hold. The key to sorting things out is to distract your dog and refocus his attention elsewhere. When you're trying to get him to stop doing something, the emphasis should be on what you *do* want him to do instead.

If, after you've tried all these suggestions, the obsession doesn't improve, get professional help. Ask around and do some in-depth research to find a trainer or behaviorist with a proven record in kind, noncoercive methods.

CHAPTER 2

BASIC GAMES

USING PLAY TO TEACH

Play is a high-value activity for both humans and dogs—you only have to look at the popularity of ball games with both species (although dogs are less enthusiastic about the spectator role than people are). As well as offering all kinds of different stimulation—new ways of thinking, exercise, and sheer fun—play also gives your dog the chance to interact with you. And because play is so valuable, it's a great tool for you to use in training your dog in the behaviors you want—and to discourage those that you don't.

PRINCIPLES OF PLAY

Your dog won't differentiate between exercises and play if he's having fun. To make sure that your training time together is both enjoyable and useful, get into good habits and stick to them. Here's how:

TEN RULES FOR TEACHING YOUR DOG SUCCESSFULLY

- **RULE 1:** Never start a session when your dog is already tired or cranky; equally, you may want to take the edge off his energy before you try to get him to play mind games with you—perhaps get into the habit of doing ten minutes of exercises at the end of a daily walk.

- **RULE 2:** Only teach your dog when you're in a positive frame of mind. If you're feeling angry or impatient, it will communicate itself to your pet, and the session probably won't be a success.

- **RULE 3:** Try a range of exercises in every session. Even if you only commit to ten minutes once a day, daily (time enough to get good results), aim to do two exercises your pet already knows or almost knows, and one that's new to him. This will keep it fresh and keep boredom at bay.

- **RULE 4:** When an exercise consists of more than one stage, don't overload your dog; teach him each stage separately before putting them together.

- **RULE 5:** Alternate active games with thinking exercises; most owners find that they get better results if they vary the pace when they're teaching.

- **RULE 6:** If your dog doesn't get it, take a step back. If you've tried something three times and your dog doesn't understand what you want and is beginning to get frustrated, go back to something you know he can do—

even if it's a simple "Sit"—and try again the following day. This reduces pressure and stops him from becoming anxious.

- **RULE 7:** Make the rewards worth it. Keep the treats small, but make them something your dog loves. For most pets, this might mean tiny pieces of chicken, cheese, or sausage—and be generous. If necessary, cut back his meals a little so he doesn't put on weight.

- **RULE 8:** Give an occasional bonus payoff. This is a trick many professional trainers use. Most of the time, when your dog successfully does what he's asked, he gets a treat. But every so often—not every session, but perhaps once or twice a week—give him six or seven treats at once when he does what you ask. Your pet will be thrilled, and the possibility of a treat bonanza will encourage him to pay even closer attention to you.

- **RULE 9:** Offer fewer treats with tried-and-tested exercises with which your dog has become completely familiar. Give him a treat, but not every time. Keep the best stuff for when he's working hard at something new.

- **RULE 10:** You can teach your dog all his life. Don't assume that training is finished because you've ironed out his bad habits and taught him to do most of what you need him to; instead, use future sessions to reinforce the bond between you and experiment with new tricks and games.

It's much more important to have short, regular teaching sessions than long, infrequent ones. "Short and often" is a good rule when training.

PLAYING LIKE DOGS PLAY

When a dog wants to play with another dog, he does a play bow: forelegs down on the ground, rear end raised, with a wagging tail. There's plenty of evidence that dogs can read this position when humans approximate it—as far as their physique allows. Lean forward and low, raise your rear end, and clap or whoop (since you don't have a tail to wag) as you run back and forth; you may feel self-conscious, but chances are that your dog will love it. Try it when you're running around the backyard together and no one else is watching—you may find that it's a hit with your pet.

ABOUT YOU
WATCH YOUR LANGUAGE

You can make training work better by preparing for it properly. If you've ever been to a class or had a private session run by a professional trainer, you'll probably have been surprised by the amount of work you have to put in yourself to get good results—at least as much as your dog. Pay special attention to your language and body language; dogs can be spectacularly skillful when it comes to picking up nonspoken signals. You may not get the results you want if body language and verbal cues clash (see pages 24–25).

MAKING IT WORK

The chapters that follow describe some simple exercises in a lot of detail. This isn't to labor the point—it's to be sure that even simple exercises are thought through and taught carefully. The majority of dogs that have problems learning games, obedience exercises, and tricks find them difficult because they're not being taught carefully or consistently enough. Make it easy on both of you by reading through the exercise you're going to teach your pet thoroughly and considering how you're going to teach it before you start. In particular, think about the following:

- Consider the words you will be using. It's difficult to give only a bare verbal direction without elaborating on it. If you're teaching "Watch Me," for instance, resolve to say just those two words and only once or twice at the most. It will not only help to make things clear to your dog, but will also give you time to check that you're not doing anything confusing with your body language.

- Think about your tone of voice. Generally, you should try to sound happy (you're thrilled to be interacting with your dog, after all), but a high, enthused tone will stimulate your pet in lively, active exercises and games, while a low, quiet one will help indicate to him that you want him to concentrate. If he gets overexcited in the course of a game, don't raise your own voice to shouting point; to a dog, it just sounds as though you're joining in the barking.

- Think about your posture. If you want a dog to move toward you, you should lean slightly backward instead of leaning forward over him. Some dogs find it threatening if you lean over them, too, so try to get into the habit of standing back.

- If you want your dog to run toward you, get down low, whistle, clap, and hold your arms out wide. This is a standard trick when teaching recall—most dogs find it hard to resist. If you have a treat ready when your dog runs over, you'll make it even more appealing.

THE BASICS 1
SIT AND DOWN

It's probable that "Sit," "Down," "Wait," and "Let's Go" were the first things you taught your dog—even if you used different cue words—but it's good to build them into your routine along with games or tricks. It is better to make sure that your pet stays responsive and reacts promptly to key commands instead of moving on to other exercises at the expense of the basics. In case your dog isn't fluent, the following pages contain a refresher course.

WHAT ARE YOU GOING TO DO?

Lure your pet into the correct sit position by moving the treat so that he is fully sitting, then repeat, using the cue word, and treat him when he responds to it. If you follow the steps, gradually the cue word becomes the call to action, and the treat he gets becomes a reward instead of a lure.

When your dog is reliably responding to the "Sit" cue, move on to "Down."

SIT

1. Stand in front of your pet, facing him.
2. Take a treat in your hand and hold it slightly over his head so that he moves his head back to look at it. As he does this, his hindquarters will automatically move down.
3. Continue to move the treat up and back until your dog is sitting.
4. As soon as he's in a full sit, say "Sit," then give him the treat. As usual, timing is key—make sure that you say "Sit" as he's in the act of sitting, not just as he's getting back up again.
5. Repeat a few times, then pick up a treat and wait. Your dog will be paying attention (you're the one with the treats) and will figure out that you want him to sit. As he sits, say "Sit" and give him the treat. Let him figure it out and take his time, if necessary. Practice without luring—don't show your dog the treat, but have them on hand, and when he sits, say "Sit" and treat him.
6. Next, start asking him to "Sit"—and reward him as he does. The treat has turned into the reward for sitting instead of the inducement to sit.
7. When he's reliably sitting every time he's asked, practice in different situations and in places where there are distractions—in fact, everywhere you go with him. Gradually reduce the number of treats; give one every so often, but not every time.

If your dog is already familiar with the basics, but you've taught them in a slightly different way, or with different cue words, stick to the cues and methods with which he's familiar so he doesn't get confused. Remember to reinforce them regularly, and make it worth his while by offering some favorite treats.

DOWN

"Down" is usually slightly harder to teach than "Sit," so practice when you're feeling patient. You may have to wait it out until your dog gets the message that pawing at your hand to get the treat isn't the behavior you're after.

Note: Some breeds—in particular, sighthounds such as Whippets or Greyhounds—find the physical transition from "Sit" into "Down" awkward and will usually find it easier to go into "Down" from a standing position.

1. It's easiest to teach "Down" on the dog's level, so kneel down in front of him before you start.
2. Ask him to "Sit," and treat him when he obliges (although see the note above about sighthounds, in which case, start by getting his attention on the treat, then go straight to teaching the "Down" command).
3. Take another treat in your hand, making sure your dog sees it, and move your hand down to the floor in front of him. Keep the treat closed within your hand so that he can't just pester you for the treat without lying down. As he stretches forward to reach it, pull it a little farther away and wait. He may keep trying to get the treat out of your hand for a while, so be prepared to be patient.
4. Eventually, he'll lie down. As soon as he's lying down, say "Down" and give him the treat.
5. Repeat until he is reliably going into a "Down" when you ask and treat; then, as with the "Sit" cue, gradually convert the bribe into a reward by using the cue word and treating when the action is completed.
6. When he's got "Down" mastered without distractions, practice the command when you're out and about and there's more going on. Reduce the rewards until he goes into a "Down" directly on request.

WHAT HE LEARNS

To sit and lie down on command.

WHY IT'S USEFUL

"Sit" and "Down" are the starting points for many of the games and exercises that follow, so your dog needs to be completely familiar and comfortable with them.

THE BASICS 2
WAIT AND LET'S GO

"Wait" and "Let's Go" are basic training exercises for dogs. As with "Sit" and "Down," if your dog already knows these exercises but in a slightly different form, don't confuse him by reteaching them. Incorporate them into your daily teaching session using the cues and methods he knows.

WHAT ARE YOU GOING TO DO?

Teach your dog to stop and wait when you ask, understanding that it's a lack of action that's being asked for, until you give him the release cue. Over time, you will be able to cut down on the treats and your dog will learn to wait on cue.

WAIT

Your dog needs a reliable "Sit" (see page 38) before you can teach "Wait."

1. Stand in front of your dog, facing him, and ask him to "Sit." Treat him, making sure he knows you have more treats.
2. As soon as he's in a full sit, walk backward a few steps (just one to start with), saying "Wait"—making the word long, low, and slow—as you do.
3. Step forward again, and—provided that he's still sitting and waiting—treat him.
4. Allow a short "Wait" to count at first. As you practice more often, ask your dog to hold the "Wait" for longer until he can reliably stay in position for ten seconds (sometimes it helps to count out loud). Young, lively dogs can find it hard to contain themselves so be patient. Reward a successful "Wait" even if it's short, practice regularly, and build the "Wait" times gradually.

LET'S GO

"Let's Go" is the release cue for "Wait." Don't try to add it as a cue until your dog can manage "Wait" for several seconds, and treat only the "Wait," not the "Let's Go."

1. Your dog is in a "Wait" and has been for a few seconds—you've drawn out the "Waaaaaiit" as long as you can.
2. Treat him for the "Wait" and then say "Let's Go" right away in a lively, upbeat voice. Your dog will respond to the tone and break the "Wait."

When teaching "Wait" and "Let's Go," don't try to increase both the distance between you and the number of seconds your dog has to wait at the same time. Dogs seem to learn the commands more quickly if you first increase the distance between you (over several sessions) and then start to add to the waiting time.

WHAT HE LEARNS

To reliably stay in a position before being given the signal to move.

WHY IT'S USEFUL

These are key commands that are invaluable in everyday life, as well as when you're teaching new games.

Tone is important here, particularly in the "Wait." Use a low tone and spin out the cue word— "Waaaaaiit." Keeping the cue long will help your dog to understand that's it's really a lack of action that's required. You can also add a hand signal, such as an upraised hand, palm out and facing toward your dog, to signify wait.

WATCH ME

Many dogs, particularly young, lively ones, lose concentration easily when they're learning. They're engaging with you and they're trying to understand what's wanted, but everything around them is just so exciting that they can't focus. "Watch Me" is a great basic exercise—it's easy to teach, and it can keep you and your dog out of all kinds of trouble, because you will be able to stop him from heading off after the nearest distraction.

WHAT ARE YOU GOING TO DO?

Teach a command that gets your pet's attention onto you when you say his name—fast and without fuss.

You can teach this exercise under any circumstances, but it's best to start when your dog is hanging out at home, perhaps sniffing around in the backyard or checking the kitchen to see if there's anything good to eat. You want to catch him when he's not thinking about paying you attention but isn't strongly distracted by anything else.

1. Arm yourself with a handful of small but high-value treats and walk around to where your dog can see you. Say his name. Use a clear, enthusiastic attention-getting tone.

2. As soon as he looks at you, return eye contact, say "Watch Me," and throw him a treat. The message you are teaching your dog is that paying attention to you brings benefits.

3. Don't wave the treat to get his attention; throw it with the cue "Watch Me" as soon as you get his attention. The treat is the reward, but paying attention and looking toward you is the desired behavior. So for this exercise, always throw the treat instead of handing it to him.

4. Don't worry about what he's doing as he looks at you. A dog might add a behavior—for example, he may sit down—when you catch his attention, but for this exercise, the eye contact is the point. Whether he's sitting or standing, he needs to be looking at you. That's what earns him the treat.

5. After you've done this three or four times, move on to something else. But remember to practice daily; this exercise is so useful that you want your dog to get it right every time.

6. Over a period, you can ask your dog to pay attention for slightly longer before he gets the treat. At first, reward him immediately, then start to build in a delay of one or two seconds, during which he still has his attention on you, before rewarding him.

WHAT HE LEARNS

That paying attention to you pays dividends—and that he should look to you the moment you ask him to.

WHY IT'S USEFUL

Not only is it much easier to take your dog anywhere with you if you know that you can catch his attention immediately, but you can also use it to distract your dog from tricky situations.

TEACHING RECALL 1
COME!

Teaching your dog to come back when you call isn't intrinsically difficult, but owners often don't put enough work into it to make their pets' recalls foolproof. The exercises here will remind you of the basic steps, but make sure you practice recall from the day you get your dog and keep practicing every single day.

WHAT ARE YOU GOING TO DO?

Teach your dog to come when you call.

Your dog should already know "Watch Me" (see pages 44–45) and be responding to his name reliably. Aim to spend five minutes on recall every day. You can split it into two or three mini-sessions.

1. Start indoors with no distractions. Arm yourself with a few treats and position yourself a few steps away from your dog.
2. Say your dog's name. As he looks at you, show him a treat. As he starts to move toward you, say "Come!" As soon as he reaches you, praise him and give him the treat.
3. Show him another treat and back away from him, saying "Come!" As he moves toward you, back away from him; he'll follow you. Stop after a few seconds and give him the treat.
4. Now call him from farther away, using his name and "Come!" in an upbeat, enthusiastic voice. When he reaches you, give him the treat.
5. Gradually move farther away until you're calling him from the across the room.
6. When your dog is coming to you in the house every time you call him, move the exercise outside into the backyard.

7. Introduce recall when other things are going on—call your dog to you at random moments during the day in the house or backyard and always praise and treat him when he comes. Start to reduce the treats a little more, but still give out the occasional windfall bonus, particularly when he comes promptly—a pleasant surprise will pay off in reinforcement terms.
8. When he's coming to you every single time he's called around the house and backyard, try out his recall when you're out and about with more distractions. Play it safe; don't let him get too far off before you call him. And never stop practicing regularly.

WHAT HE LEARNS

If you make recall rewarding for your dog, he will learn that it's always worth his while to come when you call.

WHY IT'S USEFUL

If you know that your dog will come back to you as soon as he's called, you'll be able to allow him more freedom when you're out and about. Recall is also key to keeping him safe: you don't want a "good enough" recall, you want a perfect one.

WHAT IF HE DOES COME, BUT TAKES HIS TIME?

Praise him warmly (even if you don't feel like it) and give him a treat. Never scold your dog when he comes back to you, whatever the circumstances. If necessary, take the exercise back a step or two, going back to the backyard or calling when he's already nearby.

Your family and friends can help when you first start teaching this exercise, with one or two other people calling your dog and asking him to come to them—from you or from the other side of the room. As he begins to respond to the cue, phase out the treats a little, until he's getting one only every two or three recalls.

TEACHING RECALL 2
CHASE ME!

While you should never ever chase your dog, it's a good idea to get your dog to chase you. If you turn "Chase Me!" into a game you play together, you're making yourself a focus for having fun outside. Add a squeaky toy or ball, plus a few rewards, and you'll be even more attractive to your dog.

"Chase Me!" will help to build your dog's view of recall as something fun instead of being a dull duty that can be ignored in favor of more interesting things.

WHAT ARE YOU GOING TO DO?
Turn recall into a game that makes coming back to you an attractive option for your pet.

1. Start outside in a place where you have enough space to run around freely but where there are not too many distractions. It's good to practice this command when you've already played a game or done another exercise as warm-up. Call your dog, using just his name and the cue "Come!," in an upbeat, happy voice.

2. Don't watch to see if he comes. Whether he immediately moves toward you or not, turn and run away from him. You can clap or whoop if you want to—it'll make you even more exciting to chase.

3. When you know your dog is running after you, pause for a moment and let him catch up, then immediately praise him, give him a treat, or squeak the toy you're carrying.

4. As soon as you've treated him, run away again; the aim is to turn catching you into a fun game he enjoys.

5. After you've practiced this every day for a week or two and he's reliably chasing after you, try the same routine somewhere where there are more distractions—perhaps in the local park, where there's plenty going on.

WHAT HE LEARNS
That running to you when you call can be part of a fun game.

WHY IT'S USEFUL
See the previous pages— a good recall can be a lifesaver.

Your dog is probably left- or right-pawed. If you watch him over an hour or two, you'll notice that he usually "leads" with one or the other. Teach this game using his leading paw.

SAY HELLO

Although it's not a trick that your dog really needs to know, an appealing sit-and-paw trick at the right moment can sometimes win over onlookers who aren't enthusiastic about dogs. Look on this as less of a trick than a public-relations exercise, and teach your pet to "Say Hello" willingly as soon as it's suggested to him.

WHAT ARE YOU GOING TO DO?

Teach your dog to offer his paw for a fist bump when someone suggests it to him. Your dog will need to know the "Sit" command (see pages 38–39) before you teach him "Say Hello."

A word of warning: Most dogs are sensitive about their paws, and a few are extremely sensitive. If your dog turns out to be one of the latter, you may not be able to overcome his nerves about having his paws touched—in which case, skip this exercise and instead teach him to sit politely when meeting someone new.

1. Stand facing your dog and start by asking him to "Sit." Treat him as he sits.
2. As soon as he's in a sitting position, touch his upper leg on the side of his leading paw (see left). Most dogs will instinctively lift their paw at this point; if he doesn't, go straight to step 3, but gently.
3. As his paw lifts, slip your hand under it and gently hold it from underneath. Say "Say Hello" as you do. Hold it for just a second or two, gently shaking it, while offering a treat with your other hand. Don't enclose his paw with your hand— you don't want him to feel trapped.
4. Practice regularly until he's reacting directly to the verbal cue "Say Hello" without you needing to touch his leg.

WHAT HE LEARNS

To meet and greet in a way that will please even those who don't like dogs.

WHY IT'S USEFUL

If your dog has a tendency to jump up when greeting, you can use "Say Hello" to direct him into more acceptable behavior. Warn the person he is greeting to touch him gently and not to grab at his paw. For a dog who is "paw shy," the trick can also be helpful in building his tolerance for times when someone has to handle his paws—for example, to clip his nails. Finally, if you have a dog that isn't an especially fast learner, "Say Hello" is easy to grasp and can therefore be used to build his confidence. You can practice it in between sessions when you're trying to teach him more difficult things. It's a two-stage exercise, although it's simple, so you can use it as a bridge to multistage exercises.

SPEAK AND SHHH

Uncontrolled barking is one of the most irritating habits a dog can have. Although it seems counterintuitive to teach him to bark on command, it can actually make it easier to stop him when you want to. And, practiced regularly, it encourages your dog to refer to you before he starts barking— even if it's only to see if a treat might be forthcoming.

WHAT ARE YOU GOING TO DO?

Teach your pet to bark on command— and, once he's mastered that, to stop barking on request, too.

To begin the exercise, you need a context where you know your dog will bark. Try not to speak other than to add the verbal cue at the right moment and to praise your dog when he gets it right. Use a clicker, if possible; it will help with the precision timing you need.

SPEAK

1. Ask a helper to ring the doorbell. At the precise instant your dog starts barking, click the clicker and give him a treat. He'll stop barking in order to eat the treat.
2. Repeat several times—if your dog starts to look for the treat and forgets to bark, don't treat him; wait until he barks. Try to get a sequence going: bell, bark, click, treat.
3. After a short break, repeat the exercise, but this time, add a verbal cue—"Speak"—as he starts to bark, so the sequence is bell, bark, "Speak" (said just as you click), treat.
4. Practice this for a few days until your dog is used to the sequence and has got the idea that it's the barking that results in the click, the cue, and then the treat.

5. Now practice moving the exercise away from the front door, using only the verbal cue. You can do this in stages, beginning at the front door with the doorbell, then trying just the verbal cue without the doorbell or the helper.

SHHH

When your pet is barking to the "Speak" command, you can teach him "Shhh" to stop barking.

1. When your dog is barking, indicate that you have a treat. Click the clicker exactly as he becomes interested in the treat and stops barking, then give him the treat.
2. Add the "Shhh" command when you can catch the exact moment your dog stops barking.

WHAT HE LEARNS

That barking and stopping barking can be exercises performed for rewards. It may also teach him to be more selective about when he barks—and make it slightly easier to stop him—but don't expect this to apply at especially exciting moments.

WHY IT'S USEFUL

Practicing a start/stop exercise can help to break the pattern of annoyance barking— and it's a neat trick for your pet's repertoire.

Keep your voice low when speaking in these exercises; to a dog, a raised voice can sound as though you are "barking" back at him and may simply encourage him to raise his own voice.

PLAYING WITH TOYS 1
TAKE IT

Dogs have limited options if they want to carry something: they can hold things in their mouths or not at all. "Take It" is the cue for your dog to take something from your hand and hold it in his mouth. Over time, you can extend it to encourage your dog to pick up an object from the floor, too.

WHAT ARE YOU GOING TO DO?

Teach your dog to take a favorite toy from your hand.

Choose the toy you're going to train with carefully. It needs to be something that's easy to carry and ideally something that your dog likes, but not to the point where he gets so excited that he can't contain himself around it. Often the easiest toy to persuade your dog to take is one that you can play a game with immediately afterward; two obvious options are a squeaky soft toy or a rope tug toy. You can use the same cue whether your dog is taking something from you or picking it up from the floor, but it's probably easiest to start by asking him to take something from your hand.

It's hard to teach this exercise using treats or a clicker, because both your hands and your dog's mouth will be engaged. The object itself needs to be the incentive, so this will work best with dogs who like carrying things anyway. Practice your timing; as usual, you need to say the cue at the exact moment that your dog takes the toy.

1. Pick up the object you want your dog to take and hold it in front of him. Make it interesting for him: if it's a squeaky toy make it squeak; if it's a rope tug toy, wave it around a little. Keep up an exciting commentary— "What's this? Look at this!"—until he takes an interest.

2. As he approaches it, hold it out and offer it to him. If he takes it in his mouth, repeat "Take It." If he has a firm hold of it, praise him. If it's a toy you play tug with, you could have a short game of tug with him—most dogs love this, so it's a reward in itself.

3. You can practice this exercise when you're heading outside to play. Pause by his toy, or pick it up, and offer it to him, saying "Take It" as you're headed for the door. If your dog reads it as a signal for a game with you, he's more likely to pick it up enthusiastically.

WHAT HE LEARNS

To take and hold something in his mouth, and to trust you enough to accept something from you.

WHY IT'S USEFUL

"Take It" is a great building block for a number of tricks you can teach your dog. It's one of the first stages to a number of more complex exercises that will give him a proper mental workout.

MOUTH SHY?

A few dogs are worried by picking things up on command—it's natural for them to explore things with their nose and mouth, but they balk at the idea of taking something when asked. (A study that looked at various games played across a wide number of different breeds found that nervous dogs don't always like their mouths being occupied if they aren't sure what's going on—it seems to make them feel vulnerable.) If your dog appears concerned, take this exercise slowly, praising him warmly even if he holds the toy for only a second or two.

For exercises and games where treats need to be accessible but not too obvious to your dog, keep them in a small waist bag that you can reach into easily when you need the treat fast.

THE TOYS TO CHOOSE

Bear in mind, when you're teaching "Leave It," that it's best to start teaching your dog using something that he likes, but better to avoid his favorite toy of all time—he will find it much harder to give it up and you may inadvertently provoke him into guarding behavior (see pages 30-31 for more information on toy obsessiveness). Instead, choose a toy or ball that holds his moderate interest and set it against some high-value treats such as cheese or chicken to help to make it easier for him to give it up to you.

PLAYING WITH TOYS 2
LEAVE IT

Useful as it is to teach your dog how to pick up a toy, it's more important that he learns how to leave something alone when you ask him. On the odd occasion when he's showing an interest in something that's within his reach but not yours, and which he really shouldn't have, you need to be able to ask him to stop what he's doing in the confident expectation that he'll obey you. This is generally an easy exercise to teach.

WHAT ARE YOU GOING TO DO?
Teach your dog to leave an object alone on your command.

1. Take a toy that your dog often plays with and likes and arm yourself with some treats that are accessible but that your dog can't see.
2. Pass the toy from hand to hand, waving or squeaking it to attract his attention.
3. Your dog will probably think you're starting a game and make a move on the toy. As he moves toward it and paws it, or tries to take it in his mouth, ask him to "Leave It" in a low, steady voice.
4. The moment he stops, or pauses, in his efforts to get the toy, reward him with a treat, using the hand that's not holding the toy. You'll need to use split-second timing and wait for a distinct pause, however short, before treating him.
5. Practice "Leave It" every day—you can use a variety of different toys—until your dog begins to understand that the cue means he should back off and stop what he's doing, whatever that is. As he becomes familiar with the cue and you practice more, he will learn to back off faster.

WHAT HE LEARNS
To immediately stop what he's doing when you ask him.

WHY IT'S USEFUL
It's convenient from your point of view (fewer chewed socks or kids' toys), and it helps to keep him safe.

PLAYING WITH TOYS 3
WHERE'S YOUR . . . ?

This exercise gets a wide range of reactions from different dogs: some get the idea that they're being asked to choose between two objects quite quickly, while others really struggle with the concept and sometimes never seem to understand. It depends on the dog.

WHAT ARE YOU GOING TO DO?
The aim is to try to teach your dog to choose between two objects.

Your dog will already need to know the "Take It" (see pages 54–55) and "Leave It" cues (see pages 56–57).

1. Choose two toys that your dog plays with regularly and is already enthusiastic about. In separate sessions, play "Take It" with each of these toys, asking your dog to pick the toy up from the floor. Name each toy as you play: give them one- or two-word names and use these names often when your dog is playing with one or the other—"Take the bear," "Take the tugger," and so on. Use the names independently and clearly—don't mix them up with other names or activities.

2. When you've been playing with the individual toys, naming them in each session, for a week or two, choose a moment in the middle of a training session (when you've warmed up with some easy exercises or games and your dog is already focusing on you) and lay both the toys on the floor in front of him. Don't leave any other distracting items around—just those two toys.

3. Ask him to take a toy, by name: "Take the bear." If he's used to the "Take It" instruction, he will probably pick a toy up. If it's the one you named, praise him. If it isn't, say "Uh-uh" and repeat the request, indicating the right toy with your hand. Praise him when he picks it up, then ask him to leave the toy ("Leave It") and reward him with a treat.

4. Repeat the exercise, naming the same toy. When he picks it up, praise him, and then ask him to "Leave It" and treat him when he does.

5. Now try naming the other toy: "Take the tugger." If he goes for the bear, say "Uh-uh" and indicate the rope tug toy. When he takes it, praise and treat him.

6. Continue, alternating which toy you ask for and avoiding getting into too much of a pattern. Keep the sessions short, and switch to a different activity if he is starting to get frustrated.

WHAT HE LEARNS
To differentiate between two objects by name and to select a particular one when you give him a verbal cue.

WHY IT'S USEFUL
This is a show-off trick—he can prove he's a clever dog indeed.

PLAY TO YOUR DOG'S STRENGTHS

Don't let your pet get too frustrated: if, after you've practiced it a few times, it still hasn't sunk in that he's being asked for something in particular, revert to an exercise you know that he can do—and reconcile yourself to the idea that it may not be the game for him. He can excel at something else instead.

CARRYING 1: TOYS

You've seen canine carriers on the street, proudly holding their own toy as they walk alongside their owners. It looks good, and mouth-prone dogs often enjoy having something to carry on their walks. If you have one of those dogs who loves to have something to carry around the house, you'll probably find that this exercise will come naturally; the first part encourages him to carry a toy, while the following pages focus on a more challenging object—a shopping bag. If your dog isn't mouthy in this way, the exercise will be more challenging; if he isn't happy with it after a few attempts, you may want to pick an alternative.

WHAT ARE YOU GOING TO DO?

Encourage your dog to carry an object comfortably.

To learn this, your dog should already know the "Take It" cue (see pages 54–55). Start practicing indoors—in a large room—or in the backyard, so that there aren't too many distractions.

1. Take something that your dog will be able to carry easily—a light dumbbell or bone-shaped rubber toy is ideal. If you want him to carry his own leash, knot it together so that it doesn't trail and it's easy for him to pick up.
2. Hand it to him, saying "Take It."
3. When he's holding it, start walking—your pet will usually walk alongside if you look as though you're going somewhere. Until you've taught this exercise thoroughly—or have a very big house or backyard—you may find yourself walking in circles as you teach.
4. Your dog will usually drop what he's carrying as he sets off with you. As soon as he drops it, pick it up, hand it to him with a "Take It" command, and set off again.

5. The next time he drops the item, hand it back ("Take It"), then say "Carry" as you set off again. Praise your dog as soon as he's carrying it for more than 3 or 4 yards (3 or 4 meters).
6. Practice this exercise for just a few minutes each time until your dog is happy to carry his chosen item for more than half a minute (which is longer than it might sound). Then take the exercise outside and practice it on a local walk—preferably one without many distractions.

Once your dog is used to carrying something easily, you can try the next exercise: getting him to carry a shopping bag (see pages 62–63).

WHAT HE LEARNS

To carry an object for a distance on the "Carry" cue.

WHY IT'S USEFUL

This is an exercise to get him attention—you'll get a lot of "Isn't he cute?" and "Isn't he clever?" glances, and you can both feel pleased with yourselves.

CARRYING 2: A BAG

If your pet is an eager "carrier," it won't be too hard to teach him to carry something heavier and less familiar than a toy. Even when he's learned to carry a shopping bag, you probably won't be able to get him to tote your groceries for you (too heavy), but you may be able to persuade him to transport a light shopping bag and its contents from the car to the house.

WHAT ARE YOU GOING TO DO?

Teach your dog to carry a shopping bag—which you do in exactly the same way as you teach him to carry a toy. Choose a fabric bag (one with rope handles that is easy for him to grasp is ideal), and put something bulky but light in it, such as a rolled towel.

1. Offer him the bag, pulling the handles up and out so that it's easy for him to take them, and ask him to "Take It."
2. When he grasps the handles, walk alongside him, encouraging him with "Carry" as long as he has hold of the bag. At first, just two or three seconds will be an achievement. Don't expect your dog to carry the bag for long periods—it's heavier and more awkward for him than a toy or a knotted leash. Practice indoors and in the backyard before graduating to an out-and-about walk. Ultimately, after plenty of practice, if he manages it for 50 yards (45 meters) or so, he'll be doing well.

WHAT HE LEARNS

How to carry something a little more challenging than his favorite toy.

WHY IT'S USEFUL

While your dog probably won't become a serious bag-carrier, asking him to carry your bag can be a useful distraction tactic when he's on the point of doing something you don't want him to do.

Smaller dogs won't be able to carry a shopping bag—it will be too large for them. Instead, try an alternative exercise with a folded newspaper or magazine that is about the right size for them to cope with.

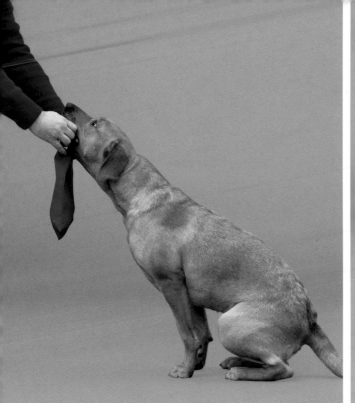

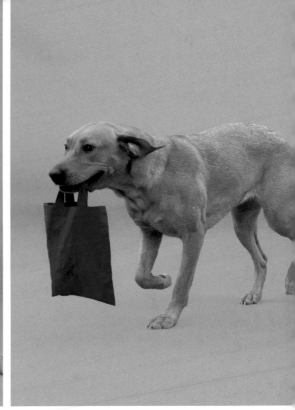

MOUTH-PRONE DOGS

All dogs use their noses constantly, but some dogs are definitely more prone to use their mouths than others—they explore things with their mouths and seem actively to like to carry things around with them. Often, they're breeds that are bred as retrievers: Labradors, working spaniels, and Golden Retrievers generally love both carrying and mouthing. Teaching these dogs mouthwork—such as carrying games—can help to discourage them from taking things they shouldn't; something like the barking-on-command exercise (see pages 52–53), giving a dog something positive to do with a natural tendency, may dissuade him from using it in a way you don't want him to.

This exercise calls for concentration over a longer time period than your pet is yet used to. Don't be surprised if he takes a rest afterward—sustained thinking can tire a dog as much as a long walk or a few rounds of agility.

TIDY UP!

When your dog has learned how to "Take" something, the logical next step is to give him somewhere to take it. The toy roundup encourages him to collect the toys he's been playing with one by one and put them in his toy box, while the laundry variation encourages him to pick up scattered clothing and place it in the laundry basket. Note, though, that you shouldn't teach your dog to pick up anything you don't want him playing with at another time, so the toy variation may be the one you prefer.

These two are essentially the same exercise, and it's up to you which version of it you teach. You'll find that the challenge usually comes in getting him to take everything to the same place—and to drop it when he gets there.

WHAT ARE YOU GOING TO DO?
Teach your dog to pick up a selection of things in one location and deposit them in another.

Your dog will need to know the "Take It" command (see pages 54–55) before you try this exercise.

1. Place your dog's toy box in one corner of the room and a favorite toy near it on the floor. You're going to start with just one toy and then add others as he gets the idea that the job is to pick up a toy and deposit it elsewhere.
2. Arm yourself with treats and get your dog ready for some activity, using an upbeat, excited voice, then run into the room with him. Keep the pace up so that he's engaged and looking to you for what you want him to do.
3. Pick up the toy and ask him to "Take It," then run over to the toy box, calling him with you, and say "Drop" when

you reach it. Show him a treat as you say "Drop," and as soon as he drops the toy in the basket, give him the treat. Reward the drop every time at first, even if it's not completely accurate.
4. Practice this exercise a few times a day with a single toy, until your dog has mastered "Take It" to the toy box and "Drop" when he gets there. Then add a second toy and repeat the instruction after the first toy is in the box.
5. As your dog becomes comfortable with the game, you can gradually add to the number of toys and place them a little farther from the box. Go around with your dog, encouraging him to get it right, and repeat each "Take It" and "Drop" until he's got them all.

WHAT HE LEARNS
To put three different stages together—taking something, carrying it to a specific location, then dropping it—within one long game.

WHY IT'S USEFUL
It's a game that combines being with you (you can pick up and put away alongside him) and having a job to do. Plus he will learn the "Drop" cue.

SETTLE

Ideally, you'll have a short session every day playing with and training your dog. And, of course, you'll also be taking him for walks, getting him his meals, and generally interacting with him a lot of the time. However, there will always be times when you need to get on with aspects of your life that don't involve him, and it's useful to have a verbal cue that he knows is the sign to settle down calmly.

The pester power of a young, energetic dog can be almost as great as that of a toddler, and it's the nature of dogs to be hopeful, so you need to harden your heart when teaching this exercise. You can help your dog get the message by keeping your voice low and calm, and being consistent, even if he continues to invite you to play. Remember, though, that teaching him this cue is to buy you some time when you need it, not a way of bypassing his daily routine—he must still be exercised.

WHAT ARE YOU GOING TO DO?
Teach your dog to understand the verbal cue to settle down.

Most dogs, even fit and lively ones, will settle down automatically when they're tired and no one is paying them attention—many will go to their preferred spot, often their bed or crate. That's the moment to try to teach this command. You can use a clicker, but the timing for this cue isn't too hard to get without one.

1. Start when your dog is already tired. Have some treats on hand. You want to attach the spoken cue to the action, so, as he's headed to the spot where he likes to rest, walk alongside him, and as he gets on his bed (or wherever else he habitually rests) say "Settle."

2. As he lies down, give him a treat (and perhaps also rub his belly if he rolls over as he lies down). Repeat "Settle" as you do so, but no more than once or twice.

3. Get up quietly and leave him resting. If he follows you, walk back with him to his bed and repeat "Settle" as he settles back down. You may have to repeat the exercise a few times before he gets the message, and it will take some practice before you can ask your dog to "Settle" when he isn't already headed for a rest. However, he'll understand eventually if you are consistent over a number of training sessions.

4. To make his "Settle" solid, introduce it in among other exercises. Don't always make it the one you finish up with—instead, ask him to "Settle," and then ask him to rejoin you for a new exercise or a game.

WHAT HE LEARNS
That he sometimes has to manage without your attention, even if you're in the vicinity.

WHY IT'S USEFUL
It's self-evident, really—you get to carry on with your own activities without being nagged by your dog.

66

USES FOR SETTLE

You can use "Settle" to distract a dog who's a pest at the front door and—ultimately—to teach him to go straight to his basket, crate, or regular hangout spot when a visitor arrives. It takes practice, but if you time the instruction and are careful to reward him on cue, you can make it work.

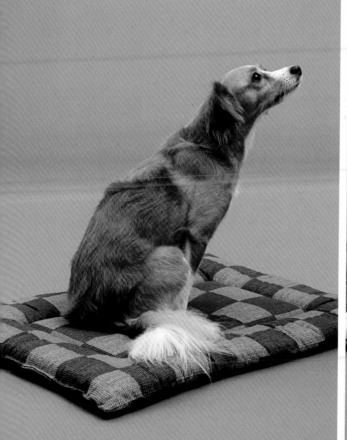

CHAPTER 3

BONDING GAMES

BUILDING YOUR RELATIONSHIP WITH PLAY

The more positive interaction you have with your dog, the more straightforward your day-to-day dealings will be. Not only that, but you'll also get to know the ins and outs of his personality in a way that the walks and games that are already part of everyday life with him won't necessarily teach you. Let your daily playing/training session become a habit, and the payoff will be complete familiarity with your pet's behavior—you'll know what you can expect from him in any situation.

BONDING WITH YOUR DOG

Much has been written about dogs as pack animals and their relationship to wolves, but it's worth clarifying what this actually means. Domestic dogs, despite having almost identical DNA to wolves, are a long way from being wolves themselves (after all, humans share more than 95 percent of their DNA with chimpanzees, but it doesn't make us chimps). Not only have dogs lived alongside humans for millennia—some scholars estimate as long as 35,000 years—but they have adapted to living in a world run by humans and to being directed by humans in most of their daily behavior.

As social animals, dogs value being part of a social group, and if you don't keep several dogs, your pet's group will be his humans (even if you do keep several dogs, your role will still be to lead—or at least it will be if you want a harmonious life). Your pet should think of you as the person he turns to when something needs sorting out and as the source of the good things in life—food, walks, and fun.

However, there are some other theories and beliefs—especially about dog dominance—that have been around for just as long and that need disproving.

THE DOMINANCE MYTH

Dominance is the bogeyman of dog behavior studies, and the idea that a dog (being really a wolf) may have a dominant personality and ambitions to replace you as pack leader is still in wide circulation. This thinking was responsible for much of the coercive and sometimes harsh treatment that was part of dog training in the past and, unfortunately, it hangs on here and there in various old-fashioned methods and ideas. If you ever hear someone talking about how you should show your dog who is "alpha," and how you have to dominate him to stop him

from thinking he's boss, these are the ideas we're talking about. Modern ethologists agree that there are various reasons why this theory is incorrect—and why using it doesn't work:

- Dogs aren't wolves; they have all kinds of ways of getting what they want (and even wolf society is much, much more complex than simply having one strong leader and a lot of followers).
- Using forceful, coercive methods to train a dog will probably result in defense aggression in a strong-minded dog and abject fear in a timid one.
- Dominance, when used between professionals, is an extremely fluid term covering a whole range of behaviors and drives; it isn't equivalent to the word as understood in general use.
- Dogs are open to negotiation; like many social mammals, they understand working through problems cooperatively with others.

Because dominance has a tendency to pop up in conversations about dog behavior and training, it's good to know the background to the theory—and know, too, that it's been discredited by most experts.

Don't cheat—give a treat only when your dog does something good without you telling him to.

ABOUT YOU
POSITIVE REINFORCEMENT

Before you start teaching more games and tricks, try this observation exercise. It's a great training tool for you as well as for your dog; it encourages you to watch him across a longer period than you usually would. Try it when you have an extra hour or two around the house— on a weekend perhaps—then continue it across several ensuing days, making sure you always have plenty of treats on hand.

WHAT ARE YOU GOING TO DO?

You're going to positively reinforce the things you want your dog to do by treating him when he does them. The tricky part—for you—is that you're not going to tell him to do anything. You are going to give him a treat and say a calm "Good dog!" every time he chooses to behave in a way you like. If you get your timing right, your dog will earn regular treats; he's bound to behave in a desirable way, even if only accidentally, several times a day.

Of course, what's important—as usual—is precise timing. Did your dog stand back politely when you opened the door? Give him a treat at that exact moment. Not only will you find that you are watching your pet more carefully, but also that you're better than you knew at predicting his behavior. Try looking for the following:

- When he automatically does something that you've practiced together in the past; for example, sitting down while waiting for his food.
- When he's polite in greeting other dogs or people—calm introductions and friendly body language.
- When he stands aside to let you through a door or up the stairs.
- When he goes to sit in his bed, as you've taught him, if you're vacuuming.
- When he deliberately leaves you at human mealtimes.

Of course, these are just a few possibilities. As you watch your dog through the day, you'll see plenty of times when he gets it right.

WHAT HE LEARNS

At first, he will be surprised by the unexpected treat, then, if you are consistent, he'll gradually link it with the behavior you like. He'll start to pay special attention to your body language.

WHY IT'S USEFUL

You get a lesson in watching your dog's behavior closely—and by paying attention, you'll see all kinds of things about the way he behaves that you otherwise wouldn't have noticed. In an ideal world, this would be your default way of living with your dog.

73

HIDE-AND-SEEK 1
FINDING YOU

In the same way that your dog loves to chase after you if you run away, he will probably enjoy finding you in a game of hide-and-seek. This game works best if you ask a friend or a family member to distract your dog while you go away and hide—then either they can look for you together (if he needs some help and extra enthusiasm), or, when he's become used to the aim of the game, he can hunt for you as a one-dog search party.

WHAT ARE YOU GOING TO DO?
Encourage your dog to hunt for you and find where you're hiding, and turn the search into a game. As he gets the idea that you're the object that needs to be found, you can make your hiding places more difficult and ask him to look for you on his own, without a human cheerleader.

1. You play this game in exactly the way you would with a small child: a friend or family member distracts your dog while you go off to hide. Build his excitement, just as you would in a child's game, by asking your friend to count aloud to ten while he or she waits with your dog and then call "Coming!"

2. Your friend should set off with your pet to look for you, keeping up a commentary about where you might be in an excited tone. (What they say doesn't matter, it's the tone that will engage your dog.)

3. Don't carry out the search for too long—half a minute or so is fine when you start to make sure your dog maintains his interest. When he finds you, make a great fuss of him, then play one or two more rounds before you switch to something else. As with the treat-hunting game on pages 82–85, this is a good activity to sandwich between more hardworking brain games during a training session.

WHAT HE LEARNS
To follow his nose and find you.
You're the prize at the end of the hunt.

WHY IT'S USEFUL
Much as the best way to teach recall is to encourage your dog to catch you, here, he's being taught to find you instead. By hiding yourself away, you're reinforcing his idea that you're someone worth hunting for and someone he wants to be around.

Try hiding at different levels: going up a level, for example, perching on a bunk bed, will pose an extra challenge because dogs don't automatically look above eye level when they're searching for something but instead rely on their noses.

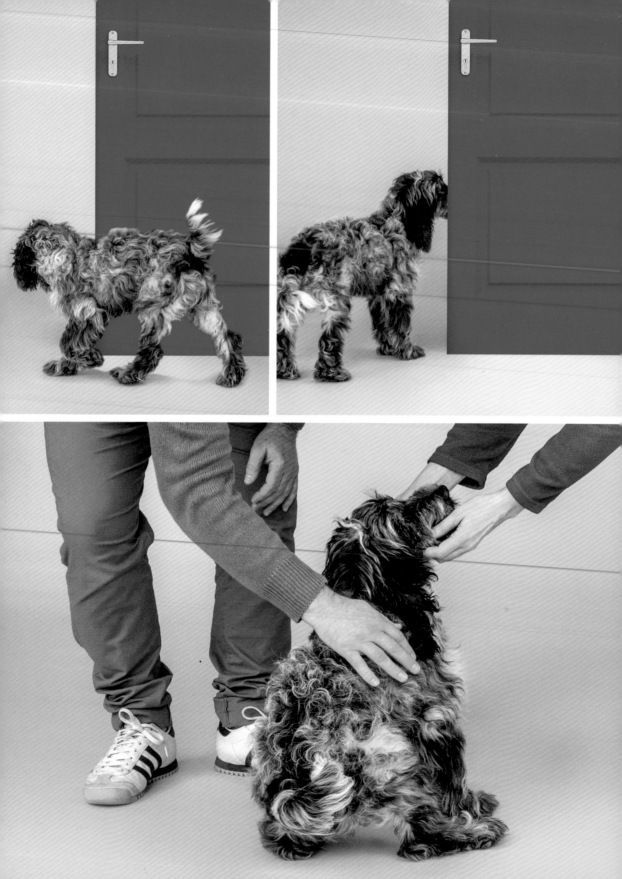

HIDE-AND-SEEK 2
FINDING OTHER PEOPLE

This is an extension of the first version of hide-and-seek. It's a great game to play with family members, and a good way to mix a range of ages, too. It's not so much part of a training session but a way to integrate your pet into a family occasion. You can involve children, because you'll be supervising. Encourage them to hide in hard-to-find places and to join in the excitement as your dog finds a succession of people. If you have a dog who becomes overly hyper easily, keep the excitement within bounds and take a minute's time out, if necessary.

WHAT ARE YOU GOING TO DO?

Engage your dog in a game of hide-and-seek with several people to hunt for.

1. As before, set your dog up in a room with a friend or family member. The rest of the group should go off and hide all over the house.
2. The friend should count aloud to ten, building up the excitement just as he or she would with a child, and then the person and your dog should run out of the room to hunt around the house.
3. As each person is found, he or she should be primed to make an enthusiastic fuss of your dog and then join in the hunt for the remaining players, until there's a crowd looking for the final member of the group. Like any other game of hide-and-seek, this is noisy, fun, and inclusive, and a confident dog will love it, because it reinforces his membership in his "family."

WHAT HE LEARNS

He'll find that he can play group games with his people and bond with the group instead of simply working with you on one-to-one exercises.

WHY IT'S USEFUL

Dogs are highly social, and playing games in a group will be especially enjoyable for him. Know your dog: If he's at all reserved with people, go gently and make sure that he's not scared. If he has a tendency to get overexcited, be sure to calm him before he gets aroused to the point of mouthiness.

PLAY DEAD
AND ROLL OVER

"Play Dead" and its continuation, "Roll Over," is a party trick for your dog to show off. Its purpose is simply for him to do what you want him to do—in exchange for treats and praise, naturally. Tricks or exercises that you teach in stages encourage your dog to concentrate just a little harder and to focus more on you, too, which makes them good for bonding.

WHAT ARE YOU GOING TO DO?

Teach your dog first to lie still on his side, and then to roll right over until he's standing upright again. Teach it on a soft surface, such as carpet (this isn't an exercise for bony dogs).

Your dog needs to know the "Down" cue (see pages 40–41) before you start teaching him "Play Dead."

PLAY DEAD

1. Kneel down facing your dog and ask him to go into the "Down" position. When he is lying down in front of you, hold a treat in front of his nose and bring it slightly over his shoulder, back toward his tail. He'll follow the treat with his eyes and, as he does so, will turn on his side. (If he scrambles up to make a mouth-on assault on the treat, simply say "Uh-uh," withdraw your hand, and start again.)
2. The second that his head hits the floor, say "Play Dead" and give him the treat.
3. Repeat the "Play Dead" trick several times over several play sessions across a week or two until he's got it, and he will happily play dead on request. You can gradually reduce the treats and make "Play Dead" the cue for your dog.

ROLL OVER

1. To convert "Play Dead" to a full roll-over, get your pet into the "Play Dead" position, then take another treat and carry it over your pet with your hand, holding it so that he can see it and taking it toward the back of his head. He'll follow it and, in doing so, will bring his body up and over into a roll-over. As he does so, say "Roll Over," and as he completes it, give him the treat.
2. Practice both stages regularly, both separately and as a sequence, until your dog can do them on request without being lured/guided by the treat.

WHAT HE LEARNS

To lie still, then go into a full-body roll-over—a trick that has two stages but is still easy for a dog to learn.

WHY IT'S USEFUL

As well as being a great trick to show off your dog, it is a useful exercise to reduce the stress of veterinarian visits— you can ask your pet to lie on one side to be examined without having to push or coerce him into position.

Don't ever force a dog into a position when you're teaching him; if he's resisting, back up and think about another way to get the results you want. Coercion can make your dog nervous of engaging with you—the opposite result from the one you want.

ADD A LEASH

If your dog is one of those (and there are a lot of them) who will dutifully return when you call them over from playing off-leash in the park, but who then create an additional game for themselves by dancing around and being skittish about being put on a leash, there's a useful extra you can add to this game. When your dog reaches you, after you praise him, ask him to "Sit" before you give him his treat. If he gets used to this routine when he runs up to you, the "Sit" will become automatic, giving you time to put on his leash.

DOUBLE RECALL

Midway between an exercise and a game, a double recall usually comes naturally to a dog; he simply has to hurtle between two people, being made a fuss of by each in turn. If you pair up with someone who isn't usually around your pet, this can be a useful game to teach a shy dog.

WHAT ARE YOU GOING TO DO?

You've already taught your dog to come to you in "Chase Me!" (see pages 48–49). "Double Recall" is easier, because your dog only has to pause briefly before dashing off again. It's best played outdoors, where there's space for him to race around. All you need are two people and some treats. If you want to, and you have enough space, you can even introduce one or two more people, so that he has up to four admirers to race to.

1. Stand as far apart from the other person as you can—ideally at least 10 yards (9 meters). Call your dog to you, using "Come!" and a happy, excited voice.

2. As soon as you've made a fuss of him and given him a treat, your friend should call him, just as excited, from where he or she is standing, catching his attention by clapping, whooping, and stretching out his or her arms. He'll run toward the person to be greeted by another treat. (If your dog isn't familiar with the other person in the game, ask them just to give him a treat—he may find a physical contact from someone he doesn't know well a little threatening, but the treats will soon establish that he's got a new friend.)

3. As soon as he's eaten the treat, call him back. You can keep this up for five minutes or so; your dog will love it.

WHAT HE LEARNS

A shy dog will become more excited and forget his reservations around new people. He'll simply concentrate on running between you and lapping up the attention—and the treats.

WHY IT'S USEFUL

If you play this game regularly but vary the cast, it will help a shy dog get used to new people. It's also a good way to start a training or play session, because your dog can burn off a little energy without having to think too hard, with the added incentive of plenty of praise and treats.

81

TRACK THE TREAT 1 FOLLOWING HIS NOSE

A treasure hunt for treats can make a popular break in between some serious training exercises. Limit the game to one room. Set it up before your daily session, shut the door, then take your dog there when he's completed something difficult. Rather like the principle of suddenly offering him an unexpected bonus cache of treats, this game is pure reward—all he has to do is follow his nose.

WHAT ARE YOU GOING TO DO?

Hide treats in a range of locations, from simple to difficult to find, to make a tracking hunt for your dog.

1. Hide a dozen treats at different levels in a room in your home; include some in hard-to-get-to corners. When you've hidden all the treats, leave the room and shut the door.
2. Start your dog's training session as you would normally. Plan to fit the treasure hunt in between a couple of the harder exercises.
3. When you've completed the first of the more difficult exercise, run to the door of the "treat room" and go in with your dog. Say "Treat track!" enthusiastically and guide your pet to his first treat, then keep up a flow of cheerleading for your dog to find the rest, asking "Where's the treat? Find the treat!"
4. He'll probably sniff out the floor-level treats without needing much help from you, but when he moves up a level, show him one of the treats placed higher up and encourage him to find the remainder.
5. When he's found all the treats, use his excited energy to keep the pace up for the remainder of his training session; move straight back into a problem-solving exercise without a break in between. You'll usually find that your dog will do well in the next tough thing you try to teach him, as the treasure hunt leaves him with both renewed energy and plenty of enthusiasm for interacting with you.

WHAT HE LEARNS

That training involves not only hard work when you have to figure things out but also breaks with plenty of treats.

WHY IT'S USEFUL

Mixing indulgent exercises and canine brain teasers in your sessions will get better results than constantly challenging your dog with the tough stuff. Offering your dog a few minutes of unexpected fun also reminds him that you are the provider of the things he loves to do and reinforces bonding.

WHERE TO HIDE
THE TREATS

Dogs will usually start by sniffing close to the ground, so leave a few easy-to-find options around the feet of furniture, under the corner of a rug, and so on, then move higher. A treat might be left on the seat of a chair, behind a cushion, or on the edge of a bookshelf. Dogs are far less likely than humans to look above their head level when they're hunting for something, so place just a few in places that your pet can access but which are high up—on the top rail of a chair, maybe, or on the middle shelf of a set of bookshelves.

Don't stage the treat track in the most immaculate room in the house. Your dog will be just as happy to hunt for treats in the utility room or the garage, and it's not fair to him to set up a game and then worry about your furniture and carpets.

Remember that you learned on page 50 that your pet is generally right- or left-pawed? Tap the paw he uses most when you're giving him a reminder that he can use it to "point" to the treat.

TRACK THE TREAT 2
USING HIS PAW

This version of the treat-tracker game calls for a more controlled approach to locating a treat by encouraging your dog to use his paw to gently "point" to where a treat is hidden.

WHAT ARE YOU GOING TO DO?

Offer your dog the opportunity to find a treat and indicate where it is to you, earning the treat itself as a reward. This isn't an exercise that calls for anything special—all you need are a few treats.

1. Kneel down in front of your dog and ask him to sit.
2. Hold out both your clenched hands in front of you on the ground. One of your fists contains a treat—choose high-value, strong-smelling cheese or sausage so that it's easy, and enticing, for your pet to smell.
3. Your dog will probably start by putting his nose down by the hand with the treat in it and trying forcefully to nose it out. Say "Uh-uh," pulling your hands back slightly away from him.
4. He may take a minute or two to figure the next stage out—you've told him he isn't allowed to use his mouth to take the treat. Give him a few seconds to think about his next move; if he's clearly puzzled, use the hand that isn't holding the treat to tap his paw. (Some dogs will have figured out without any help that if they can't use their mouths, they can use their paws; if that's the case with your pet, move on to the next step).
5. When he's figured out, with or without your help, that he should use his paw

and not his mouth, put your hand back on the floor. Your dog will start to paw the hand with the treat in it. Let him do this for a second or two, but then say, very softly, "Geeently." The low tone will make him pause.

6. You're aiming to get him to touch your hand with his paw, but without trying to get the treat out. As usual, timing is critical, but this is a tough trick to teach using a clicker, because you're using both of your hands. Instead, watch carefully, and at the moment that his paw is resting on your hand but he isn't actually pawing it, open the hand and give him the treat.
7. Practice taking him through the routine a few times in each daily session for a week or two—using "Uh-uh" only when he tries to extract the treat for himself, and he'll shortly learn that he just needs to touch your hand with his paw to win the treat.

WHAT HE LEARNS

That patience can work better than force when he wants something.

WHY IT'S USEFUL

It's a quick trick that you can play anywhere, and is easy to teach to others, so that you can have friends and family play with him in a way that he's used to.

SWAP

Giving up a valued object can be a big deal for a dog. Teaching "Swap" shows your pet that if he gives something up to you willingly, even something he values, he'll get something just as good back in exchange. What's more, as you practice, you'll end up giving him back the original object as well. Soon, he will be handing over his toy, bone, or whatever you ask for and eagerly taking the substitute you're offering, confident that you won't be depriving him.

WHAT ARE YOU GOING TO DO?

Show your pet that he won't regret giving something up to you when he's asked.

1. This is an opportunistic exercise: you need to be ready for the right situation to happen naturally. Wait until your pet is relaxed and happily playing with a favorite toy. Have a hollow treat toy stuffed with something irresistible ready, and, when you see your opportunity, fetch it from the refrigerator.

2. Simply approach your dog in a relaxed way, bend or kneel down beside him, and show him the stuffed treat toy. If he immediately drops whatever he's playing with, say "Swap," hand him the substitute, and gently pick up the original toy.

3. Sometimes he'll grab for the original toy, dropping the new one. If he does, give it to him immediately (you want to teach him that he won't lose out in any way by working with you). If he loses interest in the original toy, lay it down gently nearby, so that he can see that he ended up with both the things he wanted.

4. Practice this whenever the chance arises (it's a good idea to have a prestuffed treat toy ready in the refrigerator at all times when you're teaching your pet this exercise). Always wait until your dog gives up the initial toy willingly; don't cheat by pulling it out of his mouth, or he'll be less willing to give it to you next time. Stay patient, and return the first toy as soon as your dog is focused on the treat toy (you can wait a few more seconds before returning it as your dog learns to trust that he will get it back).

5. It may take a few weeks of regular practice, but you'll find that as your dog becomes used to giving things up to you, you can reduce the value of what you're offering in exchange. Eventually, he'll happily give something up to you as soon as you say "Swap."

WHAT HE LEARNS

To give things up to you easily, and to trust that you'll treat him respectfully around the things he values.

WHY IT'S USEFUL

On the rare occasion that your dog has something he shouldn't (he's chewing a shoe, perhaps, or he's found a chicken bone in the street) and you need him to give it up to you without a battle, you'll have already done the groundwork.

HANDS OFF!

Dog society is interesting in the way in which it views possession of objects. It's unusual to see a dog, even a larger and stronger dog, take a coveted item (whether it is a toy or a bone) away from another who has it. However, if the second dog leaves the treasure, even for a moment, all bets are off: the first dog will feel free to take it. But taking something by force that another dog is enjoying doesn't often happen in everyday canine etiquette.

CHAPTER 4

BRAIN GAMES

BOOSTING YOUR PET'S THINKING SKILLS WITH PLAY

Smart dogs learn fast, and this chapter offers a variety of ideas that are within the abilities of most dogs, provided that you're prepared to be patient. Your dog will become used to engaging with you when you take him through something new. Some of the exercises may tax him a little, and not every dog will love every game, but by the time you've taught him to balance a treat on his paw, touch a target, and bring you his bowl at dinnertime, you'll have every reason to be proud—both of him for his smarts, and of yourself for your newfound training ability.

ABOUT YOU
TEACHER TRAINING

You already know that timing is key and that you should watch your dog for clues to tell you when you're getting it right. But sometimes, even though you think you're teaching in the correct way, and the one that works best, you hit a wall, and suddenly your dog can't seem to learn anything from you. If it's not just one particular exercise that's proving difficult—in which case you may have discovered his Achilles' heel—but a range of different things, it's time to review the way you're teaching him. You may have allowed a few bad habits to sneak into your routine.

HOW YOU'RE TEACHING

Check through the following to help you find where you may be going wrong:

- Are you matching your tone to the exercise? Your tone should match the energy level that the game or exercise calls for. Upbeat, enthusiastic cues generally elicit action; if you want things to slow down, use a lower tone and stretch your words out more. Don't raise your volume much—if you get too loud, it may intimidate a shyer dog, while a more confident one may decide that you are "barking" at him and be tempted to bark back at you.
- Are you watching your body language? Try to keep still when you're teaching your dog to do something. When he's focused on you, he'll be watching what your posture/gestures are saying at least as closely as he'll be listening to what you actually say. Avoid big gestures unless you're drumming up excitement for a specific activity.
- Are you crowding your dog? Most dogs will be more relaxed and open to interaction if you stand a little back from them. Generally, dogs aren't any happier than people about having their personal space invaded.
- Are you talking too much? Keep words to a minimum when you're working with your dog—just the cue for the exercise, and perhaps a "Good dog" to direct him if he's doing what you've asked but is clearly not confident about it. The more you talk, the more you risk confusing the message you're trying to send.

ABOUT YOUR DOG
BASIC BODY SIGNS

Just as you need to be careful about what signals you send your dog, you also need to be alert to the signs he's sending you. Here's a key to some basic body language that you may see your dog using.

SIGNS THAT YOUR DOG IS FEELING STRESSED OR UNCOMFORTABLE

- Tongue flicking—just a quick flick of the tongue over his nose.
- Turning away, sniffing the ground—he isn't being obstinate or ignoring you, he's telling you that he's out of his comfort zone. To another dog, this would be an appeasement signal ("I'm not a threat, I'm just over here, doing my own thing").
- Yawning—in an active context, this isn't a sign that he's tired; instead, it tends to indicate that he's feeling anxious.
- Looking away—dogs make much less frequent eye contact than humans anyway (they interpret a direct, long look as confrontational), but if your dog is actively avoiding your eye, he's sending you a message that he isn't enjoying the activity you're working on with him, and that it's time for a break.

SIGNS THAT YOUR DOG IS OVERLOADED

- Barking or being noisy unexpectedly. If your dog suddenly seems to explode into action mid-activity in a hyper way, you may have been overloading him with different things (this isn't the same as your pet simply getting excited in the course of a game—it's more like sudden hysteria).
- Starting to wander off. Somewhat like turning away to sniff, this is a deliberate refusal to engage. Take a break; he's had enough for the day. Try again tomorrow.

To get your sessions back on the right footing, give your dog a few days' worth of extremely simple things that you know he's confident about before reintroducing any of the problem exercises. When he's relaxed and happy, introduce just one or two more difficult challenges, but let him set his own pace, and make sure to end each session with something that is both easy and well-rewarded.

TARGET PRACTICE 1
TOUCHING THE TARGET

Although humans tend to identify the idea of a target with a tangible object, a target in dog-training terms is any item that your dog can demonstrate he can identify when asked to, usually by touching it either with a paw or with his nose. You can buy paper targets (with the authentic bull's-eye marking) in many pet stores or online, but you'll find it easier to use a plastic lid from a small food package, which will also be more durable. The important thing is to use the same target every time until your dog gets used to the cue and understands what it is you're asking for.

WHAT ARE YOU GOING TO DO?

You're going to ask your dog to touch the target with his nose. Sniffing it will probably come naturally to him, especially if you've made it appealing to him by making it smell of food, such as liver paste. When he's mastered touching it with his nose, you're going to ask him to touch it with his paw. As with the other target exercises, this one is easiest to teach using a clicker.

1. Holding the target in your hand, call your dog. He may go straight to the target and sniff it, in which case, click as he does so and say "Touch."
2. If he doesn't go straight to the target, tap it with your finger; your dog will come over to see what's interesting you—tap it again, and as he goes to sniff it, click and treat him.
3. When you've practiced "Touch" daily over a period and your dog is unerringly touching the target with his nose, move on to asking him to touch it with his paw, using a separate cue. Call your dog to the target, and, after he's sniffed it, tap it, saying "Paw." If your dog seems puzzled, lay a treat on the target so that it remains interesting, and hold it in place with your hand. He'll probably start to nose at it, but if you continue to hold it, he'll eventually try to get it using his paw. The moment that he uses his paw instead of his nose, click and repeat "Paw."
4. When you've taught both cues, continue to practice, using both "Touch" and "Paw," so that he remains familiar with the two different actions.

WHAT HE LEARNS

To focus on a single item, but to associate two different actions with it.

WHY IT'S USEFUL

This exercise calls for your dog to concentrate hard. Target touching can also be a first step to some more complicated tricks and games that involve pushing things with his nose—for example, closing a door.

94

TARGET RECOGNITION

Although a number of studies have been done on canine recognition processes, the jury is still out on whether dogs are able to make a clear distinction between a noun and a verb— that is, an item and an action. No one really knows whether, when we say to a dog "Where's your ball?" and the dog trots over and picks up his tennis ball, he's thinking of the tennis ball or of the action, and whether he sees the ball in terms of something to play with, or as an object that exists whether he's playing with it or not.

What is certain is that there's a broad range of awareness in different dogs. Teaching a dog to touch and eventually hunt for a target seems to pose more of a challenge to some dogs than others— some will find the target but then have difficulty differentiating between looking at it, touching it, or (if you move on to advanced games) pressing it with a paw or nose. However well your dog does with these games, you'll find it interesting watching him trying to figure out what it is you want and differentiating between the different cues.

VARIATION:
CLOSING THE DOOR

Try placing the target low down on a door that is ajar. You can click and treat your dog to encourage increasingly hard "Touches" on the target until your dog can close the door on cue.

TARGET PRACTICE 2
FIND THE TARGET

Your dog has already learned to touch the target, both with his nose and his paw. Now you're going to ask him to find the target, placing it in a different spot each time. Don't always lay it flat; you can attach it vertically to a door or on a piece of furniture, and you can also vary the height at which you place it, so that he has to look around to find it.

Like the treat-tracker and hide-and-seek games, you'll probably have to accompany your pet as he searches out the target the first couple of times, but once he understands what's required, he should be motivated enough by the praise and treats he earns to hunt for it for himself.

WHAT ARE YOU GOING TO DO?
Place the target in different locations and encourage your dog to find it.

1. Out of sight of your dog, place the target somewhere in a room. Start with a fairly obvious location; you can make it more challenging once your dog understands what he's supposed to do.

2. Using a cue such as "Let's find!," start a hunt with your dog. He won't immediately know what you're looking for, so lead him to the target and ask him to "Touch." Click and treat him as soon as he does.

3. Repeat this a few times, placing the target in a different place every time; he'll soon understand the game. If his enthusiasm for it starts to wane, you can make it more appealing by rubbing the target with something fragrant (to a dog, that is), such as the liver paste that's sold to fill Kong toys.

4. When he's finding the target wherever you put it, you can add "Paw" to the "Let's find!" and "Touch" cues.

WHAT HE LEARNS
To build on an initial exercise and take it to three stages.

WHY IT'S USEFUL
It's a good brain workout for your pet to think through the different steps—look, find, touch. (Incidentally, this is the kind of game that most dogs find tiring, so it is a good one to incorporate into your session on a rainy day when no one wants to walk too far.)

97

ORDER YOUR DINNER

This exercise teaches your dog to bring his empty bowl to you at dinnertime. If you practice it before a mealtime, his motivation to learn will be strong. Make sure before you start that his bowl is one he can easily pick up—something made from light and sturdy molded plastic in a shape he can reasonably be expected to carry. Don't use a metal or ceramic bowl; it will be too difficult for him to hold, and he may drop it.

WHAT ARE YOU GOING TO DO?

Teach your dog to bring his empty bowl to you on request.

Your dog will need to know the "Take It" cue (see pages 54–55) before you start teaching this exercise. It has three stages and can be taught with a clicker. You will start by handing him the bowl, but ultimately the aim is for him to go and collect it from where it's kept and bring it to you so that you can fill it with food.

1. Take the bowl and practice the "Take It" exercise, asking him to take it from your hand and hold it for a second or two. Practice over a week or two, asking him to hold it for a little longer each time. Finish each practice by taking the bowl from him and feeding him his dinner, so that he expects holding it will bring good things.
2. When he's happy to hold his bowl for four or five seconds, hand it to him ("Take It"), then encourage him to bring it over to the counter, where you have his food waiting. Walk alongside him, and use "Carry" as the cue as he's carrying it over.
3. Practice these first two stages for several more sessions until he is confident taking the bowl from you to the counter.

4. The final step is to get your dog to collect his bowl for himself, instead of taking it from your hand. This is usually the hardest thing to teach him, and may take a few tries. Go with him to the area on the floor where his bowl is kept and ask him to "Take It," as he would from your hand. Make sure it is arranged so that it is possible for him to pick it up from a flat surface—it will need a rim or recessed handle for him to get a grip on. When he picks it up, praise him lavishly but keep the momentum going as you say "Carry" and turn to walk with him to the counter where his food is waiting.
5. When he can put "Take It" (from the floor) and "Carry" together, try just nodding toward the bowl until he looks at it, then use both cues without standing by him or walking with him.

WHAT HE LEARNS

To use his initiative in putting several actions together—and to prompt you to give him his meal.

WHY IT'S USEFUL

As you stop directing him from up close, he's acting more independently. A particularly self-starting dog may even start bringing you his bowl unprompted when he knows it's time for dinner.

HEALTHY DINNER

A natural diet for your dog
should be high in protein, with
some fat, bone, and small amounts
of vegetables. Ideally, it shouldn't
feature grains, potatoes, rice,
corn, or soy—all of which are added
to commerical pet food to bulk it
up, due to their low cost—or large
quantities of preservatives. Labels
can often be complicated to read,
but in general the fewer the
ingredients listed and the more
recognizable that they are to you,
the better the quality (this is also,
unfortunately, reflected in the
price; as you'd expect, cheap food
is unlikely to be good food).

FIND THE TREAT 1
UNCOVERING THE TREAT

As its name suggests, this exercise gives your dog the opportunity to find treats hidden in increasingly hard-to-access areas. Instead of hiding treats around the room, such as in "Track the Treat" on pages 82–83, you're going to try a succession of upturned cups and bowls, boxes, and so on to test his ingenuity in actually accessing the treats.

The simplest versions of this game don't need verbal cues. Your dog will have plenty of motivation; it's his dexterity and determination that are being put to the test. Most dogs enjoy a variety of different challenges and formats when they're finding the treat.

WHAT ARE YOU GOING TO DO?
Whet your pet's appetite with some simple, fast, uncover-the-treat puzzles.

1. Take three plastic cups and, with your dog watching, place them upside down with a treat under each one. Then lean back and encourage your dog to approach and find the treats. He'll have to push the cups over, which is harder than it sounds with only a nose and his paws at his disposal.

2. When he's dealt with the cups, try the same arrangement again, but this time using plastic bowls. These are harder to turn over; because your dog can't use their height to get the purchase to push them over, they tend to slide along the floor. Most dogs eventually figure out that they need to push down with their nose and flick with their paw at the same time—if your dog has been trying for a while and is getting frustrated, help him a little with the first bowl, and then see if he can manage the others.

3. Still not too hard, but a slightly different approach—put a treat in a square of newspaper, crumple it up, and push it into an empty toilet-paper or paper-towel tube. Your dog will either have to tear up the tube and then the newspaper or push the newspaper through the tube.

WHAT HE LEARNS
To use his ingenuity and dexterity to solve a new problem.

WHY IT'S USEFUL
This activity will challenge your dog and keep him engaged while he figures it out.

FIND THE TREAT 2
SEALED CONTAINERS

Once your dog has dealt with cups, bowls, and newspapers, you can offer him the same challenge in a slightly harder format. Using sealed plastic containers means that he has to indicate the treat and get you to open the container and get it out for him—he'll be looking to you for teamwork.

WHAT ARE YOU GOING TO DO?

Offer some tougher find-the-treat puzzles that he'll have to work with you to solve.

1. Take three plastic lidded food containers and use a hole punch to cut a small hole in the top of each. Put a treat—preferably a strong-smelling one—in one of the containers.
2. Lay out the containers in a line and show them to your dog. He'll sniff around them and quickly establish which has the treat in it. Ask him to "Mark It"—you want him to put his paw on the container with the treat in it. As soon as he touches the container with his paw (even if he's actually trying to paw it open), use the cue (click if you're using a clicker), open the container, and give him the treat.
3. Try some different variants. Put treats in two of the containers but not the third, and ask him to "Mark It" again—this time, twice. Then put different treats in all three containers, and see which one he cues first. You can enjoy yourselves with this exercise. Your dog is bound to engage with as many different versions as you can devise, because he's guaranteed a treat at the end of it.

WHAT HE LEARNS

To mark a container so that you can reward him with the treat hidden inside it.

WHY IT'S USEFUL

This activity requires teamwork and will strengthen the bond between you and your dog.

VARIATION:
TENNIS BALL

Using a tennis ball as a treat container will take some dexterity to crack. Use a sharp knife to make a long slit in the side of a tennis ball, then place a couple of treats inside and give it to your dog. He needs to work out the right amount of pressure to apply—and the right angle at which to apply it—to make the treats fall out of the ball. This is a homemade variant on the many commercial treat balls you can buy, but it's more challenging than most. It's appropriate for smaller dogs only, and you should always supervise your dog while he's working on the tennis ball—put it away if you're not present.

COMMERCIAL GAMES

Some of the more difficult commercial treat-finding puzzles call on your dog to use directional pressure to solve. These games aren't inexpensive, but if you have a determined treat hunter in your dog, it may be worth investing in one of them, because they can offer a great source of entertainment for an indoor day, and they can be substantially more complex than your homemade versions.

Pet stores will usually have a couple of examples out of their boxes so that you can do a dummy run and try before you buy. Most have different levels and a variety of blocks that prevent access to the treats and need to be pushed, lifted, or levered out of the way.

FIND THE TREAT 3
MULTITREAT VARIETY

Now you can see how your dog does with a more complex puzzle. The final round of Find the Treat games includes a well-known trainer's trick that uses tennis balls and a muffin pan to really challenge your dog.

WHAT ARE YOU GOING TO DO?

Set up a multitreat bonus game using tennis balls and a muffin pan. You'll need a nine- or twelve-cup muffin pan and a matching number of tennis balls.

1. Drop a treat into each cup of the pan, and put a tennis ball on top of it.
2. Show the pan to your dog and watch him figure it out—he'll smell the treats, but it may take him a little time to realize that he can't just push the balls aside. Because the cups of the pan are deep, he'll have to lift each tennis ball out of its hollow in order to get at the treat.

WHAT HE LEARNS

To work in stages: He has to lift the obstacles to get to the treats.

WHY IT'S USEFUL

The more complex the puzzle, the more it will intrigue and engage many dogs.

HEAR ME WHISPER

Dogs often respond to quiet sounds with closer attention than they do to louder ones. This exercise is simple: Take your pet through a range of activities that he already knows, but cue at a low volume, or even try working in complete silence. (Unless your dog is elderly and getting deaf, his hearing will be considerably sharper than yours—dogs not only hear a wider range of pitches, but can also hear at a lower volume than we can.)

Even humans often pay more attention to a whisper than they do to a normal speaking voice, so it will be interesting for you to see how your pet reacts to this particularly quiet exercise. Almost every dog is insatiably curious, so you'll find it easy to get your pet's attention simply with your unusual behavior.

WHAT ARE YOU GOING TO DO?

Teach two or three of your regular exercises, but in a whisper.

1. Line up two or three of your usual exercises that have cues—for example, try "Say Hello" (see pages 50–51), "Play Dead" and "Roll Over" (see pages 78–79), or "Swap" (see pages 86–87).
2. Arm yourself with treats, then settle down beside your dog and take him through the sequence you've chosen. Make sure any noises you make— whether cues or encouraging noises— are particularly quiet.
3. Keep to the pattern you usually use in playing—just take the volume right down. Most dogs' reaction to this will be to concentrate harder.

WHAT HE LEARNS

That the familiar (the exercises) can sometimes come with a twist—and that it's still worth playing along. With less clearly voiced cues, too, your dog will be looking at your body language to see if it will help tell him what you want him to do.

WHY IT'S USEFUL

A change of pace can mean that your dog will probably pay closer attention to what you are teaching him—surprises can sometimes be useful motivation in training.

SENSITIVE HEARING

Occasionally this game will scare a dog (a research study speculated that this could be when a dog has especially sensitive hearing). If your dog seems to be reacting in a fearful rather than an intrigued way to your whispered instructions, move on to something else.

TRACKING A SCENT TRAIL

Dogs use their noses over and above their other senses. It's well documented just how much more acute our dogs' sense of smell is than ours, so setting up up a scent-track activity for him will be playing to any dog's main strength.

WHAT ARE YOU GOING TO DO?

Lay a scent trail for your dog to follow with a payoff at the end.

A scent trail needs setting up in advance, but don't leave it more than ten or fifteen minutes—the scent shouldn't fade to the point where it isn't obvious to your dog. A really effective, smelly scent trail can also be somewhat messy, leaving broth or gravy in its wake, so it's better to set it outdoors.

1. Put together a bag with extra-smelly contents that will appeal to your dog. You may be able to use leftovers from a family meal—a chicken carcass with some broth poured over it would be a good choice, as would ground meat, again with added broth so that the moisture will be left, with its scent, along the trail. Wrap what you've chosen in a piece of fabric—a piece of cheesecloth would be ideal—knot the corners together, and tie a piece of string to it so that you can pull it around.

2. Lay the bag on the ground and set the trail by pulling it around after you over as wide an area as you can. The track can meander about, but don't go over a path you've already laid—try to leave a distinct trail behind you. When you've taken it as far as you can, pick the bag up and wrap it in plastic as you take it away to give the trail a clear end.

3. Leave a puzzle at the end of the trail to give your dog a final challenge before he gets his reward. It could be some cooked chicken or small pieces of cheese placed under a bowl, as you did on pages 100–101.

4. Take your pet to the start of the scent trail. Most dogs won't need any extra encouragement; they'll start to follow their noses immediately. You can lay a small piece of chicken or cheese at the starting point to set him on the right track. Run along with him as he follows the trail, encouraging him back on track if he starts to follow his nose elsewhere.

5. As your dog gets used to the scent trail game, try subtler scents and see if he can pick them up. Make scent bags with just meat or fish remains but no extra liquid, so that the scent is fainter. Once your dog has got the idea, he should be able to follow them.

WHAT HE LEARNS

To track a specific scent alongside you.

WHY IT'S USEFUL

Really, this is just fun. But a dog's strongest sense is his sense of smell, and if you never make use of it, you're losing an important way in which you could interact with him. This game is also a particularly good way to fulfill a dog with an innate need to use his nose.

BALANCE THE TREATS

An accomplished or agile dog may learn to balance a treat on his nose and hold it there until he's given permission to flip it in the air and eat it. This is a big ask of most dogs, however, so here's a simple version that you can turn into a mini-practice anywhere you happen to be. If you've got a dog with extra-good balance and excellent self-control, there are also some tips on how to teach the more difficult version of the trick.

WHAT ARE YOU GOING TO DO?
Teach your dog to balance a treat on his paw and wait to eat it until he's told he can.

Your dog will need to know both the "Leave It" (see pages 56–57) and "Take It" (see pages 54–55) exercises before you teach this trick.

Depending on your dog, you can teach him either sitting up with a paw held up (for the pet who's always looking to put even more into a trick or game), or lying down flat with his paws in front of him (if he's more of a laid-back personality, or an older dog who's a little stiff in the joints).

1. Pick the pose you want your pet to take and ask him to either sit or lie down. For the sitting-up pose, when he's in position, ask him to give you a paw. Holding it gently from underneath, place a treat on the top of it.
2. As soon as the treat is on his paw, your dog will either dip his head down to eat it, or look at you for guidance ("What am I supposed to be doing?"). If he moves to eat it, say "Leave It."
3. Make the cue last for two or three seconds—then cue him with "Take It."
4. A confident dog will gobble up the treat; if he hesitates, you can pick it up and hand it to him on the "Take It" (you don't want to confuse him).

This game is about self-control, and your pet needs to know that he can have the treat, but only when you say so.

WHAT HE LEARNS
That sometimes he has to wait to be told it's OK to take what he wants.

WHY IT'S USEFUL
Anything to build a little self-control in your pet is a good thing, and this exercise sends him the message that permission must be granted by you. As an added bonus, your dog gets to practice his "Leave It" and "Take It" exercises.

SAFETY
If you have to hold your dog's paw or steady his head while he's balancing the treat, don't use your hand to restrain him, only to help him balance.

VARIATION: NOSE BALANCING

If you want to try to balance a treat on your dog's nose instead, first practice the version opposite until your pet understands the cue, then ask him to sit and carefully place a treat on the flat part of his muzzle, just beyond his nose (for obvious reasons, you won't be able to try this with a flat-faced breed, such as a Pug or a French Bulldog). You may have to steady his head with a hand under his chin for the "Leave It" cue, then on the "Take It" cue, remove your hand and he can flip the treat and eat it.

Before you start this exercise, make sure that your dog really loves his den, whether that's a crate lined with comfortable bedding, or a basket or padded bed. Giving him somewhere to go for downtime that gives him a view of what's going on but that isn't on the main path through the house will appeal to him.

OFF TO BED

Whether you want to answer the front door without your dog's assistance or are dealing with a family situation and just want your dog to be elsewhere for a short time, it's useful to teach him to go to his bed or crate and stay there for a few minutes. The challenge here is that you'll be telling your pet to leave his place at the center of what's going on, and most dogs (except the shy ones) like to be in the thick of the action. For this reason, it may take sustained practice to get your dog to go to his corner every time you ask.

WHAT ARE YOU GOING TO DO?

Teach your dog to go somewhere specific for a limited time, and not just to settle down wherever he's comfortable.

1. Once you've established that your pet's rest area is as appealing as possible (see opposite page), start to train when the opportunity arises, and reinforce him when he goes there of his own accord. The cue for this is usually "In your bed" or "In your crate." (If it's something you've taught in some form already, use the cue that your pet is already used to.) As your dog heads off there, follow him, and as he goes in his bed or crate, say "In your bed" and give him a treat. Repeat this whenever you see him go to his bed of his own accord.

2. When you've established that going to his bed, if noticed, equals a reward, try sending him there with the cue. Again, do this over a period of time—don't rush it, and consistently cue and reward.

3. When he is reliably going to his bed as you ask him to, set up a situation in which things are going on around him—get a family member to ring the doorbell, or ask several people to gather in the kitchen—and then cue him to go to his bed. This is usually the slowest step; many dogs will rush to their bed in a token gesture, then rush back out to take part in whatever activity is going on. If this happens, accompany him back to his bed, with the cue, and treat again. With patience and persistence, most dogs will manage a stay of a few minutes—just long enough for you to do something, such as answer the door, without an enthusiastic canine interruption.

WHAT HE LEARNS

That sometimes he can't be in the middle of everything, and he has to stay out of the way for a short period.

WHY IT'S USEFUL

When you don't want your dog underfoot, it's good to know that the "Off to Bed" exercise is solid enough for him to obey you without fussing.

113

CHAPTER 5

FITNESS GAMES

GAMES TO BUILD YOUR DOG'S FITNESS AND AGILITY

Whether your own idea of staying fit is a peaceful walk in the countryside or a two-hour stint at the gym, the idea of a healthy mind in a healthy body doesn't just apply to people. Any trainer will tell you that exercise is a key element in any plan for a happy and well-behaved dog. Teach your dog some agility exercises and sequences as well as offering walks and brain games and you'll be giving him the ideal combination for a thorough mind-and-body workout.

HOW FIT IS YOUR DOG?

If you know that your dog's health is generally fine, if his veterinary visits are usually limited to an annual checkup, and if he's got that desirable combination of bright eyes, wet nose, and shiny coat plus a general enthusiasm for any physical activity offered, he's probably in good enough shape for some agility work. Because you're extending his activities, use the opportunity to check his weight and review his diet so you can get him in the best physical condition possible.

Beyond weight and diet, if your dog is sedentary, elderly, or has developed back or joint problems or any condition, such as hip dysplasia, get him checked before you embark on a fitness program. Most dogs can increase their activity levels without any problem, but particular activities sometimes need to be approached with caution or left out altogether.

IS HE THE RIGHT WEIGHT?

In the United States, canine as well as human obesity is on the rise. Does your dog need to lose weight? Veterinarians use a basic rule of thumb when they're looking at dogs. If you run your hand down his ribs, you should be able to feel them distinctly, but if you run your hand down his back, you shouldn't be able to feel the knobs of his spine (if you can, it's probable that he's actually underweight). If there's a discernible layer of fat blurring the shape of his ribs, he should probably lose a pound or two; if you can't feel them at all, he is definitely too fat. Look at him from above, too—there should be a distinct waist between the end of his ribcage and his hindquarters. If his waist definition is negligible and he tends more toward a box shape, he needs to lose weight. Of course, breed, natural build,

and body shape will also affect what he should weigh—for example, a healthy Greyhound will be much bonier in both look and feel than an equally healthy spaniel. If in doubt, check with your veterinarian.

IS HE EATING WELL?

You know that if you eat junk, you won't have the body you want. The same goes for your dog—but he's not the one who puts the food in his bowl. There are direct advantages for you as well as for him in feeding him high-quality food. Dogs on a good diet usually have better breath and don't experience gas. They also eliminate in smaller, drier quantities—poor-quality food contains a lot of fillers, which tend to pass straight through—so there's less picking up to do. Feed him the best you can afford; it will pay in terms of his health and well-being.

When you're shopping for dog food, try to ignore attractive packaging or upbeat words such as "natural" or "healthy" (which have no legal meaning). Instead, look for specific ingredients rather than generic labels, such as "oats" or "lamb" rather than "cereals" or "meat derivatives."

FLYBALL

Agility isn't the only choice when it comes to activity classes you can take with your dog. Flyball is an option for true canine athletes. It's a knockout competition played in teams, in which dogs race down a course, taking in hurdles on the way, then press a pedal to release a tennis ball from a box before racing back up the course carrying the ball. At professional level, it's extraordinarily fast, and at a more achievable amateur level, many dogs adore it. Local clubs run classes, so take your dog for a tryout if he's one of those that always seems to be slightly ahead of the game when it comes to agility; you may find it's his natural forte.

ABOUT YOU
WORKING WITH YOUR
DOG ON FITNESS

Games that concentrate on fitness are just that: they make sure that your dog gets and stays in good shape. Agility is something a little different. The professional version, taught in classes and seen in shows and competitions, takes you and your dog around a carefully orchestrated obstacle course, with the aim of improving your dog's fitness and flexibility and showing it off, together with his ability to work alongside you as a team.

You can take agility as seriously as you want to, picking a few exercises you know your dog will enjoy and putting them together in a short sequence or, if your pet turns out to have a natural talent for agility courses, building up to agility classes and competitions. There's a middle way, too, in which you can compete with a few friends and their dogs by setting up a short backyard obstacle course. Be aware that professional agility has plenty of rules about how a dog approaches the obstacles on a course, so if you think you have a potential agility star, check the way the professional courses are run so that you can teach him the correct way from the start.

YOUR OWN FITNESS
To give your dog a good workout, it helps to be fit yourself. Running an agility course has to be done at speed—you must keep up with your pet and encourage him when necessary—and even individual activities, such as hurdles or flying disk games, are much easier and more enjoyable if you are fit and active.

You've assessed your dog's fitness; now make an honest judgment of yourself. Do you sometimes cut a walk short because you're feeling tired? Do you tend to focus on games and exercises that develop your dog's brainpower instead of on ones that demand more physical activity? If that's the case, let your dog be the inspiration for you to improve your own fitness. Instead of making drastic resolutions, add five or ten minutes to your regular walks, and aim to include at least two active exercises in your daily training session with your dog. Small steps like these, provided that you commit to incorporating them daily, improve your stamina surprisingly quickly. By the time your dog has learned enough to try a homemade agility course (see pages 138–39), you should be fit enough to run it alongside him.

CATCH 1
PLAYING FETCH WITH A BALL

For most dogs, a ball is the absolute best toy, and classic "Fetch" is one of the most enjoyable games you can play. Other dogs may need a little encouragement. If your pet is one of the latter, start by playing indoors and throwing the ball only a few feet at first. Arm yourself with two or three balls, so that you can keep the pace up, and use "Swap" (see pages 86–87) to encourage your dog to return the ball by offering an alternative.

WHAT ARE YOU GOING TO DO?

Play "Fetch," while teaching your dog to return the ball to you.

Unless your dog is a particularly small breed, a tennis ball is ideal for this exercise—small enough for most dogs to carry easily in their mouths and with some bounce in it if you're playing on a hard surface. For giant breeds, a tennis ball is too small to be safe, so you will need to use a larger, soft version instead.

1. Until your dog's got the hang of bringing the ball back, play in the backyard or another relatively confined space. Have two balls ready—you're going to reinforce his retrieving efforts by reminding him of the "Swap" exercise.
2. Bounce one ball on the ground, or throw it up in the air and catch it until you have your dog's attention (keep the second ball out of sight).
3. Throw the ball—a medium-strength throw, not too far. As your dog picks it up, call "Come."
4. As he looks toward you, call again, and as he starts to head in your direction, get down close to the ground and hold your arms out.
5. As he gets close to you, take the other tennis ball out so that he can see it. He may drop the ball he's holding and head over to you, in which case, say "Uh-uh," walk back to where he dropped it, and hand it to him again.
6. If he gets to you but doesn't want to drop the ball, don't grab at it—instead, remind him of his "Swap" cue while offering the second ball. Bounce it on the ground or throw it from hand to hand if you need to make it more appealing.
7. As soon as you've reclaimed the original ball, make sure he's watching and throw it again. Remember to ignore any behavior you don't want and praise any that you do. "Fetch" is exciting for dogs and it may take a few sessions to teach him that only giving up the ball will win him another throw.

WHAT HE LEARNS

To use his mouth to pick up a ball that you have thrown, return it to you, and then give it up.

WHY IT'S USEFUL

An enthusiastic game of "Fetch" is a great workout for your dog.

If your dog loves "Fetch," and you have a busy day ahead of you and need to tire him out quickly, an inexpensive plastic ball thrower is your best helper.

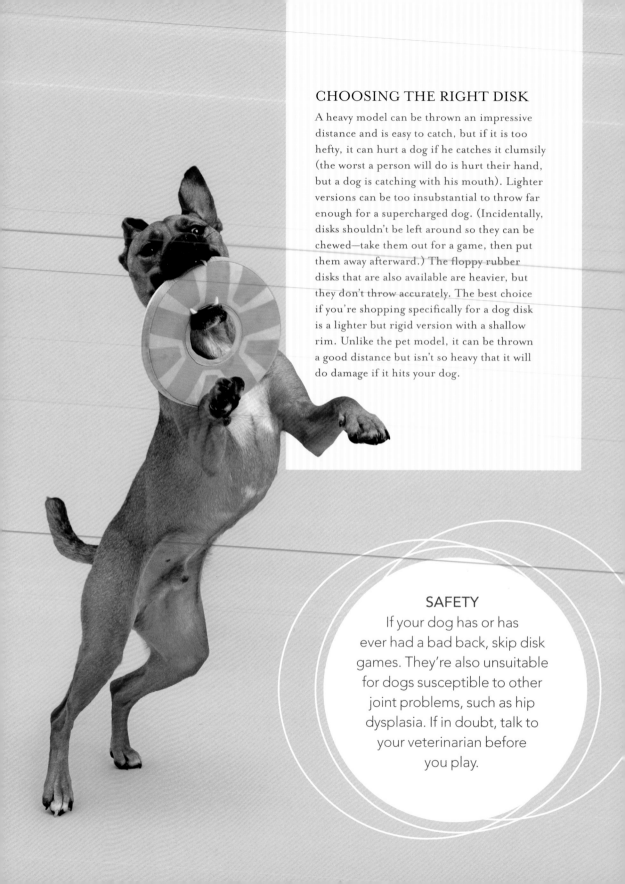

CHOOSING THE RIGHT DISK

A heavy model can be thrown an impressive distance and is easy to catch, but if it is too hefty, it can hurt a dog if he catches it clumsily (the worst a person will do is hurt their hand, but a dog is catching with his mouth). Lighter versions can be too insubstantial to throw far enough for a supercharged dog. (Incidentally, disks shouldn't be left around so they can be chewed—take them out for a game, then put them away afterward.) The floppy rubber disks that are also available are heavier, but they don't throw accurately. The best choice if you're shopping specifically for a dog disk is a lighter but rigid version with a shallow rim. Unlike the pet model, it can be thrown a good distance but isn't so heavy that it will do damage if it hits your dog.

SAFETY
If your dog has or has ever had a bad back, skip disk games. They're also unsuitable for dogs susceptible to other joint problems, such as hip dysplasia. If in doubt, talk to your veterinarian before you play.

CATCH 2
PLAYING WITH A FLYING DISK

When flying disks first appeared in the 1950s, it wasn't long before they became favorite toys for dogs as well as people. They have plenty of advantages for dogs: the curve in their flight makes them less predictable to chase and catch than a ball, and they're easy to throw a long way.

WHAT ARE YOU GOING TO DO?

Give your dog a gentle introduction to disk play.

Manufacturers' advice soon after the disks were first produced (when it became clear that dogs liked playing with disks, too) suggested that you serve your pet his dinner on the upturned disk. You probably don't need to go that far, but if your dog hasn't ever played with a disk before, take a few steps to engage his interest before you play outdoors.

1. Take the disk out and roll it across the floor. When your dog takes it in his mouth, ask him to give it to you (arm yourself with treats and ask him to "Swap;" see pages 86–87).
2. Throw it gently and low (just a few inches above the floor), and let him go and retrieve it.
3. When he's become used to the disk, take it into the backyard or another open space and try a few low throws—not too high and not too hard. Most dogs will get the idea quickly and try to catch it immediately.
4. Ask your dog to return and "Swap" each time. When you're throwing gently, he's not too far away, but as soon as he's in a larger space and

you're throwing hard, you need to be able to get the disk back easily. Reward him with a treat when he brings it back and gives it up. (If he doesn't want to bring it back, whatever you do, don't chase after him—the simplest fix is to turn and run away from him so that the game turns into him chasing you. When he catches you, you can reclaim the disk and he can have a treat.)

5. Keep the pace brisk, but don't throw too extravagantly at first; your dog should be able to catch the disk fairly easily without having to jump extremely high or twist midair. Increase the height and distance of your throws gradually, over several sessions.

WHAT HE LEARNS

To catch, retrieve, and return a flying disk. Dogs that love to jump will do their best to get to it midflight.

WHY IT'S USEFUL

Plenty of leaping and running equals a well-exercised dog. Flying disks are more of a challenge to catch than a regular ball, making them an especially great tool for athletic dogs.

123

USING A LURE

Some dogs love pouncing games, and if you make a lure, they will track or stalk it almost as a cat would. This game uses a retractable leash with a toy or lure attached to create a chase-and-pounce game for your dog. It works best with smaller dogs, because retractable leashes are usually only 7 yards (6.5 meters) long—not enough for a larger, fast dog to build up any speed before it reaches its "prey."

WHAT ARE YOU GOING TO DO?

Use an extendable lock-and-release leash to entice your dog into a chase.

The prey should be something small and fluffy. A fake-fur foxtail toy will create plenty of excitement by flipping about in a lifelike fashion, while a soft squeaky toy will offer a gratifying noise when your dog catches up with it. If you play in the backyard, you can tempt your dog at the start of each chase-and-pounce by letting the tail of the toy extend from a clump of grass or stick out from behind a tree.

Your dog should already know the "Swap" trick (see pages 86–87) before he plays this game.

1. Take your chosen toy and attach it using the leash's clip.
2. Holding the toy in your hand, release several yards of the leash and then press the button to hold the leash in position.
3. Lay the toy on the ground and walk a short distance from it. Call your dog—you can jerk the line a little to make the toy move realistically.
4. As your dog looks and starts to move toward the lure, release the lock so that the toy whizzes along the ground. As the prey suddenly comes to life, your dog will chase it down and pounce on

it. You can lock the leash again and let him play tug with it for a while before tempting him away from it with a treat and starting the process again.

5. If your dog finds the chase too exciting to allow you time to set the lure again between bouts of pouncing, enlist a friend to hold him back until you're ready to go again. Terriers and other small hunting breeds, in particular, find this game exciting, and you can incorporate it into a family walk, involving children in distracting the dog while you set the lure.

WHAT HE LEARNS

How to chase and pounce upon a fast-moving object.

WHY IT'S USEFUL

Most dogs enjoy the suspense of the lure, and turning it into a chase game both entertains them and keeps them fit.

You can also play a lure game with a long line instead of a retractable leash. It will let you lay a longer trail, but it will turn into a straight game of tug when your dog catches up with you as you reel the line in.

GETTING READY FOR AGILITY CLASSES

In agility competitions, a dog must lead into the poles with his left shoulder. If you'd like your dog ultimately to attend agility classes, start him off correctly by teaching him to lead on that side from the beginning.

WEAVING GAMES 1
THROUGH CONES

Practicing with plastic cones is a soft way to introduce your dog to weaving. The easiest way to start to teach it is to use a set of small plastic cones, spaced well apart. As he gets used to the principle, you can move the cones slightly closer together to encourage him to make a tighter weave through them. If he takes to the exercise enthusiastically, you can try a set of weaving poles (see pages 128–29), which are used in agility classes and offer a slightly more challenging option.

WHAT ARE YOU GOING TO DO?

Teach your dog to weave between a set of plastic cones on cue.

1. You'll need a set of four plastic cones. Set them up in a line, with even gaps between them. Judge the gap according to the size of your dog—he should have plenty of space to walk between them.

2. Arm yourself with a handful of treats and stand with the cones to your right. Your dog should be standing facing front with the cones to his left. If necessary, you can use a treat to lure him into position.

3. Holding the treat just in front of his nose, lure your dog between the first two cones, leading with his left shoulder. As he walks between them, give him the treat and continue to lead him through the next gap with another treat.

4. Carry on weaving through the remaining gap, around the end, and back around the line. When you start, you will need plenty of treats, because, at this stage, you're luring your dog rather than rewarding.

5. Practice over a few sessions. When your dog is weaving between the cones easily, following the lure, you can start to use a cue word, "Through," as he moves into each gap.

6. Keep practicing, but gradually reduce the number of treats. Continue to use the cue until your dog is getting to the end of the cones before receiving a treat.

7. If the cones are widely spaced apart, you can reduce the space between them slightly as your dog gets more confident with the exercise.

8. When he is happily weaving through on cue, try adding a speed element (agility encourages both speed and precision)—you can run alongside him as he races through the cones.

WHAT HE LEARNS

How to weave in and out around a set of evenly spaced obstacles.

WHY IT'S USEFUL

Weaving through cones is a great introductory activity if you're thinking of taking your dog to agility classes.

WEAVING GAMES 2
USING WEAVE POLES

If your dog has enjoyed weaving using plastic cones, try him out with weave poles. These upright poles call for a tighter, more precise weave than cones; they're a classic part of all agility classes and competitions.

WHAT ARE YOU GOING TO DO?

Teach your dog to weave through a set of six weave poles. If he has learned "Through" in the previous exercise, the cue is used in exactly the same way here.

1. Line up the weave poles in position in an open area so that there is plenty of space for you to walk around as you guide your dog through the poles and for him to move freely.
2. Arm yourself with plenty of your dog's favorite treats. Just as with the previous weaving exercise using plastic cones, you'll start by luring him in and out of the poles. (If you've already taught the exercise with cones, go straight to the "Through" cue and the reward instead of luring).
3. Position yourself with the poles to your right, and your dog to the other side of them, ready to walk between the first two, leading with his left shoulder.
4. Lure your dog between the first two poles, holding a treat close to his nose as you guide him.
5. As he passes between the poles, if you are using a clicker, click and treat him (or just treat him if you're not). Direct him around the second pole, right shoulder toward it, and into the next space. Click and treat again, then around the third pole, left shoulder first,

and so on, until he passes between the last two poles, at which point, click and treat (or treat only) for the last time.

6. The weaving will probably be very jerky and uncoordinated for the first few sessions. Keep the practice short but regular. Take your dog through the exercise a couple of times per session, and persist until he begins to weave more fluidly.
7. Start to use the cue "Through" as your dog becomes more comfortable, and gradually convert the lure to a reward, keeping the treat to when he's farther along the poles each time.
8. As he gains in confidence going in and out of the poles, speed things up a little by moving faster yourself. You can gradually reduce the treats as he increasingly responds to the cue; instead, reward him as he reaches the end of the line and completes his weave through the last two poles.

WHAT HE LEARNS

How to weave with tighter, more precise movements than in the previous exercise.

WHY IT'S USEFUL

It challenges your dog to move both precisely and fast, and it is a good introduction to the skills needed in formal agility classes.

WEAVE POLES

In a competition, there will usually be twelve weave poles—which are always set 2 feet (60 centimeters) apart—but you only need six poles to teach your dog effectively at home. You can buy inexpensive standard half-sets of six poles from dog agility suppliers or online. They are made of light tubing with attached bases so they won't fall over, and many are dual-purpose, converting into simple jumps, with bases and clips to fit them together.

If your dog finds weaving one way and then back difficult, practice with two plastic cones placed 2 feet (60 centimeters) apart, luring him through a simple figure-eight pattern to help him get used to bending his body into a weave.

WEAVING GAMES 3
THERE AND BACK

When you've taught your dog to walk the weave poles in one direction, it's not a lot more work to turn him around and take him back through the other way. Don't expect miracles: If your pet can walk a six-set of poles, there and back, leading with the left shoulder and (eventually) moving easily through them without being lured, all for a treat at the end, you can both be proud of yourselves.

In agility competitions, dogs run just one way and then onto the next obstacle, so if you want to try agility classes, skip this exercise and concentrate on getting your dog to weave just one way, then immediately move on to another exercise.

WHAT ARE YOU GOING TO DO?
Teach your dog to walk the weave poles in both directions, going seamlessly back to the beginning without pausing when he gets to the end of the row.

Don't ask your dog to weave both ways down the poles until he's confident going one way without skipping poles or walking around them the wrong way.

1. Walk the six weave poles with your dog, as on pages 128-29.
2. When you get to the end, guide your dog around the last pole and turn him so that he's headed between the last two poles, going back the other way, and, as usual, leading with his left shoulder toward the first pole as he starts his weave. You'll have walked around the end pole, so although you're now headed the other way, the line of poles is still to your right.

3. Continue to the end of the row, using the "Through" cue and treating your dog as he completes it.
4. Practice daily (but just a couple of rounds per day) until your dog is confidently and easily walking first up and then down the row of poles.
5. When he's mastered the sequence, add an element of speed—jog instead of walk down the line.

WHAT HE LEARNS
To turn around and move back through the weaving poles in the opposite direction once he reaches the end of the row.

WHY IT'S USEFUL
It will allow your dog to familiarize his body with the weaving rhythm, so that he can eventually make the movements without thinking about them, just like when you're learning to dance.

131

JUMPING

For obvious reasons, jumping comes easier to some breeds than others (a French Bulldog probably won't be able to jump as high, or as elegantly, as a Saluki or a Border Collie), but even short-legged dogs can enjoy appropriately scaled jumps, especially if you're cheerleading them on.

Several kinds of jumps are used in agility classes and competitions, from the basic—a light pole balanced across supports—to more complicated setups, such as double jumps (two or more sets of bars placed a little apart), a tire suspended at jumping height, or frame jumps, which look like a window held in a frame. To teach starter jumping at home, stick to the basics. Buy a length of light plastic tube and a few supports; plastic cones of various sizes are inexpensive and make it simple to adjust the height of the jump. The bar should be light enough to fall easily if your dog knocks into it.

WHAT ARE YOU GOING TO DO?
Teach your dog to clear a hurdle of an appropriate size.

In competition, dogs are usually expected to jump hurdles that are set at their shoulder height. Start lower to build your dog's confidence, and raise the height of the jump slightly every couple of sessions.

1. Set up a jump with a length of plastic tube supported on books or pieces of wood (most cones won't be small enough to support the lowest jumps), just a couple of inches from the ground. Your dog should be able to hop over it.

2. Holding your dog on a leash, run up to the hurdle with him and jump it alongside him, saying "Over" as you both jump. Don't tug on the leash—it's there only to keep him alongside you.

3. Repeat several times, jumping yourself, even if he hesitates. Don't raise the height of the jump until he's jumping with you every time.

4. When he's jumping happily, introduce another jump or two, leaving plenty of space between them, so that you can jump in a sequence. Stop jumping and remove the leash; instead, run alongside the jumps, cuing him with "Over" and treating him when he manages the sequence by himself.

WHAT HE LEARNS
To jump over an object on cue.

WHY IT'S USEFUL
It's good practice for agility classes. If your dog happily clears streams and fallen branches when you're out walking without seeming to give it much thought, he'll really enjoy organized jumping, too.

SAFETY
Don't play jumping
games with dogs
under twelve months
old, or eighteen
months in the case
of giant breeds.

VARIATION: JUMPING THROUGH A HOOP

To teach your dog to jump through
a hoop, enlist a helper to hold the
hoop steadily at one side, and start
with it held just an inch or two
above the floor, so that your dog
only has to hop over the barrier
(he shouldn't be on the leash). Lure
him through it to begin with, saying
"Over" and offering a treat from
the other side, then, as with the
hurdles, raise the height of the hoop
gradually (although not above his
shoulder height) and run toward it
alongside him as he jumps through.

Whatever you are using for your pause table, use that and only that when you practice. If your dog isn't allowed on the furniture at home, he may need encouragement to jump on the table; keep it limited to this exercise.

USING A PAUSE TABLE

A "pause" table or box is part of every agility course; dogs are required to jump onto it and wait there—either sitting or lying—usually for a count of five seconds, after which they're asked to jump off again. Pause tables need to be sturdy with nonslip tops (this is important, because your dog may be jumping onto them from a fast speed) and are usually shoulder height to the dog.

WHAT ARE YOU GOING TO DO?

Teach your dog to jump onto a low table, stool, or ottoman, and wait there for a count of five.

Your dog should already know the "Wait" trick (see page 42) before you start. You can teach this exercise with a clicker, if you want to.

1. Choose a suitable box or small table for your dog to use. You can improvise, but be sure that it's stable, that the top has a nonslip surface, and that it's a height he can easily jump. A footstool or upholstered ottoman will work, provided that it's big enough for him to sit or lie on comfortably.
2. Arm yourself with treats and go over to the table. Call your dog to you, place a treat on the table, and tap the top of it, saying "Hup." Your dog will hop up to get the treat. If he hesitates, tap the top of the table again.
3. Before he can jump down again, say "Sit" (lure with another treat, if necessary, and if you're using a clicker, click as he sits), then hold your hand up and say "Wait," drawing out the word and keeping your eyes fixed on your dog.
4. As you speak, mentally count to a slow five in your head. When you reach five, say "OK" in an upbeat voice, and your dog will jump off the table.

5. If he gets down while you're still counting, go back to the beginning and start again.
6. Practice the jump, sit, and wait for a few sessions. When he's going through the stages consistently, put the pause table into a sequence with some active routines—perhaps between weaving and jumping exercises—so that you're using it as professional trainers do: to stop and calm their dog midcourse. As you complete the previous exercise, run up to the table, encouraging your dog to do the same, so that he goes straight from full action into a sit and wait.

Over time, if you're working toward a homemade agility course, you may find that a five-second wait isn't long enough to calm your dog down. If so, gradually build the wait time to ten seconds, counting it out for your dog slowly and calmly, before raising the pitch of your voice to say "OK" when he can recommence the action.

WHAT HE LEARNS

To take a moment's time out on cue, even when he's excited.

WHY IT'S USEFUL

In agility competitions, this exercise provides a breathing space in between high-speed activities.

INTRODUCING THE TUNNEL

If you've watched professional agility competitions, you'll have noticed that the tunnels they use are long enough to have a curve (so the dog can't see the open end of the tunnel as he enters it). When you're first introducing your dog to running through a tunnel, he'll be happier if he can see the open end as he runs into it.

WHAT ARE YOU GOING TO DO?
Teach your dog to run through a tunnel without hesitation, even if he can't see through to the other end.

1. Shorten the tunnel to around two-thirds of its full length and lay it out straight so that you can see from one end to the other. Ask your dog to sit at one of the open ends.
2. Go to the other end, bend down, so your dog can see you through the tunnel, and call him to you.
3. Many dogs will get the idea immediately and rush through the tunnel, others will run around it, discovering you with great excitement at the other end. Be ready with a treat and praise if he gets it right the first time; if he came around the wrong way, say "Uh-uh" and start again. Kneel down and lean into the far end of the tunnel to call him if he's slow to get the message.
4. When he's going through the tunnel every time, pull it out to its full length and change your position; instead of luring him through, stand with him at one end, say "Go!" and run alongside the tunnel as he runs through it, meeting him at the other end with enthusiastic praise. If he constantly tries to run with you outside the tunnel, enlist a friend to help out. One of you should call your dog from the far end of the tunnel, while the other runs alongside it as he runs through.
5. Finally, bend the tunnel, extended to its full length, into a curve, so that your dog can't see through to the far end, and ask him to run through it as usual.

WHAT HE LEARNS
To enter and exit a tunnel on cue.

WHY IT'S USEFUL
Learning to enter a tunnel on cue when he can't see through to the end helps to build your dog's confidence and his trust in you.

BUYING A TUNNEL

Invest in an inexpensive lightweight tunnel that can be used at varying lengths and is at least 10 feet (9 meters) long when expanded to its full length. Tunnels are available in a range of diameters. Pick one between 1½ and 2 feet (45–61 centimeters), which is wide enough for most dogs; the standard diameter used in competitions is 2 feet (61 centimeters). Even if your own pet is a small breed, if you are planning on practicing with friends, you want the tunnel to be wide enough to work for bigger dogs.

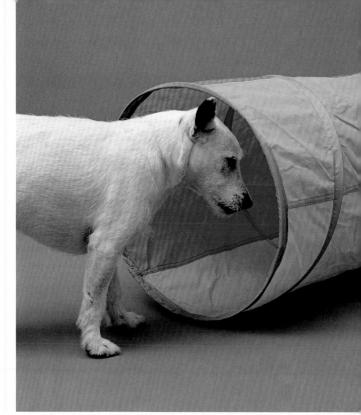

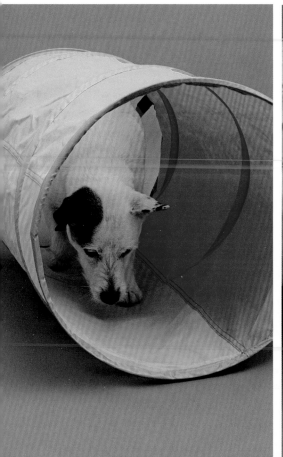

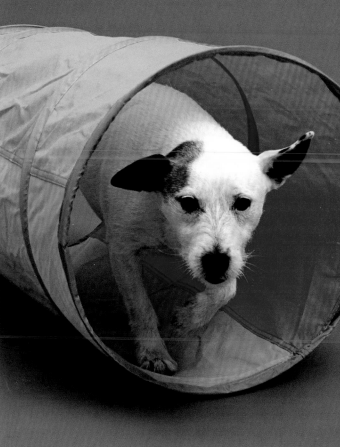

HOMEMADE AGILITY

When you've taught your dog to manage simple jumps, weave poles, the pause table, and the tunnel, you can put them together into a basic home agility course. And if you have like-minded friends who have been teaching their own dogs to negotiate the same obstacles, you can set up sessions where the dogs can play and practice agility at the same time.

THE COURSE

For a home agility circuit, you need plenty of space. If you don't have a large enough backyard, find a friend or neighbor who does and who will let you set up there, or look for a quiet public space where you'll be able to hold an improvised agility session for an hour or two.

If your dog is confident with all four of the exercises you've taught, you can add one or two elements to increase the challenge you're offering and make the course take a little longer. For example, you could arrange three jumps to start, followed by a bench for your dog to run along (new element), followed by the weave poles, followed by the pause table, then some plastic cones set up so that you can ask your dog to do a figure-eight around them (new element), and finish up with the tunnel. Set the elements out with plenty of space between them, and decide on a route that your dog and any other dogs taking part will have to follow.

Run around the route several times with your dog, correcting him with an "Uh-uh" and a pause to regroup if he takes a turn onto the wrong piece of equipment or runs off-course for a moment. Keep up the momentum as much as you can, so that your dog takes the obstacles with enthusiasm. He may

actually find it easier to do an improvised agility circuit than to take on some of the obstacles individually, because he'll be fueled by your excitement and praise as he tackles each of the exercises.

As your dog becomes more familiar with the course, scale down the number of lures and treats you offer to help him over and around the obstacles. Your eventual aim should be to take him through the course without distractions and treat him only at the end of the round. However, some of the exercises, such as the weave poles, may need the lure of treats to help him complete them for a longer time than others.

TIMING

If you would like your dog to compete in formal agility classes and shows, introduce a timing element as soon as he's familiar with your homemade course, and you and he can run it against the clock. If friends and their dogs join you for agility sessions, use a stopwatch or a phone timer to set up a competition— you could stage a knockout between half-a-dozen dogs to see who can run the course fastest. This is fun for both owners and dogs, and it will also be helpful experience for your pet if you decide to take him to agility classes.

WORKING UP TO AGILITY CLASSES AND COMPETITION

If your dog is enjoying his home-agility program, let him try his skills on a full-scale course. Look for a local agility class that offers trial sessions. These will give him the chance to make a few experimental circuits of the course before you commit to a class. Some classes require your dog to have his Canine Good Citizen certificate (proof that he's obedient enough not to disrupt the class), but many welcome complete novices and hold introductory sessions so that you can run the course in your own time and try out some of the equipment that you won't have at home.

Don't be surprised if your dog's previously well-rehearsed individual exercises fall apart when he's faced with a whole course for the first time that contains a variety of activities, only some of which he'll be familiar with. Take him around the course gradually, encourage him gently over and around the unfamiliar pieces, and let him refuse if there's anything that seems too much for him on a first try.

NEW EQUIPMENT

A typical agility class will offer all the things you've practiced: simple bar jumps, a tunnel, weave poles (usually a row of twelve), and a pause table. Other obstacles at the class may include some or all of the following:

- Tire jump and window jump: Teaching these is similar to teaching a bar jump, but they're both harder for the dog because they call for him to jump through a narrower space. Most are adjustable in height, so it's easier to start teaching these jumps at a low height until your dog is used to the smaller space around him.

- A-frame: Two wide boards, propped in an A shape, linked by a chain underneath, and adjustable to make the ramps steeper or shallower. Your dog scrambles to the top, then runs down the other side. It should be set to a wide "A" with a shallow incline while he's learning; you can make it gradually steeper as he becomes used to it.

- Dog walk: A narrow plank with shallow slopes at both ends that your dog has to run along, making contact with the colored areas at each end (these ensure that your dog runs the whole length of the walk and doesn't jump off).

- See-saw (also known as the teeter-totter): This is just like a child's plank see-saw, but without handles at each end, and with a base that extends at each side at the center point (this will act as a visual reminder that it's the point at which the plank starts to tip—in time, your dog will learn to slow down at this point). Take this one slowly; it's one of the hardest obstacles for your pet to learn, and he needs to be supported to discourage him from jumping off partway along.

140

- Closed tunnel or chute: This is a tunnel made from nylon or light canvas with one open end. Beyond the frame that holds the end open, it's soft, so that the fabric collapses onto the ground. Your dog has to learn to tunnel through it, pushing his way by using his nose. Because he has to go into a dark, confined space, he may take some time to learn to go through the chute confidently.

While these aren't all the possible obstacles or equipment you may find on an agility course, most or all of them will feature on the majority of courses.

FROM FIRST CLASS TO COMPETITION

From a trial class—when your and your dog will usually be going around the course in your own time, with one-on-one advice from the trainer, and perhaps just a handful of other dogs and their owners present, waiting their turn—to your first class, which will be louder, faster, and more exciting, is a big step. Get as much private practice as you can to accustom your pet to the obstacles he finds more challenging. Some clubs and classes have times when you can reserve the course for a solo session, so take advantage of this if it's available, and use the time to concentrate on the obstacles that your dog finds hardest, with short breaks for simpler exercises he can do easily when his confidence needs a boost.

Most classes will only introduce an "against-the-clock" element when your dog is confident on every piece of equipment. The excitement of a timing element—with plenty of encouragement from you as you run the course alongside him—may get better results from your dog than you expected. If adding speed to the other requirements makes your dog stressed and results in a poor round, however, take the pressure off and let him go back to doing the course at his natural pace until he feels more confident.

SAFETY

Help your dog around the course and don't press him on any particular obstacle that makes him nervous. Support him when he is on raised obstacles, and jumps should be set low until he's used to them.

Here's an example of a course layout used in an agility competition. The circuit the dog should take is marked on it. Layouts can vary a lot, but the different elements shown here in this beginner-to-medium course are typical. As well as five assorted jumps, the course incorporates two pipe tunnels, one closed tunnel, weave poles, a seesaw, an A-frame, a dog walk, and a pause table.

Begin by walking your dog to the course's entrance. When he starts to move, run alongside him, directing him over the first jump (1) before encouraging him to go through the pipe tunnel (2) and guiding him over the second jump (3) and through the closed tunnel (4).

Keeping the momentum going, direct him through the second pipe tunnel (5) and through the tire jump (6). Utilize his running start to take him up and over the A-frame (7), enabling him to take his time as he comes down the other side, before jogging alongside him as you navigate your way back through the first tunnel (8).

Take your dog over the seesaw (9), letting him control the pivot before encouraging him to jump up and onto the pause table (10). He must then wait in either a "Sit" or a "Down" position for a designated period of time.

Following on from his momentary respite, approach the set of ten weave poles (11), making sure that your dog leads with his left side as he negotiates in and around while not skipping any of the poles.

Guide your dog over the fourth jump (12) before approaching the dog walk (13). Finally, take your dog over one last jump (14) before finishing the agility course—taking a moment to appreciate the teamwork required of you both.

SCALE:

Each square is 10ft x 10ft (3.3m x 3.3m)

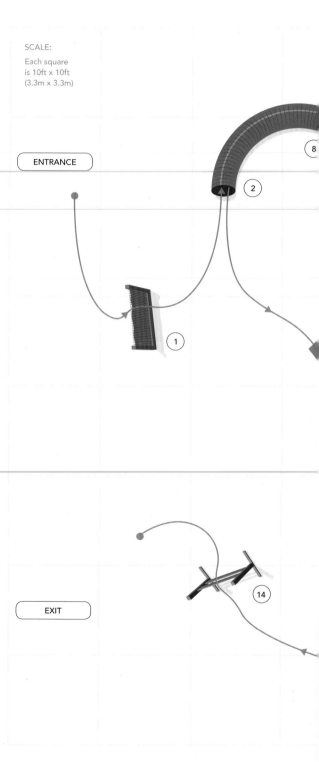

ENTRANCE

EXIT

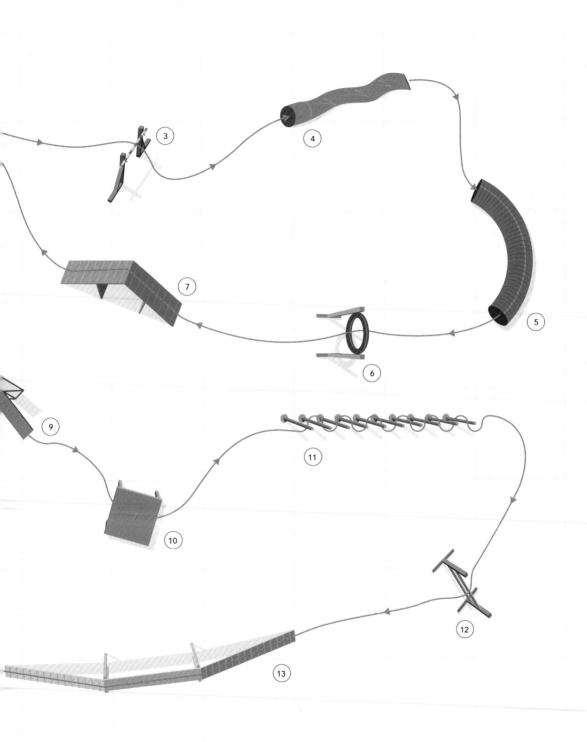

CHAPTER 6

FIGURING IT OUT

GAMES TO STRETCH YOUR DOG

If you've already taught your dog a range of skills and tricks from the earlier chapters in the book, this chapter contains a handful of different options that may prove a little more challenging. There are tricks here to impress an audience—calling for your pet to fetch your keys and getting him to follow instructions in a foreign language—as well as a get-the-treat agility game and even a couple of exercises to develop your pet's soccer and skateboarding skills.

FIND MY KEYS

If you taught your dog the beginner's versions of fetching and carrying (see "Take It" on pages 54–55, and "Carrying" on pages 60–63), and the "Swap" exercise (see pages 86–87), this exercise is a good progression. It combines the earlier versions into something more complicated, and the keys are smaller and harder to carry than a soft bag or toy, too.

WHAT ARE YOU GOING TO DO?

Ask your dog to collect your keys, which you've left on a low surface nearby, and to bring them to you.

Your dog should know the "Take It," "Carry," and "Swap" cues before you start. Be ready to practice the different stages separately, rewarding each one, before you put them together.

1. "Find My Keys" has three different stages: your dog has to pick the keys up, carry them in his mouth, and bring them to you. Start to teach it by handing your dog the keys, then asking him to carry them. Hold the keys out to your dog and ask him to "Take It."

2. Choose a spot to which you want your dog to carry the keys. Now he's holding the keys, so accompany him over to the spot, asking him to "Carry." If he drops the keys on the way, repeat the "Take It" command, and wait until he has a firm hold before going back to "Carry."

3. As soon as you both reach the spot, hold out your hand and ask him to "Swap." When he gives the keys up, give him a treat—take one from the bag if you opted to use one (see opposite page); otherwise, have one ready to give him.

4. Practice the exercise in this form for a while. If he seems confused, go back to the basic steps, rewarding each one,

for a few sessions. When he has the different parts mastered, lay the keys on a low surface or the floor for him to pick up instead of handing them to him.

5. After a few more sessions in which he practices picking up the keys himself, place them on the floor, making sure he sees where they are, then go and stand next to the spot where he usually brings them and ask him to "Take It."

6. Usually the dog finds the most challenging part of this trick is picking up the keys when he and they are at a distance from you. Once he's holding them, the "Carry" cue and some encouraging noises are usually enough to get him to bring them over to you, and "Swap" is easily managed with a treat. Stay a few yards away from your dog as he practices combining the stages, stepping in only with extra guidance if he seems to be getting really confused. Practice regularly until he can manage all three stages at once without hesitating between them.

WHAT HE LEARNS

To manage a trickier version of the pick-up-and-carry exercises he already knows.

WHY IT'S USEFUL

It's a multistage exercise that will give him a good brain workout.

KEY TRICKS

To make it a little easier for your pet to pick the keys up, attach a large, soft fob to them while you're practicing, so there's something for him to get hold of. If you need an extra incentive to get his interest when you start, attach the keys to a small zipper-top purse that contains treats—he'll be able to smell the treats but not access them.

SAFETY
This game isn't suitable for a dog with back problems or joint stiffness, nor for long-backed breeds that are prone to back problems. It's best for young, agile dogs, over a year old, who love to jump and who will be able to extract the treats from the toy.

HANGING TREATS

We've already noted that dogs don't tend naturally to work above their heads, although many are accomplished jumpers, so going after a treat toy hung up high makes the most of an agile dog's skills. Ideally, your dog should be familiar with the treat-dispensing toy before you start. If he's already rolled it around on the floor to get the treats out, he'll have a better idea of what he needs to do when he sees it hanging up.

WHAT ARE YOU GOING TO DO?

Encourage your dog to use a treat dispenser that's hung on a stretchy bungee cord at head level.

You can set this game up to be played inside or outdoors. You'll need a secure suspended line, such as a clothesline, that won't give way mid-game; an elasticized bungee cord (the kind that is adjustable in length and fastens with clips, not hooks); and a treat dispenser with a hole in the center that goes all the way through. The latter should give up its treats fairly easily—the balancing as your dog tries to extract them will already be challenging for him.

If you're playing indoors, set the line up over a nonslip surface so that your dog doesn't slide around when he's trying to extract the treats.

1. Put two or three treats in the toy and encourage your dog to play with it so that his interest is engaged.
2. When he's taken the treats out by rolling the toy on the floor, thread the toy onto the bungee rope, refill it with treats, and hang it over the secured line, clipping it together so that the bungee is in a loop and the toy is hanging a little above your dog's head.
3. Call your dog and swing the toy back and forth a while, then sit back and watch him jump up and try to work out how to get the treats.
4. Adjust the length of the bungee if the toy's hanging too high for your pet to get any purchase on it; he needs to have enough chance of success to keep him interested, but not enough for him to empty the toy quickly.
5. This game can be a tough challenge, because the toy will both swing back and forth and slide up and down the line. If your dog is not having any success after a few minutes and is becoming frustrated, you can hold the bungee so that he has to deal only with the swinging motion and is more likely to snag a treat.

WHAT HE LEARNS

To use balance and agility to extract treats from a familiar toy.

WHY IT'S USEFUL

This game helps build on your dog's natural balance and coordination—and can rekindle interest in a toy that's become familiar to him.

SPEAK MY LANGUAGE

Sleight of hand, or rather mouth, is what makes this trick work. Your dog can't really learn a second or third language (truthfully, he doesn't speak English, either). But you can introduce alternative cue words in another language for simple actions and accompany them with gestures that give your dog an extra indicator of what he should do. When he's mastered a few alternative instructions, show off his bi- or trilingual skills. He should win plenty of applause for his new accomplishment.

The easiest instructions to cue in another language—tying into actions that your dog already knows—are "Sit" and "Down" (see pages 38–39), and "Say Hello" (see pages 50–51). You can choose any other language you want as an alternative; the equivalents to these three cues in German and French are, respectively, "Sitzen," "Platz," and "Hallo sagen," and "Assis," "Couche," and "Dis Bonjour."

WHAT ARE YOU GOING TO DO?
Teach your dog to learn new cue words for tricks he has already mastered.

1. Start with "Sit." Even if your dog is so used to sitting on request that he sits the second you ask, without needing a treat, take him back to the beginning and lure with a treat, taking it slightly over his head, exactly as you did when you were first teaching him. Practice with the familiar "Sit" cue for a day or two as part of your daily teaching session.
2. When you've reintroduced the cue-sit-treat sequence, introduce a new cue, keeping the rest of the exercise exactly the same—use the treat to lure, and as your dog sits, use the new cue, such as "Assis." Because the situation is so familiar, most dogs will sit automatically.

3. Practice daily, swapping between English and another language for the cue, but keeping everything else about the trick the same. After a few sessions you should be able to abandon the lure and the treat, and just use the cue. Alternate between the two different language cues, and praise your dog when he sits.
4. Use this sequence to extend your dog's repertoire to "Down" and "Say Hello," going over each exercise in exactly the way you originally taught it, and gradually introducing the alternative cue. Only introduce one alternative cue for each exercise at first—you can add more languages once he's mastered one set of alternative cues.
5. When your dog is happily responding to one or more extra languages, get him to perform to an audience.

WHAT HE LEARNS
To connect a particular behavior with more than one cue.

WHY IT'S USEFUL
This one is purely for entertainment—although you can flatter foreign friends by teaching your dog to follow instructions in their own language.

Some owners are concerned that introducing different cues for familiar actions will confuse their dog. But the familiarity of the everyday exercises means that you will tend to ask the dog in the same way every time, so tone and body language are usually enough of a reinforcement for your dog to understand what you're asking for.

You will probably use a lot of treats teaching this game, so give your dog slightly smaller rations in his meal to balance things out.

SOCCER

Chances are that you've kicked a ball around with your dog already—most owners have enjoyed a game in the backyard or the park, and few dogs don't enjoy playing with a soccer ball. In this game, you're going to teach your dog how to direct the ball; once he's learned that, you may even be able to get him to make a goal.

WHAT ARE YOU GOING TO DO?

Teach your dog to dribble with his nose, using careful luring and treats.

It's best to teach this game outdoors, although you can play indoors, provided you have enough clear floor space for your dog to get a few yards of dribbling in without bumping into the furniture. You can use a clicker if you want, although you'll have to be dextrous, because you'll also be juggling treats and the ball. Start with a ball that's completely inflated; if it's even a little spongy or soft, your dog will get a grip and puncture it with his teeth.

If your dog is mildly enthusiastic about soccer balls, it's easy to teach him to dribble a ball. It's much harder if you have a die-hard ball fanatic, because your dog will be so desperate to play with the ball that it will interfere with his concentration on the game you want to teach him. If that's the case, allow plenty of time for this exercise and start by enjoying an energetic game with him for twenty or thirty minutes; when you've taken the edge off his energy, it will be easier to teach him.

1. Arm yourself with a supply of treats. Place one on the ground under the ball and hold it lightly with one hand. If your dog isn't already eagerly nosing the ball, call him over and encourage him to reach the treat.

2. As your dog starts to nose the soccer ball, let it go, so that it rolls as he pushes it. While he's still pushing, say "Push." As the ball rolls, he'll stop to eat the treat. While he's eating, roll the ball a little farther and place another treat under it.

3. Repeat until you have a rhythm going—push, treat, push, treat—being careful to say "Push" only when he's actually pushing the ball.

4. Gradually, over a number of sessions, reduce the number of treats you reward him with, keeping up the cue word. At first, you reward every time he pushes, then every couple of pushes, then every third push.

5. As he gets gradually enthused by pushing the ball for its own sake, back off and roll it toward him, then away from him. Try to set up an exchange in which you roll the ball to each other.

WHAT HE LEARNS

To improve his agility by learning to direct a ball using his nose.

WHY IT'S USEFUL

You can incorporate a soccer ball into your dog's agility exercises to add an extra level of complexity: he can weave the ball between cones, push it in front of him, or follow it through a tunnel.

SKATEBOARDING

Of course, you'd love a dog who skateboards—who wouldn't? And it may well be possible if you have a confident dog and are prepared to spend a lot of time teaching him. Even with a confident dog who's eager to learn new things, teaching him to skateboard is a big project, and it will take many, many sessions for him to learn. It has to be his decision, and not every dog will want to try, so respect his choice if you've patiently spent time trying to encourage him and he's anxious and has decided against it. As usual, the trick has to be fun for both of you, so use your judgment when teaching this one.

WHAT ARE YOU GOING TO DO?

Teach your dog to climb onto a skateboard and balance on it as it moves.

Your dog should know "Say Hello" (see pages 50–51) before you start.

All teaching should be done on a flat surface so the skateboard can't roll unexpectedly. You need a sturdy skateboard and two large, heavy books to block any movement of the skateboard while your dog is learning. Start to teach indoors—ideally in a carpeted room—and without distractions. You will need to repeat each tiny stage many, many times with this exercise to be sure your dog is relaxed with the process.

1. Put the skateboard on the floor and place the books so they securely stop it from moving. (Any sudden movement before your dog is happy and comfortable with the skateboard will probably unnerve him, so be careful to block it properly).
2. Call your dog, kneel down next to the skateboard, and encourage him to sniff around it and check it out.
3. When he's had a good look, ask your dog to "Say Hello," and allow his front paw to drop onto the skateboard. Reward him for leaving it there, and repeat the exercise until he's used to his paw dropping onto the board and expects a reward for keeping it there. Always let him place his paw on the board himself; don't ever pick it up and put it there.
4. When he's happy to keep one paw on the board, repeat the process with his second front paw while his first is still on the board, and reward him for keeping both front paws on the board. Again, be ready to repeat this stage many, many times before moving on.
5. Introduce a cue for your dog to put both front paws on the board— "Skate"—and start to use it, while reducing the number of treats.
6. With your dog's front paws on the board, gently move the front book blocking the skateboard forward a few inches, so that the board can move a little. Have treats on hand so you can immediately reward your dog when the board moves. Control the movement carefully by steadying the board with your hand—you shouldn't let it move more than an inch or two at first.

(continued)

You need quiet surroundings to practice outside; be sure to choose somewhere well away from the road, ideally also without much pedestrian traffic.

7. When your dog moves the board—as he will by rebalancing his front and back feet—give him a reward. Again, be ready to practice this step many, many times before moving on. If he jumps off, don't coerce him back on the board, but take him slowly through the stages, one paw at a time, until he's back on.

8. Gradually, you should be able to allow the board to move a little farther each time your dog gets on, offering him a treat just in front of him as the board begins to move. The carpeted surface will stop the board from traveling too far or too fast.

9. Practice regularly until your dog is hopping onto the skateboard and traveling a few more inches each time, with regular rewards. Eventually, you should be able to remove the second book support at the back of the board, because your dog will understand how much movement on his part it takes to move the skateboard.

10. When he is perfectly confident skating short distances on a carpeted surface, try out his moves outdoors, on a smooth surface on which the board will move more easily, such as a cement path. Take it slowly, as with the previous steps, until he gets used to the different movement the board has on the cement.

Always stay close to the skateboard while your dog is on it—remember that although he's moving the skateboard, he isn't in control of it.

WHAT HE LEARNS
Skateboarding can be exciting—for the right dog. It's the ultimate balance challenge.

WHY IT'S USEFUL
It really isn't useful, except as the ultimate audience pleaser—ideal for a pet who loves the limelight.

CHAPTER 7

GETTING ALONG

DOG-TO-DOG PLAY

However much time you spend with your dog—playing, training, walking, or hanging out together—you won't ever be able completely to replace dog-to-dog interaction and play. Playing with other dogs can be an important part of most pets' lives, and if a dog has been well socialized in puppyhood, he won't usually have problems. Overall, dogs tend to communicate well with one another with only occasional misunderstandings— which are usually easily corrected, if necessary, by owners calling time out—and you can learn a lot from watching dogs having fun together.

HOW DOGS READ OTHER DOGS

You can use your pet's playtime with other dogs to learn some canine signals. They may not be able to speak, but dogs "talk" all the time, using both their facial expressions and body language. One study of more than thirty dogs, interacting in pairs and trios, estimated that each animal was sending around a dozen signs a minute, from tongue flicks and eye squints to play bows and body freezes. This is language your dog may not always share with you—you've given him no ideas that you're fluent in "Dog."

So why is it useful to learn a little dogspeak? First, a lot of this book has been about building a bond with your pet. Any experienced owner knows that their pet generally does most of the heavy lifting when it comes to making himself understood to his humans. A little effort going the other way can only be a good thing—and may help to eradicate misunderstandings as to what your dog is trying to tell you. Second, getting used to watching his reactions in all kinds of different scenarios is definitely helpful when it comes to teaching and training him—you'll be quicker to see when he's confused or uncomfortable with what he's being asked to do, or even when he's reaching a level of excitement that may render him obsessive about a particular game or activity.

WHAT ARE YOU LOOKING FOR?

Just as people do, dogs talk in different ways: there is the unconscious body language that happens naturally, and there are the signs that they seem to use deliberately to tell others something specific. Earlier chapters have touched here and there on some of the signals dogs send, but only regular observation will familiarize you with a particular dog's messages and tell you which body language leads to which results.

People sometimes think they know what a dog is saying but get it wrong, because they're unfamiliar with the finer detail. Take a simple example: A dog is looking toward another and wagging his tail—but he is actually highly excited in a tense, overaroused way that will probably lead to a fight. Still, most people think they know that dogs wag their tails when they're happy, so the situation is easily misunderstood. A loose, sweeping tail accompanied by a relaxed body does usually indicate a happy dog, but if the wag is from a stiff tail, held tensely, and consists of short, staccato movements from side to side, chances are that the dog isn't feeling relaxed and happy at all, and it would be best to intervene before trouble starts.

GOOD-TEMPERED PLAY

If you don't normally watch dog play closely, start by looking out for some

160

of the following reliable signs that he's enjoying himself and is behaving sociably with his playmate:

- Slightly closed, almost squinty eyes.
- An open mouth and relaxed, lolling tongue.
- Frequent play bows (front paws extended, bottom in air—the universal sign that a dog wants to play), during momentary pauses in the game.
- Body held loosely and tail wagging in a broad, sweeping motion.
- Regular changes in play, every minute or two, marked by a momentary pause—for example, a dog who was being chased becomes the chaser, and vice versa.

WHEN PLAY ISN'T GOING WELL

Here are a few signs that the game is not as good-tempered as you'd want it to be, and that the dogs may need distracting:

- A dog looking at another with a sustained stare, with hard eyes and slightly lowered head—giving a stalking impression.
- A dog with a closed or nearly closed mouth with tightened commissure

(mouth corners)—you usually see this tight mouth before things turn into growling or snapping.

- Hard body slamming, in which one dog repeatedly barges another, hitting him hard, without the second dog reciprocating in the same way. Some dogs enjoy this tough form of play, but if the enjoyment isn't mutual, it's not generally received as good etiquette on the part of a play partner.
- Longer pauses in play, when the dogs freeze before starting again—if the freezes are accompanied by a lowered body stance and increasingly slow body movements, it's time to interrupt.

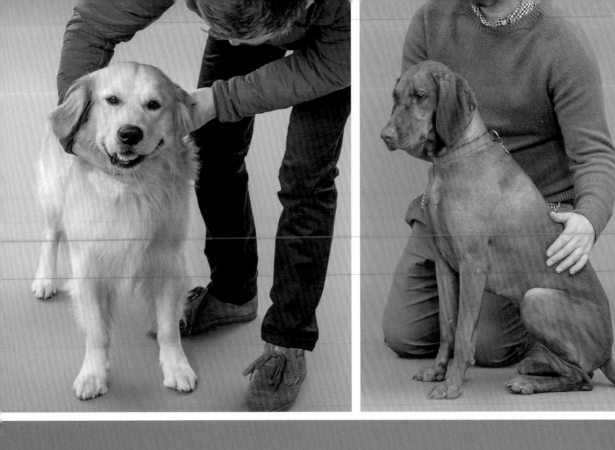

ABOUT YOU
HOW TO HELP WITH SOCIALIZATION

If your dog was socialized as a puppy, he's probably already enthusiastic about meeting other dogs and will have learned a few canine manners to be sure that other dogs are happy to meet him. With well-socialized dogs, a first meeting will usually be enough for you to see if they're merely going to tolerate one another, or, best of all, take to each other immediately and seem likely to become good friends.

Play with another dog teaches your pet to match his energy to that of another dog and offers him the opportunity to practice his fluency with his own species. The more positive play experiences, appropriately supervised, that a dog can enjoy, the more comfortable he will probably be in the company of other dogs.

The advantages of having a dog who is relaxed around other dogs are obvious; it's also helpful to you to see how your dog behaves socially, because it can highlight areas you can work on together.

SETTING HIM UP FOR SUCCESS: FIRST MEETINGS

Even with well-socialized dogs, there are a few dos and don'ts for first meetings. If you know the dogs well, start outside, walking them side by side on-leash a few paces apart; if they seem eager to interact, gradually walk them closer together so they can perform canine introductions. If it goes well, switch to off-leash interaction in an open space, so that they don't feel confined in a situation in which they don't have any control.

First meetings are best held on neutral territory in an open space, where there's plenty of room to run around. When dogs have met a couple of times and you know that confrontational behavior isn't likely, you can try meetings at home, first in the backyard, then in the house. It's best not to leave any favorite toys lying around when meeting at home, whether in the house or backyard. If a visiting dog helps himself to a toy that the resident especially values, it may result in fireworks.

Always supervise dogs at play, making sure that their energies are evenly matched and there's no bullying. If the energy in a game seems to be rising to a point where overexcitement could turn into barging, nipping, or other problems, call both dogs over, ask them to "Sit," and give them each a treat, refocusing before play starts again. Signs that you may have a problem include persistent power plays—when one dog keeps mounting the other, or repeatedly places a paw on the other's back—and increasingly tense body language. If these persist, call an end to the play session and try again another day.

MATCHING PLAY TYPES

Play to your dog's strengths when you arrange for him to spend time with other dogs. Take an in-depth look at his favored style of play and try to be sure that he's matched with dogs who like playing in the same ways.

The well-known trainer and author Pat Miller made a study of different styles of dog play, dividing the kinds of games and activities she observed between dogs into six broad groups: Body Slammers, Wrestlers, Chasers, Tuggers, Cheerleaders, and Soft Touches. Most of the dogs didn't like to play in every different style, and some mismatches between styles—mixing a Body Slammer with a Chaser, for instance—rarely worked out. Two play types often didn't join in with play at all: a Cheerleader—the same type sometimes nicknamed "the play police" by dog owners—tends to run around the outside of a game, often jumping and barking, but rarely actually risking contact; while the Soft Touch, as the name implies, is intimidated by fast play with a lot of hard body contact, and tends to look for a quieter personality to have fun with.

WHAT'S HIS NATURAL STYLE?

Watch your dog playing with others. He may be a dog who loves to run full out as much of the time as he can, in which case, you have a Chaser; he may seize the opportunity to grab one end of a tug toy and tease another player with it until the dog grabs the other end—in which case, he's a Tugger. Of course, he may be both, but although dogs switch between activities and some will be enthusiastic about several types of play, few enjoy every kind. Establishing his favorites not only helps you to see which kind

of playmate suits him best, but also which games he may enjoy most when he's playing with you.

DOGS ON THE PERIPHERY

If your pet is a natural Cheerleader, he's more likely to play easily with you than with other dogs. The Cheerleader seems to have cast himself as the one in charge of other dogs' play: what style of play they prefer, who's allowed to play, and how excited the players are allowed to get. He'll usually do this by circling and barking while other dogs play, sometimes actually putting himself between two players in order to call a halt to things (perhaps the players are having too much fun). If that's a description of your dog, he should find it easier to relax into a game if he's with only one other—ideally familiar—dog at a time.

SHY DOG

At the other end of the spectrum, the Soft Touch dog is gentle and easily quashed. He'll usually be happiest playing with dogs who aren't too bold and assertive, either. If this is your dog, go gently with introductions, and watch for signs that he's looking overwhelmed by another dog's play style—if he's spending a lot of time at the bottom of a wrestling pile or freezing in chase games in a way that doesn't look relaxed, or evidently trying to escape a game by backing off or out, call time and look for a more suitable play companion for your pet.

WHEN YOUR DOG IS NERVOUS

What if, despite your best efforts, you have a dog who appears nervous or even aggressive in the company of most, or all, other dogs? Can you help him overcome his fears and learn to play? Often the answer will be yes, but you need to take a cautious and careful approach and you should call in professional help—a nervous dog needs knowledgeable handling. This is a special subject that we can only treat briefly here, but if you have a nervous dog, there are some useful resources listed on page 174.

WHY DOESN'T HE LIKE OTHER DOGS?

It can be hard to establish the reason why a dog is nervous in the company of others, but the most common cause is inadequate socialization when your pet was going through his key development stages. If he wasn't socialized as a puppy, this can be hard to fix later on. Some dogs, too, even when socialized, still find play with other dogs stressful and a little unnerving. If your dog is a rescue dog who came to you as an adult, you may never know what happened in his past that makes him less socially skilled now.

WHAT NOW?

The most important thing with a nervous or fear-aggressive dog is that both he and the other dogs and people he encounters be kept safe. Don't try to work it out alone. As soon as possible, do some research and seek out a reputable behaviorist or trainer who will give you some one-on-one help.

ONE OF THE GANG

Sometimes you may have to leave your dog in circumstances where he's mixed in a big group—whether it's going to be a daily occurrence with a familiar dog walker coming to take him out while you're at work, one day a week at a dog day-care center, or a dogsitter integrating him into his or her canine group while you're on vacation.

Before you leave your dog in a big group, check how comfortable he is with the specific group in advance—don't just leave him in the situation and expect him to manage. Any good day-care center or dog walker will be happy to have you tag along for an hour or two to check that your pet will be comfortable and happy playing and socializing as part of a group.

Check the formalities with both dog walkers and day-care centers—make sure they are insured and qualified to care for your dog—and ask plenty of questions. Day-care centers should have sufficient staff to watch with and interact with dogs, instead of leaving groups mixing unsupervised. Dog walkers should limit the number of dogs they take out per walk; some local governments may specify a maximum number of dogs that a single walker can take out at any one time, but in any case, the dog walker should only walk as many dogs as he or she can easily control.

EPILOGUE
PLAYING FOR LIFE

We've already said that you can play with your dog all his life. The same holds the other way—if you find yourself immobile or with limited mobility for any reason, there are still plenty of games and exercises you can use to vary the daily routine.

PLAYING WITH AN OLDER DOG

Don't let your dog's routine get into a rut just because he is aging. There are plenty of ways to keep his day-to-day life enjoyable and varied that don't depend on peak physical fitness. In some cases, just a few tweaks to his usual range of activities can make them fun for him again.

- Try out some variations on "Hunt the treat," with some small but high-value and tempting food rewards. You may find it easier with an older dog that won't try to tackle everything at a hundred miles an hour.
- Take treat hunting outside, too, by scattering a handful of small treats into the grass in the backyard and encouraging your dog to hunt for them.
- Consider teaching him some extra tricks. A dog that already knows how to give a paw might be encouraged to do a high five, or if he's learned to lie on cue, try encouraging him to "Play Dead" on his side. Practice the tricks on a soft surface.
- If your dog has taken to plodding around on his regular walks, take him on some new routes in different places. To a dog, a huge part of every walk is based on scent, and even a short walk in a new location will offer him a completely different scent landscape to explore.

- Cut back on more energetic activities a little, but don't give them up. A dog that used to run 50 yards (45 meters) after a tennis ball you hurled with a ball thrower may still enjoy a more leisurely game of "Fetch" in the backyard.

WHEN YOU CAN'T PLAY

If you can't run around with him as much as usual, look at games you can practice together in one spot. The only challenge is keeping your dog's interest.

- A trash picker is useful if you're not mobile. Use it as an extended hand to move toys around on the floor or challenge your pet to a game of tug.
- Get your dog chasing bubbles around the room—all you have to do is blow them for him, using a children's bubble-blowing kit with a wand.
- If you're using a cane, make it into an improvised low jump for your dog to clear.
- Teach your dog to jump up onto a nearby stool or ottoman.

You can use enforced immobility to concentrate on your verbal cues overall. It's a useful reminder that you don't always have to move around much for your dog to grasp what you want him to do.

DOG GALLERY

Dotty

Bella

Chunk

Patch

Rufus

Milly

Buster Blades

Bear

Amber

Bailey

Vizzy

Nugget

Treacle

Zara

Alfie

Buster

Itch

Polo

FURTHER READING

GENERAL BOOKS

Bradshaw, John. *In Defence of Dogs.* Allen Lane: 2011.

Clothier, Suzanne. *Bones Would Rain From the Sky: Deepening Our Relationship With Dogs.* Warner Books: 2005.

Coppinger, Raymond and Mark Feinstein. *How Dogs Work.* University of Chicago Press: 2015.

McConnell, Patricia. *For the Love of a Dog: Understanding Emotion in You & Your Best Friend.* Ballantine Books: 2007.

McConnell, Patricia. *The Other End of the Leash.* Ballantine Books: 2002.

BASIC TRAINING

Dennison, Pamela. *You Can Train Your Dog: Mastering the Art & Science of Modern Dog Training.* Shadow Publishing: 2015.

FEEDING DOGS

Bendix, Kate. *The Dog Diet.* Short Books Ltd: 2016.

Macdonald, Carina Beth. *Raw Dog Food: Making it Work for You and Your Dog.* Dogwise Publishing: 2011.

Morrison, Henrietta. *Dinner for Dogs.* Ebury Press: 2012.

Olson, Lew. *Raw and Natural Nutrition for Dogs: The Definitive Guide to Homemade Meals.* North Atlantic Books: 2015.

DEALING WITH PROBLEMS

Aloff, Brenda. *Aggression in Dogs: Practical Management, Prevention & Behavior Modification.* Dogwise: 2002.

Brown, Ali. *Scaredy Dog: Understanding and Rehabilitating Your Reactive Dog.* Tanacacia Press: 2009.

McConnell, Patricia. *The Cautious Canine: How to Help Dogs Conquer Their Fears.* McConnell Publishing Limited: 2005.

Miller, Pat. *Do-Over Dogs: Give Your Dog a Second Chance for a First-Class Life.* Dogwise Publishing: 2010.

Stewart, Grisha. *Behavior Adjustment Training 2.0: New Practical Techniques for Fear, Frustration, and Aggression.* Dogwise Publishing: 2016.

INDEX

Puppies

for dummies®

A Wiley Brand

Puppies

4th Edition

by Sarah Hodgson

A Wiley Brand

Puppies For Dummies®, 4th Edition

Published by: **John Wiley & Sons, Inc.**, 111 River Street, Hoboken, NJ 07030-5774, www.wiley.com

Copyright © 2019 by John Wiley & Sons, Inc., Hoboken, New Jersey

Published simultaneously in Canada

For general information on our other products and services, please contact our Customer Care Department within the U.S. at 877-762-2974, outside the U.S. at 317-572-3993, or fax 317-572-4002. For technical support, please visit https://hub.wiley.com/community/support/dummies.

Wiley publishes in a variety of print and electronic formats and by print-on-demand. Some material included with standard print versions of this book may not be included in e-books or in print-on-demand. If this book refers to media such as a CD or DVD that is not included in the version you purchased, you may download this material at http://booksupport.wiley.com. For more information about Wiley products, visit www.wiley.com.

Library of Congress Control Number: 2019935454

ISBN: 978-1-119-55847-7; 978-1-119-55848-4 (ebk); 978-1-119-55850-7 (ebk)

Manufactured in the United States of America

C10008881_031819

Contents at a Glance

Table of Contents

Introduction

To say that I love puppies would be an understatement. So, when asked to write the fourth edition of *Puppies For Dummies*, I jumped at the opportunity. There has been an explosion of changes in how to raise and train dogs over the past few decades, with fancy terms you'll read about in a new Chapter 6, "Bonding with Your Puppy Using the New Science of Modern Dog Parenting." Researchers from across the globe are doing fascinating studies — even some you can get involved with that reveal how dogs communicate and learn best. The good news for trainers who use positive reinforcement and encouragement to teach their students how to behave? Many studies show that dogs learn most quickly in the first months of puppyhood and respond best to training that encourages their focus and reinforces good behavior. Goodbye to the alphacentric approach, where correcting the puppy for what they're doing wrong instead of teaching them how to act right, is the order of the day. Research has shown what many dog lovers have long recognized as common sense:

>> A domineering approach is inextricably tied to the practice of physical punishment.

>> Electronic collars that buzz, spray, or shock clearly terrify puppies.

Alphacentric training philosophies create fear and (as studies show) don't train or teach puppies to be friendly, happy, well-mannered family members. Trust me: You won't find support for that approach in this book.

What you will find is a common-sense approach to selecting your puppy, loving hints to help you through those first critical months, and support in problem-solving and training. You'll find straightforward info in plain English on what to do and how to do it. Nothing more and nothing less — I promise.

Even though raising a puppy is also a daily responsibility (and a huge one, at that), it's like many other projects in life: After you understand how to determine what your puppy is thinking, and after you find out how you can communicate with them effectively and structure your environment to limit your frustrations, the day-to-day tasks and problems immediately become simpler. The comment I hear most often from clients after our initial visit is this: "You are a miracle worker!" But I know that the real miracle is the puppy. Like an interpreter, I just facilitate the communication between the two species.

About This Book

Raising a child is a big project that is only made easier by reading a stack of how-to books and organizing systems, like mealtimes and potty routines, that eventually become habits. Fortunately for you, puppy raising is nearly identical, with the bonus that, unlike children who take a couple of decades to mature, a puppy matures within a year. *Puppies For Dummies,* 4th Edition, will help you simplify this whole adventure from the onset of choosing a puppy for your family to managing your puppy's day-to-day needs, training and playing, and dealing with everyday frustrations. Behind every happy puppy is a supportive, understanding, and nurturing family cheering them on!

If you're feeling overwhelmed by this project now, don't despair: This book gives you a whole new outlook, provides easy steps to resolve annoyances, and helps you civilize your puppy in no time flat. In this book, which is meant to be an all-inclusive guide, I walk you through the early decisions — purebred or rescue, low shedding or superfuzzy, big or small — and then provide everything you need to know to raise your puppy right. I'm excited to get started!

Conventions Used in This Book

While writing this book, I used a few conventions that I'd like you to know about ahead of time:

- » To avoid any "puppy gender bias," I use plural pronouns: that is, *they* and *their,* throughout the book. Except for anything that's strictly related to females or males, you can be sure that the info applies to your puppy regardless of gender.

- » Anytime I introduce a new term, I *italicize* it.

- » Keywords in lists appear in **boldface.** Also, when I present a list of steps to perform, the action you need to take is in **boldface.**

Optional Reading

Please don't be stressed by the size of this book. I know, right? Who has the time to read a 400-page book from cover to cover? Of course, you can, but I wrote each chapter as a stand-alone unit and would be just as pleased if you used this book as a quick reference guide. If you're pressed for time, use the trusty index guide to find what you need and go there. Don't need help choosing the right puppy or talking to breeders or shelters? Then there's no need for you to read chapters that help with those situations. And, though the sidebars contain information that fascinates me, it's not Required Reading. Finally, if you're in a real hurry, you can skip any paragraphs that have the Technical Stuff or Just for Fun icons attached to them.

Bottom line? I'm thrilled that you've picked my book off the shelf — I've written it with you and your puppy in mind. As far as how you read it? That decision is up to you.

Foolish Assumptions

Here's what I've assumed about you, dear reader, when writing this book:

>> You know that puppies have four paws and a tail — or at least a stump of a tail.

>> You either have a puppy right now or are considering getting one, but you don't know much about raising a puppy.

>> You don't want to obtain a PhD in training techniques and dog physiology or psychology. You just want the basics on topics such as what supplies to buy, how to train your puppy to perform basic commands, the best dog food to use, how much exercise to provide, and how to keep your pup healthy in general.

If you fit into any or all of these categories, this book is for you.

How This Book Is Organized

This book is divided into parts, each one having its helpful theme. Here's a quick rundown.

Part 1: Choosing a Dog to Love for a Lifetime

In Part 1, you find the scoop on choosing a puppy — big or small, pure breed or rescue, super-young or a little bit older? In this part, I cover lots of typical questions and buyer-beware scenarios to help you make all the right decisions. Are dog breeds all that different? What's with the new designer mixed breeds? Can a pup's personality be predetermined? Where's the best place to find a puppy? You will find all the answers and more in this part.

Part 2: Living and Loving Your Puppy: The Early Days

Everybody loves bringing a puppy home: the buildup, the shopping, the rush of serotonin and oxytocin, the happy love hormones. Few things can beat that! Living with a puppy, especially one that's just been separated from their mom and littermates, can be a bit of a buzzkill. What should you expect? How should you deal with the barking and whining — especially when it happens in the middle of the night? How do you act when your puppy grabs something you'd rather they didn't, or chases the cat or nips the kids? You can find all the answers in Part 2. Plus, you learn about the new science of modern dog training, which reinforces techniques I've long encouraged. Research shows that puppies, like young children, can pick up routines almost immediately, making those early weeks super-important. In this part, you'll learn about how your puppy's needs affect their behavior, why sleep training is crucial for a happy life, and why consistency with friends and family helps to shape good behavior from the start.

Part 3: Training with a Positive Spin

Whether you're starting this book with a little pup or an adolescent, this part of the book speaks to the off-leash wannabe in all of us. Leashes are often hard to wrangle, and no one wants to get hauled around in the name of training, least of all your dog. In this part, you'll discover how off-leash training is something you can shape at any age with the use of some cool tools and groovy gadgets. As you master lessons, I'll delve into different training styles to find the approach that works best for you and your puppy — from clickers to target training.

In Part 3, you'll explore an array of frustrations that many people experience with their adolescent dogs: This isn't a pretty stage, no matter what your species! Rather than look at your puppy's behaviors as good or bad, examine them from your puppy's perspective. Everything your puppy does has value as it communicates their worldview; over the course of this book, you'll find out how to interpret their reactions so that you can develop a mindful approach to training and resolving stress. You'll feel proactive and empathetic when dealing with specific issues such as separation stress, noise reactivity, anxiety, and even aggression. The best part is that your relationship with your puppy will grow stronger from working together to resolve whatever issues arise.

Part 4: Conditioning Good Manners in Your Puppy

Your first choice is whether you want your puppy to learn good manners and listening skills or whether you'd rather condition annoying routines and dismissive behavior. You read that sentence correctly: The choice is up to you. If it's the former, Part 4 is for you. I cannot wait to show you how to encourage your puppy's cooperative behavior from the start. In these chapters, I go over first lessons (how to teach your puppy to sit, stay, and come) before moving on to more complex routines, like where to potty and how to greet people at the door. (*Hint:* On all four paws.)

Part 5: Creating a Wellness Plan

Puppies are a lot like kids: They act well when they feel good. If your goal is a happy, friendly, well-mannered dog, take good care of them inside and out. In this part, you'll find all you need to know on nutrition, exercise, and grooming. Also, since no one wants to get sick or be sidelined by accident, least of all your dog, it's important to know the signs and symptoms of an illness and be on the ready should anything bad happen. Part 5 provides lists and quick skills as well as a do-it-yourself doggie first-aid kit to prepare, just in case life ever presents your dog with the unexpected.

Part 6: The Part of Tens

Last but not least, in Part 6 I give you ten of my favorite games and ten crowd-pleasing tricks. Enjoy!

Icons Used in This Book

You'll find icons throughout this book on the left side of the page that point to different sorts of info. Here's the list of the various icons you'll encounter:

TIP

This icon highlights useful tidbits and helpful advice — such as how to lift your puppy and hold them just right to give them that loving feeling.

REMEMBER

Here is where I get to stress the main points — such as rewarding what your puppy is doing right and responding in such a way that the wrong behavior doesn't result in more attention.

WARNING

"Warning, warning!" Need I say more? Don't skip this one.

TECHNICAL STUFF

This icon alerts you to factoids and technical information that, though fascinating, is more for the dog-obsessed folks than everyday folks just trying to get a handle on their puppy's behavior.

JUST FOR FUN

I love to have fun, so this is my favorite icon! Though not necessary to learning, these tidbits give you a fresh and fun way to spin requests so that your puppy will use a behavior, like sitting, to get you to throw their toy again and again and again. You can skip these tips, but who'd want to?

Beyond the Book

In addition to what you're reading right now, this product comes with a free access-anywhere Cheat Sheet that offers a ready schedule for housetraining and a list of helpful directions (sit stay, come and nope) for sharing and easy posting on the refrigerator door. To get this Cheat Sheet, visit www.dummies.com and type **Puppies For Dummies Cheat Sheet** in the Search box.

Where to Go from Here

The coolest thing about this book is that you can jump in anywhere. It's a no-rules reference guide whether you're in the early stages of thinking about getting a puppy or you have one already chewing on your shoelace.

Though you can read the book from cover to cover, feel free to take a quick skim of the table of contents to choose your topic and dig right in. Regardless of where you start, remember this principle and you can't go wrong: Puppies are a lot like babies. They need to be nurtured but not spoiled, loved but not overindulged. Just like kids, they need guidelines and limits, not unlimited freedom. At the end of the day, you're the dog parent, and it's your responsibility to keep your puppy safe. Use the training lessons — mainly formatted in Chapters 10-13 but sprinkled throughout the book — to teach your puppy what words mean, and then use those words to organize where they should go and what they should do in every situation.

Thank you for picking up my book and adding it to your library. Everyone needs help sometimes, and raising a puppy is no small task. But with time and information, things do get easier — even enjoyable. I've taken special care to organize this book so that each section teaches you how to successfully communicate with your puppy and raise them to be a wonderful family member, now and always.

1

Choosing a Dog to Love for a Lifetime

Chapter **1**

Welcome to the Puppy Love Club: Here's All You Need to Know!

Choosing to bring a puppy into your family is one of the more exciting decisions of your lifetime — but it's also a little scary. If you're feeling overwhelmed, don't be discouraged. I've written this book to help you no matter where you are on the puppy continuum. Adopting a puppy is more like bringing home a baby than, say, a fish or a hamster, but with a child, there's usually a lot more build-up, with months to mull over magazine articles and room décor. And even the infant stage is pretty tame — not so with puppy. Unlike other pets, puppies bond and engage with you from the minute you meet them, and they depend on you like a child from that day forward. In return for your kindness, they offer you their unconditional love and enthusiasm every day of their lives. Dogs are like toddlers in their adoration and attentiveness, delighting in every interaction and weaving their way into every social interaction that goes on in your household.

Puppies and toddlers have even more similarities: Both are nonverbal and reliant on you. Both depend on you to shape and fulfill their everyday needs, from learning where and what to eat and drink to figuring out where to sleep and go potty. A puppy matures a lot faster than a baby, so that's a plus (the first year of a puppy's life equals about 20 of a human's), but a dog's emotional capacity parallels a 2- or 3-year-old, so they never leave for college, wreck the car, or max out your credit cards!

Civilizing a puppy is a project to be approached mindfully — and, fortunately, this book makes it a positive and fun experience for everyone. This first chapter lays the groundwork for what lies ahead. With these guidelines in hand, you'll have no trouble getting through the first year.

Looking at All Your Options

Dogs come in a lot of shapes and sizes. Until now, you may not have given dog breeds and personalities much thought. Instead, you may have believed that the only characteristics separating one pup from another were coat color and body size. Unless your plan is to choose a dog who complements your couch cushions, you have to know a little bit about the types available.

Before you consider the differences between dog types, in Chapter 2 I help you peek into your lifestyle to get a handle on what it is you want from your relationship. Puppyhood is a quick window, lasting about a year, but dogs live a long time (generally, 10 to 14 years, depending on the dog breed or breed mix), so it's important to think about your life now as well as 5 to 10 years from now. For example, your heart's pick may be a high-energy breed from the Sporting group, but if you're at work most of the day and you prefer "vegging out" to jogging, this puppy will lose their appeal when you find them climbing your walls or curtains.

In Chapter 3, I explore different types of dogs, both purebred and natural breed blends (also known as *mutts* or *mixed breeds*) and what are known as *designer* mixes (two breeds mindfully bred to create a new breed — a Chiweeny, Pomski, or Goldendoodle, for example). A quick peek at the concept of *hybrid vigor* will help you to appreciate a dog who looks and acts unique. I'll also help you explore the ideal home environment for different types of dogs as well as the necessary exercise, training, and socialization commitments of each one.

REMEMBER

After you have an idea of the personality you want, you can consider breeds. Over time, hundreds of known breeds have been developed worldwide. In the United States, the breeds are grouped into seven categories: Herding, Hound, Non-Sporting, Sporting, Terrier, Toy, and Working. Each of these breeds has specific characteristics that allow the dogs to withstand the environment of the lands of their original descent. Each breed has a defined look, temperament, and interest that continues to get passed down from generation to generation.

In Chapter 4, I show you how to start your search. Talking to various rescue organizations and breeders is a project in and of itself. To help you, I've created a list of questions that are important for you to ask — and I also fill you in on the kinds of questions you may be asked as a potential parent to their dog.

First impressions count. When you visit your puppy's birth home — whether it's with a breeder or at a shelter, store, or private home — do you get the sense that the puppy is in a safe, positive, and relaxed environment? While there, do you feel comfortable asking any pertinent questions and voicing your concerns? And, because many good breeders will question you (because, let's face it, they want to find good homes for the puppies they love like their own babies), do you find their questions insightful and/or appropriate?

REMEMBER

Puppies, like children, have distinct personalities. In Chapter 3, you'll find a temperament test that you can take with you when checking out a particular puppy. Visualize the ideal characteristics you value in a dog and list them in the margin. For example, do you want a dog who's devoted to making you happy and who's needy for attention and delighted to do your bidding? Or are you more comfortable with a puppy who's affectionate but independent? Maybe your heart is set on a timid puppy who needs patience, coaxing, and love to come out of their shell. Believe it or not, you can make accurate behavioral predictions such as these when puppies are just eight weeks old.

YOUR PUP'S INGRAINED NEED FOR A JOB

A puppy's instinctual skills, with a few exceptions, are no longer necessary to human survival. But please don't let any puppies in on this secret. Their skills are their life's talent, and employing them gives their lives a sense of purpose. No sheep to herd? The neighborhood kids will do. No snow in Savannah? Pulling a skateboarder will satisfy a Siberian husky. No ducks to retrieve? A tennis ball will do just fine. Dogs love to work, and they can't quell their passions just because you have a late meeting. So, be sure to take the breed's job instincts into account when picking a pooch, and always make time to indulge them.

Helping Your Puppy Jump into the Family Groove

You've been looking forward to bringing your puppy home for days, weeks, and perhaps even years. Few events in life are as exciting as adopting a puppy.

REMEMBER

Regardless of your mood, this initial trip can be scary and overwhelming for your puppy, who may be separating from their original family for the very first time. Plan ahead by organizing both the trip home and your arrival. Make your puppy-supply purchases, which are listed in Chapter 5, well in advance. Also set up your pup's room before they come home, and explain your routines to family and friends. Having a plan puts your mind at ease, which will help your puppy survive this transition stage. Your puppy will bond to you and their new life in no time, though the first few days can be jarring for both of you.

Understanding your puppy's point of view

The most important task to focus on in the early months is socializing your puppy to people, places, and normal stimulations. As far as developing good habits early on, your puppy will thrive on consistency and predictability, and so will you. In Chapter 6, I explore the new science of modern dog training and describe what science has proven about living with dogs. Researchers used to scoff at us crazy dog people, reminding us that dogs were incapable of reason and emotion; now those researchers have come full circle. Studies show that puppies and human toddlers have a tremendous amount in common: Now it's the academics who are telling us that dogs think and feel, and will mature to the capacities of a 3-to-4-year-old child. This chapter helps frame out just how capable and eager your puppy is for learning and how making the most of puppyhood — by investing in play, socialization, and training — will reward you for a lifetime.

In Chapter 6, I also focus on describing your puppy's daily needs and how to structure a schedule around them. Knowing how your puppy likes to organize their day takes the guesswork out of this experience and humanizes many of their communication skills and dependency issues. Chapter 6 points out just how much a human toddler and a puppy have in common — from a routine bathroom-and-sleeping schedule to predictable stages of development. In that chapter, I help you structure a realistic day, which must include secluded nap times, and bring some regularity back into your life.

Raising a puppy in the modern world

Think of puppyhood as your golden opportunity to influence and civilize your puppy. The chapters in Part 2 of this book introduce you to directions and problem-solving techniques that are personality, size, and age-appropriate. Each chapter is broken into easily understandable exercises that are fun to do and easily repeated by others.

Training and conditioning your puppy starts from the moment they step into your home. From first introductions to family, friends, and other pets to conditioning and bonding in the first days and weeks you have them home, Chapter 7 will guide you through these first days and experiences.

Your first goal regardless of the age your puppy is when you bring them home is to teach them early manners — from where to go to the bathroom to how to greet family and friends when they come through the door. Conditioning good habits from the start doesn't happen magically, of course, and in Chapter 8 you'll discover how learning to listen to your puppy makes teaching basic habits easy and fun. (*Hint:* You use your eyes to read their body language.)

If you have kids or grandkids, having a puppy will add a new dimension to your months ahead. In a puppy's mind, kids are often pigeonholed as other puppies and can be perceived as rivals for toys, food, and attention. Chapter 8 offers a proactive (rather than reactive) approach to raising a puppy with children — from phrases to use to groovy games and activities to play. By organizing fun activities, you're giving the child license to both control and enjoy the puppy while the puppy learns respect for everyone who walks on two legs.

Positively overdoing bonding and socialization

TIP

If you want a well-rounded, gentle-mannered dog, follow this secret tip: Overdo socialization in puppyhood. Go overboard with socialization, even more so than with training. Expose your puppy to everything — objects, surfaces, sounds (inside and out), places, and people of all ages, races, sexes, and sizes. Expose your pup to other animals and pets, too. (Until your puppy is inoculated, surround them with healthy, friendly dogs.) Even changes in weather patterns must include mindful handling. If your puppy is startled or concerned, a soothing reaction from you may be misinterpreted as mutual fear. To teach them how to manage themselves, reassure your puppy with your confidence and direction. Knowing how to calm them when they're stressed can make the difference between a pet who rolls with the changes and one who locks up emotionally or reacts defensively. Chapter 9 gives the lowdown on socializing your pup.

Tackling Training Throughout Your Puppy's Growth Phases

Here's just some of what you have to look forward to as your puppy grows through their first year (turn to Part 3, Chapter 10–13 for more on training during each stage):

>> **Taking Baby Steps (8 to 16weeks):** Infancy is a curious time for a puppy. They're encoding your home and all the people in it for the very first time. This is where you get to make a positive impression, shape their personality for the better, and socialize them to sound and daily routines that they'll discover in your home. They're needy and dependent on you, so make the most of this time together. Chapter 10 will guide you!

>> **Teaching Your Pre-Adolescent Puppy (16 weeks to 6 months):** Before the terrible twos start, you may be convinced that you've adopted an angel. Then it happens almost overnight: Your puppy falls from grace. If it's any consolation, all their mischief is a wonderful sign of normal development. Your puppy is growing up. Most people notice more confidence during this stage and less of a help-me attitude and more of a can-do spirit. Embrace it. Chapter 11 shows you the way!

>> **Surviving the Teenage Months (6 months to 9 months):** Okay, by now you're getting a good glimpse of your puppy's lifelong personality quirks. Are they needy, confrontational, strong-willed, dependent, focused, obstinate? Your puppy is maturing faster than you can keep up. Now is the time to start fun, positive training routines and to increase games that encourage interaction. Fortunately for you, bad habits are easy to phase out during this stage if you can remember to stay cool. Puppies are still eager to please during this stage and are motivated to behave to get what they want — from treats to toys and attention. Chapter 12 tells you what you need to know.

REMEMBER

The hardest behavior to control during your puppy's first year isn't your puppy's — it's yours. Anger and frustration will spell your ruin — your puppy won't understand you, and they'll react with confusion and, possibly, defensiveness.

>> **Striving for Off Lead Control (9 to 12 months):** At this point, for the most part you can see the light at the end of the dark tunnel. During this phase, if you've been consistent with training, you'll often have a super puppy — devoted, responsive, and mindful. Well, that is to say, *most* of the time. Sometimes your almost-adult puppy still tests their independence; sometimes that incorrigible 3-month-old puppy reemerges, and they're up to their old tricks.

REMEMBER

Does committing the next year to train a puppy sound like a project? Well, you're right — it is. After you commit to the role of your puppy's parent and teacher, they can learn all they need to know throughout the first year — from where to potty and what to chew to polite greeting manners and how to conduct themselves in a crowd. They won't learn these things overnight, however — like school for children, puppy training is a stage-by-stage process.

Teaching words your puppy should learn and love

Teaching your puppy commands is similar to teaching English as a second language. Though your puppy can't understand sentences or phrases, one spoken word — paired with a posture or routine — will make your puppy feel directed, connected, and safe.

Here are a few of the commands you can find in Chapter 11:

>> **Follow:** This command says, "I'll lead the way. Follow me!" You use this one whenever you and your puppy are out and about.

>> **Stay:** This command is all about self-control. Saying "Stay" tells your puppy to relax and be patient. After you've perfected some early lessons at home, you'll be able to use it everywhere you go.

>> **Come:** A must-have item in your command vocabulary, this one calls your puppy back to your side. You *must* teach this command positively if you want your puppy to listen.

>> **Leave it:** Most dogs think their middle name is No, so try to avoid that one. To teach your puppy to leave stuff alone, you need to teach them a word or short phrase that says "That's not for you."

Picking a consistent approach

REMEMBER

You can find many gadgets to help you convey and emphasize your directions, from clickers and target sticks to training collars and leashes. Keep in mind, though, that if you randomly try these objects or mix and match your approaches simultaneously, you're likely to confuse your puppy.

Read Chapter 5 to find out about equipment for your home, and read Chapter 13 to discover how various leashes and training gadgets can help shape your puppy into a trust-worthy companion. If you have family members involved in your pup's training, have a group discussion to ensure that you're all on the same page. Consistency is oh-so-reassuring to your puppy.

Handling Day-to-Day Frustrations — and More Serious Problems

In the chapters in Part 4, I dissect all areas of frustration, from housetraining (in Chapter 14), nipping and jumping to the more serious infractions, such as aggression. Just remember that many of your puppy's naughty behaviors — the ones that frustrate you to tears — are fun and enjoyable to them. Even though this book doesn't take the place of professional advice when your situation is dire, use this book to shed light on Everything Puppy — from a wagging tail and puppy breath to adolescent defiance.

At times, you and your puppy just don't see eye-to-eye:

>> You'll want them to come and be near you when they want to explore and play.

>> You'll want them to chew on their bone, and they'll favor an item perfumed with your scent, like a sock or slipper.

>> They'll think digging is fun — sometimes indoors and other times outdoors.

>> Barking will be their way of alerting you that visitors are approaching, whereas you may be happier with the sound of a doorbell.

>> There will be nights when you're exhausted and your dog will want to play.

Habits are formed at many an aggravating moment, leaving you stranded and in a vicious cycle. Ironically, this cycle is *your* creation. Sure, it feels like you must do something when your puppy tears off with your napkin, but screaming is perceived as prize envy (you want what they have) and only guarantees a repeat performance. Think about it: If cruising the counters brings you back into the room, your puppy will repeat this tactic no matter the consequences. In Chapter 15, I help you to understand your puppy's mindset and try a whole new approach to resolving your differences.

REMEMBER

Your puppy is easily overwhelmed by your frustration. Even though a young puppy may look like they knows what you're talking about when you shout "No," their reaction is only fear and confusion. And I *know* you don't want to scare your puppy. In Chapter 15, I discuss how to teach your age-appropriate puppy the concept of No. They can learn it, but not until their brain has developed some maturity.

Of course, more serious issues — what I call *red-flag issues* — warrant concern and reaction. Aggression comes to mind, as does separation anxiety, excessive barking, and destructive chewing. I'll go over these issues in Chapter 16. Bear in mind that a puppy exhibiting this behavior isn't happy; your corrections won't lighten the intensity. Find a more cheerful approach, modify your behavior, and help your puppy develop a more cheerful, go-with-the-flow attitude. You'll all be a lot more relaxed.

REMEMBER

A sensible reason is behind every puppy behavior, whether it's counter surfing, separation anxiety, or jumping on guests. Investigate and understand why your puppy is reacting in a certain way. Then juggle the variables to meet their needs as you redirect them to more appropriate activities.

Ensuring a Clean Bill of Health

If you take care of the inside of your puppy, the outside can better take care of itself. Chapters 17,18, and 19 help you make pertinent healthcare decisions, balance your puppy's diet, stay on top of their daily hygiene, prevent parasites and disease, and understand their healthy vital signs so that you can react calmly in an emergency.

Spaying or neutering your puppy (see Chapter 17) is crucial. It's a responsible action, and everyone must stem the growing overpopulation, for which widespread euthanasia seems to be the only other solution. Even though controversy abounds when it comes to all sorts of issues involving spaying or neutering — appropriate age, competing surgical choices, and after effects, to name just a few — knowing the facts will give you the ability to choose your course of action wisely.

A sick puppy is like a toddler: When they're ill or troubled, your puppy is unable to articulate it in words. They will, however, respond in ways that would be obvious to another dog. In Chapters 18 and 19, I help you decipher your puppy's signals so that you know how to keep them healthy and happy *and* how to respond to them when they're ill or in case of an accident.

REMEMBER

Reading these chapters doesn't take the place of having regular check-ups or consultations with a veterinarian. Your veterinarian has a medical degree and may recommend tests or blood work to determine a specific ailment. So, use these chapters to educate yourself on the signs and symptoms to watch for and how to read what your puppy feels when they're unwell. Sharing this information with your veterinarian is more than invaluable — it can save your puppy's life.

Chapter **2**

Finding the Puppy That's Right for You

Getting a puppy leaves people in one of two camps: bursting with excitement or completely overwhelmed. Your puppy plans may be in the exploratory stage, or you may be actively campaigning for a furry bundle of joy. Wherever you are emotionally, the truth is that this may be the only time in your life when you can choose a family member — so make the most of it by picking a puppy who fits in.

Whether your home is big or small, you live alone or with others, or you're the president of a company or a stay-at-home mom — some type of puppy is perfect for you. Puppies are faithful to the people they love, no matter their lifestyle or living conditions, but you can make your future puppy happier and better behaved by considering a few aspects of your habits and way of life before choosing a breed.

In this chapter, I walk you through several important considerations when choosing a puppy to suit your lifestyle. By thinking thoughtfully about these topics, you can start to narrow in on the best puppy for your home. (And, after you develop a sense of your ideal dog, the breed discussion in Chapter 3 helps you hone in on just the right pet.)

Living Your Dream: Pinpointing What You Really Want

Everyone wants a perfect dog: a well-mannered, loving companion who gets along with the family and is a joy to be around 24/7. But the reality is, perfect dogs aren't born that way — they develop from good-enough puppyhoods. As with children, your dog's behavior is a direct reflection of the time you've spent conditioning their cooperation and socializing and training them during their puppyhood phases. Throughout this book, I outline the effort that goes into coaching your puppy into a well-balanced, friendly, responsive dog.

The best place to start isn't even with the puppy — it's with *you*. If you're in the early stages, just considering what type of dog will best fit into your lifestyle, use this chapter to lay out all your options. Use the following questionnaire to help you focus on what you want and determine the type of puppy that will fit in best.

Getting in the right mindset

When forming the mental picture of your perfectly suited companion, don't ask yourself what sort of puppy you want. Instead, ask what sort of *dog* you want. All pups traverse their first year through the typical phases, from the curious, nipping early days to the defiant adolescence and dismissive teen, but they spend the bulk of their lives in a mature state that's largely predictable based on breed-specific characteristics.

The first step in choosing your forever puppy is to select a dog breed or mixed-breed dog type — select it down to the size, coat type, and exercise requirements that will mesh with your personality and lifestyle. Most people find an 8-week-old Golden Retriever puppy irresistible, and you may melt at the sight of a shar-pei puppy, but fast-forward ten months: Will your likes and dislikes line up with the adult versions of these puppies?

To improve the likelihood of a happy and lasting relationship, think about what you're looking for in a dog. Big or small? Active or less energetic? Dependent and responsive off-leash or independent and spirited? There's a dog for every description! The questionnaire in the next section helps you narrow down your wants from the many possibilities.

Considering yourself before you choose your puppy

Living with a dog is more like having a toddler than sharing your life with a cat or containable pet. A hamster or chinchilla can fill their minimum daily exercise requirements (MDER) by jogging on an exercise wheel as he basically lives and dies happily within the confines of their living space. A dog will go insane left in a cage all day. Puppies are sociable creatures whose main focus in life is food and fun. Because they're reliant on you for basic care and well-being (just like a toddler), you'll be correct in thinking of yourself as a dog parent versus a dog owner or master.

How much time your puppy-soon-to-be-dog requires for exercise fun, grooming, and attention depends largely on these three factors:

>> **The breed or mixed breed:** If you haven't chosen a breed, let this chapter and the next one help you narrow your options.

>> **Early imprinting before bringing them home:** *Imprinting* is a fancy term for how puppies are influenced by the way they are treated in the first six to eight weeks of life: Chapter 4 helps you find and dialogue with breeders and rescue associations so that you can gauge their puppies' early life experiences.

>> **Your puppy's training and socialization:** I get to these topics in Part 2 of this book.

The following questionnaire helps you get a handle on choosing a breed, rescue, or mixed breed that has the best chance of living up to your expectations. Consider the next decade plus a few years: Do you have hopes for the future? It's time to be honest with yourself and your family so that everybody wins!

REMEMBER

Sure, a 6 a.m. run with your well-trained companion sounds great on paper, but if you're addicted to the Snooze button, you'll quickly grow to resent a puppy who just can't be shut down.

On the other hand, if you're an athlete, psyched to have a running companion, spend time choosing a breed or mix that will be eager to keep up with you. Got young kids? A protective breed of any size, bent on alert barking every time someone ventures near the front door, may not be the best choice if your home is the hub of weekly PTA and after-school get-togethers.

This questionnaire is split into three subsections to better help you gain perspective on yourself and your choice in selecting a breed or mixed breed. If you're committed to caring for a puppy and meeting their needs, and if you can muster up the patience to deal with typical puppy phases, you're certainly on your way to a lovely, lifelong bond with your puppy. Good luck!

The Look

1. What size dog do you want?
   - ☐ Extra Large
   - ☐ Large-Bulky
   - ☐ Large-Agile
   - ☐ Medium-Bulky
   - ☐ Medium-Agile
   - ☐ Small-Bulky
   - ☐ Small-Agile
   - ☐ Tiny

2. Do you have a coat preference?
   - ☐ Short-coated
   - ☐ Long-coated
   - ☐ Wavy
   - ☐ Hair (non-shedding)
   - ☐ Shaggy (needs regular professional grooming)
   - ☐ Shaggy (hand brushing at home)
   - ☐ Curly-coated

3. You prefer a dog whose ears are
   - ☐ Folded
   - ☐ Tipped on the end
   - ☐ Always standing straight up
   - ☐ Cropped

4. You like a tail that:
   - ☐ Curls
   - ☐ Is cut short or is naturally short
   - ☐ Is slightly curved
   - ☐ Is straight

5. As far as facial definition, you admire a
   - ☐ Long snout
   - ☐ Square snout
   - ☐ Rectangular snout
   - ☐ Pushed in face

Day-to-Day Behavior

6. Which personality do you prefer in a dog?
   - ☐ Interactive
   - ☐ Needy
   - ☐ Independent

7. How much attention are you able or willing to give your dog?
   - ☐ Lots
   - ☐ Occasional
   - ☐ Little

8. How much exercise will you give your dog?
   - ☐ A lot of rigorous exercise
   - ☐ Daily walks
   - ☐ A couple of outings a week
   - ☐ Playtime with other dogs
   - ☐ Yard freedom
   - ☐ Little exercise

9. You want to take your dog along with you whenever possible.
   - ☐ Yes
   - ☐ No

10. Your dog will sleep in or near a bedroom at night.
    - ☐ Yes
    - ☐ No

11. You want your dog to sleep on the bed.
    - ☐ Yes
    - ☐ No

12. You're planning to limit your dog's house freedom to a specific area.
    - ☐ Yes
    - ☐ No

13. How do you want your dog to act toward newcomers?
    - ☐ Welcoming
    - ☐ Accepting
    - ☐ On guard

14. With regard to children, you want a dog who is
    - ☐ Trustworthy
    - ☐ Playful
    - ☐ Accepting, but aloof

15. How often do you want your dog to bark?
    ☐ Rarely or never   ☐ When hearing a noise

16. When considering training, how much time can you devote?
    ☐ A lot and it will be a hobby   ☐ As much as necessary and no more and no less
    ☐ Very little and I want a dog who doesn't need a lot

17. How much time can you devote to grooming?
    ☐ Every day   ☐ Couple of times a week   ☐ Occasional   ☐ None

18. Please check some favorite pastimes you hope to share with your dog.
    ☐ Jogging   ☐ Hiking   ☐ Walking   ☐ Gardening
    ☐ Water activities ☐ Outdoor   ☐ Sporting events ☐ Watching television
    ☐ Computer games   ☐ Reading   ☐ Knitting   ☐ Sitting at the cafe
    ☐ Cooking   ☐ Elderly care   ☐ Volunteer work   ☐ Visiting with friends

19. What other pets do you have?
    ☐ Dogs   ☐ Horses   ☐ Cats   ☐ Rodents
    ☐ Amphibians   ☐ Bird/birds

20. Any other considerations? Circle or list others.
    ☐ Special-needs home arrangements   ☐ Child on the way ☐ Other

What About You?

21. Have you owned a dog before?
    ☐ Yes   ☐ No   ☐ What kind?

22. Have you trained a dog before?
    ☐ Yes   ☐ No   Were you successful?   ☐ Yes   ☐ No

23. What size home do you live in?
    ☐ Large   ☐ Medium   ☐ Small

24. Do you have a yard?
    ☐ Yes   ☐ No   Is the yard fenced in?   ☐ Yes   ☐ No

25. How committed are you to reorganizing your life around the needs of a puppy?
    ☐ Very   ☐ Somewhat   ☐ I don't want to change my schedule

26. Which adjective best describes your personality and home life?
    ☐ Organized/scheduled   ☐ Laid back   ☐ Chaotic

27. When you're around a child you feel
    ☐ Unsettled   ☐ Uncomfortable   ☐ Relaxed   ☐ In control

28. The thought of being with a group of children is
    ☐ Scary   ☐ Unappealing   ☐ Tolerable   ☐ Fun

29. When your house is out of order you feel
    ☐ Out of control   ☐ Stressed   ☐ Like cleaning   ☐ No concern

30. When in charge of some task or game you are
    ☐ Rigid   ☐ Structured   ☐ Democratic   ☐ Placating

Interpreting your answers

Now that you have all this information about what you want, what should you do with it? In this section, I help you analyze your answers to the questionnaire. As you read this section, make a mental sketch of your ideal dog. Your answers will help you get some ideas of the type of dog that will suit your lifestyle in the long run. Keep the questionnaire in mind (make a copy if you need to) as I walk you through the description of the various breeds or mixed breeds in Chapter 3.

The Look: Considering your dream dog's appearance

Even though your dog's appearance shouldn't be a chief motivating factor in your breed selection, it's still important. You may have strong preferences based on aesthetics, such as what tail or facial features make you smile, and you can narrow down the breeds you look at based on those criteria. You may also be concerned with practical matters — what care is involved in owning a curly or thick-coated dog. Questions 1 through 5 guide you along and help you narrow your decision.

Certain features affect the cost of owning a dog, and that consideration may be an important one for you. When you're considering your dream dog, consider hidden perks and drawbacks tied to the appearance of each individual breed: For example, breeds with nonshedding hair will save you from fur- covered furniture, but they do require regular trips to the groomer. Long-, thick-, or curly-coated dogs also need professional grooming periodically. And you may love the look of bigger dogs, but they cost more to feed than small or tiny dogs.

The look you prefer in a dog may also have health implications. Various breeds tend to have specific health considerations that you'll need to be mindful of and research in order to prevent. For example, short-snouted breeds are beyond adorable, but they're prone to skin irritation and respiratory difficulties. Giant-size breeds have shorter life spans than other dogs.

WARNING

I often note the similarities between puppies and children, so if kids make you uncomfortable, think carefully about whether you're ready to take on the challenge of raising a puppy. And, if some of the other questions concern you — for example, if you don't want to have to change your schedule or train an unruly puppy — you may want to consider not getting a dog at this time in your life. Wait for a dog until your schedule frees up some more.

Day-to-Day Behavior: Thinking about your dog's energy and attitude

The next part of the questionnaire gets into the meat of the matter, considering dogs' personalities, behaviors, and exercise requirements.

» **Questions 6 and 7:** These questions target the essence of your dog's personality. Some breeds are fiercely self-contained and independent and need little human direction in order to shape and reinforce their behavior. Other dogs watch you closely and can't seem to make a decision without weighing your opinion. And some are interactive, in-between breeds that choose to follow you when they can but don't destroy the furnishings if you go out to do errands. What appeals to you: A dog who needs you desperately (for example, a Shetland sheepdog or a Cavalier King Charles spaniel) or a dog who's content with time apart (such as a Cairn Terrier, a Rhodesian Ridgeback, or an Airedale)?

» **Question 8:** The amount of exercise you're able to give your new pooch should be a key factor in choosing a dog breed. If you're honest here, this question helps you discover what energy level you can match. Even though an active breed may sound dreamy, if you can't consistently provide plenty of exercise for the next decade, cross it off your list. A high-energy dog who is pent-up, isolated, or underexercised can become destructive, clingy, and impulsive. These behaviors will no doubt be frustrating for your family, so be sure you can provide what your dog needs.

» **Questions 9 through 12:** How involved in your life would you like your dog to be? If socializing is high on your priority list, choose a breed that was bred to take direction and follow humans around instead of a breed that was bred to guard, hunt, or protect your home. Although any dog will enjoy being near you 24/7, breeds that were designed to work independently of man are more mentally equipped to handle periods of isolation.

» **Questions 13 through 15:** These questions pinpoint why you're getting a dog. Does the thought of a dog's protection appeal to you? Do you like being alerted to outside noises, or do you want a companion who just rolls with the comings and goings of the outside world? Are you interested in a playmate for your children? Make a big mental note about what your goal for the pet is.

» **Questions 15 and 16:** These questions dive deep into the time commitment issue. And yes, Question 15 relates to time commitment as well as core reasons for getting a dog. Training a dog of a protective or hunting breed to bark only at the right things and for a limited period of time are key considerations throughout their first year. The amount of time you need to commit to training and shaping your puppy is directly determined by the breed and the personality of each individual puppy. Strong, independent, and dominant puppies need more structure and stern reinforcement than passive, dependent, and sweet-natured puppies.

» **Question 17:** Grooming is another time consideration. All dogs need a good brushing occasionally, but long-, thick-, curly-, or wavy-coated breeds need a commitment (daily brushings) and periodic professional grooming, which may become costly!

>> **Question 18:** Sharing time with your puppy is a healthy way to establish trust and friendship. Consider your favorite pastime and find a puppy who will grow up to be in the same groove as you. For example, if you've got a fetish for Frisbees, you have to decide whether you want a dog who fetches them relentlessly or one who shows no interest (so that you can actually play a civilized game with friends or family). A dog bred to course fields all day herding, hunting, or retrieving waterfowl will grow insanely restless and destructive if they're cooped inside all day. A companion dog, however, will enjoy the serenity of calm, predictable activities and will need far less exercise to stay on an even keel.

>> **Question 19:** Introducing a new puppy to other pets in your household can be tricky, so take this question seriously. If you breed prize-winning rabbits or own cats, avoid breeds genetically programmed to kill them. If you have another dog, choose a breed that will mesh with their traits and personality. Other pets? Even those in glass cages can elicit your dog's drive to chase and capture. If you have any other pets, consider a breed with a more chilled reaction to other animals.

>> **Question 20:** If you have other considerations, think through them in terms of the future. For example, if you're planning to have a child in a couple of years, do you want a protective dog to stand guard, or a cheerful spirit to welcome your child at the door?

What About You? Determining what you're ready for

Questions 21 through 30 target you and your lifestyle. They're meant to simply make you think for a minute about your ability and readiness. Getting a puppy is like falling in love: The lines between your commitment and your own needs aren't always clear. Sure, now you may say you'll groom your long-haired puppy every day, but what happens when you miss a day and notice they've become a knotted mess? Can you afford a groomer? Are you really willing to commit to this daily task?

You should also consider how well you handle stress. Puppies can be annoyingly impulsive and scattered. Are you going to need medication to get through the early years, or can you roll with it? If you're a neat freak, pick a dependent, composed breed that will (hopefully) have greater respect for your wishes.

I often note the similarities between puppies and children, so if kids make you uncomfortable, think carefully about whether you're ready to take on the challenge of raising a puppy. And if some of the other questions concern you — for instance, you don't want to have to change your schedule or train an unruly puppy — you may want to consider not getting a dog at this time in your life. Wait until your schedule frees up some more!

WARNING

I often note the similarities between puppies and children, so if kids make you uncomfortable, think carefully about whether you're ready to take on the challenge of raising a puppy. And, if some of the other questions concern you — for example, if you don't want to have to change your schedule or train an unruly puppy — you may want to consider not getting a dog at this time in your life. Wait for a dog until your schedule frees up some more.

Deciding on the age to bring your puppy home

The age you bring home a puppy is an important consideration. The earliest age you bring home a puppy should be eight weeks old, although this should not be the first time your puppy is around people. You will learn a lot about choosing a rescue puppy or breeder in Chapter 4, but for now remember that your puppy should be raised inside and around people and household noises from the moment's they're born. You may hear the term *impressionable* or the even fancier term *imprinting*, which relates to how often your developed puppy was handled and exposed to different noises and stimulations. Although you may think that your puppy should grow up in a bubble during their early weeks, you would be wrong. Studies show that puppies exposed to the chaos of everyday life and handled by friendly people are better able to adapt to life with you when they come home.

If you bring home a young-young puppy (younger than 12 weeks of age), they'll need a lot of socialization, supervision, and consideration. You'll need to continue to expose them to lots of sights and sounds, bringing them out in a carrying case or on leash after your veterinarian says it's safe to do so. (More on this adventure in Chapter 9.) Little puppy bladder muscles aren't fully developed; their teeth are falling out at a rapid pace, they're unsure of themselves, and, in short, they can be overreactive to everyday occurrences, spelling out hyperexcitement or distress. If the thought of midnight potty runs leaves you feeling cool to the idea of raising a young puppy, perhaps you'd be better suited to adopting an older puppy or dog. Puppies older than four months begin to have better bladder control and are well through their nipping and teething phases, so you may have an easier time with them.

If you like the idea of getting an older puppy (between four months and a year, for example), make sure you do a thorough background check, paying close attention to the type of social experiences your candidate had during the first critical months of life. Find one that has been raised inside a house and around lots of people and other dogs. The first six months of a dog's life is a critical socialization period, where your dog either grows comfortable of their surroundings or wary of new experiences. If you adopt a little puppy, you have control over this time and can shape your puppy's life experiences; if you adopt an older puppy, make sure they've had the right type of social experiences to fit in with your lifestyle.

As far as where to go to find an older puppy, start by visiting a local shelter or perusing rescue organizations online through sites such as www.petfinders.com or www.adoptapet.com. Shelters are filled with older puppies and dogs, and you can easily find rescue clubs for specific breeds on the Internet or through a local kennel club. (In the United States, www.AKC.org is a good place to start.) Sometimes a breeder may hold on to a puppy longer for various reasons, such as an adopter backed out, the puppy displayed show potential, a puppy is returned, or a puppy is held for medical reasons. If this option sounds promising to you, ask the same essential questions I list in Chapter 4, such as where the puppy was raised during their critical imprinting stage (from birth to four months old) and whether they are housetrained and socialized. Your puppy cannot change their early influences and you do not want to get stuck with a puppy who has spent their whole life in a kennel or living outside.

Considering Your Household

The dynamics of your household will affect how your puppy adjusts to their new lifestyle. Are you living alone, or are other people, kids, and/or pets at home with you? Consider your *current* lifestyle: your routines, your schedule, the demands of your home life. Are you expecting? Retiring soon? These are questions you should ask as you begin the process. And don't forget that dogs live a long, long time (8 to 12 years on average; some, even longer), so you need to consider the big picture. For example, though you may be single now, are you envisioning marriage and children? If so, get a breed or mixed breed that will groove with the chaos and taunting of young children. Where are you now, and where do you think you'll be five or even ten years from now?

REMEMBER

Children add a lot of pizazz to anyone's life. Your furry, 4-legged child is no exception. If you're half of a newly married couple eager to title your puppy "our first child," you'll have to socialize your puppy extensively with babies so that they don't feel displaced when you welcome your second (human) child someday.

Me and my shadow

You're single and free and have few responsibilities to tie you down. Even though the constant companionship of a puppy may sound dreamy, it's a major responsibility and one you'll have to shoulder 100 percent. When bringing a puppy into your life, you'll suddenly become a parent of sorts. With that responsibility comes all the commitments and demands that properly raising a puppy requires. If you dig sleeping until noon, forget it. Your puppy will have you up before dawn and often in the middle of the night for several weeks. If the joy of sitting at the cafe for hours at a time tops your list, cross it off or forget about getting a puppy. Most cafes frown on inviting in anything but the human species, and your puppy will not sit still for hours at a time. Walking, grooming, and feeding your puppy all require a mindfulness that leaves your carefree days in the dust.

TIP

If you're truly up for the challenge, remember that your puppy will be your responsibility for a decade or more. If you plan to share a household with someone eventually, socialize your puppy well so that they won't get their hackles up when that special someone sweeps you off your feet. Also, think about whether you may have a family of your own someday. If it seems likely, choose a breed that enjoys children, and start socializing your puppy with kids from the get-go. (Flip to Chapter 9 for more on puppy socialization.)

Just the two of us — plus pup

It's just you and your honey, but a puppy makes three. Owning a puppy together is your first true test of cooperation. Raising a puppy is a lot easier with two people to share the responsibilities, but consistency is a key factor. If the two of you join forces, following similar guidelines for structure and training, your puppy will mature quickly and thrive in the consistency. But if one of you wants the puppy to feel at home on the furniture and eat from a dish at the table and the other person prefers a more structured approach, your puppy's worldview will be skewed, and they won't know which rules apply or when.

REMEMBER

To avoid arguments, discuss ahead of time how you'll raise this puppy and which rules make the most sense for your lifestyle and future situation. Have a heartfelt talk with your partner — ideally, before bringing your puppy home. Be sure to discuss the following topics:

>> What are your separate visions and hopes for adding a dog to your life?

>> Where will the puppy sleep?

>> How will you share responsibilities, from feeding and walking to exercise and training?

>> What are your feeding philosophies, from kibbles in the bowl to handouts from the table?

>> How much money will you apportion to training, grooming, and maintaining the puppy's health?

Your puppy will live and love most serenely in a household where you can both agree.

TIP

If you and your partner are retired empty nesters, now may be a terrific time to get a puppy, because you're probably home more often and have time to be attentive to your puppy's schedule. However, remember that a young puppy's needs can be quite demanding. If you already completed the 4 a.m. diaper-changing routine and you'd rather skip these experiences than relive them, consider an older puppy who has been in a supportive environment or one whom the breeder is willing to socialize and train for you. Also, pay close attention to the exercise requirements when choosing a puppy. You need to ensure that you and your soon-to-be-adult dog are a solid match.

A family with young kids

If you're getting a puppy to raise with your young child, you may suddenly feel like you have twins (except that one is slightly furrier than the other). Raising a puppy with children younger than the age of 5 is a tremendous undertaking, and it's one that often creates more stress than it's worth.

Until the ages of 5 to 7, children have trouble grasping others' feelings — whether the others are people or pets. Though a tight squeeze may signal love from your 3-year-old to you, it can instill panic or frighten a young pup. A squeezed puppy may feel trapped and bite defensively, even if under normal circumstances they wouldn't react this way. This puppy can mature into a dog with an innate fear of young children or into a dog who's immediately tense in their company.

WARNING

If you have a needy toddler, postpone getting a puppy for at least a couple of years. Your child needs all your attention to develop a strong sense of self. A puppy will pull you away from your parental duties and rival the toddler for your attention. This situation is almost guaranteed to cause some headaches. Introduce the puppy after your child is more emotionally steady and is also excited and ready for the addition.

TIP

If you're convinced this is the right time to add a puppy to your family, consider the option of an older puppy who has been well socialized to children during their first few months. Find a 6- to 10-month-old puppy who has been given up for reasons such as a move or human allergies to the puppy. After they're past the intense nipping phase, puppies are less likely to think of the kids as littermates, also known as siblings. As a bonus, an older puppy has better bladder control and may already be completely house-trained.

Are you ready to take the plunge? Flip to Chapter 8 for tips on raising kids and puppies together.

A family with older children

Got kids older than 5 years old? I'd guess that at some point they've begun lobbying for a dog as a holiday or birthday gift with the plea, "We'll take care of him ourselves. *Please?*"

If you feel yourself about to cave, realize that no matter how much your children promise to take part, the puppy will always be your responsibility. Kids can't be expected to remember everything. Many kids still have to be reminded to tie their shoes or flush the toilet. Even though they may take part in the daily responsibilities, you won't be able to relax on the sidelines. You'll be the coach, the cook, and the social director for your children and your new puppy.

Your best bet is making the puppy a fun family project from the start. Involve the whole family in all the early decisions, from what breed type and personality to choose to where the puppy should eat and sleep. Encourage your kids to read this book. Activities like walking, training, and grooming the puppy may fall into your hands, but if you make those activities look like fun, you may have your kids clamoring to take part. The greatest joy is seeing your children parent the puppy. Only yesterday they were the ones in diapers!

WARNING

With all the chaos and comings and goings of a family with children, I caution you against protective, or guarding, breeds, especially if your home is the hub of a lot of activity. These breeds may suffer from career stress when trying to keep track of all the activity in your home, and they may subsequently lash out at the unsuspecting children. Unless you can dedicate your family to a consistent and extensive training program, stick to rough-and-tumble, ready-for-play breed or mixed-breed types who accept everyone as long-lost friends. If you end up choosing a breed who is home proud and stranger wary, spend loads of time socializing and training them how to act at the entranceway, to ensure that your next decade isn't spent running interference.

A whole menagerie (other pets)

Is your house a zoo? Do you run the risk of creating a dog pack in your living space? Sharing your life with many animals can mean a harmonious existence — or a complete nightmare. How you plan and introduce and treat each pet are the dominant factors here.

TRAVEL CONSIDERATIONS

When considering adding a puppy to the household, you can't leave travel out the question. Do you enjoy the flexibility of flying out on a moment's notice? Does your career pull you away for days at a time? If you're nodding your head yes, think through what that means for your puppy. Do you have friends or family members lined up who welcome the responsibility of a puppy and can tolerate the adolescent mischief that strikes puppies from the ages of 7 to 11 months? Or can you afford to pay someone to kennel your puppy or dog or to stay in your home while you're away? Kenneling a dog can cost between $15 to $100 each day, depending on where you live and what extra bonuses you purchase to embellish your dog's stay, such as extra walks, training lessons, or deluxe suites. Perhaps you'll want to take your puppy along with you. Bear in mind that any change in schedule, caregiver, or location will upset your puppy's routine and may result in hyperactivity, nervousness, or backsliding in training (including house-training).

If you already have a menagerie, look for a breeder who has exposed his or her puppies to other animals at a young age. If the breeder had cats and you also have cats, your puppy may think they're a cat! With a little food, fun, and positive encouragement, you can encourage a strong friendship to develop. Choosing a puppy with the right temperament also influences how well they will be accepted into your existing group.

WARNING

If you're adding a dog to a household of other critters, spend a long time searching out a breed that isn't genetically programmed to corral, maim, or kill those other critters. Even though your Siberian husky may accept a bunny rabbit in a hutch, your growing puppy may not be able to curb their impulses when Hopper comes out to play with the children.

Other dogs

Do you have an older dog or a multitude of other paws parading through your kitchen? Even though most dogs play well with other dogs when introduced properly, few relish the relentless chaos and interaction of a young pup. As your puppy matures, a strong relationship may develop. However, some dogs would prefer to remain your only pet. Imagine if your significant other brought in a new, younger version of you to keep you company. If your dog can't get enough of you, adding a puppy may not be their first choice. For more tips on introducing a puppy to your resident pets, flip to Chapter 7.

If you're trying to decide which breed is compatible with your dog, put yourself in their paws. Two Golden Retrievers can chase balls all day and wag their tails at everyone in your neighborhood. A Golden Retriever and a rottweiler, on the other hand, are a combination similar to oil and water. By nature, rottweilers are stoic, serious-minded, self-contained dogs who are mindful of their surroundings. A Golden Retriever is friendly, engaging, impulsive, and passionate about new experiences. Though I'm sure some exceptions exist, bringing these two under the same roof will be anything but relaxing for the dog, the pup, or the members of the household. Think about both the breed you have and the one you're thinking of adding, and make sure that, at the end of the day, they have enough in common to coexist.

Personality is also a factor. If you coexist with a sweet, gentle dog and then bring home a dominant, bossy puppy, be aware that the new pup will likely lord over your resident dog in no time, which is sad to see. After all, you know who came home first. A bossy puppy may rule your roost in the end, regardless of house order or your wishes. However, you can simplify your life by choosing dogs whose personalities mesh.

Chapter **3**

Browsing Breeds and Rescues: Choosing One That's Right for You

Sure, almost all puppies love dog biscuits and a scratch behind the ears, but the similarities end there. If you're new to dogs and puppies, you may be surprised to learn that even though they're all built pretty much the same, each one has its own personality, and each one faces the world in unique ways. Some thrive on human interaction; others prefer an independent lifestyle. Some love the general mayhem created by small children, whereas others find it less than thrilling. Some see houseguests as long-lost friends, and others see them as potential enemies. Some dogs cherish quiet, solitary times; others eat your house if you come home too late. What sounds good to you? Fortunately, you can choose with reasonably good predictability!

If researching the right dog for your lifestyle sounds overwhelming, you'll love this chapter. In moments, you'll be in the know after reading advice that's streamlined and tailored just for you. In the pages ahead, you'll learn the difference between mixed-breed, designer-mixed-breed, and purebred dogs, as well as where to find them. If you already know what type of dog you want, you can reference this chapter for clues to where to find your puppy, or flip ahead to Chapter 4 to get tips on temperament testing your potential candidates and how to finesse a conversation with a breeder or rescue staff. First impressions do count — the more you know, the more confident you'll feel. Meanwhile, use this chapter to take one final look at just how a puppy's breed or mixed-breed traits will impact your life now and in the future.

REMEMBER

Getting a puppy is no short-term thrill. In fact, the thrill is relatively short-lived. As your puppy grows, you'll be responsible for all the care, love, and training of a developing dog who will share the next decade-plus with you and enrich your life in many ways. Use this chapter to prepare yourself for the adoption process.

Figuring Out Whether You Want a Purebred, Mixed-Breed, or Designer Dog

The first decision you need to make is whether you want to adopt a dog from a reputable breeder or from a shelter, an online site, or a rescue organization. Puppies, no matter the size and coat type, are nearly identical in terms of their natural instincts (to chase, explore, sooth pain or frustration and alert to distractions) and daily needs (to eat, drink, sleep, play, and eliminate). But the similarities pretty much end there.

The biggest difference between adult dogs, aside from their size and weight, are their interests and interactive needs. Big dogs need more exercise outdoors and may require more investment in time and energy to handle their impulses to chase and explore than would a small dog with limited or no access to going outside. That said, all dogs need attention and involvement, and each one is excited to learn new words, games, and fun tricks like a toddler. (You'll find more on the importance of teaching, socializing, and positively conditioning your puppy to all your life has to offer in Chapters 8 & 9.)

JUST FOR FUN

Though dogs are one of the most varied species on the planet (thanks to people tinkering with their mating choices), they are still the same on the inside. The tiniest little teacup-size puppy, weighing less than one pound, will have similar thoughts, emotional capacities, and reasoning abilities as a 20-pound giant puppy of the same age, especially in the first four months of life. You could even mate the two — although I wouldn't recommend it.

HOW BIG IS "LARGE"?

Dogs come in all shapes and sizes. Unfortunately, the sizes aren't as simple as "big" and "little." The following table can help you figure out how big large is and how little small is — just in case you ever need to know. The measurement is from the floor to the top of the dog's shoulder: These figures represent adult dog sizes.

Category	Height	Weight
Small	Up to 10 inches	2 to 20 pounds
Medium	10 to 20 inches	20 to 50 pounds
Large	20 to 27 inches	50 to 90 pounds
Giant	More than 27 inches	More than 90 pounds

REMEMBER

When you're first starting on your puppy finding journey, you may discover much arguing and much unnecessary animosity between people who advocate adopting a rescue or random mixed-breed dog and those who are comfortable adopting a purebred or designer-mixed-breed dog from a reputable breeder. Each will have valid points that may tug at your heart, but where you get your puppy and how you chose to raise them is your decision (to be made with your family, if you have one). Raising a puppy is a huge commitment, one just below raising a child, so do it right. This chapter educates you on the difference between the choices of rescuing a puppy and buying one from a breeder.

Choosing the breeder route versus the rescue route

When you purchase a purebred dog, you're buying into a multigenerational breeding effort. Individuals, known as *breeders*, devote their lives to matching dogs in their never-ending quest to produce healthy, conformationally sound, and emotionally consistent puppies. That's a good deal for you if you're the one purchasing a puppy.

A puppy bought from a breeder costs money; a shelter, transfer, or abandoned puppy costs far less. Here's the reason. Breeders are individuals whose only focus is to raise a specific breed of dog — or to design a specific mix of breeds, such as a Labradoodle or Maltipoo — to produce healthy puppies. These breeding programs find the healthiest parents for their puppies and ensure that the puppies they produce have a head start in socializing and training before you even bring them home. Your money is paying for that service.

Consciously raised puppies have been shown to be less agitated and stressed than other puppies who may be experiencing the sounds and stimulation of indoor living for the first time. This is not to say that you cannot condition these pups to life as you live it, but you'll need to invest a lot more time upfront, especially if your puppy is wary or defensive of new experiences.

TIP

Do you have the time and presence of mind to socialize a puppy who is unfamiliar with new experiences? If not, are you willing to pay a trainer or puppy daycare center to do extra socialization for you? If not, seek out a reputable breeder or find a shelter or rescue organization who has raised your potential puppy with its birth family to be sure that their early experiences were crafted from the start.

Of course, you will have a lot to do after your puppy comes home (see the chapters in Part 2), but early social experiences with home and family life must be crafted to condition your puppy to roll with the punches, so to speak. That's what takes extra know-how and time if your puppy has had no experience before you adopt them.

Deciding on a purebred dog

If you decide to take the purebred dog route, remember that well-respected breeders are worth their weight in gold. These individuals start socializing and handling their puppies from the second the puppies are born so that, by the time you pick up your puppy (around eight weeks), they'll be familiar with human handling, being restrained, and living life indoors.

WARNING

When choosing a breeder, keep in mind that some are better than others. How can you tell? For starters, good breeders will have as many questions for you as you do for them and will insist that you sign a contract that includes health and behavior guarantees. This document also insists that you return the puppy to the breeder should anything happen that causes you to rehome them. (To learn more about what qualifies a good breeder, flip to Chapter 4 and find a list of their qualities.)

REMEMBER

What are some other differences between a purebred and a mixed breed? Purebred dogs cost more — between $600 and $6,000. (The high end of that range is rare, but some championship show dogs and unique designer-mixed-breed dogs can fetch this price).

Opting for a random-mix puppy

Mixed-breed dogs, also known as *random* breeds or *mutts,* are created when pure-bred dogs (or other mutts) mate with another breed or mixed-breed dog. This dog will have a random mix of traits from two or more parents. No two mutts are ever alike in look or personality.

Just as capable of love and devotion as purebreds, mixed-breed puppies often happen by accident when people don't spay or neuter their dogs and then forget to contain or watch their dogs. Because this often happens in parts of the world where leash laws and spay-and-neuter ordinances aren't reinforced, many of these "oops" litters are uploaded to sites like petfinder.com or adoptapet.com or transported to shelters or adoption agencies where there's a bigger need for precious "adoptables." The bottom line? A mixed-breed dog is every bit as delightful as a purebred dog and is, some argue, healthier mentally and physically by virtue of hybrid vigor.

TECHNICAL
STUFF

The term *hybrid vigor* refers to a mixed-breed dog's gene pool. Though the theory has been questioned, it claims that you get a larger range of possible traits by matching two completely different breeds.

REMEMBER

Purebred or designer-mixed-breed dogs generally offer more predictability regarding their looks and interests, which can be both a plus and a minus, as you'll soon discover. A random mix will have a more blended look and feel, with certain qualities of either parent more dominant than others. Finding a breed that's predisposed to a trait or look you admire, or figuring out which breed types you'd prefer in your mixed-breed puppy, takes much of the guesswork out of assessing the puppy's developing look, behaviors, and needs.

Designing fancy (and expensive) mixed breeds

The designer-mixed breed is the latest craze to hit the dog world. To create a designer-mixed breed, breeders mindfully mate two purebred dogs to create a new, unique breed. This idea began with an attempt to create hypoallergenic seeing-eye dogs by mating standard poodles with Labrador retrievers. The resulting dogs were coined *labradoodles,* and though they didn't catch on as seeing-eye dogs, the craze caught on in the public sector. Now breeders have created designer mixes of every shape and size, and the list of designer breeds is nearing 100. Table 3-1 shows just a few of these fun new breeds.

TABLE 3-1

The New Designer Mixes

Designer Breed Name	Breed Combination
Cavachon	Cavalier King Charles spaniel + bichon frise
Chiweenie	Chihuahua + dachshund
Doodleman pinscher	Doberman pinscher + poodle
Jack-a-Bee	Jack Russell terrier + beagle
Labernese	Labrador retriever + Bernese mountain dog
Pomimo	American Eskimo dog + Pomeranian
Puggle	Pug + beagle
Shorgi	Corgi + shih tzu
Torkie	Toy fox terrier + Yorkshire terrier
Zuchon	Shih tzu + bichon frise

These designer dogs often cost much more than purebred or mixed breeds, to the tune of $2,000 to $6,000. Are you wondering how a breeder can get away with selling these mixed breeds at such high prices? Some are in it just for the money, following current trends and selling their puppies online to any buyer. Other breeders are as serious about their lines of designer breeds as breeders of single breed lines, making the same effort to choose healthy parents with health clearances and stellar temperaments to create puppies with these same qualities.

For example, the puggle (a pug-and-beagle cross) has a longer snout than the pug, which is genetically healthier, hands down. Most owners hope that with this cross, personality-wise, the beagle's scent-chasing obsessions will be toned down and that the marginally higher trainability of the pug will seep in.

REMEMBER

If you're considering a designer breed, you can't exactly be sure of what you'll get. A purebred dog's size, weight, and interests can be predicted. A mixed-breed dog, designer or not, has a random mix of either trait in no particular order. If you're thinking of buying one of these fun and fancifully named breeds, make sure you like both mixes — you can end up with the look of one and the personality of the other.

TECHNICAL STUFF

Everything about your puppy is predetermined by the combination of traits available from each parent. The dog pros would say that each puppy has its own, unique *genetic inscription* — for the coat color and the tail type right down to the sound of their barks and their reactions to strangers. Just as humans are pairings of their parents' traits, so are dogs. When similar dogs are bred consistently over *many* generations, the puppies will begin to look and act like their parents. Each set of dogs having these same traits, or genetic inscriptions, is classified into groups called *breeds*. When dogs of different breeds get together on their own to create a litter, their offspring will have a random blend of traits from both parents.

Because purebred dogs have a limited number of genetic bundles available to them, their appearance may not vary much from generation to generation. A West Highland white terrier, for example, is always white, with little variation. If this breed mated with a black-and-tan cocker spaniel, however, the puppies would have varying coat colors. Because the coat types of those two breeds are also different, each mixed-breed puppy would come out with its unique look.

WARNING

Because purebred dogs have a more limited pool of genetic choices, health-related considerations can often be passed from parent to puppy: Some examples are hip or elbow dysplasia; chronic skin, eye, and ear conditions; heart murmurs; and eyelid malformations. Because mixed-breed dogs have a larger pool of genes to work with, they have more random occurrences of these ailments and, some would argue, are healthier for it. In Chapter 4, you learn the right questions to ask potential breeders (or rescue organizations, if they know the parents) to ensure that your puppy's parents have clearances on every one of them.

Choosing the Type of Dog That's Right for You

Now it's time to select your chosen puppy. Finding one that's best suited to adapt to your lifestyle and family comes down to discovering the breed or mixed-breed whose worldview is most similar to your personality. Are you hardworking, sporty, sensually oriented, feisty? Finding a dog with qualities you can relate to is easier than you think. The first step is to get a better handle on the term *purebred*, a term lots of people use without really understanding what it means.

Purebred dogs are a relatively new phenomenon on the dog evolution trail. Having lived alongside us for over 14,000 years, the mindful breeding of dogs began only a few hundred years ago. Until that time, dogs generally reflected the landscape of where they lived: short-coated dogs in the hotter climates, thicker-coated dogs in the northern hemisphere, sure-footed dogs in the mountains, and so on.

Once people figured out that they could mix and match dogs to produce puppies of similar size and temperament or to suit their fancy, they began to pair dogs to serve their individual needs. Farmers bred dogs to guard or herd their flocks; merchants used dogs to move their produce or deliver goods from one town to the next; and hunters developed breeds to retrieve or to alert to their chosen quarry (a fancy term for a defenseless animal such as a bunny, bird, or fox). Breeds were created for many other purposes too, from border patrol to dog racing to mere cuddling. Dogs have been bred to do so many tasks over the millennia that scientists view dogs as integral in our species evolution.

More than 320 breeds are now registered worldwide. These days, being a purebred dog is like belonging to an exclusive club: Only dogs with similar looks and interests get in. Although most breeds are no longer asked to do the work they were developed for, fanciers continually devote themselves to breeding and selling puppies that reflect their traditions.

Choosing a specific breed enables you to predict the size, weight, and interest of your puppy. Selecting a one-of-a-kind mixed-breed puppy, and predicting or discovering the various breeds that combine to create them, allows you to make accurate descriptions about their interests and energy level as an adult dog.

When researching a breed, mixed-breed, or designer-mixed-breed, try to meet at least three adult dogs of the same breed or mix-breeds. All puppies are cute and adorable, but they grow up in the blink of an eye, so make sure you like the look and personality of the dog your puppy will become.

Whether you're considering a purebred, mixed-breed, or designer-mixed-breed, take a good, hard look at your lifestyle now and project out five to ten years. How might a certain breed's or mixed breed's interests and energy level play out in your home?

Different Breeds for Different Folks

With hundreds of different dog breeds and millions of mixed-breed combinations out there, it's hard to keep them all straight! To remedy the confusion, dog fanciers founded breed clubs whose job it is to track litters down to each puppy: Think of a gigantic family tree, doggie style. Various countries have parent clubs that not only register dogs but also organize get-togethers (known as *dog shows*) and sporting events to highlight different breeds' form and functionality. In the U.S., this not-for-profit club is known as the American Kennel Club, or AKC. The club is also responsible for defining how dogs should look, move, and act (known as the breed's *standard*), and it recognizes dogs who come closest to the organization's ideal.

The AKC, as well as other breed clubs — the Canadian Kennel Club, the Nordic Union Kennel Club, and the original Kennel Club located in the United Kingdom, for example — organize the different breeds they recognize into various subgroupings that highlight similarities between the breeds. In the following sections, I give you a quick description of the seven breed groups listed by the AKC.

The Sporting group

A proactive lot, dogs in the Sporting group were bred to help man sustain themselves by *flushing* (scaring out of hiding) birds and retrieving the ones that their masters shot. In this day and age, you're unlikely to shoot your supper from the sky, but don't tell that to your dog. Born with a fetching fetish, these breeds thrive on an active and involved lifestyle and won't retire just because you're well fed. No ducks to claim or birds to point out? Your slippers will do, and so will the pigeon perching on the windowsill.

When these puppies are exercised, directed, and included, no group is more happy-go-lucky and accepting of life's random chaos. But when they don't get enough playtime or training, they can be hyperactive and destructive.

The Cocker Spaniel, Golden Retriever, German Shorthaired Pointer, and the Irish Setter are in this group.

WARNING

Even though the loyal and cheerful dogs in the Sporting group have well-earned reputations as patient family pets, they need both mental and physical stimulation. They can't cope with long hours of isolation; coupled with a lack of exercise, this isolation fuels anxiety. An unhappy Sporting dog is destructive, hyperactive, and impulsive. This isn't a good mix — especially for your couch and end table.

The Hound group

The dogs in the Hound group are a happy lot with a 1-track mind; their fascination with hunting propels them through life and allows them plenty of opportunity for employment. Though you may have no interest in hunting a fox, chasing deer, or treeing a raccoon, your hound puppy probably will.

Originally teamed in pairs or packs, each hound was prized for their instinct to follow game without depending on human direction. As a result, a hound's friendly manner and pack mentality result in a dog who enjoys family life yet is generally independent enough to entertain themselves.

The Beagle, Greyhound, Irish Wolfhound, and the Foxhound are in this group.

WARNING

There are two types of hound: those that hunt by following the scent of their chosen pre, and others who trail animals by sight — commonly referred to as Scent hounds and Sight hounds. Both should be kept on a lead when outdoors, because their instinct to chase hasn't been bred out of them and you can't outrun them. In addition, you should socialize both to common household pets (like cats, birds, and rabbits) at an early age; otherwise, they may confuse them for lunch!

The Working group

The breeds in the Working group vary in chosen occupation, but their work passion unites them. Whether participating in guarding, pulling a cart or sled, water retrieval, protecting, or performing police work, they're a task-oriented group.

The breeds in the Working group may be large, but if they're nurtured with consistency, training, and exercise, they can adapt to any lifestyle with ease. When living in the country, these dogs must be contained to keep them from roaming off in pursuit of some self-assigned task. They can adapt to apartment dwelling when given daily walks and an occasional romp in the dog park.

WARNING

Carefully consider your situation before choosing a guard dog. Raising children and dogs is challenge enough. Territorial breeds can overstate their job as guardian, protecting your home and children against all intruders — including friends, extended family members, daily workers, and even other children. These dogs quickly suffer career stress in busy houses. If your heart's set on a territorial breed, structured training is a must.

The Alaskan Malamute, Bernese Mountain Dog, Giant Schnauzer, and Rottweiler are in this group

The Herding group

The Herding group breeds were developed during the agricultural age, when their herding skills were prized by caretakers of sheep and cattle across the globe. Man put great effort into fine-tuning these herding instincts when developing the breeds in this group. Even though these skills are no longer a priority, each dog's behavior in the home is reflective of them. For example, a dog bred to herd sheep is often seen herding children. If properly socialized as to not view your home and the people in it as field and flock, these dogs — trained and exercised — are deeply loyal.

WARNING

If the herding breeds aren't given an outlet for their impulses, they can develop obsessive, patterned behaviors, like circling a table or chasing fast-moving targets such as automobiles or joggers. For herders that are understimulated, their pacing creates a well-trodden path in a yard or field. Herding dogs must be trained, lest they adopt their people or children as sheep to protect. Cattle dogs are serious-minded, strong, and stocky dogs who can develop repetitive behaviors such as nipping your (or your children's) moving ankles.

The Rough and Smooth-coated Collie, Bouvier de Flounders, German Shepherd dog, and Belgian Malinois are in this group.

The Terrier group

The breeds in the Terrier group were designed to either track down vermin in barns or fight other animals for sport. Determined and tenacious by design, they work independently and don't prioritize human direction. Because they're spirited and spunky and not easily impressed or persuaded, terriers aren't a great match for control freaks. Even though they thoroughly enjoy human companionship and a good romp, they must be confined or leashed to prevent roaming or hunting.

REMEMBER

Don't be surprised if your terrier lifts their lip as you reach, or anyone else reaches, for their bone or food bowl. It's a natural reaction called *spatial aggression*, and it's similar to what a young child does when he doesn't want to share a favorite toy (although, hopefully, your kid doesn't growl). Other dogs known for this behavior include some Working breeds, hounds, and certain toy breeds. For suggestions on overcoming this dilemma, refer to Chapter 18.

Although terriers traditionally bred to fight other animals have a combative history, most of the breeding lines have all but extinguished this impulse. Extensive socialization can ensure a friendly attitude toward other dogs and pets.

The Cairn Terrier, Bull Terrier, Lakeland Terrier, and Parsons Jack Russel Terrier are in this group.

WARNING

Though the practice is rare, some owners still use fighting breeds for sport. These owners usually don't neuter the dogs (because doing so would diminish their fighting tenacity) and often neglect them. Because of this mistreatment, these dogs may have many litters of puppies, and their genes can seep into the domesticated gene pool, possibly causing the breed to be more aggressive. When choosing a dog from this group, trace its history or talk openly with the breeder or previous owner about their breeding philosophy and the temperaments of the dog's parents.

The Toy group

The lovable little miniatures in the Toy group have been bred down from larger dogs. Even though they can be cuddle companions, many still have their original breed characteristics firmly set. Take the miniature pinscher (or min pin), for example. A distant relative of the Doberman pinscher, the min pin is an astute watchdog who sounds visitors' arrival before they even knock at the door.

When assessing specific breeds, research their ancestry. Even though their size is different from their ancestors' size, their genetic impulses may be undeniably similar. Don't pass on training them simply because of their toy-like appearance.

Constant affection without direction results in a Napoleon-like complex, which is reflected in behaviors from chronic barking to marking and, often, aggression. You'd be surprised at how much damage a 5-pound dog can inflict!

WARNING

Toy breeds are fragile by design. Even though certain breeds are stockier (the pug and the Cavalier King Charles spaniel, for example), they're all tiny — especially as puppies. Be mindful of this puppy around larger dogs and young children: Toddlers can easily hurt or overwhelm the puppies if they mistakenly confuse them for a stuffed animal.

The Chihuahua, Pekinese, Maltese and Toy Poodle are in this group.

The Non-Sporting group

The Non-Sporting group is the catchall group. When a dog's orientation is too varied to fit anywhere else, it ends up here. Dalmatians, for example, were bred to follow horse carriages over great distances and, when parked, to lie under the carriage and guard both the contents and the horses from vagabonds. The Keeshond, a Norwegian breed, was bred to accompany men on sea travels, cheerfully alerting them to any commotion. Though each dog's ancestry is varied, they're threaded together by their devoted participation in human affairs.

Whether you're considering a pure breed or a mixed breed, consider what type of dog sounds good to you. Do you relate to the more serious nature of dogs in the Working group? Many breed books explore the different breeds in depth. Does the zest and intensity of a terrier excite you? You'll have many choices!

The Bichon Frise, French Bulldog, Finish Spitz, and the Miniature Schnauzer are in this group.

Chapter 4

Deciding Where to Go to Get Your Puppy

I f you're at that stage in the puppy-searching process where you have a pretty good handle on what type of dog you want to live with, it's past time for you to finally find your forever puppy. The thing is, you'll soon discover that you can find puppies to purchase everywhere — on the Internet or from a breeder, shelter, rescue organization, or pet store. They even sell puppies on craigslist! So, where's a future puppy owner to start?

I recommend that, before you start surfing the Internet for that perfect puppy, consider the differences between well-respected dog breeders and those brokers who may not have your or your future puppy's best interests in mind. And, if your heart is set on a rescue dog, consider the differences between highly rated dog shelters and those rescue organizations that often have more dogs and puppies to manage than they can care for adequately. Because your puppy is the one relative you get to choose, take your time to pick one that has had a proper start. After all, if you're going to pay top dollar for a puppy, you deserve one that has a head start in life and hasn't been raised like livestock.

REMEMBER

Puppies grow up fast and are more like children than cats when it comes to their demands for your attention and their need for care. Choosing a puppy is a decade-plus relationship, so resist the immediate gratification of buying puppies online or over the phone in place of selecting a respected organization or breeder who'll take care of your puppy (and take the time to socialize them) from their very first breath.

After you've narrowed your search, you need to choose a few places or people to contact. You'll find a handy cheat sheet in the pages ahead listing the best questions to ask a puppy provider, like where the puppies have been raised (inside is best), whether or not they have been seen by a vet or given inoculations, and whether they have a jump start on crating or house-training.

Finally, because every puppy has sensory reactions and a budding personality that can be scored as early as 8 weeks old, ask the breeder whether they have tested the puppy or, if not, whether you can observe the litter before choosing the one that best connects with you and the rest of your family.

WARNING

When you go to a breeder or shelter, there's a small chance you won't click with any of the puppies you meet. It doesn't often happen, but be prepared. Always remember that nothing is more disappointing (for you and the pup) than bringing a puppy home and finding that it isn't a good fit. Finding your forever puppy is worth the wait. Think of the advice and tips in this chapter as my way to teach you how to find a puppy that connects with you and each member of the family.

Searching High and Low for Your Puppy

One vital stage of any puppy's life happens before you even bring them home. During that early stage, from birth to 8 weeks old, the type of environment surrounding them forms them in ways that will impact their behavior in your home. A puppy from a peaceful environment, where the owners mindfully nurture the parent dogs and puppies, is generally better equipped to handle the transition into a new home than a puppy who has lived in an overcrowded, neglected kennel and who has been severed from their litter at an early age. The reason is simple: A puppy's brain is still developing even after they come out of the womb, and it continues until they're 12 weeks old. Life stress can have a much greater impact at this time.

TIP

Lots of people are eager to know what's better — a male or female puppy. Personally, I've loved both. Boys, however, are known, generally speaking, for being more clinging and dependent than females. If you have dogs at home, avoid having two female dogs under the same roof. Adult females can be a little ornery while living together (just imagine!) and often get along better with male companions. Of course, if you have a male dog, they can roll either way.

Finding puppy love on the Internet

Unless you have a direct connection to a breeder, shelter, or rescue organization, the first place you may want to look into finding your puppy is on the Internet. Nowadays, you'll find direct sites for breeders, shelters, and other sources, as well as sites that review such businesses. And though it used to take time to contact other people who have had experiences with a shelter or breeder, you can now send instant messages to people to see how their puppies developed. The web has brought dog lovers together, and you'll be pleasantly surprised to see how happy everyone is to help you get started on the right paw.

That being said, I don't recommend that you actually buy a puppy over the Internet. You should meet with and talk directly to representatives of shelters and rescue organizations or breeders. And do all the necessary research to find your forever puppy from a good source. Scammers are everywhere: Beware of the "breeder" who demands that you wire money immediately through Western Union. Puppy mills (facilities that basically farm dogs like livestock) advertise their litters online, misrepresenting their devotion to their puppies' well-being. Welfare organizations and shelters post haunting photos of mixed-breed puppies who need homes but may not be a good fit for *your* home. A pet photo is like the cover of a book: You can't tell much just by looking.

Some websites rate potential breeders and list the ones who have litters for sale. Good places to go for information are `www.adoptadog.com`, `www.puppyfinder.com`, and `www.puppyfind.com`. However, some people in the puppy industry make the argument that no ethical breeders would sell puppies online because, much like a child-adoption agency, anyone with an ethical bone in their body would want to meet a prospective parent so that they know who is adopting their "furry children" and what kind of home they'll be providing. So do your research *carefully* before traveling down this road. Anyone can advertise themselves as a breeder, and you don't want to give your heart away to a mishandled puppy!

WARNING

Unless you're a fan of mail-order brides (or grooms), don't buy a puppy from an ad on the Internet. You will overpay for a puppy who has likely spent their early days in an outdoor pen or living on a puppy farm like a pig. You'll be nearly guaranteed a puppy whose high levels of stress will play havoc on your lovely home or apartment. It's far better to find either a rescue that has used a foster home or a breeder or shelter who's helped your dog to adapt to life in your town and will be on call to help you to settle your puppy in as they start life with you.

Here are some tips for finding a good pup on the Internet:

>> **In addition to emailing the puppy's shelter, owner, foster family, or breeder, speak to the other party by phone.** Ask about the breeds and genetic health of the puppy's parents, if they're known. If the parent's histories are supposedly known, but no one has health certifications to back that history up . . .think twice: Puppies are everywhere, and you want the one with a healthy future.

>> **Ask for a copy of the puppy's health records.** People can easily and immediately send them via text or email. If you're even slightly suspicious about the information, call and speak to the veterinarian's office directly. Ask the hospital staff questions about the puppy and the owner: Was the puppy raised with their mother and littermates, where were the puppies housed, and how much social interaction have they received? If the people caring for the puppy are unwilling to share this information, reconsider this puppy. The ideal puppy is one raised indoors with the birth family and with lots of loving social interaction — anything less may spell trouble for you in the long run.

>> **When talking to people in contact with your puppy, listen for loaded words like** *spunky* **(which probably means hyperactive or reactive),** *shy* **(timid), or** *self-assured* **(meaning strong-willed).**

>> **Request a video of the puppy with their mother and littermates or with other dogs at the shelter.** Is the location clean? Does the puppy look happy and healthy?

>> **If the puppy is already separated from their mother, ask what age they were at the time of separation.** Puppies removed before 7 weeks lack their mother's formative influence, which is invaluable for learning emotional regulation, bite inhibition, and respect. These puppies may never make up for the valuable time lost and may need a lot more structure and time to socialize and train.

>> **Ask the owner to send you the purchaser's contract outlining the agreement between you.** Don't buy a puppy without an agreement that clearly states what will happen to the puppy if you discover that they have a health issue or find that their temperament isn't a good match for your family. If you're unable to return the puppy for any reason, do not proceed. All good breeders should let you return their puppies, no questions asked.

>> **If the breeder checks out and prefers that you pay online, use an online escrow account to hold the funds until your pup has arrived safely and you've had them checked out by your veterinarian.** A reputable breeder should agree to this plan if they're more devoted to the placement of their puppies than to their dollar value.

>> **Beware of the bargain-basement puppy.** A puppy whose price is reduced may be undersocialized, maturing out of the cute phase, in poor health, or temperamentally unsound.

When choosing a mixed-breed puppy from a photo, be mindful of the mix. Although all puppies look adorable onscreen, if the puppy is a combination of two breeds that you wouldn't otherwise choose for your lifestyle, mixing them won't help. Research all breeds that may be in the mix, and evaluate each one's fit with your lifestyle.

Adopting a pup from a shelter or a rescue organization

You may be wondering what the difference is between a shelter and a rescue organization and how it relates to choosing your forever puppy. The short explanation is that shelters operate out of a municipal building or kennel-type facility and often care for a range of pets, whereas rescue organizations generally focus on one type of animal, and foster those animals out to live in homes until they are find their forever homes.

TIP

Although puppies are generally born in litters ranging from 3 to 13 puppies, occasionally a mother dog gives birth to just one puppy, called a *singleton*. These puppies are at a disadvantage because they would normally learn much more about the world by way of interaction and play with their doggie siblings. Unless you're a seasoned dog owner, avoid singleton puppies: These dogs need someone who can help them learn boundaries and good manners. The same advice applies to *hand-raised* puppies — puppies who, for whatever reason, lost their mothers early on and had to be rescued and raised solely by humans. Even if raised with littermates, without their mother's influence and lessons on self-restraint these puppies often develop pushy, unyielding mannerisms and a tendency toward resource guarding. Explore other options and leave these puppies to someone with lots of special needs' puppy-raising experience.

Shelters

The local animal shelter (also known as animal control, the dog pound, or the Humane Society) is often a government-run facility that harbors various types of animals that have either been abandoned at its doorstep or found roaming within its jurisdiction. Shelters are often full of various types of animals available for adoption. Many shelters, especially in areas where spay-and-neuter laws aren't enforced, if they even exist, are overrun and forced to euthanize animals who aren't claimed or adopted within a set period. Although no-kill shelters exist, often having more animals than they have space to contain them makes them controversial; an unadoptable, ill, or poorly mannered dog may be preventing another dog with better adoption potential from reaching the public eye. Unfortunately, it's a problem with no ideal solution.

If you choose to adopt a puppy from a shelter, the puppy will have detailed health records and if not spayed or neutered already will generally have you return the puppy to their chosen veterinarian for the procedure at a designated time. Most shelters will have a greeting pen or room where you and your family, if you have one, can spend time with various candidates before choosing the one you like best.

WARNING

Shelter puppies come from all walks of life. Some of the pups' situations are known, although others aren't. Many shelters and animal welfare organizations rescue puppies from dire situations and care for them until they're adopted. Some of these puppies are removed from their mothers at an early age (before 8 weeks old) and need special care before they can be put up for adoption. Other puppies are brought in with or without their mothers and left at a shelter. Those pre-adoption weeks are *critical:* If you adopt a puppy whose early life was stressed, you cannot make up for lost time. Even if you're able to increase the socialization and touch conditioning levels in the first weeks you bring them home, there may be certain wary or dramatic reactions you can never completely condition out of your puppy.

Rescue organizations

As you surf the web, you may notice a lot of rescue organizations within a 1- or 2-hour drive from your home. Rescue organizations are similar to shelters in that they are not-for-profit, tax-exempt organizations. They differ from shelters because they generally focus on one species — say, dogs — and gather volunteers to serve as foster families until their rescues find their forever homes. Adopting a puppy from a rescue organization versus a shelter may be a longer process, involving home visits and lengthy questioning to ensure that the rescue you like is best suited for you and your family (if you have one).

WARNING

When people think of hoarders, they generally think of people who like to collect stuff, but do you know about animal hoarders? Though few people scoff at people who collect worthless stuff like newspapers and old cellphones, people who hoard pets affect more than themselves. Raids occur across the country, discovering individuals who hoard many dozens of animals (often, dogs and cats) at a time. These animals often live in squalor, and though the hoarder-person likely loves their animals on some deep emotional level, they're often long past the number of animals they can manage.

The recent development of not-for-profit rescue organizations often supports a person's fixation on rescuing animals, making it easy for a hoarder to masquerade as a rescue organization. If you come in contact with such a place, resist rescuing an individual animal and contact the authorities (the local animal shelter). Puppies raised in these conditions need professional help to undo the damage of a stressful start.

Whether talking to shelter staff or emailing rescue organizations, you will be asked for a lot of important information, including your current employment status, how much time you'll be able to spend at home during the day, whether you have a fenced-in yard, and what you will do with your dog when you go on vacation. Answer honestly; if your application is turned down, ask why and consider whether you're willing to make changes in your lifestyle to increase the chance of getting the next puppy you consider.

Here are some important questions to ask the staff or foster family. These people, often volunteers, all have one thing in common — they love their dogs and want the best for them:

» Do you know anything about the puppy's history?

» Have you spent time with the puppy? If so, what do you think of their personality?

» Has the puppy been introduced to children or cats? If so, what was their reaction?

» Has the puppy been vetted? That is, do they have a health clearance from a veterinarian?

» Has the puppy been neutered? Many shelters routinely alter puppies at a young age or offer you a discount at their clinic.

TIP

If you have other pets or kids, arrange a meeting to gauge a potential puppy's reaction to them. Although you may adore a puppy, if they don't light up to the rest of your gang, find one who does. The last thing you want is to have to bring the puppy back.

Most, but not all, of the puppies found at shelters and rescue organizations are mixed breeds. Consider how each breed in the mix will fit into your lifestyle. For instance, if you're looking for a low-shedding, small- to medium-size dog who will sally up to anyone, pass on the Chow-Akita mix, no matter how cute they look sitting there in the cage. As an adult, they'll be large and aloof to strangers and will have heavy shedding seasons — and those characteristics do *not* match your initial criteria!

TIP

A staff member can give you their opinion of the breeds that went into the mix, but if you have a friend who knows breeds, you may want to send them a photo or bring them along for a second opinion.

Buying a puppy from a professional breeder

If you've decided that you prefer the predictability and breeder assurances of adopting a purebred puppy or designer mixed-breed puppy, go for it! Although you may get some flak from those who feel that everyone should "adopt, not shop," don't let anyone guilt-trip you out of your decision. In your case, be sure to purchase a puppy from a well-respected breeder who raises their litters indoors and exposes them to many of life's everyday stimulations.

As is true in all professions, you'll come across good breeders and not-so-good ones. Top breeders conscientiously raise dogs with good genetic lines. Reputable breeders test dogs before breeding them to ensure that they're free of any congenital defects and to guarantee the health of the puppy they sell. Good breeders also socialize their puppies to everyday sounds and stimulations, including children, men, as well as various other animals; many breeders submit every puppy to temperament testing to help pair each with an ideal home.

Here are some other ways to determine whether a breeder has their dogs' and puppies' best interests in mind or is breeding just to make money. If you sense hesitation or lack of expertise when speaking to a breeder, move on. You want to raise one puppy who'll mesh into your lifestyle with ease: Find a breeder who supports your vision, not the one who treats their dogs like livestock.

Remember that these people are giving you their time; thank them for speaking with you and be prepared to answer their questions first. If they don't build the answers to your potential questions into the conversation, ask politely and note their answers. Here are some questions to ask when talking to a breeder:

>> Are litters raised in the home and mindfully exposed to the sounds and stimulations of everyday life? Litters raised in the kitchen or living room are best; see if you can find one.

>> Is the potential breeder aware of their breed's (or mixed breed's) genetic defects — defects passed down from one generation to the next, and which may include hip elbow dysplasia, eye or heart maladies? (Conscientious breeders avoid breeding dogs with such defects.) Do both your potential puppy's parents have all their health clearances up-to-date?

>> Does the breeder you're speaking to have a contract to sign? If so, could they send you a copy of it to review? If a breeder doesn't have a contract to sign when buying your puppy, do not use that breeder. Contracts should contain policies for returning the puppy, no matter what the age, if your situation

demands it. Many top breeders have you sign an agreement guaranteeing the health of your puppy and a stipulation regarding spaying or neutering your puppy. This contract also lists the inoculations and deworming medications that may have been given before you bring your puppy home.

>> Has your puppy seen a veterinarian? If not, that would be a good indication that this breeder doesn't have their puppies' best interests in mind. Veterinarians are costly, but that's part of the high price you pay when buying a puppy from a breeder in the first place. A good breeder will have their litters checked at least once and will provide the first set of inoculations.

>> Ask if the puppies are bred for the show ring — pretty, yes but they may not have a pet's more chill personality or temperament. Reputable breeders breed for temperament, which means that the breeders are just as interested in puppies that act delightfully as ones that look good. If you want your puppy to be a pet, this attribute in a breeder trumps all others.

>> Has the breeder begun training their puppies to a crate or pen? Many breeders would already have provided their puppies with chew toys, such as ropes, hard plastic or rubber bones, or hollow bones stuffed with dry food, and would have also already begun training their puppies to use a separate potty area to eliminate before handing them over to their new owner. All this prep work gives you a tremendous leg up on housetraining and chewing habits when you bring the puppy home.

>> Good breeders take notice of each puppy, using colored paper collars to identify pups early on. Has the breeder you're considering spent time interacting with and holding each puppy or developing a simple training protocol to encourage good manners? One thing a mindful breeder does is withhold food or treats until their puppies stop jumping, which results in good manners from the start.

>> A good breeder also observes and handles each puppy to determine their sensory sensitivities after 7-weeks of age. Breeders often do (or allow a potential family to do) a short series of temperament tests to determine which puppy would be ideal for a given home. In the later section "Testing a puppy's temperament," I include a temperament test that you can give as you consider each candidate, if your breeder hasn't done a test already.

REMEMBER

Breeders who can help you understand both the positive and negative aspects of the breed they work with are worth their weight in gold. If they're serious about the placement of their puppies, they'll ask you a whole list of questions to ensure that you're a good fit for their breed and their puppies. You may feel more scrutinized than if you were adopting a child, but don't be put off by their questions, because in the end you'll receive a puppy who has been loved and well cared for since its very first breath. If the breeder rejects you, ask why and ask whether they can provide information that can help you determine what dog would work best with your lifestyle.

When evaluating breeding facilities, go with your gut. If you drive up to a breeder's kennel and get a bad vibe for any reason, such as dirty facilities, an inability to answer your questions, or not being allowed to see your puppy's mother (or father, if he's on the premises), leave. The urge to save a puppy from a bad environment may be overpowering, but unpleasant facilities or mistreatment can result in sickly or poorly socialized puppies. You will pay in the long run for having a puppy who may need more time and attention than you can devote in order to undo the isolation from real-life experiences your pup has endured. It's better to back out of the driveway and place a quick call to the local chapter of the American Society for the Prevention of Cruelty to Animals (ASPCA) to report bad breeders than to buy a puppy and possibly live to regret it. You'll be doing yourself a favor, and you'll help put people who are breeding purely for financial gains out of business.

Checking out a home breeder

Puppies who are bred in someone's home may be purebred or mixed. These home-bred puppies usually come from dogs who are beloved pets, but who may or may not have health clearances, or from dogs who have mistakenly escaped their owners' yards and mated with unknown sires. However, sometimes these pups come from dogs who live with people who thought breeding two purebred dogs would be fun, educational for the kids, or lucrative. If you follow a sign advertising a puppy for sale, talk to the owners about the following points:

>> If the puppies are a mixed breed, is the mix of breeds known or considered?

>> Were the parents tested for genetic defects known to the breed(s)?

>> Can you meet the parent dogs?

>> Have the puppies seen a veterinarian? If so, how far along are they with inoculations?

>> What sort of stimulations have the puppies been exposed to (cats, kids, daily mayhem, and so on)?

>> If the puppy turns out not to be a good fit for your family, would the breeder consider taking the puppy back?

WARNING

A home breeder is unlikely to take the puppy back, so if the situation turns ugly, you may be left with the prospect of rehoming your puppy or dropping them off at a local shelter.

Because purebred puppies bred at home generally cost the same as a breeder would charge, give this option a second thought if this individual cannot provide health clearances or reassurances should this puppy not work out in your home.

WARNING

Don't adopt a puppy younger than 8 weeks old. (Seven weeks may be okay only if you're experienced with very young puppies.) You don't want to adopt before 8 weeks because a pup's mother normally spends weeks 6 through 8 socializing and teaching their puppies. The result of this socialization is good for you because the puppies will have more organized elimination habits, respect, and bite inhibition.

Puppies taken home early are often coddled by well-meaning, adoring humans. During a developmental stage, when the puppy's mother would be teaching respect and impulse control, a person is placating and inconsistent. In this case, everyone becomes a target for nipping and bullying behavior.

Avoiding puppy brokers, puppy mills, and pet stores

Okay — there are a few places where you should definitely not get a puppy. Here are my top five:

>> **Puppy brokers or agents:** Puppy brokers (also known as puppy agents) are smooth-talking dog people who will promise to get you a puppy from their list of top-of-the-line breeders. Initially, these folks seem like saviors, descending to save you from the hassle of locating a puppy on your own. Do *not* be fooled. Most brokers are just out to make a buck and fill orders as fast as they come in — but no decent breeder will ever sell their puppy through a third party. Puppy brokers will go who-knows-where to find you a puppy when you want it and mark up the puppies they find in order to lace their pockets. After you decide where you want to concentrate your search, finding a puppy on your own isn't hard; Chapter 3 and this chapter walk you through the process.

TIP

If you've already paid a broker to find you a puppy, insist on speaking to the breeder, ask the broker to provide reviews from other customers, and check the health clearances on both parents.

>> **Puppy mill breeders:** Puppy mill breeders aren't breeders; they're farmers. They offer many different types of puppies and house their dogs like livestock instead of beloved family members. Mother dogs are often bred every heat cycle (a horrific practice) and then killed off after they can no long produce large litters. Puppies are produced under tremendous stress and often live to wallow in feces. The noise of the dog's barking is deafening. Individual puppies have little socialization or handling before they're washed and primed for sale. Buying a puppy from this sort of situation does nothing but feed this practice. Do you want your money to go to someone who has such little regard for a dog's life? Puppies from these situations are often more difficult to housetrain, chew to relieve anxiety that started long before you brought them home, and

are hypersensitive to touch and sound. Sometimes it's hard to determine if your puppy came from a puppy mill, but generally if you are buying your puppy from a middleman it's highly likely that seller bought the puppy wholesale from a puppy mill where puppies are sold cheaply and not from a breeder who would never dream of selling their pups to a middleman.

>> **From a box on the corner:** If you ever pass a box with a sign that reads "Free to good home" or any similar message, promise me that you won't look. Puppies are a mix of their parent's genes and their early upbringing. In this case, you'll likely have no proof of either. I have two words for you: Walk away. Repeat this mantra: One puppy, one choice, one life.

>> **Pet stores:** When a store owner purchases puppies for resale, they have to find breeders who are willing to sell puppies cheaply enough that they can be marked up and resold for a profit. A reputable breeder would never sell puppies to a pet store. So the pet store then contacts resale breeders who often breed many dogs simultaneously to meet the demands of the pet store. The resale breeders often stretch both themselves and their breeding dogs to the limit, and many of the facilities called — you guessed it — puppy mills (see the preceding bullet point) are understaffed. These conditions result in puppies who don't get proper care or socialization with the human world. They may also be sickly, as puppy mills are notorious for being understaffed, resulting in filth, dirty unchanged water, and feces-encrusted cages that attract parasites and flies. Bacteria and illness frequent these environments and quickly spread from puppy to puppy. Why take the risk?

>> **Craigslist, Facebook, Twitter:** Although I'm not saying a breeder won't have an online presence, online interactions don't take the place of reaching out and speaking with the breeder, shelter, or rescue organization. If you want to begin your search online, explore sites like www.petfinder.com to locate rescue dogs or www.akc.org to locate breeders. After you've researched places and checked their reviews, and perhaps even reached out to some of their puppy owners on Facebook, it's time to make the phone call and speak to the people in charge. Take the time now to research this project. Otherwise, you may have more than a decade to regret your impulsivity — and that's one hard lesson to swallow.

WARNING

More calculating breeders who choose to send their puppies out for resale don't usually send the pet stores the cream of their litters. The puppies they send are usually undersized or of poor conformation, from an ankle joint that's out of place to an undershot jaw. Resale breeders aren't likely to spend money to ensure that their breeding dogs are free from genetic defects.

LOOKING PAST THE DAZZLE OF TRENDY MIXES

Although many people are now purposely mixing different dog breeds, coming up with fancy-sounding names and then selling them at a high price, few of these "breeders" have much experience. Generally, when you pay for a puppy, you're paying for generations of careful breeding and reliable temperament. A breeder who is generating mixed-breed puppies, giving them names like Chi-weenie and Shorkie and selling them at a premium, may well be someone who owns a puppy mill and is just pairing dogs they have housed in kennels. Be careful when paying money for mixed-breed dogs. Use the same considerations you would if you were buying a purebred dog.

Meeting and Assessing Puppies

Whether you're choosing a mixed-breed or purebred puppy, you can tell a lot about them just by meeting them. If you're visiting a shelter, see how the puppy (or the litter) deals with the anxiety of a new introduction, Do they hesitate, get excited, or take it all in stride? If visiting a breeder, ask if you can meet the parents and spend a couple of hours observing the litter. Like all kids, all puppies have distinct personalities and varying degrees of sensory awareness. A puppy with a strong sense of themselves is forceful in play and with toys; a more passive puppy hesitates in new situations and often watches and considers before they jump up and responds. A playful puppy gets excited more easily and tries to engage their littermates in interactive activities like wrestling and tug-of-war. When choosing your new puppy, watch how they interact with their first family — that's how they relate to their world.

TIP

Before you drive to a breeder, ask about the visiting procedures: Can you meet individual puppies on your own, or will you be in an open room with the breeder present? The following section presents some guidelines for meeting and assessing your potential puppy and provides exercises (also known as a *temperament test*) that check for certain qualities and lets you know what the different reactions to stimuli tell you about your prospective puppy.

Finding out what to expect when visiting puppies

When the day finally arrives to go meet your potential puppy, you may be headed to different kinds of places to check out lovely puppies. The procedures for visiting pups differ depending on the type of place, so I break down the basics for you here:

>> **In a private home:** If you're going to visit a foster family or a breeder, you'll likely go to their home. Ask to visit in the morning or late afternoon because that's when most puppies are awake and playful. If that isn't possible, ask about the puppy's schedule and how long you can stay. Avoid nap times or late-night visits. When possible, ask to stay for a couple of hours so that you can watch and interact with the litter over an extended period.

>> **At a shelter:** Speak with a staff member ahead of time to find out how many puppies are available for adoption. (You can also ask ahead of time whether they know the breeds or mix of breeds so that you know whether the type of dog you want is available.) Find out whether a private meeting area is available and whether you can observe a litter together. Ideally, you want to see your candidate interacting with other puppies to determine their sociability within a group.

>> **At a pet shop:** If you've settled on purchasing your puppy from a pet store, you'll visit on your schedule. When possible, visit in the morning after the puppies have had a good rest. Ask to meet individual puppies separately: If one seems like a good fit, bring other puppies into the greeting room, too, to see how your candidate interacts with them.

Profiling puppy personalities

Selecting a puppy from a litter? You can tell a lot about each puppy's evolving personality and coping skills by 7 weeks of age. Though you can shape your puppy's habits once you get them home — redirecting your playful puppy if they jump on you, for example, or having them learn to fetch a toy when you come home — their worldview is set early on. In this section, I tell you how to evaluate a pup's personality based on simple exercises and on watching how they act with their littermates. These are basic categories — a litter may have more than one, or may not have one, of the personality types:

>> **Assertive:** Assertive and playful puppies have a lot in common, so it's easy to confuse the two. At first glance, both might seem social and interactive. You may think, "Wow — that one has spirit." However, keep watching. Do they steal the toys from the other puppies or play too rough? Do they scale the enclosure or climb on the backs of their littermates as though they don't exist?

These bossy behaviors are sure signs of determination, smarts, and willpower, but unless you're in the market for a dog who'll win agility competitions, think hard about how those characteristics will mesh with your home life. If you have the time to channel (and challenge) this puppy, take them home.

However, if you have other demands on your time and you're hoping for a puppy to reduce your stress, another personality type may suit you better.

>> **Playful:** Puppies in this group are quick-thinking, fun-loving, and engaging. They're equally fascinated by toys and socializing with their littermate or with you. When playing with different puppies, they adjust their tempo to reflect the other puppies' demeanor. Another term for this personality type is *social butterflies* because they're all about engaging without being too headstrong. This temperament is ideal for an active person or a family with older children.

>> **Independent:** These puppies interact in playful encounters some of the time, but are also happy sitting or playing with a toy on their own. Stoic and contained, these independent thinkers seem to have been born with an old soul.

These pups are ideal in structured homes where owners fully respect their sense of self and make a commitment to teach them. Because these puppies are mindful and alert, they're best suited to calm homes with older kids or no children.

Dependent: This type loathes solitude and wants to please. If socialized with people, they gravitate to you as if seeking your approval. That attitude leads this puppy to the head of the class or into the doghouse, depending on how you play it: If you direct and reinforce good manners, you'll have more than 100 percent cooperation; but if you try to discipline your puppy, they'll see your interaction as a reason to replay bad behavior over and over and over.

REMEMBER

Because of their trainability, dependent puppies are wonderful companions, but they can end up on the B list if they don't receive direction.

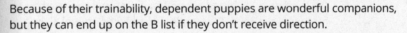

>> **Relaxed:** This calm personality type beautifully balances play, interaction, and sleep — doing all three on their own time. Perhaps less intelligent than their more active siblings, pups with this personality type simply do what they want, when they want.

Having relaxed puppies may sound dreamy, but remember that motivating them takes some creativity. They're not ideal for controlling owners, but they complement most households and fit beautifully into a home environment with young children, as long as the breed is suitable (see Chapter 3 if you need help selecting a breed) and the puppy shows an immediate affinity for the children upon first meeting them.

>> **Sweet:** Soft-natured and gentle, these puppies are often buried under their littermates who are playfully aware of their docile nature. These pups are also passive and eager to please, so their sweetness is palpable. Within their litters, these puppies stay close to their mothers and use their protection as a shield.

The sweet personality is good for owners who prefer doting attention over rigorous training. Puppies with this personality are less likely to roam, because staying close to home is a top priority.

>> **Timid:** These puppies, who are clearly not born with a strong sense of self, may appear to have been abused, even though it's more symbolic of their dislocated character than misguided nurturing. When approached, they often creep on their bellies or arch their backs in total submission.

Your heart may go out to pups with this personality, but select this type only if you have the time and patience to devote to fostering their self-esteem.

Regardless of your effort, timid puppies may always be overwhelmed and in need of direction, so they aren't a suitable choice for families with children.

WARNING

Testing a puppy's temperament

In this section I give you 10 quick exercises, also known as *temperament tests,* that you can administer while you're deciding whether you and a puppy are compatible. Of course, you can't get a completely accurate snapshot of your adult dog — other factors are equally if not more important, like socialization, training, and consistency — but these tests are a good way for you to determine each candidate's sensitivities and get a realistic view of their early conditioning.

In the following section, you'll find a testing sheet to keep track of your candidates' reactions: Feel free to cut out or copy the form and take it with you when interacting with a candidate. I ran through these exercises with more than 20 dogs before I found Whoopsie, our Labrador retriever. Truth be told, I wasn't looking for them when I found them. I had scanned the shelters in the area, testing puppy after puppy. Then I was called to select a puppy from a litter for a client. That's when it happened: I temperament-tested a puppy who hit the score I was waiting for. (See "Rating the results," later in this chapter, to find out about scoring the test.) Now it's your turn!

REMEMBER

If you're testing an 8-week-old puppy (a common age for puppies to become available), remember that their brain won't be fully aroused or awake until they're 12 weeks old. Try to schedule your visit just before feeding or stay for a few hours to watch them during various activities. Test your puppy when they're active, not when they're tired or sleepy.

TIP

If you have children, involve them. If you have other pets, ask if you can bring them. Some facility staff or breeders may balk, but it's essential that your puppy meet and make a connection to every member of your family. You want your puppy to succeed in your home environment, which means getting along with your sometimes-disgruntled resident schnauzer or your shy 6-year-old son. Finding a puppy who best suits their temperaments can be a plus because not every puppy personality will jive with them. Let children older than 5 take part in the exercises, and ask whether other pets can meet your chosen canidates.

REMEMBER

A puppy's breed influences their reaction to many of these tests and can skew the results. A retriever breed is more interactive, a terrier is squirmier when restrained (terriers like to stand firm), and smaller breeds are more hesitant when bent over (they're so tiny and you're so big) and more reactive to loud noises.

Using the scorecard

Bring the form shown in Figure 4-1 with you when you're testing puppies. Score each puppy's response to test items with the following scale:

A = Active   N = Neutral   P = Passive

Puppy Assessment Form

Name / Number of Pup	1. Observe	2. Play	3. Cradle	4. Call Back	5. Tuck & Pat	6. Bend Over	7. Back Leg Hold	8. Toe Squeeze	9. Startle Sound	10. Crash Test	11. Uplift

FIGURE 4-1:
Use this assessment form whenever you're testing puppies.

REMEMBER

Active puppies are smart and full of fun, which means there will suddenly be a whole lot of life going on under your roof. Spirited and intelligent, active pups are adored by owners who have the time and determination needed to train and socialize them. Neutral puppies are relaxed and undemanding — sort of the regular guys of the dog world. Passive and shy puppies appreciate love and support but are fearful of change, so they do best in consistent environments and with people who have the patience and time for extra socialization. (I tell you more about the importance of early socialization and how to do it in Chapter 9.)

After you perform the tests in the following section, you can interpret the scores using the information in the later section "Rating the results."

Performing the tests

If possible, do these gentle exercises with each prospective puppy to assess their socialization to everyday handling and sensory comfort levels (how well they adapt to sudden sounds, sights, and commotion, in other words). This will give you insight into the puppy's personality and how they will mesh with your lifestyle:

1. **Observe.**

   You can tell a lot about a puppy before you've even said hello. Watch the puppy, for up to 30 minutes when possible, if they're playing with other puppies in order to observe their personality. Do they prefer jumping into group activities (A), hanging in the midst of the activity (N), or staying on the sidelines (P)? Are they stealing the bones (A) or submitting when approached (N or P)? After you've observed the pup for a few minutes, assign them a score in the first column.

2. **Play.**

   When you first take a puppy aside, play with them, offering both treats and toys if permitted. Do they squirm to get away from you, look anxiously for their littermates, or engage and climb on you like a long-lost friend? Rate their energy level and persistence: Are they hyper or demanding (A), easygoing (N), or just wanting to be petted (P)? Bring out some toys. Do they show interest in them? Do they share willingly, instigate tug-of-war (A), or covet the object immediately? Coveting is an early sign of possessiveness, which may lead to aggression.

   I brought a ball when I was searching for a dog who would catch and retrieve. If being able to play a particular game with your puppy is important to you, see how the pup does with a related toy or activity.

3. **Cradle. (See Figure 4-2.)**

   Cradle the puppy in your arms. Do they relax (P), wiggle a bit, and then relax (N) — or kick like crazy (A)? Which action matches your expectations? See how quickly the puppy recovers after being put down; recovery is measured by how quickly they return to you and willingly takes a treat or engages with a toy.

WARNING

   Don't choose an A type if you have children. That type is bright and engaging, which is a plus if you're sporty or you want to be involved in obedience or sportier activities like agility or freestyle.

4. **Call back.**

   While holding out a treat or a squeak toy, call to the puppy as you back away from them. Do they race after you while jumping or nipping your ankles (A), follow happily (N), or hesitate and need coaxing (P)?

FIGURE 4-2:
Performing the
cradle test.

Illustration by Barbara Frake

5. **Tuck and pat.**

   Kneeling on the floor or sitting in a chair, settle the puppy between your legs.
   Pet them in long, gentle strokes as you praise them softly. Do they wriggle free
   as they nip (A), wriggle and then relax (N), or simply melt in your embrace (P)?

6. **Bend over.**

   Stand up, stretch, and relax. Now go to the puppy and lean over to pet them.
   Your doing this may seem overwhelming to the pup because you're so large
   and they're so small. Do they jump up to your face (A), cower in confusion (P),
   or just relax and let it happen (N)?

7. **Hold the back leg.**

   In this exercise, you're testing the puppy's reaction and sensitivity to discomfort.
   While petting the puppy, gently lift the back-right leg 2 inches off the floor and hold
   it for a count of 5 seconds (although either leg would do). Do they react defensively? If so, they're definitely an A type with high pain sensitivity. An N puppy may
   lick or place their mouth on you gently, whereas a P puppy will show concern.

   When choosing a puppy for a home with young children, I look for a puppy
   who has a very low sensitivity to touch — one who barely notices a toe squeeze
   and doesn't ruffle at being petted the wrong way or restrained for a short burst
   of time (fewer than 5 seconds).

8. **Startle with sound.**

   When your prospective puppy least expects it, tap two metal spoons together
   behind their back, then drop them 3 inches from where they're standing.
   Gauge their reaction: Do they startle and freeze? How quickly do they recover
   to explore the spoons or take a treat from your hand? If the puppy shows
   intense spoon interest, score A; a nonchalant glance, an N; and a fear reaction
   noted by cowering or withdrawal, a P.

9. Do the crash test. (See Figure 4-3.)

Stand and wait until the puppy is no longer interested in you. Suddenly fall to the ground and exclaim "Ouch!" Does the puppy race over and pounce (A), come to sniff or lick your face (N), or cower and run in fear (P)?

TIP

If you have a family, choose a puppy who rolls with unpredicted reactions and noise. You have enough on your hands without your puppy getting involved.

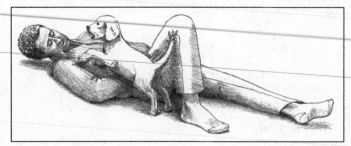

FIGURE 4-3:
Falling down for the crash test.

Illustration by Barbara Frake

10. Uplift. (See Figure 4-4.)

Lift the puppy 4 inches off the floor by cradling their midsection. Hold them there for at least 5 seconds. Do they wriggle and bite furiously (A)? Do they relax and look around (N)? Do they look fearful and constrict their body posture (P)?

TIP

When testing giant breeds, the uplift may not be physically possible. (They're heavy even at 8 weeks.) You can modify this test by standing behind the puppy and, with two hands supporting their ribcage, gently lifting their front legs 3 inches off the ground.

FIGURE 4-4:
Checking the puppy's reaction to the uplift test.

Illustration by Barbara Frake

Rating the results

After you've completed the tests in the preceding section, see how many of each letter (A, N, or P) the puppy scored. Don't be surprised if you get mixed results. Here are some tips for interpreting the tallied score:

>> **All A:** This interactive puppy is bright and self-assured. Raising them will take concentration, consistency, and time. Their favorite expression: "What's next?"

>> **All N:** Easygoing and contained, this puppy will be pleasant and self-assured, though perhaps not motivated to follow your agenda when it conflicts with their own. Their favorite expression: "Is this necessary?"

>> **All P:** This puppy has weak self-esteem and needs your reassurance to feel safe. Without proper lessons and socialization, they'll be shy. Their favorite expression: "It's been three minutes — do you still love me?"

>> **Mix of A and N:** This active puppy will want to be in the middle of everything but will show slightly more impulse control when stimulated. Their favorite expression: "Let's do it again!"

>> **Mix of N and P:** This puppy will be easygoing and gentle, yet with a stronger sense of self than a completely passive pup. Because they're more composed, they'll be an ideal puppy for a calm house with or without older children. Favorite expression: "Another back-scratching, please."

REMEMBER

If you've found a puppy whose score matches what you're looking for, great! If not, keep looking. Don't get discouraged, and don't settle for a puppy who doesn't quite suit you, just because you've been looking for a long time. I've been there — finding the right puppy is worth the wait.

Going for an Older Puppy

If you've decided to adopt an older puppy, you may be hoping to skip the tasks involved with the younger set, from curbing the nipping habit to house-training. With the right pup, you may be able to avoid some of these situations. However, no situation is perfect, and very few puppies can glide into a new life without a few setbacks. In this section, I walk you through some of the special considerations you should have when picking out an older puppy.

Considering the source

Depending on where you go to look for an older puppy, read the following questions to ask and points to consider before taking your little guy or gal home:

>> **Breeder:** A breeder often keeps a puppy for showing purposes. If the puppy doesn't grow into "show dog" potential, they'll be made available for sale. Sometimes, finding this puppy is like hitting the jackpot — provided the puppy has been living indoors, has received individual attention, and has been well socialized. At other times, it's a disappointment, especially if the puppy has lived in a kennel for the past 6 months.

REMEMBER

Because a breeder's older puppy may be unfamiliar with the routines of home life, they may not know what stairs are or may not have spent time in a yard. And, no matter what the breeder tries to tell you, a puppy who has spent the majority of their time in a kennel isn't housebroken. Find out where this puppy spent their early months before racing into this venture. A puppy who can't emotionally acclimate to your home life isn't a reasonable candidate for you.

>> **Rescue organizations:** Rescue organizations foster their puppies in homes, and you'll be able to both visit the home and question the foster parent about your puppy's socialization, temperament, and training. This can be a good option when considering an older puppy. The same rules apply, however, to the important question to ask: Has the puppy been raised indoors around other pets and people? How are their reactions to everyday sounds and stimulations? How is their house-training going? Don't be afraid to ask or test for more detailed information, like whether the puppy enjoys snuggling or being held, what toys are their favorites, whether you can remove high-value items like a bone or food dish, and how they behave on a leash. If you have a family, make sure the puppy relates to everyone, including other pets.

WARNING

You may find a puppy, young or old, who is being fostered in another state. Visit if you can; otherwise, look for a different puppy. People who are fostering are in the business of getting their puppies adopted, and they want to do it especially quickly if a puppy is a lot to handle. Sometimes, these people may enhance a dog's behavior traits and disregard others. See Table 4-1 for alternative interpretations of general behavioral descriptions. Buyer beware.

WARNING

After a puppy's peak socialization period, around 16 weeks of age, it's impossible to turn back the clock. People, places, sights, and smells that your puppy would have conditioned to naturally at an early age will seem suspicious to an older puppy. Do you want a dog who can't warm up to everyday stimulations?

Puppies who are overisolated or stressed during infancy are shown to chew more destructively and may wreck your furnishings if they aren't conditioned to chew their toys. The early turmoil created nervous energy that needs to be displaced, and because running to the refrigerator is off limits and nail-biting isn't an option, your puppy will chew on whatever is available. Provide plenty of satisfying options or else you may see your sofa disappear, one cushion at a time.

» **Shelter:** If you find an older puppy at a shelter, ask about their history and try to find out why they were left there. Were they found on the side of the street, or have they grown up in the system? Has the puppy in question been returned more than once? Ask what the reasons were — you may be adopting a dog who couldn't be house-trained, was fearful of kids, or showed aggression when chewing a bone. Find out what the staff thinks of the puppy's personality.

» **Pet store, puppy broker, craigslist, and other sources:** Discount shopping isn't for puppies. Do *not* buy a puppy without meeting and talking to the breeder or rescuers first. Though you may read a phrase that makes you feel like you'll be the winner, there are no winners in the online puppy shopping game. Buying a puppy in this manner ensures that more puppies will be bred this way, which doesn't take their interests to heart.

Puppies obtained online, especially those past the cute phase, sell for a discounted price. Though your heart (and mine) goes out to each of them, consider their reality before you adopt. A virtual lifetime spent behind bars can take an emotional toll, and house-training is a project for puppies never introduced to a designated potty area or the concept of holding their bladder. Also, these puppies have had little to no exposure to living in a home and the natural exposure to everyday sounds or objects, like stairs, cars, and tile flooring.

TABLE 4-1   ## Putting the Best Spin on Things

Clue Word(s)	Alternative Interpretation
A spunky puppy	Hyper; has a hard time transitioning calmly; manic
Doesn't get along with kids	Not socialized with children during the critical period; will likely show a lifetime caution with them
Not good with cats or other animals	Likely has a high prey drive, making leisurely strolls a nightmare
Not good with other dogs	Probably has been attacked by other dogs or lived in a shelter situation
Cautious of strangers	Has not had proper socialization to people; may be highly reactive to strangers and visitors throughout life
Better with women	May always be defensive and untrustworthy of men (who are walking plumes of testosterone) if they don't have positive experiences with them before 3 months of age

(continued)

TABLE 4-1 *(continued)*

Clue Word(s)	Alternative Interpretation
Better off leash	Terrible on a leash or no formal leash conditioning
Nervous/shy of new situations and people	Unable to cope with unpredictable or unfamiliar situations
Fearful	No socialization to life whatsoever
Unpredictable	Uncontrollably and inconsolably reactive with little to no forewarning
Aggressive	As with a mood, cannot be eliminated, only managed
Independent	Not trained to listen and cooperate with people
Stubborn	Headstrong
Submissive	Fearful
Needs room to run	Likely confined during early life; has a hard time calming down; hyper
High energy level	Same as the preceding entry — hasn't learned to self-soothe
Nippy	Hasn't learned to regulate play with people and may develop into a dog who bites when excited or when guarding toys and bones
Prey drive	Chases everything that moves

Testing older pups

If skipping over the mayhem and inconsistencies associated with a young puppy sounds good to you, your adoption outings will target puppies who are older and (hopefully) wiser. Though you can apply the exercises for testing young puppies, here are a few additional guidelines when meeting to see whether an older pup is a good match for your lifestyle. Always remember to let your head lead your heart. Nothing is sadder than rescuing a dog only to have to return them because they couldn't cope with your lifestyle. Be strong — find out ahead of time whether you and the puppy are suited to each other by performing the following tasks:

>> **If you have kids, introduce them to the puppy before you bring their home.**

>> **If you have an animal menagerie at home, make sure the puppy can cope with the creature chaos.** Ask whether the owner has other pets at home (if the puppy has been living there) or whether anyone has conditioned this puppy to other creatures.

>> **Ask a staff member (or the previous owner) to lift the puppy.** What happens? Intense fear or frustration isn't a good sign. The ideal puppy may squirm but is still accepting of restraint. Also, ask to see how the puppy acts when approached while chewing on a bone or eating a meal.

>> **To see how they handle contact, bring a soft brush and try to groom the pup while feeding them treats.**

REMEMBER

Older puppies who lack intensive early socialization are less accepting of strangers and strange or unpredictable situations than infant pups, so allow some room for edginess. But if you see anything more extreme, use all your willpower to back off, especially if what you see is aggression or excessive fearfulness. Unless you want a major training project, look for a puppy who's been socialized to living indoors and shows comfort with each member of your family (other pets included).

Chapter **5**

Shopping for Your New Baby and Looking to the Months Ahead

Before embarking on your first pre-puppy preparation shopping spree, prepare yourself. You'll see a lot of stuff — many of the brands will seem pretty similar, and most of it will be made overseas. (Look for a Made in America sticker if that aspect is important to you.) Initially, your puppy will need only a few simple items, such as bowls, some toys, and a crate, gate, or pen for an enclosure. This chapter can help you make the right choices about purchasing puppy supplies, from what kind of toys and self-soothing objects to buy to where to place the crate. A little planning will give you peace of mind and ensure that your puppy comes home to a calm, consistent, and supportive new environment.

Shopping for the Early Days with Your Puppy

The first few days after you bring your puppy home will be a bit of a blur; the most important task to focus on is your puppy's sleeping and house-training routines. Quick responses to commands like Sit and Come are important (and you'll learn about early puppy conditioning in Chapter 7), but your initial focus is on helping your puppy adapt to your schedule and getting comfortable living with you.

TIP

To avoid overstimulating your puppy or blowing your budget before the puppy has cut their baby teeth, remember that less is more, at least initially. Though you may have the temptation to buy everything you can for your pup — from the latest toy to a designer raincoat — I suggest that you bring a list and stick to it.

Your puppy's safe place

Your puppy needs a safe place, like a crate, enclosure or small gated pen for sleep and a free-play room to call their own. Puppy-proof these places by removing any "mouthables" (items that a young puppy can grab, chew, or choke on), and decide where you'll sit and what you'll do when supervising your puppy for the first few days they're home — more about this in Chapter 7!

TIP

I strongly advise using a crate for house-training and chew training; it's also the best place for your pup to rest during the day and sleep at night. Think of it less as a cage and more as a bedroom. You'll find tips in the next several sections to help your puppy bond with their room.

Gate

A gate can be used to blockade a door and prevent your puppy's passage from room to room or on a stairway. Gates come in handy when you want to

>> Enclose your puppy in a room when you're around to supervise or play with them

>> Control your puppy's access to dangerous or off-limits rooms and stairs

>> Teach your puppy that people, food, and fun happen only when they're calm. (Do not enter the free-play area until your puppy is sitting calmly or engaging with a toy.)

WARNING

Some people feel less guilty when leaving their puppies in large gated areas rather than in small rooms or crates. Big mistake. Big rooms make a puppy feel displaced and lonely so that they may potty or chew out of sheer anxiety. Dogs are den animals who feel safest in small, manageable spaces. If your goal is peaceful separations, enclose your puppy in a crate or small enclosure when you leave for more than a few minutes. If you're leaving for more than six hours, consider the playpen as a happy medium and hire a dog walker to break up their day. See the next section for more info on playpens.

Playpen

A *playpen* — essentially, a movable enclosure — is quite the multifunctional purchase. It can be used to

>> Acclimate the puppy to other pets by keeping them apart until they're familiarized with one another

>> Contain your puppy when you can't watch them

>> Keep your puppy from wandering about large, open rooms

>> Paper-train them, if that's your goal

>> Contain them outside temporarily

A folding playpen (see Figure 5-1) can be tucked away or transported easily.

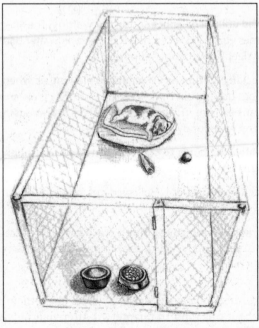

FIGURE 5-1: A playpen is a safe and portable place for your puppy to stay.

Illustration by Robert Golinello

Teach your puppy to stay calm for greetings from day one. One of the first lessons your puppy will learn is how to act when people approach you. Anytime you approach the gate or playpen, or whenever you're letting your puppy out of their crate, pause. Ignore your puppy if their jumping, squirming, or vocalizing. Do not engage them until they're calmly standing on all four paws.

Crate

Yes, some dog crates look like oversized guinea pig cages, but the truth is that your puppy, with the right conditioning, will love their crate like a child loves their bed. The trick is in the training! Make positive crate training one of your first goals — you'll find it especially useful during the early stages of potty and sleep training.

Because you'll want your puppy to sleep and nap in their crate, put it in a quiet room with little traffic. Ideally, your puppy should sleep near someone at night, so your bedroom is a good location. Keep the shades in the crate room drawn during the day. If you find it inconvenient to traipse through your home to an upstairs crate during the day, buy two crates — one for the bedroom and another to place close to your front door.

Here are a few things you can do to make your puppy's crate a little cozier:

>> **Have a stuffed animal or another dog toy waiting.** The Snuggle Puppy, for example, comes equipped with a heartbeat and hot water bottle to radiate the feeling of sleeping with other puppies.

>> **Prepare a docking station or CD player to play music when your puppy is left alone.** Dogs don't like silence in general and may grow anxious of distant noises they can't explore. The point of music is to drown out the sounds of silence and help your puppy tolerate on being alone.

>> **Install light-blocking binds to create a den-like atmosphere at night and during the day for nap times.**

>> **Provide a pacifier equivalent.** Hollowed-out toys stuffed with kibbles are ideal.

>> **Induce calm and sleeping by adding a crate cover.** The first goal with quiet time is to teach your puppy how to relax and soothe themselves when no one can be with them.

For the first weeks after you have your puppy home, help them pattern sleep routines. (See more about this topic in Chapter 7.) After your puppy establishes good sleeping habits, begin to vary their nap locations by moving their crate or playpen to different rooms of your home or by tethering your puppy near you as described in Chapter 7.

Still not sold on crating your puppy when you're out or can't be watching them? Think about it this way: Giving your pup their own special place to play and rest is synonymous with giving a child their own bed and tucking them in when it's time to rest. You wouldn't make a child sleep on the floor in the middle of a large room, would you? Your puppy will appreciate having their safe place.

When you shop for a crate, you'll find all sorts of different sizes, materials, and colors. Should you get a divider or leave space for potty paper? Should the sides be covered or open for air flow? Here's the scoop:

>> Plastic crates are standard for travel and can also be used as everyday crates. If you plan to travel with your pup, buy this type.

>> Wire crates allow for better airflow and viewing and can be covered with a blanket at night to create a more den-like experience. Dividers are also available to size the crate according to your puppy's size.

>> A wicker, wood, or canvas crate is less of an eyesore than other models. However, you have to pray that after you pay top dollar, the puppy won't decide to chew their way out.

A crate can be an invaluable training tool. It's ideal when

>> You're leaving a puppy alone for a duration of time not to exceed 3 hours for puppies younger than 4 months old or 6 hours for older puppies.

>> You're teaching a young or mischievous puppy who isn't house-trained to self-soothe or rest.

>> You're feeding an easily distracted puppy.

>> An overly excitable pup needs a timeout. In this case, don't use the crate as a form of punishment; simply lead your puppy there with a toy and toss treats in the back section of the crate as you calmly guide your puppy in.

A crate does have some drawbacks, however. It can be emotionally destructive to your puppy if it's overused, because puppies are social creatures and aren't accustomed to long spells of isolation. Left alone regularly for more than 4 to 6 hours often results in *hyperisolation anxiety* — a lonely puppy who's overreactive and hyper, in other words. If you must leave your puppy for long stretches, consider a playpen–crate combination.

A crate isn't a teaching tool. Your puppy needs lessons from you to learn how to act in all areas of your home and in everyday situations, such as mealtimes and family interactions and when people come to visit.

If the idea of a crate still turns your stomach, you have other options. To contain your puppy when you're not home (necessary for house-training and to teach your puppy to rest when you're not home), you can use a playpen or a very small, gated room. If your puppy is older, you can use a leash to keep your puppy with you when you're home and show them how to act in the rooms you share.

WARNING

Though playpens are ideal enclosures for young puppies under 12 weeks of age, and can be used to supervise a puppy in multiple areas of a home, they begin to lose their magic when your puppy reaches 4 months of age. At this time your puppy won't want to be separated from you, and the use of a playpen may lead to excessive barking or frustration chewing. Hopefully, by this time you'll have a handle on house-training and can begin to give your puppy more freedom in supervised areas.

Comfort stations

Even though you'll find some adorable and comfy dog beds on the market, resist the urge to buy a collection until your puppy is house-trained and past the chewing phase: Either habit can make waste of your cozy purchase.

Meanwhile create a comforting area in each room you share that your puppy will look for and return to each time they enter it. Lay down a flat mat, towel or blanket, spreading them near your sitting areas to help your puppy identify their place. Place chew toys and bones on their mat to create a calm vibe.

WARNING

If the puppy has a strong chewing tendency, skip the bedding altogether. Ingested blankets and towels can cause serious intestinal problems in puppies.

TIP

Take your pup's mat with you wherever you go. It helps your puppy feel safe and at home whether their visiting the vet, staying at the kennel, or riding along on a family trip. It's like having a security blanket.

Bowl

Organized feeding times in organized places is a relatively new phenomenon in the dog-human relationship; dogs used to spend their days poking about and looking for food outside or patiently waiting for discarded table scraps. The issue with feeding your puppy at a set hour and all at once is that they will grow restless and excited near their designated mealtime and then be rewarded with a big jackpot of food for annoying behavior. Instead, consider feeding your puppy their daily ration of food throughout the morning or late afternoon, using the food to reward their attention and patience. I tell you more about early puppy training and socialization in Chapter 9.

TIP

Doggie mealtime is a purely human concept. Yes, it's more convenient to feed your puppy in a bowl, but when you're able, portion out meals into reward pockets or treat cups and use the food to motivate good habits, such as coming when called, chewing toys on their mat, or pottying in the proper place.

For now, purchase a few bowls to start — two for water and one to contain your puppy's meals. Keep bowls for water inside the house and out, but sequester your puppy's food dish to control and vary feeding locations based on your early socialization efforts. For example, you may choose to feed them on their comfort mat one day, saying "On your mat" as you lead them there; in their crate the next day, saying "In your room"; and in the car another day, saying "To the car." Meals are powerful motivators and are useful in conditioning and socializing your puppy during the first month you spend together.

As for the type of bowl, stainless steel is ideal because it's easy to clean, it doesn't break, and its weight reduces the chance of the bowl being knocked over. Size the bowl to your puppy's breed: small, medium, or large.

You can buy bowls with stands that raise the dish to make eating more ergonomically comfortable and that are advertised to help prevent bloat (which they do not). These bowls certainly make eating look more comfortable, but they aren't totally necessary, because dogs are physically designed to be ground-level feeders.

WARNING

Bloat is a fairly common and fatal dog disease if not caught immediately. Caused by gas, the stomach presses on the diaphragm and twists, cutting off all circulation. Learn about the signs and symptoms and avoid the number-one cause of bloat — exercise directly after eating a large meal.

JUST FOR
FUN

Sometimes dogs do the darnedest things, like carrying their food dish to private locations or burying their food (or attempting to, anyway) in cushions and rugs. Modern convenience is lost on some dogs, who still like to interact with their food instead of gobbling it up in one sitting.

Rewards, toys, and self-soothing activities

Your puppy will repeat behaviors that get your attention, food, and fun. The simplest way to motivate your young puppy's good manners and routines is to reward positive choices — sitting for attention, for example, or standing on all four paws instead of jumping. In addition, if you praise, pat, or play with your puppy each time they make a good chewing choice, you'll save yourself a lot of destruction in the long run. The following sections present other tips to get your new puppy started on the road to good behavior from the moment you adopt them.

Food rewards

A food reward is often the best way to encourage your puppy's focus and make a positive association with learning. If your puppy's excited for the dry food you've chosen to feed them, look no further. Ration out all or a portion of each meal, and divide that amount into treat cups or reward pockets (as described in the following list).

If you feed your puppy moist or raw food or they don't excite to their kibble, find another type of treat that gets them excited. Remember that your enthusiasm with the treat is more important than the amount or size of the food reward. Here are two great ways to use food to train and motivate your puppy's earliest learning:

>> **Treat cups:** Keeping your puppy's treats in a specific container helps them connect the sound of the shaking cup with a food reward, which is a valuable training tool. (I discuss this training technique in Chapter 10.) To create a treat cup for your puppy, purchase an inexpensive plastic container (or use an emptied deli container), cut a small, round hole in the lid, and fill it halfway with dried kibbles or broken-up dog treats.

>> **Reward pockets:** Place your puppy's treats in one of your pockets or purchase a food pouch to stow snacks. With food bits at the ready, indoors and out, teach and reward your puppy whenever the opportunity knocks. Did they sit before you opened the door or go to their mat or crate — reward them as you say "Good puppy!" Are they nervous going down the stairs? A few tidbits tossed on the ground may be all the incentive they need to try a little harder. Use meals or treats for rewarding your puppy for returning to you and for outdoor pottying. Check out Chapter 10 for more uses of reward pockets.

Toys and bones and puzzling for dogs, oh my!

Although you may be tempted to buy every toy and bone available to you, don't! Puppies, like children, have specific likes and dislikes, and overwhelming your pup with options is disruptive. They'll grow up thinking everything on the floor is fair game — even your beloved, oh-so-broken-in slippers. Keep in mind, though, that a new puppy will spend their first few days nosing about and won't be interested in interactive play for another two to four weeks.

HOLLOW TOYS

Many people, myself included, swear by objects that can be stuffed with moistened kibbles and frozen, or a mix of kibble and a creamy spread that can be safely left in your puppy's enclosure to soothe their chewing impulse each time it strikes. Some puppies can't figure it out at first, so show yours how to explore the contents by digging out a little of it with your finger. Puppies learn from mimicking, and nothing is more fun than discovering food and rewards locked inside a stuffed bone. When cleared of foods, this toy can be tossed in the air or chewed, making it the ultimate 3-in-1 object.

TOSSING TOYS

Toys come in as many different shapes as you'd find in a high school geometry book, so prepare yourself. Puppies like objects that bounce, squeak, and roll. You'll have plenty of selection, and, for the record, your puppy won't mind if you choose a bird squeak or a fox, or a red ball or a blue one — it just needs to bounce, roll or squeak (or all three) and you're all set. Choose a couple of toys to discover what captures your puppy's heart, and look no further.

WARNING

Stuffed toys can be great fun for puppies who think of them as small prey animals, especially when they squeak. Some puppies, however, go beyond the toss-and-play mode and insist on ripping them from limb from limb until the squeaker is removed. This isn't an ideal game for puppies, because squeakers can be dangerous when you remove them, and the stuffing can be ingested. Search for toys with the word indestructible on the packaging.

TUG TOYS

Puppies love interactive games, especially as they mature. Tug is a great game for puppies and can be used to teach your puppy to Give on command, as well as learning what is and isn't okay to tug on — your hair or slippers, for example. Here's a quick lesson on playing tug with a young puppy:

» Start with a rope or doggie play pole, which can also be fashioned out of a stick and a toy tied to it with a 3-foot rope.

» Bounce the toy in front of your puppy or wait until they show interest in playing with it. Reward their interest by saying "Tug" and providing resistance.

» Take a smelly food treat in your hand (like liver, hot dog, or jerky-type treat) and, as your puppy releases the toy, say "Give."

» Let your puppy have the toy back right away and continue playing or say "You win" as you congratulate them and walk away.

Soon your puppy will learn that sharing and releasing toys means more fun and interaction, not less.

Self-soothing bones and interactive toys

When picking out *self-soothing* toys for your puppy (objects they can play with alone), keep the analogy of giving a child your smartphone to keep them busy when you're present but not accessible. Self-soothing objects come in many forms: What calms your puppy best?

BONES

Though you generally can't go wrong with indestructible plastic bones, some puppies find them, well, boring. Rawhide, which is made in America, is a satisfying chew, but it's problematic with some dogs who chew obsessively because they gulp it as they go and can choke or get indigestion. Destructible bones also cost money to replace — just saying.

Personally, my clients have had the most luck with pressed rawhide, animal-part sticks (hooves and bully sticks), and vegetable-matter pulp bones. Test out a few kinds yourself to find a bone that satisfies your puppy's craving and that can pass the "systems" test (their digestive system, that is); then buy it in bulk.

PUZZLE TOYS (ALSO KNOWN AS ENRICHMENT TOYS)

Puppies love a challenge, so use puzzle toys to keep them busy and on their toes. As you might expect, you have plenty of store-bought options when it comes to puzzle toys, but you can come up with your own pretty easily. Here are a few ideas:

>> Place food in a muffin tray, and then cover the tidbits with a ball.

>> Fill a hard plastic bottle with food.

>> Toss treats onto the carpet or ground as you encourage your puppy to play Find It, as described in Chapter 7.

Some puzzle toys are safe enough to leave in your puppy's enclosure to keep their mind and spirits occupied when you leave them alone.

Freedom lines (indoor and out), collars, and early leash skills

For your puppy's homecoming, you need to purchase only two leashes: a short, lightweight nylon leash that your puppy will drag behind them (for easy and calm redirection) for indoors and a long freedom line for outdoor playtime in open areas (away from streets) and, later, for advanced training. You can purchase a lightweight mesh harness or thin, adjustable nylon collar (also known as a buckle collar). Buckle collars don't slide or choke. Their purpose is to carry your puppy's ID tags. (For more on collar conditioning and leash training, check out Chapter 11.)

WARNING

Small-breed puppies are fragile, and their throats are particularly sensitive to the restraint of a collar. Although the collar is important for sporting an ID tag, if you have a small puppy, attach any leashes to a harness instead of a collar.

Freedom line

Freedom line is a fancy term for a lightweight lead (leash) that your puppy can drag behind them. You can make or purchase this lightweight leash and let your puppy wear it whenever you're together in the house or yard. Ideal for dragging behind your puppy, the light weight lead gives them a sense of freedom while your supervision ensures their safety. Stay close to the line so that you can easily redirect your puppy or guide them from one activity to another without stress or frustration, whether the activity you want to avoid is jumping on the counters, chasing another animal, digging up a plant, or nipping at the kids.

The indoor drag leash should be 4 feet long and be attached to your puppy's buckle collar (or harness, in the case of small-breed puppies). When giving your puppy freedom outside, use a 25- to 50-foot-long lead to allow them freedom to play while giving you plenty of leash to interfere with a rambunctious puppy and/or hold onto to retrieve them if they should wander off. For young puppies, long lines are great for wandering in a yard or field — take along some favorite snacks and reward your puppy every time they "check in" with you. You can also use long lines to encourage off-lead training as your puppy matures.

I discuss training leashes used on older puppies in the section "Exploring Future Needs, Modern Gadgets, and Training Tools," later in this chapter. For now, let your puppy explore on a drag lead or long line so that their first experiences of walking with you doesn't involve you choking them.

TIP

MICROCHIPS: BUILT-IN LIFESAVERS

Your veterinarian and breeder are likely to suggest that you microchip your puppy, and I also strongly recommend it. Your veterinarian can inject into your puppy's neck or shoulder (no more painful than a typical shot) a preregistered, computer-recognizable identification chip. If your puppy gets lost or ends up at a shelter, a simple wave of the wand reads the embedded information (typically, your contact info) so that your puppy can be returned to you. Many breeders have a microchip inserted in each puppy's shoulder before sending them home. If your pup isn't one of them, make an appointment immediately.

ID collar and tags

When your puppy is conditioned to a collar, you can secure an ID tag to it. Some national-chain pet stores now have machines that create personalized tags in minutes. You can also find fancy ID tags online: Search the Internet for the phrase *ID tags for dogs.* I find that the best message to write is *Need meds! Help me home [555-555-5555].* Of course, your pup probably won't need meds, but this message discourages would-be dognappers and stresses the urgency of getting your puppy back home if someone finds them straying. I recommend using an ID tag in addition to a microchip because people can't identify the information on the microchip without the appropriate device.

Socialization carrier and sling

Your biggest efforts in the early days will be house-training your puppy and socializing them to everything your life has to offer. Though your veterinarian will rightly advise you against walking your puppy into town until they've had their inoculations, this doesn't mean you can't carry them about in a sling or carrier or take them along on short car rides. The whole socialization process, from meeting new people to conditioning to loud sounds to getting your pet accustomed to all the nuances of your life, is so important that I've devoted an entire chapter (Chapter 9) to it.

Meanwhile, here are a few products you may choose to get a head start on the socialization routine. Two of the options involve carrying your puppy, something only you know whether you can do. If your puppy is a miniaturized breed, remember that life can seem quite overwhelming when you're on the ground. Nestling near to your heart in a sling or curling up in a carrier provides an extra buffer of safety and helps in all your early socialization efforts. Puppies initially startle to unfamiliar noises and, without their birth family to reference, can develop fear if they're not comfortably contained.

REMEMBER

The objects described in the next four sections come in various sizes, shapes, and colors. Read the reviews and reference the sizing charts to help you decide which ones to purchase.

Snuggle sling

I'm a big fan of the sling, no matter what the species. A sling rides over your shoulder and allows you to tuck your puppy into the pouch when they're in a calm mood so that you can keep your puppy close when conditioning them to new sights and sounds or when moving about your home or building. To accustom your puppy to the sling, lay it flat in or near their sleeping area and hide food in the folds, so they can smell, explore, and find treasure in it. To familiarize them with your smell, put a shirt in the pouch, too.

Most puppies are transitioning from full-time companionship with littermates to a singleton lifestyle in your home. Though you don't want to carry them about full time, lest they develop an overdependence on your presence, using a sling to condition them to your lifestyle and to socialize them in the world beyond can be as reassuring as it is convenient.

If you have other pets agitated by seeing a newbie having so much direct contact, make a different selection from the products in the following sections.

Carrier

Small travel kennels, especially if you plan to travel with your adult dog, should be conditioned early and used to provide your puppy with a feeling of safety. Condition your puppy to their carrier by sprinkling food, treats, and toys around them in the carrier. If your puppy is wary, you may also unzip the openings and play in and around it.

The sooner you get started with the carrier, the faster your puppy will grow to accept that being in it means more time with you. Use the carrier as you would a sling — to transport your puppy about, slowly conditioning them to the sights, smells, and sounds in and about your home. More socializing tips in Chapter 9.

Alert bell

Your puppy will start communicating with you and signaling their needs by 12 weeks, and sometimes even younger. To get a jump start on the process, hang a bell by the outside door or by the gate that leads to the papered area if you are training your puppy to potty inside. (Flip to Chapter 14 for tips on house-training your puppy.) Tap the bell every time you take your puppy to potty. Your puppy will learn the system and tap the bell themselves whenever they want to be let into the potty area. Pretty nifty! Here are a couple of other bell systems that work:

>> If you have a fenced yard, hang a bell on the outside door to encourage your puppy to ring it to come in. This will save you the hassle of replacing screens or listening to your dog bark when you can't get to the door immediately.

>> Have a bell by the main water dish. Tap it for each refill and watch as your dog learns to tap it should they ever find it empty.

For more on teaching your puppy to ring a bell to go to their potty area, check out Chapter 14.

Exploring Future Needs, Modern Gadgets, and Training Tools

As your puppy gets older, they'll develop in ways you can't imagine. Sure, they'll grow like a rose, but, like a child, your puppy will shed their inhibitions and become more confident and curious by the day. You may notice that your puppy listens less, explores more, and tests the boundaries of their everyday interactions with you.

Though you won't need any of the items listed in the following sections for the homecoming, you can read about what you'll need in the future or mark these pages for later consideration.

Compassion wear (also known as walking restraint)

After your puppy gets settled into your home and is old enough to socialize around town and with other dogs and people (which happens around 16 weeks of age), you'll need to bone up on the leash training and choose the right type of body restraint. Neck collars were the norm until very recently, when they were shown to have stressful effects, especially when placed on young puppies. Imagine being led about by a necklace: you'd pull away and feel trapped, too (a phenomenon known as *oppositional reflex*). Unless you're a pro with leash training and you have your timing down to a science, consider using compassion wear, which conditions your puppy to walk near you through a system of guiding, not jerking or pulling. These user-friendly collars require little to no strength to control and allow you to focus on positive reinforcement to encourage your puppy's focus and cooperation. The two types of conditioning collars are no-pull harnesses and head collars.

TIP

You can reference my website, SarahSaysPets.com, for photos and video clips specifying leash use and collar options.

TIP

Stick to buckle collars and freedom lines when guiding puppies younger than 4 months old. Other types of collars restrict your puppy's breathing and teach them that walking near you is uncomfortable.

Easy-walking, no-pull harness

I've found a few types of no-pull harness designs that are effective in encouraging good following skills in puppies. A harness that loops around the front of the puppy's body is also an ideal system for puppies of all sizes and can be used safely if a puppy's neck is too fragile to bear the resistance of a neck collar.

Front-attached, easy-walking harness

This type of harness braces your puppy across their chest. The leash clips in front of your dog's chest and restrains their forward momentum as you lead them forward. It may look and seem awkward at first, but it works amazingly well after it's fitted properly. Some puppies get distracted by the leash and grab for the strap incessantly, but most pups learn to accept the restraint in a couple of walks. (Figure 5-2 shows one of these harnesses.)

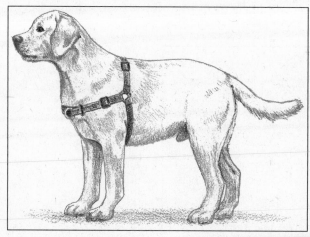

FIGURE 5-2:
A front-attached, easy-walking conditioning harness.

Illustration by Barbara Frake

WARNING

If your young puppy is one obsessed by the leash dangling in front of their face, wait awhile before attaching the leash to the front clip: Most grow out of this obsession by 4 months old. You can either start out with a mesh neck collar first and then transition to a harness or flip the front clip harness so that the leash attachment rests between the shoulder blades rather than on the chest (a trick not possible on every version of the front clip design — see if it works with yours).

Head collar

A head collar is like a horse halter for dogs. It can be used from the start — even with puppies as young as 12 weeks of age. It's a nonconfrontational conditioning tool that encourages cooperation and good following skills.

REMEMBER

You may think this collar looks like a muzzle when you first see it, but it's not. Puppies can eat, chew, and play happily while sporting a head collar; it simply eliminates internal or external pressure around the neck.

How does this wonder collar work? It works on the "mommy" principle: When your puppy was very young, their mom would correct them by grasping their muzzle and shaking it. This communicated the statement, "Hey, wild one, settle down!" The head collar has the same effect. Left on during play, the pressure on the nose discourages rowdiness and mouthing. By placing a short lead on your puppy when you're expecting company, you can effectively curb jumping habits. Barking frenzies are drastically reduced, and training is made simple as you guide your puppy from one exercise to the next. Another plus is that leading by the chin demands minimal physical strength, so nearly everyone can use it — kids too. (See an example in Figure 5-3.)

FIGURE 5-3:
After your puppy is used to the nose strap, you'll be able to guide them like a horse on a halter.

Illustration by Barbara Frake

How often you should leave the head collar on is a question best answered by your puppy. If yours is relatively well behaved, you can use it exclusively during walks and lessons. If they're the mouthing, jumping, or barking type, leave the collar on whenever you're able to supervise them.

TIP

The head collar must fit properly around your puppy's neck. If it's too loose, your puppy can pull it off and perhaps chew it. You want the neck strap to fit snugly, with one finger's worth of space between the neck and the strap. (My website, SarahSaysPets.com, offers a short video on sizing the head collar and putting it on.)

REMEMBER

If you give this collar a try, you may have to tolerate some resistance. Initially, puppies don't love the idea of a head collar. Their reaction reminds me of the first day my mother dressed me in lace — I hated it, but after an hour or so, I hardly noticed it at all. And your puppy will learn to tolerate the head collar. When you see them flopping about like a flounder, be patient. After they realize that they can't remove the collar, they'll forget about it. Some puppies take an hour to adjust to the feel of the collar; some take a day or two. Place it on their head three times a day for 20-minute intervals until they accept it.

WARNING

Neck wear collars, also known as choke or prong collars, are available but not recommended for modern-day dogs and dog lovers. The idea behind a neck wear collar is that it applies pressure around the dog's neck when the dog strays, bolts, or chooses to explore in another direction. This causes a feeling of entrapment or worse, affixation, which leaves a dog feeling more stressed by situations like seeing another dog or walking with you. Long term? Neck collars do more harm than good.

Check chain or martingale collar

If you're confident that you can guide your puppy by their neck, choose a check chain or martingale collar. This collar slides over your puppy's head and rests high on the neck, just behind their ears. The check chain has a section of chain that should be centered between your puppy's ears. The *martingale* is a cloth collar that is especially useful with long-necked dog breeds because it has a wide midsection that distributes the weight of your pull.

TIP

I rarely encourage the check chain or martingale collar because it often pits the owner's strength against the puppy, and the puppy is left pulling against the owner's grip instead of walking with them.

Leash training

In the long, intertwined history of people and dogs, the leash and leash walking are relatively new inventions, designed for convenience and safety. When out walking with their dogs, humans tend to go in straight lines, confident in the belief that they are in charge because they are holding the leash. But restricted, linear walks are unnatural to puppies, who prefer to meander and explore. Your puppy will pull on the leash in an effort to increase the meandering. You will pull back, increasing the restricting. This combination of pulling away and pulling back puts pressure on your puppy's collar, and they'll start to choke and feel very, very anxious.

Walks should bring about the calm you experience when walking hand in hand with someone you care deeply about. It's a learned habit: Getting it right takes some practice and the right leash and training restraint. The following sections have some tips about finding the right equipment; be sure to review the earlier section on freedom lines and the joy your puppy feels when exploring naturally.

Leash options

As your puppy matures, they'll be less tolerant of being left alone. If they're still too curious to turn loose in your home, it's time to begin leash training. (Flip to Chapter 7 for specific instructions.) After your puppy is comfortable on a leash, guide them room by room using a 4- to 6-foot leash that you can hold or clip to your side.

When it comes to starting these walkabouts, the sooner you move beyond the confines of the kitchen, the better. I recommend no later than 12 weeks of age, but remember to take your puppy to potty before exploring together.

After you've taught your puppy the basics of cooperative walking skills indoors, begin to use the training leash outdoors. Vary between the freedom line and the training leash so that your puppy learns to understand the difference by the weight of the leash.

When practicing your puppy's walking skills on a training leash, stop whenever your puppy pulls and wait until they turn or walk back to you or sits to begin walking again. If your puppy does circle back to your side, drop a treat inches from your shoes and say "Find it" to reinforce the decision to check in.

Seat belt safety wear

When driving a little puppy under 16 weeks old in a car, use a small crate to encourage calm manners and for safety purposes. As the puppy matures, continue leading them to one door and area of your car; if crating a large dog as you drive isn't feasible, consider using a safety harness and/or seat belt attachment when you drive.

A seat belt safety lead can be used in the car or left secured to your puppy's collar for easy guidance when you're out and about. Letting your puppy ride in your lap or hang their body halfway out the window when you drive may seem fun, but it's a bad idea. Here's my rule: Confine your puppy while driving. It's safer for you, your puppy, and other motorists.

Retractable leash

A retractable leash is fun when used in the right setting, such as meandering on a beach or in an open field. The longer, the better. Initially, this leash is great for exercising. Your puppy can run like mad while you stand there reading the morning newspaper. When you progress to off-leash work (see Chapter 13), the retractable leash is a staple.

Don't use a retractable leash near roads or heavily populated areas. Its high-tech design takes getting used to, and even a seasoned pro can lose hold of the slack. If you're out with other people, watch their legs. If a person gets sandwiched between you and your prancing puppy, they're in for a rope burn.

Clicking and targeting tools to simplify learning

Puppies have been shown to respond to learning games and clicker training as young as 7 weeks old, so feel free to begin these lessons now. Anything that encourages your puppy to repeat activities like pottying in the right place, chewing on their toys instead of yours, or going to their mat is a good thing.

Clicker

If you've never formally been introduced to the clicker, allow me: This small, handheld device (see Figure 5-4) makes a sharp clicking sound each time it's pressed. Pair this sound with a food reward and you'll discover power that would make Pavlov proud. Your puppy will alert to the sound, and when they connect this noise with a food reward, they'll be prompted to repeat whatever action makes it click. Use the clicker properly to condition good behavior in mere seconds. Sounds too good to be true, right? It isn't, and you can get started with puppies of any age. Check out Chapter 11 for more tips on how to use your clicker to help your puppy use good habits.

FIGURE 5-4:
A clicker is a handy training tool.

Targeting disc

Teaching your puppy to go to their targeting discs is a fun and useful way to teach your puppy lessons like Go to Your Place and Stay. You can purchase discs or make them out of a heavyweight paper or the top of a plastic container. This technique requires some ingenuity and patience until your puppy catches on — then prepare yourself for some fast-paced excitement. Check out Chapter 11 for more tips on how to use a targeting disc (and how to play the Lily Pad game).

Targeting Stick

Think of a targeting stick as a long finger. Purchase a fancy one (some have clickers built into them) or use a kitchen utensil or toy wand. Once you've chosen your targeting stick, teach your puppy to mark the end of the stick by rewarding their interest. Check out Chapter 9 for more tips on how to use a targeting stick to help direct and socialize your puppy.

Bringing Puppy into the Digital Age

Are you a tech-head? Don't let adopting a puppy slow you down. Check out the options described in this section for products that can make your life and your puppy's life safer, organized, and more fun.

WARNING

Never attach anything to your puppy that delivers a shock, spray, or vibrating sensation. Marketed as training tools, these items are inhumane and have lasting effects on your puppy's otherwise trusting and cheerful demeanor. Outlawed in many countries, using these battery-operated items is a big no-no.

Two-way camera

These devices allow you to watch, record, or interact with your puppy when you can't be with them. After purchasing the camera, you'll be instructed to download an app to your phone or tablet. The camera allows you to interact in a variety of ways, from talking to your puppy to dispensing treats, food, or water. A new one allows video chats. Though a camera is convenient and nifty, remember that nothing truly takes the place of your being home. Too much interruption from virtual you may cause anxiety — whereas, left alone, most puppies are quite able to cope with isolation by chewing from a selection of appropriate toys.

I often ask my digital clients from around the world to record their puppies' behavior and share these clips with me before sessions; I send video back (using my dogs, of course), sharing protocols that are as effective as they are fun.

Automatic feeder and water fountain

These devices can be programmed to allow your dog access to food and fresh water at set times throughout the day. Though fresh water can never be argued with, feeding devices should only be used in a pinch. Meals are better used as rewards for good behavior and offered during social times when you and your puppy are together.

Treat dispenser

I love a good treat dispenser — it has *so* many uses. If your dog suffers from isolation anxiety that leads to barking or destruction when left alone, consider a device that can be preprogrammed to dispense food when they settle on their mat and stop barking. These machines can also be used when you're home to teach your puppy to stay on the mat or to settle down during greetings. App-controlled as well as personalized to release treats when barking stops, a treat dispenser is one conditioning tool that few homes should be without.

Tracking collar

If the thought of losing your dog keeps you up at night, purchase a tracking collar and rest easy. This device is linked to an app on your phone and allows you to trace your puppy's whereabouts inside and out.

Automatic poop-picker-upper

Why stop to scoop when motorized devices or mini robots can scan your yard and clean up the poops for you. I've seen these in action — brilliant!

Treadmill and hamster wheel

I dare you to search for the term *hamster wheel for dogs*. You're going to get an *eyeful.* If exercising your puppy inside appeals to you, you'll have many options, whether you settle on a treadmill or a self-paced running wheel. (Yes, a running wheel looks exactly like a giant hamster wheel for dogs.)

Mechanized brush, hair remover, and bathing apparatus

If settling on a traditional dog brush and using your sink or shower head to bathe your puppy sound a little boring to you, modern inventions that make bath time zippier and sometimes less stressful await! From circular shower heads to full-body hair dryers and brushes that do most of the work for you, your puppy will be the best-groomed dog on the block. Just take good care to condition your puppy to the feel and sound of these devices before using them. See Chapter 17 for tips.

Bluetooth music cube

Your puppy won't like silence and will sleep better with noise. New studies show that dogs respond best to calming noises versus variety in voice and sound. What better way to ensure that your puppy hears calming sounds than to purchase or download music specially created for their ears only?

Light-up leash and collar

The light-up leash and collar sound like just what they are: Either is a great way to keep track and provide safety in traffic when out after dark.

Activity monitor

Think Fitbit for dogs. Easily clipped to your puppy's collar, this item lets you track and record your puppy's daily activity.

All these gadgets, and more, are available just about everywhere you'd normally shop for your puppy products; read reviews before making any purchase to ensure that the one you buy is reliable.

2

Living and Loving Your Puppy: The Early Days

Chapter **6**

Bonding with Your Puppy Using the Science of Modern Dog Parenting

When I began teaching dogs and people, 30-some-odd years ago, there was no research supporting any of it. Anyone calling their puppy "baby" got an eye roll from the scientific community who declared that dogs were biological automatons, incapable of thought, reason, or attachment. How far we've come! Nowadays, dogs are the hot new research model, and it's the professionals who are shouting, "Dogs think, feel, and have complex reasoning ability." As if we didn't know. In this chapter you find out about the latest and greatest discoveries in dog science and see how it confirms what you already knew in your heart.

In the pages ahead, you'll also find essential tips, from organizing a routine schedule and inspiring healthy sleep habits to shaping your puppy's earliest memories of you and motivating associations to words like *Sit, Stay,* and *Come.*

That all sounds pretty neat, but truly the best thing science has done for us has been to demonstrate beyond a reasonable doubt that our dogs, even as young puppies, respond best to calm direction, routines, and praise. As you'll discover if you haven't already, your puppy has an uncanny ability to recognize and respond to you in ways that resemble the attachment between parents and children; just being around your puppy creates loving feelings. (In science-speak, our bodies release the loving hormone oxytocin). So, doesn't it make sense that we treat these sensitive, intelligent creatures kindly? Dogs — like kids — raised with compassion and respect grow up happy. And happy is good.

JUST FOR FUN

The word *anthropomorphic* gets tossed around a lot in the dog world. It's a fancy term for our very human tendency to project our feelings onto other animals. It's a no-no according to many, but a little anthropomorphizing could be a not-so-horrible thing if it keeps people from being too harsh or cruel with their doggies. After all, it's science that's telling us of the similarities between puppies and little kids. I'll show you how to balance your anthropomorphic impulses with the realities of what makes your puppy separate and unique.

WARNING

Dog training methods are like parenting philosophies: You can choose from lots of different approaches, and what works for one kid may not work for another. Thanks to science, more and more professionals are swinging to the proven studies demonstrating that dogs actually learn best when routines and language are positively reinforced. But some training advocates still rely on decade-old alphacentric methods that stressed the need to dominate and relied heavily on traditions passed down from a time when dogs lived primarily outside and worked hard for a living. Few dogs embrace that lifestyle now, trading cold nights for comfy couches, and trading chores for companionship.

Should you feel the need to hire a professional to help you raise your puppy, first explore the trainer's approach. If someone uses a word like *dominant* or suggests methods that involve using prongs or battery-operated collars, find someone else. You are your puppy's only advocate. If you love your pup like a baby, as many people do, be as discerning in your choice of helpers. If you're having trouble finding a class or trainer in your area, ping me at sarahsayspets.com or search online at sites like https://apdt.com/https and https://m.iaabc.org.

Domesticated Wolves or Little Children?

Until the 21st century, most trainers borrowed from the growing philosophy that dogs were domesticated wolves, with many of the wild, unruly survival skills that captive wolves used to cope with being locked away. It wasn't until the mid-to-late 1900s that a scientist named David Mech, trudging into various Northern reaches of the United States, revealed the truth about how wolves live and relate to each other. Funny thing — wolves have strong family ties and devotion to their young that's not so different from how humans live and love.

As far as the evolutionary debate and how it relates to your relationship to your puppy goes, suffice it to say that dogs are no longer considered domesticated wolves, but rather a subspecies that split off to form a friendlier, more pleasing species that continues in their eagerness to please us. Imagine that! Brian Hare, a researcher from Duke University, wrote a compelling essay stating that, with both dogs and people, our survival was less survival of the fittest (as another great naturalist, Charles Darwin, proposed) than survival of the friendliest, because we required group cooperation to thrive.

With all eyes focused on our parallel evolutions, dog cognition has become a global obsession. In the past decade alone, a scientist has figured out ways to monitor dogs' brain activity, decode their DNA, and do comparative analysis with human and other mammalian brains. Electrodes and MRI scans track the brain centers that alert to strong scents, familiar faces, various expressions, and spoken words. I've listed three of the more important findings, and how they help you to relate to living with and loving your puppy.

TIP

Interested in reading more about dog cognition? Research the topic online or at your local library. Periodicals like *Science Daily* and *Nature* (both online) stay abreast of all the current studies. Have fun exploring the new science of your beloved puppy.

Brain science

Until recently, the scientific community had a hard time admitting that dogs have feelings. Why? Because in academic circles nothing is real unless there is measurable data to prove it. Since no one in academia could show that dogs were capable of feeling emotions, reasoning, and attachment, it just wasn't so.

Enter two scientists: Dr. Stanley Coren began as a psychology professor and neuropsychological researcher at the University of British Columbia, whose lifelong hobby with dogs finally realigned his professional career. In 2008, he did what at the time seemed like a simple comparative analysis showing beyond a reasonable doubt that dogs have similar cognitive abilities to 2–2½-year-old children. Researching at the University of British Columbia, Coren set out to determine which breed of dog was the smartest based on a set of questions that tested their responsiveness to human direction. Although the findings caused quite the ripple in the dog world, the significant undisputable discovery was that all dogs, regardless of their breed or intelligence rating, are capable of processing information, reasoning linear outcomes involving getting something they desired (such as a bone or freedom), and deducing simple arithmetic. He also showed that dogs could learn up to 150 words.

Dr. Coren's publications opened the floodgates, and soon studies from around the world were conducted on topics including a dog's musical preferences to similarities in the body chemicals released during petting.

Fast-forward to 2012 when another human neuroscientist, named Gregory Berns, an MD/PhD who specialized in MRI analysis, did a similar experiment with dogs. By tracking their brains' responses to familiar smells, sights, and verbal directions, he discovered beyond a reasonable doubt that dogs show similar proactive and excited reactivity to everyday routines and people as we do.

Further studies with Dr. Berns' team of scientists showed that dogs and people have similar brain centers, chemical releases in response to anticipation of positive outcomes, and neurological wiring. His revelation set the scientific world on fire. proving to people everywhere that, yes, dogs

» Recognize familiar faces and are more attracted to cheerful expressions than angry, frustrated ones

» Respond positively to the smells of the people they love

» Are capable of problem-solving and modeling behavior (monkey-see-monkey-do-type learning).

TECHNICAL STUFF

The major difference between a dog's brain and a human's brain? The size: "A large dog's brain is about the size of a lemon," says Dr. Berns. So, what's going on in all those empty pockets of your puppy's brain? Much of it is devoted to olfactory receptors and sensory tunnels that collect information about your puppy's present situation: from the noises they hear to the sights and smells surrounding them. We people swapped out sensory awareness for complex thinking skills, in the process growing the frontal lobes of our brains, or what's called the *cerebral cortex*.

What the nose knows

With all the hoopla about dogs, some naysayers still claim that dogs are just not as smart as everyone thinks. Rather than point out what dogs excel in, they point to how a dog's intelligence can't compare to a dolphin, chimpanzee, or person. Yes, I'll admit that I can't teach a dog to make me breakfast in bed or balance my checkbook, but dogs can do plenty of things people won't try, either.

Dogs have stellar hearing and response rates, fully capable of alerting to an unfamiliar noise or intruder if they're prone to doing so. I, on the other hand, slept through a hotel fire detector; needless to say, had I been home, my dog's barking would have roused me.

Most dogs have acute scent-detection abilities, too — far surpassing human comprehension. In her book *A Dog's Nose*, Alexandra Horowitz, PhD, lays out your puppy's most sensitive appendage for all the world to see. Sure, their brains may be smaller than our own, but they make up space by devoting *40 times* the sensory surface area to interpreting a world we cannot fathom — a world full of scented rainbows. Here are some other points Horowitz makes:

>> In a side-by-side analysis, your adult puppy will have up to 300 million *olfactory cells* (your puppy's sniffing receptors) in their head, in comparison to a human's 6 million — that's a 50:1 ratio.

>> If trained, a dog can identify a single teaspoon of sugar in 2 million gallons of water — that's two Olympic-size pools of water. I can't even smell sugar in my morning coffee.

>> Every dog has a secondary olfactory center located in the roof of their mouth, called the *vomeronasal organ*, that alerts them to slight changes in body chemicals (known as *pheromones*) that help to distinguish the age, sex, and sexual receptivity of other dogs.

>> Dogs can smell moods. Slight changes in our perspiration cue our dogs into reading whether we're happy, sad, or afraid.

Sure, dogs aren't smart like people are, but it's precisely because they are *not* people that dogs are brilliant in their own right, and the sooner you can recognize, respect, and reward your puppy for their version of *clever*, the sooner you'll be navigating your own love story.

JUST FOR FUN

When walking your puppy, allow some time for sniffing — especially in areas where dogs congregate. Sure, the idea that your dog is sniffing other dogs' eliminations sounds gross to you, but you're not a dog. To your puppy, reading the morning "pee-mail" is the highlight of their day.

Master emotions

Now that science is up to speed on the emotional life of dogs, it's time to tip my hat to one of the most renowned neuroscientists of all time, Jaak Panksepp, PhD. He discovered that all mammals (humans, too) are born with five master emotions that rule all their behavior, day in and day out. I'll relate the five emotions to dogs only, but don't be afraid to let your imagination run wild — we have more in common with our dogs' emotional landscape than you might think.

Seeking

Seeking is the master emotion that drives a dog's survival: They hunt to find food, water, and companionship. As a social creature, your puppy can't survive on their own and will form close bonds to whoever they spend time with, which often surpass their connection with other, unfamiliar dogs.

JUST FOR FUN

Scientists have recorded 100 expressions that dogs use to communicate with people. Many of these expressions are easy to identify: I want some, play with me, pet me now, time for breakfast, let's go for a walk! See how many expressions you can read — you know your puppy best.

Playing

Play is somewhat of a mystery: No one can put their finger on why it happens — it just does. Dogs play when they feel safe where they are and who they are with: It's a good measure of your puppy's mood.

TIP

Playing and seeking are baseline emotions that you can use to measure your puppy's mood accurately. When taking your puppy out and about or introducing a new distraction in your home, if your puppy will take a treat or engage with a toy, rest assured that they're feeling secure enough to access their positive emotions.

Fear

Fear is a tricky one: It's a sign that your dog is feeling unsure and stuck. In the next section on body language, you'll learn the telltale signs of fear, but you don't have to imagine too deeply — fear is a universal feeling. It freezes joy and leaves dogs immobilized, not sure of what will happen next and unsure what exactly to do about it.

TIP

I address a puppy's fearful reactions throughout the rest of this book. Pay close attention to Chapter 9: Socialization is the best insurance that your puppy is comfortable with all the sights and sounds he'll experience in your world: Otherwise, you'll never know when fear-of-the-unknown might strike.

Frustration

Frustration hits when a puppy is caught between what they want to do and what they can't do — or what they can't reach. Low-level frustration often happens when a toy rolls under the couch or when a puppy whines behind a gate. Higher-level frustration mounts and may develop into more dramatic reactions in response to people passing by a window or fenced yard or to suffering from excessive isolation. You can find tips for dealing with these specific issues in Part 5.

Panic

Panic is fear on steroids. Puppies panic when imminent death or peril seems at hand: It can happen in the early weeks of life when a puppy is separated from her litter, or at some point later on. I once worked with a husky who was crated during a small house fire, while the alarms blared and fire crews arrived to douse the blaze; after that experience, that pup panicked every time he was asked to go into a crate. Panic shuts down all other emotions and leaves a puppy in a state of, well, panic.

Your Puppy Is Talking — Are You "Listening?"

Another great influencer who shaped modern dog thinking long before it became scientifically cool to do so was Nicholas Dodman, DVM. His books outlined dogs' emotional lives and communication styles. When it comes to communicating, dogs and humans differ in these key aspects:

>> People talk with language and need to listen to one another for meaning.

>> Dogs use postures and subtle gestures to symbolize meaning: If you want to hear what your dog is saying, you need to use your eyes.

It took nearly two decades for scientists to follow Dr. Dodman's lead, but when they did, they confirmed roughly everything he'd already taught us. Here's an overview of your dog's body talk: Consider how learning how to listen to your puppy will improve your relationship. Puppies are like kids — they are much more eager to listen to you if you learn to listen to their side of the story, too.

Posture

Your puppy's posture is a funny thing: It's easier to remember if you compare it to yourself or someone you know well. Both pups and people "shrink" when they're confused, fearful, or anxious; they also rise with excitement. They have a resting pose when life is least stressful, and a few favorite sleeping poses. Observe your pup and note, down to the very last detail, their body language, paying special attention to tail and ear positions.

TIP

Consider how your puppy will read *your* posture when something extraordinary happens, like a visitor's arrival. All puppies get excited when people visit: Your home is their den, and the door is the mouth of the den. If you, in your desperation to save face, start shouting and pushing your puppy as someone enters, the whole arrival scene is one big fiasco. Instead of redirecting your puppy or showing calmness by example, you've just taught your puppy that greetings are a wild-'n'-crazy scene.

Learn to translate your puppy's postures and to redirect or soothe them when the mood they show doesn't reflect the scene. In the remainder of this chapter you'll also learn how their ears, eyes, mouth, tail, mouth, and vocalizations can be interpreted — use Figure 6-1 and Table 6-1 for quick reference. I help you explore different ways to interact with your puppy throughout the rest of this book, using these tables and illustrations as a guide.

FIGURE 6-1: Understand what your puppy is telling you in these five postures.

a. Fearful   B. Unsure   c. Relaxed

d. Defensive   e. Alert

Illustration by Barbara Frake

TABLE 6-1   **Reading Your Puppy's Body Language**

Body Part	Fearful	Undecided	Relaxed	Alert	Defensive
Eyes	Squinting, darting, unfocused	Focused or shifting	Focused or dozing	Attentive, focused	Glaring, hard
Body	Low, arched, pulled back and down, hackles possibly up	Shifting from forward to pulled back, approaching but then immediately avoiding the person	Relaxed	Comfortable posture, leaning toward an interest, moving from side to side, or jumping if excited	Pitched forward, rigid, tense
Tail	Tucked under belly, wagging low	Tucked low under belly, arched slightly over the back, or fluctuating between the two	Tail down in a resting position	Still or gently swinging in a relaxed or slightly elevated position	Still above rump or above arched back in a tight, repetitive wag
Mouth	Pulled back, often in a tense, nervous semi-smile	Tense, trembling, or nervous licking	Relaxed	Panting, normal, possibly parted in a vocalization	Tight, unflinching, and possibly parted in a growl or vocalization

Eyes: blinking, social gazing

Your puppy's eyes will tell you a lot about how they're feeling, from adoration to hopefulness to outright fear. Learn how you can interpret your puppy's five key expressions to help adjust to eye situations:

>> **Relaxed eyes:** Notice your puppy's eyes when you're enjoying a moment together. Comfortably gazing at you in calm and mutual adoration, pupils (that dark circle in the center of their eye) in proportion to the colored ring, AKA the iris? That's their relaxed eye.

>> **Squinty, appeasing eyes:** If your puppy is squinty it means one of three things — they are trying to appease you (or another person or dog), they are slightly fearful (you can tell if they're rump is lowered), or there is something actually caught in their eye. (Not usual, but if they scratch or rub their eye, you should check.)

- » **Hard eyes:** A dog who stares with hard eyes and a rigid body is feeling threatened or defensive. If pressed this dog — or puppy — will bite.

- » **Whale-eye:** This happens, and is not a good thing, when a puppy is so stressed, frustrated, or anxious by a stimulus or situation that you can actually see the whites of their eyes. If this happens to your puppy, do whatever you can to calm them by removing the stimulus or taking them out of the situation.

- » **Avoids eye contact:** If your puppy avoids your eye contact, they are either feeling overwhelmed by your interactions (are you staring down at them intensely?) or are just trying to ignore you altogether (not an uncommon behavior when they are in their adolescent phase — see Chapter 12!). If you can't tell right off the bat, check out their other indicators (ears and tail, in other words) to see if they are up (attitude) or down (conflicted).

Tail talk

Like your puppy's eyes, the tail is extremely expressive and can be used to gauge how they're feeling throughout the day. As you'll discover, there's more to a tail wag than what meets the eye: Its position as well as the tempo of the wag determine whether your puppy is happy or anxious or feeling more assertive.

To get a read on your puppy's tail, observe its position. First, figure out their neutral tail — where it sits in relationship to their rump when they're calm. Using that position as tail-neutral, see whether you can identify these "tell-tail" emotions:

- » **Happy:** Your puppy will lift their tail slightly and wag it from side to side when they're happy.

- » **Excited:** When your puppy is excited, they will raise their tail a bit more and wags more frantically; this often happens when you return home.

- » **Arched:** A puppy who feels threatened (generally a behavior not seen before 7 months of age) may arch their tail stiffly over their rump. This puppy will stand their ground! Proceed with caution!

- » **Tucked:** A puppy who tucks their tail beneath their body is trying to look small. Often accompanied by cowering, this one is signaling fear or anxiety.

REMEMBER

Your puppy's tail wag doesn't always signal joy. Learn these tempos so that you can distinguish a happy wag from an anxious or aggressive wag:

- » **Happy swing:** Puppies who wag their tails so hard that their bodies wiggle are extremely happy: Discover what makes your puppy feel this good — maybe a special treat, toy, or happy voice — and use these things to train and reward your pup as often as possible.

- » **Sway:** A sway is a shorter wag, and the emotion varies depending on where it's held. A sway on a slightly elevated tail expresses interest or arousal. If the tail is swaying at rump level, your puppy is showing submissiveness. A below-rump sway on a puppy displays fear.

- » **Twitch:** Twitching tails convey intense emotion. One that's raised above the rump signals agitation. A low twitch? This puppy is panicking.

JUST FOR FUN

Want to know just what your puppy thinks about Aunt Edna's visit? Look at their tail — if it's wagging on the right side, they're happy. Tails that wag to the left communicate caution or insecurity.

Ears

Your puppy will also use their ears to express emotion and will often use them in concert with their tail: Ears and tail up convey confidence and a bold curiosity; ears and tail lowered communicate caution or fear. Learn these poses and all the other ear expressions in between these two extremes.

- » **Relaxed:** All puppies have different ears. Some flop, others point, and some stand part way up. Study the ears when your puppy is relaxed to determine their resting pose.

- » **Seal-like:** This adorable, seal-like look is copped when your puppy draws their ears back: When it's paired with a full swing of their tail, you no doubt have a happy and excited puppy on your hands.

- » **Antenna:** This is the classic one-up, one-down expression that lets you know your puppy is focusing on two different noises at the same time. Your puppy is one of a very special species that can be tuned into different sounds simultaneously.

JUST FOR FUN

Did you know your puppy can move their ears independently of one another? This adaptation helps them track sound coming in various directions — neat!

- » **Pitched forward:** When a puppy pitches their ears forward, they're making a statement: Generally paired with a raised tail and forward body lean, this puppy is trying to make themselves look bigger. Look around you — whatever your puppy is staring at may be causing excitement or frustration.

- » **Pinned back:** With ears pinned back, and body curved and lowered to the floor the puppy's message is feeling small and powerless.

Mouth: Grin or grumble, stress panting, play panting, yawning

Your puppy's mouth is similar to your own: When cracked in an open, smile-like curve, it generally conveys joy (unless the puppy is panting due to hot weather or excessive activity, like bone chewing, a stint at the dog park, or exhaustive play). A closed mouth is common when a dog is sleeping or playing independently. A tightened lip pout is seen in puppies who are concentrating or doing something unpleasant, such as meeting a new dog or smelling something foul. A growl where facial muscles are tightened and lips are curled communicates that your puppy is feeling either defensive or seriously afraid. Note your pup's mouth positions so that you become fluent in their lip language.

>> **Mouth slightly open**: A relaxed jaw that's slightly open is similar to a child's impish or happy grin. The lips are loose and wrinkle-free.

>> **Mouth shut:** Dogs generally keep their mouths shut when relaxed or sleeping, but if your puppy closes their mouth in a social situation, pay attention to what's going on around you. If your puppy is feeling stressed, a tightly clenched mouth or puckered lip communicates growing agitation.

>> **Lip licking:** Your puppy will lick their lips when they're anxious or over-stressed. If you can, remove your puppy from the situation or calm them by holding them to your heart or tucking them behind or beneath you.

>> **Taut face, lips in *C* position:** If your puppy's face is stretched and taut, check their lips for a quick gauge of their emotional state. If your puppy feels threatened or trapped, their lips will pull back into a "c" curve.

>> **Taut face, lips in *V* position:** If your puppy is feisty and reactive, clearly ready to take on the world, their offensive reactions can be noted in lips that pull back into a "v" curve.

>> **Yawning:** Puppies yawn when they're tired, or when copying another dog or person; yawning may also be a way of releasing stress. Keep your puppy's emotional landscape in mind when determining a mood or emotion.

>> **Panting**: Your puppy will pant when they're thirsty or hot, but may also pant if they're stressed or overstimulated. Keep the situation in mind when interpreting this behavior.

Vocalizing

Your puppy will have a variety of vocalizations, starting with small, pitiful whimpers when they're newborn and helpless to the ear-splitting, headache-causing yaps of a puppy feeling lonely, frustrated, or defensive.

Although I address how to manage or redirect your puppy's barking habits in Chapter 16, I've listed various types of barking here:

>> **Bratty barking:** These puppies want attention! They space the barks out, and the level is monotone and consistent.

>> **Stress whining:** These puppies want something they can't have or reach: It might be a toy or your attention or a completely random item — but you'll know the instant it happens, because it will pull on your heartstrings. Beware, though — if you reward whining, you get more and more and more whining until it becomes a lifelong habit.

>> **Reactive barking:** These puppies alert to any sound or stimulus. Because the sound is high-pitched and repetitive, your goal will not be to stop your puppy — reactive barkers are born, not made — but to develop an off switch so that you can curb the barking once it starts. Want a clue? Flip to the barking section of Chapter 16.

>> **Baying, or howling:** This is generally a breed-specific sound isolated to hound-type dogs and Nordic breeds. These dogs use their voices to communicate with other dogs and to express frustration when left alone or feeling stressed.

>> **Play growl:** Puppies often growl during play, especially during confrontational games like tug-of-war, physical wrestling, or face-to-face sparring. It can and should be easily calmed or diffused by redirecting the play to an object or chewing type of toy.

>> **Pleasure seeking:** Many dogs growl or moan when enjoying a rub or scratch. Unless the sound is paired with a stiff posture and direct, hard-eyed stares, it's a pleasurable sound.

>> **Throaty growl:** A warning growl that's paired with a stare and tense body posture often occurs over resources. It's common for puppies to communicate their boundaries with other dogs; however, if they're growling at you, get professional help. Though you can redirect your puppy if this type of aggressive stance continues, it may become a habit. And you know what they say about habits: They're hard to break.

>> **Belly growl:** A more serious growl emanates from the belly. This growl means the dog is about to bite. Often paired with raised hackles, flattened ears, and exposed teeth, this dog will lunge and snap or bite the source of its frustration.

There's a direct parallel between dogs who bark and people who yell: See if you can make the parallel. A puppy barks at seeing the neighbors walking their dog. If you yell, your puppy will interpret your raised and frustrated tones as barking. Though your puppy may stop barking for the moment, they'll go back to barking the next time around, because your yelling was simply interpreted as backing them up. Yelling isn't helpful. Find a better solution to your barking problems in Chapter 16.

Fur

Your puppy's fur is filled with lots of scents that signal — to every dog they meet — their demographics as well as their latest poop-rolling adventure. None of it matters much to us humans, although when their fur stands up on end, take notice. When your puppy's hair lifts along their spine (technically referred to as piloerection), your pup is definitely trying to tell you how they're feeling at the moment — and it's not always confident. Pay close attention to these instances

>> **On the offensive:** A thin line of hair that stands up along the spine and continues down the back. Dogs with this pattern of piloerection may appear overly confident, but will likely turn aggressive.

>> **Anxious:** A broad patch around the shoulders. On the flip side, this pattern is spotted in dogs that are less confident and even fearful.

>> **Aroused and conflicted:** Patches of hair raised at the shoulders and the base of the tail and no raised hair on the back. This pattern covers a range of reactions that a dog may be feeling, from ambivalent to conflicted.

Piloerection is just another fancy word for *goose bump*.

I've never understood the lure of being a dog whisperer. Dogs don't listen to whispering people. Pride yourself instead on being a dog listener, because taking the time to listen is most important.

Understanding Your Puppy's Basic Needs

One of the most helpful similarities between puppies and babies is their basic needs: All of them need to eat, drink, sleep, go potty, and play. The main difference is the way they express their need confusion. Babies cry when a need overwhelms them; puppies, though they may occasionally whimper, get nippy and restless.

As kids mature, they learn to communicate their needs with words; your puppy can't talk, but they'll mature, too. In place of spoken language, they will gesture their needs if you've laid the groundwork by pairing each need with a routine. Involve everyone in your household in these rituals, and within a week you'll create habits with your puppy that will stick for life. See Table 6-2 for a mock chart you can use as a model for training, or take it as Square One and modify it.

TABLE 6-2   **The Puppy-Needs Chart**

Your Pup's Need	The Word or Phrase You Say	The Routine You Follow
Sleep	"On your mat," "In your crate," or "Bedtime"	Designate one spot in each shared room, or use a crate or pen to condition good sleeping habits. Take your pup to their area, provide a chew toy, and secure them, if necessary.
Drink	"Water"	Keep the bowl in the same spot. Encourage your puppy to sit before drinking.
Go to the bathroom	"Outside," "Papers," "Go potty," or "Get busy"	Follow the same route to the same potty spot. Restrict attention until your puppy goes. If they're going outside, tap a bell to encourage them to alert you when they need to go out.
Play	"Bone," "Ball," "Toy," or "Go play!"	Establish a play area inside and outside the house. Make sure all four paws are on the floor before you toss a toy or give a bone.

WARNING

Dogs become frantically fussy when overtired or confused by hunger, exhaustion, thirst, or the need to potty. Nearly all puppies will start by nipping in confusion, but if these initial nips are met with harsh discipline, the puppy may develop defensive reactions, such as aggression or barking back.

REMEMBER

Whoever satisfies a need is held in high regard. Though your puppy may take some time to "pay it forward" with their love and devotion, each passing day brings you closer to that ultimate connection. Need by need, your bond grows.

Sleeping

Your puppy is most awake at dawn and dusk: The fancy term is that they're *crepuscular*. People are diurnal; some animals, like raccoons and owls, are nocturnal; dogs are crepuscular — they rest a good 75 percent of the day. Though this makes them ideal companions, they can grow frustratingly fussy when overtired: Think of a toddler having a meltdown. Now imagine that toddler with teeth. If your puppy is mouthy to the point of snapping, it may have little to do with their personality and more to do with needing a routine rest. Turn to Chapter 7 for a proper sleep schedule. (Keep in mind that your goal is to have a dog who is active with you twice per day — before 9 a.m. and after 4 p.m.) Too much stimulation can create a chronically frenetic dog: You don't want that, now do you?

Young puppies (younger than 6 months) require two 2- to 3-hour sleep cycles daily. Like kids, some puppies have a hard time putting themselves to sleep, especially when excitement levels are high. Designate a quiet room for napping (using a crate, pen or gate to contain your puppy), and place them down for scheduled naps during the day. In my house, having 9 a.m. and 1 p.m. naps helped me schedule my day, too. Each time you lead your puppy to their resting area, say a cue word or phrase, like "In you go." Eventually, your puppy will go to this area on their own when they're tired.

Eating

Puppies enjoy predictable routines. A hungry puppy is understandably upset and may show you by eating anything — even difficult-to-digest items such as tissues or walls. Schedule feeding times and stick to them, whether you feed all or a portion of your puppy meal by hand or from a bowl. If you notice your puppy getting nippy or difficult, check your watch. The behavior may be a result of hunger tension.

JUST FOR
FUN

In Chapter 5, I argued for hand feeding your puppy their meals when possible. If you're out of the house around normal feeding times, however, you can now buy timed feeders that you can set or program with an app. If your schedule is less than predictable or you know you may be called away during mealtimes, consider this option.

A young puppy has a high metabolism and should have more frequent meals. Schedule three to four meals throughout the day, slowly phasing out meals as your puppy matures. At some point after your puppy reaches 10 months to a year, they may naturally drop one meal. Most dogs, however, prefer two feedings a day.

JUST FOR
FUN

Does your puppy love their food? If so, use it to reward them throughout the day. Portion out some or all of the food and use it to motivate quick responses and self-control. (For more on how to use food to inspire learning, check out Part 4 of this book.)

Drinking

Water is critically important for your puppy's well-being: it should be left out and available at all times. That said, try to monitor their drinking habits while housetraining them. Establish a drinking station for your puppy and keep their dish there, whether it's empty or full. Give water with meals, after playing, chewing, or napping, and as you're on your way to the potty area.

TIP

Restrict water after 7:30 p.m., unless you want to be up all night taking your puppy outside. If your puppy needs a drink, either give them a small amount or offer a couple of ice cubes.

JUST FOR FUN

Although dogs have many fewer taste buds overall (humans have 9,000 to their 1,700), your puppy has a ring of taste buds on the tip of their tongue that make water taste sweet. Pretty cool.

Going to the bathroom

I don't think house-training can be summed up any better than with the wonderful maxim "Whatever goes in must come out." Your puppy's biological clock will have them eliminating on demand. When their bladder or bowels are pressed, they'll let loose whether they're outside or on the papers — or the rug, if you're not watching.

REMEMBER

Your goal is to teach your puppy where to go and how to let you know when an obstacle (such as a door) is stopping them from getting there. Fortunately, you'll find this task easy after you commit to a routine and can relax your expectations. Tension or expressed frustration is confusing; your puppy won't learn quickly and may grow increasingly more afraid of you. Your puppy needs a schedule, a routine, and a consistent pattern — all of which are within your grasp.

If you're having house-training difficulties, refer to Chapter 14.

Playing

The urge to play and express themselves energetically is one of the most natural responses in your puppy's repertoire. As with children, play and lighthearted interactions can be fabulous instructional tools and can be used exclusively during your first few months together.

REMEMBER

How you play with your young puppy determines your long-term relationship. Rough games, such as wrestling or chase communicate confrontation, which can be scary and may lead to aggression or mischief. Great games such as the 2-ball toss or soccer and name games (which I describe in Chapter 20) instill cooperation and a fun-loving attitude — this puppy won't ever want to leave your side.

Chapter **7**

Establishing Good Habits from the Start

The answer to the age-old question "When should I start training my puppy?" is, if possible, before you even bring your puppy home. Because dog training is 90 percent people training, it's ideal to begin by preparing your home, your family, and even your other pets long before the big day arrives. In this chapter, you learn how to arrange spaces with your puppy in mind and how to prepare and introduce the kids and resident pets; I also give you tips for when you have to leave your puppy alone; an answer to the recurring question "Are crates necessary?" My goal in this chapter, however, is to cue you in on the first and most valuable lessons your puppy needs to learn during their first month at home. Puppy training doesn't need to be a drag — just be sure to organize and share your insights ahead of time so that everyone in your household is on the same page.

Training, training — the kind you might think of when someone says the word doesn't need to be a formal process, if you focus on creating consistent routines and condition the right attention-getting habits. *Hint:* If your puppy wants your attention, wait until they have all four paws on the floor before you address them.

Preparing for Your Puppy's Arrival

Preparing for your puppy-baby's homecoming is a lot like getting ready for a baby. You'll have fun shopping (see Chapter 5 for suggestions) as well as setting up your puppy's playscapes and nursery, and if you organize your puppy's potty plan ahead of time, you'll be surprised how quickly that will go.

Puppy-proofing a free-play zone

Designate an open room, like a kitchen, as your puppy's *free-play zone*. A carpet-free space is ideal; rolling up area rugs at the corners may tempt a pup to chew, and the absorbent texture may prompt elimination. Tape wires down, remove all low-sitting temptations, and place your shoes elsewhere. Place the puppy's comfort station at the corner of this room as well. (See the next section.)

REMEMBER

The free-play zone should be free of items that the puppy shouldn't play with (such as the hanging towels and doll shown in Figure 7-1). A little puppy-proofing can prevent a lot of problems.

FIGURE 7-1:
Look at this space from your puppy's perspective and clear away any temptations.

Illustration by Barbara Frake

TIP

If your puppy's free-play zone blocks another pet's domain, reorganize your resident pet's area well in advance of the puppy's arrival. For example, if your cat's bowls and litter box are within the puppy's area, relocate them before you bring your puppy home so that your cat won't feel displaced by the new arrival. For more tips on introducing your pup to the resident pets, flip to the section "Introducing other pets," later in this chapter.

Setting up a food and water station

Feed your puppy by their comfort station in their free-play zone or, if they're distractible, in a gate or crate within the free-play zone. Have two dishes — one for water, one for food. Take up the bowls at appropriate times and wash the dishes after every feeding. (See Chapter 6 for more on feeding times for puppies.)

Help your puppy identify an area of the free-play zone that is home base. This area will be your puppy's comfort station, where they'll rest, find their bones and toys, and go when directed to "Go to your place." Place a flat mat, folded quilt, or bed in a corner area or a nook created between furniture. Put your puppy's toys and bones on the mat, and if possible, arrange the water dish nearby. Sit by your puppy's calming station with them and treat them so that they think the area is special. If you make this area the focal point of your interactions, your puppy will bond to it quickly. (See Figure 7-2.)

FIGURE 7-2:
Give your puppy an area in all the rooms you share.

Illustration by Barbara Frake

Your puppy should have a pre-established comfort station in each room you plan to share. Choose a spot that's close to where you spend the most time. As you introduce your puppy to new rooms in the house, either bring their familiar bed or use a similar one in each room.

Establishing your puppy's sleeping area

Puppies need a lot of sleep to support their rapid-fire growth and mental development. If your puppy isn't getting enough sleep, you'll know it — though sleep may not be the first thing that comes to your mind. An overtired puppy may become hyper and nippy to the point of being aggressive if you try to interfere with their constant motion.

Because a tired puppy can become ornery (just like you), you'll want to address their sleep schedule immediately! Designate a gated area as their sleep space, or put their crate in an area free from a lot of foot traffic and incoming light so that they can sleep undisturbed. (It wouldn't hurt to pull the blinds or drape a towel over your puppy's crate to create a den-like feeling.) Because puppies are attuned to all sounds, block distant noises by leaving on soft rock or lullaby music so that your puppy doesn't feel left out. Whether you choose a crate or a gated room, make it cozy by laying down a mat and an article of your clothing, as well as a puppy pacifier (see Chapter 5) or bone to self-soothe your puppy if they should grow restless. Avoid fluffy beds or cushions because either can encourage chewing or accidents.

Sleep training

Sleeping is one of your puppy's basic needs — just as important to their development as eating and drinking. When puppies don't get enough sleep, they act frantic to the point of distraction, often becoming incessantly mouthy. Many show aggressive tendencies when continuously overtired, much like a colicky infant.

Unlike people, who as adults are *diurnal* — resting 8 hours or one-third of a 24-hour cycle — dogs are *crepuscular*, most awake at dawn and dusk and resting for the remainder of the day. This factor makes them ideal pets because your day can be organized to play 20 minutes an hour with them before 9 a.m. and after 4 p.m.

As far as creating a habitual daytime sleep schedule goes, organize their nap times during the day for those times when you're busy or working anyway. Until they reach 8 months of age, your puppy should have a noontime visit to feed, take comfort, and relieve themselves.

See Table 7-1 for a daily schedule, including ideal nap and potty break times. As tempted as you are to provide your puppy with daytime activities and late hours filled with dreamy snuggles while watching T.V., resist the urge. If you overstimulate your puppy, they will have a harder time settling down, may be overreactive, and may develop extreme separation anxiety during adolescence and puberty stages. For more on potty breaks and house-training, see Chapter 14.

TABLE 7-1   **Daily schedule for growing puppies**

Time of Day	Activity	Potty Time
6-7AM	Early morning wake-up	Go outside/papers; offer self-soothing toys and activities
7:30AM	Breakfast	Create a feeding routine, feeding by hand, in a toy, treat cup or bowl
7:45AM	Potty and Play Time	Go to your potty area; use play as reward
8AM-8:30AM	Quiet self-soothing play or interaction	Give your dog puppy pacifiers. chews, and blankets while you get ready
8:30-9AM	Last outing then mid-morning nap	Give attention after your puppy goes potty; next put in crate with pacifier or chew
11-11:30AM	Potty run after nap	Go outside/papers
11:30A	Lunch for puppies	Feed or portion out food and use for play or training
11:45AM	Potty and Play Time	Take to potty areas after meal, then play with multiple toys!
12:15PM-1PM	Self-soothing play with chew toys, other dogs, or an adventure	Assign words to everyday routine like Car, Walk, or Bone
1PM-3PM	Outing then nap	Take your dog out before crating them for afternoon nap
3PM-4PM	Outing then games and fun	Go outside/papers; reward with play
4:15-4:30PM	Dinner	Early is better; let 15 minutes pass before rough play
4:30PM	Outing	Go outside/papers
4:30-6PM	Self-soothing play, exploration, or interaction	Reward your puppy with play or a self-soothing activity
6PM	Out and attention	Potty run and loving attention
8PM-9PM	Last out then to bed	Last outing then bed
10-11PM	Final out	Take your dog to their area to go then back to bed. No attention

TIP

If your puppy is having a hard time sleeping solo, consider a Snuggle Puppy sleeping buddy toy, as described in Chapter 5.

Crate training

To some, maybe even you, crates seem confining, even dungeon-like torture devices that trap poor puppies against their will. But crates aren't awful — I promise. Puppies grow to love these enclosures like kids love their big-kid beds.

And though you can phase off the use of their crate as your puppy matures and their house-training and chewing habits are under control, no one says you have to: Some puppies even become crate-dependent, entering the crate on their own when life gets too overwhelming. Every time I see our sweet Tally dog curled up in his crate, I start wishing I had a crate to crawl into when days are long and times get tough.

Here are ten steps to introduce your puppy to their create. (For more about what type and size of crate to purchase, flip to Chapter 5.)

TIP

If you live in a large home, consider two crates — one in the kitchen area and the other in the bedroom or quiet place to encourage rest. Place the crate in the free-play zone, placing old clothing articles or a pad on the bottom (unless your puppy pees on them — then keep the bottom bare until your puppy learns to hold their bladder).

1. **Initially have the crate in the open area, using it as toy central.**

   Place toys, treats, and bones just inside the crate, and then let your puppy's curiosity take over. From the start, place their food near the opening, gradually moving each meal closer to the door.

2. **After a couple of days, play the "in-we-go, out-we-go" game.**

   Take high-value treats and sit by the opening of the crate. This is a hands-off exercise — *no touching or forcing* your puppy into the crate. Shake the cup or hold a treat to your puppy's nose, and then toss in the treat. Say "in-you-go" as your puppy goes into the crate to find it, and "out-you-go" as they leave the crate. Play this game three to five times and quit before your puppy loses interest.

3. **If your puppy is comfortable moving in and out of the crate, begin to feed a portion of their meals scattered in the crate.**

   I use commercial foraging mats or place a bowl in the back corner.

   As your puppy is eating their meal, slide a bone or extra-high-value treats in the open side slats while still leaving the crate door open.

4. **Place all high-value chews or favorite toys and note any time your puppy enters the crate to play or rest.**

5. **After your puppy is comfortable in the crate, say "In-you-go" as you lure them in using a fist of kibble or a few high-value treats.**

   Sit down at the opening, say "Bye for now" and shut the door; ask a helper to drop in a favorite chew through a side opening or do so yourself. Within 5 seconds, open the door and place another treat inside the crate, before your puppy has a chance to pop out.

6. **Gradually lengthen the close-door time until your puppy is accustomed to varying closures from 10 to 60 seconds.**

   Again, either drop in a chew as you walk away or ask a helper to feed treats in the side window while you walk away.

7. **When you're confident that your puppy can settle inside their crate with a self soothing toy, choose a natural nap time and leave them alone for 15 minutes with a favorite chew and gentle music playing, and then dim the lights.**

8. **If they're frantic, you can return to the area — but don't rescue them. Just let your presence calm them.**

   Do not remove your puppy from the crate when they're distressed or else they'll grow frantic every time they're left alone. Wait until your puppy is settled to calmly open the crate.

9. **When they have settled down, feed high-end treats through a side opening, and then open the crate and take the puppy to potty.**

10. **After your puppy is calm being left alone, use the crate for nap times.**

REMEMBER

Young puppies need lots and lots of sleep, and are most awake at dawn and dusk. Puppies need two full nap periods and a good night's sleep to mature into calm, sensible dogs. When overstimulated and chronically entertained, puppies develop into impulsive dogs who need a lot of activity to self-soothe. Use your puppy's natural sleep cycles and chew toys to teach them to self-soothe or rest when left alone.

WARNING

Crates aren't ideal for older puppies who may be suffering from separation anxiety. If separation anxiety is a concern, read more about that topic in Chapter 16.

Establishing a route to the bathroom area

Whether you're paper training your puppy or teaching them to potty outside, establish a schedule as the one outlined in Table 7-1 and decide on a route to speed through shared rooms to the door or to the papers, which should be set in a specific spot. (See Chapter 14 for a diagram of a sample route.) Place papers in the specified area or select a door to use and a potty area no more than 10 to 20 feet from your home's entrance.

TIP

Containing your puppy in certain areas of your home is important, especially if your house is large and you have other pets or children. Too much freedom or activity can set bad habits in motion, especially if your puppy is fearful or easily excited, so you'll want to determine which rooms your puppy is allowed into at first and set up the potty route accordingly.

Bringing Puppy Home

The day has finally arrived to bring your puppy home. You've thought ahead, prepared family members and friends, and probably shared your excitement with a few strangers. This trip will be a real thrill ride for you. Your puppy, however, may feel a little differently. Leaving the place and people they're used to and being separated from their dog family can be stressful and scary.

TIP

Make every effort to plan a calm trip home. See if you can arrange the trip during their usual naptime. Also, think through the possible scenarios so that you'll be prepared for anything that may happen:

>> **Best case:** Your puppy may sleep the entire way home. Keep your energy subdued and speak softly to your puppy if they wake up. Calming music may also be effective.

>> **Worst case:** Your puppy may throw up, howl, or have diarrhea. The worst-case scenario is a drag, I know, but be prepared, just in case. And no matter how disappointed, disgusted, or frustrated you become, don't stress or correct your puppy.

REMEMBER

To be prepared for any mishaps, bring the following items on the trip:

>> Paper towels and cleaner

>> Pet safe carpet or upholstery cleaner

>> Plastic bags

>> An appropriately sized plastic crate

>> A towel to spread under the crate to prevent slipping or to clean up accidents

>> A lightweight collar with an identifying phone number in case of emergency or accident

>> A few chewies or a soft toy

TIP

Crating your puppy in the vehicle is important for safety and comfort. Ask the breeder or caretaker what size is most appropriate for your pup. In the car, secure the kennel by bracing it with pillows or tying it down on a level surface. If other people are riding with you, ask someone to sit near the opening of the kennel and speak softly to the puppy while feeding them whatever food they're accustomed to eating if they're awake.

WARNING

Never let (or make) your puppy sit in your lap while driving. It's too distracting and, to make matters worse, a slight fender bender may release the airbag. Like infants, your puppy won't survive the blow.

Introducing Puppy to Your Household

When planning your first day with your new pup, remember to keep it simple. If you have kids or other dogs, tire them out and use bribes to ensure their cooperation. Don't tolerate fighting and commotion between siblings — your puppy will have enough on their mind. Keep all stress at bay for the first 24 hours. If you have other pets, keep the puppy separated with a puppy playpen, praising your residents for sniffing or approaching the puppy.

In this section, I walk you through the best way to introduce the puppy to your family — including both people and pets. No doubt everyone will be fast friends after puppy settles in, but you can ease the inevitable initial fears and discomfort by handling day one well.

Forming a welcome circle

To introduce your family to the puppy, gather everyone involved in Team Puppy, hand everyone some puppy kibble, and create a large circle by sitting on the floor or grass. Place your new puppy in the center of the circle and let them approach everyone on their own. Dole out toys or small food rewards so that everyone can give the pup a present when first meeting them.

Calming the kids

If you have kids, the day that your puppy first comes home may be on a future fondest-memories-of-childhood list — talk about excitement! However, part of your job is to keep the kids calm because too much squealing and loving in the first 5 minutes can be somewhat overwhelming for a pup. Explain the situation ahead of time and ask your children to help you make the puppy feel comfortable by speaking quietly and petting gently.

Here are a few tricks I've found useful in dispelling early tension, frustrations, and fights:

>> **Model, model, model.** The saying "Monkey see, monkey do" applies to children, too. Because your children pick up on habits by watching you, show them how to act with actions instead of words. I can assure you that

something is bound not to go as planned, but if you stay calm and ignore the impulse to badger or boss, you'll have a more relaxed home on your hands. Kids react poorly to negative reprimands. Stay cheerful and model the right behavior while your children are watching. Like monkeys, they see — and then they do.

>> **Assign tasks.** Make a chart assigning everyone a job ahead of time. Make raising the puppy a fun family affair where everyone plays the role of the parent.

>> **Talk to your kids ahead of time.** Get them involved in your plans and warn them of all the possible situations that may arise. For instance, the puppy may be sad and withdrawn and may not want to interact with anyone — they're missing their littermates. Though the kids may be let down, everyone must respect the puppy — they'll snap out of it in a few days. On the other hand, the puppy may be nippy and want to play rough — again, a carryover from their first family. (See Chapter 15 for tips on handling a mouthy puppy.) Make sure the kids are aware of the possibility, and help them interact with the puppy when they're calm.

Remind the kids that puppies need a lot of sleep — especially during the first 6 months. Let them decide on the music choices and placement for the puppy's nursery, and show them the sleep schedule so that they can take a role in putting the puppy down for naps and bedtime.

>> **Take the puppy away.** Your puppy will get easily excited by your children and may express themselves by nipping, jumping, and tugging. Help create a plan if a situation with the puppy gets out of hand, referencing Chapter 8 for some creative ideas like Alligator Island (every kids favorite), Fishing for Fido and the Run Run Stop game.

REMEMBER

If redirecting your puppy doesn't work teach your kids to clear the area!

Saving your friends for another day

Everyone gets excited when they hear the word *puppy*. Friends and neighbors crawl out of the woodwork and want to welcome you home. Don't be persuaded! Limit early introductions to only the closest friends and family. Resist extracurricular visits and drive-by welcomes until the next week, when your puppy has fully transitioned and has bonded with the household.

WARNING

Sometimes your friends can be the hardest to control. Many will, without provocation, share their views on everything from house-training to how to discipline your puppy when they misbehave. Listen respectfully, but stay the course. Even though your friend may speak the gospel about what worked for *their* puppy, you're not raising their puppy — you're raising your own. As children, what works for one pup may not work for another. If you follow everyone's advice, you risk confusing your puppy. If you need more help than this book offers, skip your friends' advice and sign up for a class or call a respected professional.

TIP

When the time has finally come for you to introduce your new pup to your friends, gather some treats and offer them to your visitors as they come in. Offer them a chair or ask them to sit on the floor as your puppy approaches. Ask them to extend the treat but not release it until your puppy is calmly standing or sitting on all four paws. By ignoring them when they're excited and petting them when they're calm, you're getting a head start on encouraging good manners.

Managing resident dogs, cats, and other animals

Though you and your family want all the pets to be friends, you have to realize that your resident pets will not be wearing party hats when you walk through the door with a new companion in your arms. Young puppies are especially annoying to other animals — and the oodles of attention they get will be off-putting to the resident pets. Some time must pass (up to 6 months, in some cases) for everyone to get used to each other.

The following sections highlight some species-specific tips to help ease the tension.

Resident dogs

Try to organize the introductions at a time when your resident dog is the calmest and, preferably, after play, meals, and exercise. If your dog doesn't know the Find It game, teach it to them by casting treats or parts of their meal on the floor while instructing "Find it." (See Chapter 20 for a more detailed explanation.)

When introducing a young puppy to an older dog, ask a friend or family member to help out supervising the puppy during the introduction. Place the puppy in a crate or playpen either in someone else's house or apartment or outside in a clean and safe environment as you approach with your dog on a loose leash. Each time your dog sniffs or looks at the puppy, mark the moment with a word like "puppy-good" or use a clicker as described in Chapter 5, and then toss a treat to the floor: Find it! If you're unconcerned about your dog's reaction, let the two sniff each other while your friend either holds the puppy in their lap or sits with the puppy on the floor.

Next, proceed into the house. Use a pen off to one side of the house or gate the puppy away from the main living area until your first dog is familiar and more at ease with the presence of the puppy. From the outset, give your resident dog the royal treatment, feeding and greeting them first (dividing their meals into as many meals as you're feeding the puppy). If your resident pet approaches you while you are, or anyone is, interacting with the puppy, turn away from the puppy and address them immediately. Don't allow the puppy to push the other pets aside for your attention; just ignore them or gently block their inclusion by turning away.

When allowing your puppy to mingle in your home, affix a light indoor freedom line (see Chapter 5) or leash onto your puppy's collar to allow for quick redirection if the puppy is too playful or is annoying your resident dog.

WARNING

Be prepared for the resident to growl, snap, or pin your puppy — and stay calm. If you yell at your resident dog, they'll be more resistant to the newbie's presence. If you're able, praise your resident, reminding them that they are still the queen and lead them away from the puppy with a promise of a treat. Your puppy must learn that your older dog is not its mother or another puppy. Reassured and given more treats for tolerating the pup's presence, they will slowly grow on each other.

REMEMBER

Growling, teeth snarling, and pinning are not unusual dog behaviors when two dogs first meet. Dogs organize their relationship based on seemingly odd interactions. Almost immediately, one dog appears to yield while the other controls the interaction. However, if one dog appears vicious or the discourse continues for more than 30 seconds or escalates to where both dogs are fighting each other, separate the dogs immediately and call a professional to help smooth the introductions. I'm often called to introduce a new puppy into a household to ensure everyone starts on the right paw.

Some older dogs, when faced with a new puppy in their home, completely withdraw, going so far as to act as though they've never met you. Don't be put off. Instead, just shower them with love and attention. If your youngster badgers or bullies your resident dog for sport, discourage it immediately by using a drag lead or a quick spritz of water from a spray bottle

TIP

If you bring a new older puppy into the group — one who is old enough to be walked on a leash — it's best to have a friend help you and let the dogs meet on a walk at a location unfamiliar to both dogs. Manage the two dogs so that when walking side-by-side, you can guide them to sniff bottoms instead of being forced at one another face-to-face. Let your resident sniff first, and then guide the puppy back so that when walking slightly behind, you can gradually walk the puppy to greet your dog, rump facing.

TIP

If you're earnestly concerned that your resident dog may harm the puppy, muzzle them or keep hold of their leash to enable easy interference. You can also call in a professional to walk you through it.

HANDLING A TWO-PUPPY HOUSEHOLD

Adding two puppies to your house is more like having twins than adopting two hamsters, two fish, or two cats. The first year is quite the balancing act. House-training, frantic chewing escapades, and nipping and jumping habits are often more than twice the effort because one puppy influences the other and, in the end, may tune you out. You need the 3 *P*s — patience, persistence, and positive attitude — to keep the training ball moving forward at a steady pace. That said, raising two puppies can give you hours of entertainment watching them play and experience life together; just keep this image in mind while you're devoting hours to raising your twins.

When left together 24 hours a day, your puppies will form a strong bond to each other, which is good. However, that means they'll also be less attached to you, which makes influencing their behavior difficult. To prevent that level of bonding, separate them at least twice a day and, if possible, let them sleep in separate bedrooms. Have two crates so that each pup gets used to having their own space.

Here are additional hints for making life a little easier for everyone in the 2-puppy house:

- **Remember that each puppy is different.** Sure, certain similarities string all puppies together. However, like humans, each one has their unique personality and temperament that affect the way they relate to their world. In a multidog household, everyone must be sensitive to the needs of each puppy.

- **Let your puppies establish their hierarchy.** Personality affects the way puppies relate to one another. Groups of two or more puppies form a hierarchy, with the most outgoing, assertive one assuming the bossier position and often the more protective, demanding role.

  You may have trouble figuring out which puppy is the leader of your group because it's not often a straightforward delineation. Puppies don't base hierarchy on who's the biggest or who came first. Nor do they base it wholly on who's the toughest. Hierarchy is most often based on who's the most responsible or level-headed in a given situation. The puppy with both the brains and the brawn wins out. Regardless of your feelings, you must support their arrangement.

- **Remember the discipline rules.** The best advice I can give you here is don't get hot-headed with your puppies. Your puppy won't understand things that happened moments ago, and together, both pups will view you as a buzzkill. Sure, you'll get frustrated when you find a mess of any kind — I get that! My family rescues problem dogs, and sometimes I think it's just to test my resolve.

  Directing your frustration at either puppy only weakens your connection to them and strengthens their bond. For suggestions on specific problems, see Chapters 15-17.

(continued)

(continued)

- Allow wrestling, to a degree. Teach your puppies to go outside or to certain areas of your home to play. If they tend to get out of hand, make treat cups (see Chapter 5) and teach them a universal name like "Pups!" Clap your hands when the play escalates, say "Pups," and then direct them with the treat cup to their play area or redirect them to a bone.

- **Play the name game**. Teach your puppies two names: their names and a universal one that you can use when they're together, such as "dogs," "girls," "boys," or "babies" — whatever works for you. Using a single name makes calling them easier; "Girls, come!" rolls off the tongue easier than "Buddy, Fifi, Daisy, Marlo, come!" Play the name game with the treat cup, shaking it as you run from them, and then turning and saying "Wait!" Reward them by tossing the treats down (see the Find It game described in Chapter 20) so that you don't mistakenly encourage jumping.

- **Feed your pups separately.** If you're having difficulty keeping the puppies separate, create two separate feeding stations. (See Chapter 5.)

- **Avoid starting a toy war.** I know you want them both to have a toy. But one puppy keeps insisting on having both. You give it back to the other puppy, and they take it away. The giving and taking can go on all day. Remember your leadership rule: If the more assertive puppy wants both, the more assertive puppy gets both. Period.

If your puppies begin to fight with each other to the point of making you nervous, *call a professional* to help you resolve the situation. Additionally, if you catch a fight before it begins, shame the underdog and reward the leader with attention. I know it feels unnatural, but remember that your dogs aren't human. If the situation repeats itself, call in a professional.

Cats

Most cats would prefer to live without a puppy in the house. Some are fearful of puppies, and others are outright annoyed. Your cat may head for the highest cabinet and stare at you reproachfully when you bring home a puppy. If you have a confident cat, they'll probably wait stoically for the puppy to approach close enough for them to give the pup a solid bat on the nose. In any case, keep your responses low-key. Overreacting can put all species on edge.

Following are some suggestions to help the introductions go smoothly:

>> **Place the puppy in a gated room or open playpen (with a special chewy for diversion) and let your cat wander around the room at their own pace.** Don't try to influence or interfere in your cat's reaction. Reward any interest your cat takes in the new addition with a favorite treat or toy. If you

can, teach your kitty "Up, up" by gently luring or lifting them onto a high counter or cat tree. If your puppy starts acting up, however, step in to calm the puppy.

>> **When your cat behaves nonchalantly around the puppy (it may take a while; perhaps a week), place the puppy on a light drag lead and bring the two together in a small room.** Hold the lead if your puppy acts up and redirect them with a toy. In the coming weeks, have your puppy drag a lead (inside and out, if needed) and continue to use a treat cup to teach them to focus on you when you call and divert their attention to a treat and toy when excited by the cat's presence.

WARNING

Don't be too surprised if your cat growls or bats at the puppy. Directing your frustration at the cat will only make matters more stressful. Your cat is defining their space, which is a necessary boundary for coexistence. Reward any initiative your cat takes to stay in the room with the puppy, erecting shelves or cat trees to satisfy your cat's instincts to mark (they will scratch an upright post) and climb safely out of reach.

Other animals

If you have farm animals or other pets in the house — such as ferrets, birds, or rodents — give the puppy a few days to acclimate to your home before introducing the rest of the menagerie. If your pup's reaction concerns you, attach a leash to curb their enthusiasm and redirect them to a toy or bone. If your puppy seems too assertive (generally experienced with older puppy rescues), they may not have had the proper conditioning for living harmoniously with other animals during their socialization period. Consider using a head halter to reduce their staring or a basket muzzle to reduce your worry and possible mishap.

When introducing caged critters, bring your puppy in to see them after playtime and with a portion of their meal or high-value treats. Play Find It, gradually inching closer to the enclosure. The goal is to let the puppy habituate to the sound and smell of the critter before becoming fully alert to the animal's presence. After three sessions of play, see whether you can prompt the critter's motion and calmly stroke your puppy, saying "Gentle," or continue to play if they seem unphased by the introduction

If you have free-roaming animals, introduce them as you would a cat, with the puppy gated in one area or in their playpen or dragging a leash.

Planning Out the First Days and Weeks

Well, you've made it home. All the anticipation has come to this very moment. Even though you may want to rush in and give your newest member the full tour, hold your huskies. Simplify the first day by showing them the free-play zone, the room they'll call home until they're grounded and potty-trained. Think through the coming weeks and how you can bring your household together to make the most of this impressionable time.

WARNING

Speak to your puppy softly and don't correct them or respond if they have an accident or chews on something they shouldn't. In the beginning, they're too disoriented to retain any information; they're just getting familiar with their new surroundings and their funny-looking furless family members, so you'll only succeed in frightening them. Relax. You'll do fine. This is just the beginning.

Surviving the first 24 hours

Prepare yourself and your family for the fact that the first day home with your puppy can be a little odd. After all the anticipation and preparation, your puppy is *home.* They may jump right into the mix, or they may pass out for days. You may get one who sleeps straight through the night, or they may be up on and off, whining mournfully. Your puppy may be rough, sweet, or completely aloof. Don't take anything personally; it may take them a few days or weeks to adjust.

When you get home, let your puppy have a drink of water, and then show them to the potty area, whether you've planned a place in the front yard or papers in a corner inside. After they have relieved themselves, bring them into the secured free-play zone or gated enclosure.

Though you and your family will be overjoyed, your puppy will likely be disoriented and confused. Stay calm, either watching or validating their interests by getting down on their level and taking a virtual tour with your nose. Though you may rely on your eyes when it comes to familiarizing yourself with a new place, puppies orient themselves through their sense of smell. If your puppy wants to rest, place a cozy blanket in your lap and be a quiet presence. You're showing them that this new space is okay, and acting like a calm and cool adult dog gives your puppy reassurance that they have someone to lean on. Discourage anybody who overwhelms your puppy with their interests or affections. Your puppy will need time to adjust.

Time for bed

Ideally, your puppy should sleep near someone at night. Because your puppy won't be used to sleeping alone, they'll often be distressed and up all night calling for their littermates. Keep your newbie close to you for the first few nights at least. If you must leave them alone, play soothing music to ease the fear of unfamiliar noises.

Adjusting, week one

The first week is quite progressive. By day two or three, you'll notice your puppy watching you and getting excited when you walk through the door. You may be surprised to note the different reactions, but their emerging reactivity is a sure sign that they feel safe and welcomed. Try to keep yourself calm, especially when your puppy gets excited, because you don't want to encourage hyper greeting manners before your puppy has cut their baby teeth.

Organize the day, using the sleep and house-training schedule shown in Table 7-1, and remain patient with accidents or exploratory chewing, especially if your puppy is in the infant stage (younger than 16 weeks of age). If you notice your puppy chewing furniture or wires, use a distasteful bitter-apple spray to discourage their curiosity, or tape the wires out of reach. Puppy-proof each area you share by placing objects such as dish towels and shoes out of reach. Prevention is worth pounds of cure.

Avoid loud or physical interference, because it only overwhelms your puppy and discourages bonding. Running and shouting "No" to a puppy may make them stop at the moment, but you'd stop too if someone shouted at you. Your puppy doesn't understand; you'll only succeed in making them afraid of people.

REMEMBER

During these early days, the most important lessons are

>> **Helping your puppy learn their name**: Fill a plastic container with some of your puppy's food or favorite treats. Voilà — you now have a treat cup. Shake it and reward your puppy until they make the association between the sound and getting a treat. Next, call their name when they're unsuspecting as you shake the cup and reward their attention. Within a day or two, phase off the cup and watch as your puppy alerts happily to their name.

>> **Teaching your puppy where to go to get each of their needs met**: Your puppy will be most focused on where to go for food, water, sleep, and potty. Assign words to each routine, as detailed in the Needs chart (Table 6-2) at the end of Chapter 6, to help your puppy associate words with actions.

Bonding with Your Puppy: The First Month

The first month with any puppy is a critical bonding time. As the days and weeks pass, you'll notice your puppy's confidence and awareness of you growing. They'll initiate routines by going to the door when they have to go out or standing by their bowl at mealtime. Your puppy is communicating with you! Now you can continue the magic by thinking of early efforts as though you were teaching a newly adopted baby English as a second language. Your puppy's first language is posturing and body cues; though they can learn words, you'll need to pair them with gestures and routines. By paying attention and interpreting the meaning behind their actions, you'll forge a bond that will last a lifetime.

When puppies are very young, their whole bodies and brains are absorbed in encoding new experiences, from the smells in your kitchen to the sound of the dishwasher. How puppies react to these sensations depends on their temperament and how you engage and interact with them.

Here is a quick list of habits and words to get started on during the first month you're together:

WARNING

>> **"Get your ball or toy."** When playing with your puppy, say "Go get your toy" as you toss a toy and let them chase it. I love the toys that are attached to a pole — they're perfect for exhausting and diverting your puppy's hunting and grabbing energy. Use the phrase to play and redirect your puppy whenever they're excited; when greeting people, for example.

Don't worry about retrieving games at this stage: Most puppies are too young to share. The goal of this game is to teach your puppy what they can grab, have, and hold ("Go get your ball or toy!") and what they can't — namely, you.

>> **Play treat cup games. Make a treat cup as described in Chapter 5. After your puppy makes the sound-treat connection, teach them the 4-paw rule. Shake the cup and reward your puppy if they hold still; if they jump, lift the cup above your head and look up.** Flip to Chapter 8 to learn how to condition an automatic Sit, and then incorporate Sit into this routine. You can use the treat cup to teach your puppy to come to their name — shake the cup and run 5 to 10 feet away from your puppy as you call their name; say "Come" as you release the treat.

>> **"Say hello."** To encourage proper greeting manners, wait to greet your puppy until they're calm enough to sit for a treat. As you reach out to pet them, say the words "Say hello." Eventually, they will learn that this phrase means to greet people on all four paws. Remember that good manners start at home.

>> **To encourage licking on command, spread a thin coat of butter on your hand and say "kisses" as you offer your puppy your open palm.** When your puppy nips your hand, let your hand go limp until they stop, or remove their mouth gently as you remind them to give "kisses" instead. More tips in Chapter 15.

WARNING

Puppies aren't perfect: Not all their messages are heartwarming. Sometimes your puppy will be bored and demand your attention by jumping up, barking, or grabbing a shoe or paper towel. As you work through the many joys and frustrations of puppyhood, remember that even bad behavior is a sign of healthy development — it signals that your puppy is engaged, focused, and dependent on you. This is the time to start communicating your routines and rules to your puppy in a calm, consistent manner.

A lot of what they learn happens when you don't even know it, like when you approach their gate or crate. Wait until your puppy is relaxed and standing on all four paws in their enclosure before you open or step over a gate or lift them out; otherwise, you'll teach the opposite. It's the same with food or water: Wait to lower the dish until your puppy can sit still. Whining and barking are other habits that start early. Ignore your puppy's vocal demands unless you're certain that they need to go out. More tips on dealing with all sorts of frustrating behavior are in Chapter 15; skip ahead, if you need to.

REMEMBER

Puppies, like kids, love attention. And, like kids, they don't care if the attention is negative or positive. Shouting, pushing, and grabbing wont' discourage a puppy — they're interpreted as confrontational play and make a puppy *more* reactive, not less.

Handling fears

During the first month, your puppy will experience everything for the first time. Given all the sounds and stimulations they face, there is sure to be something that will likely startle your puppy: Fear of the unknown is completely natural and your puppy's startle reflex, a powerful force. Stay calm. Though you'll be tempted to soothe your puppy when they're fearful of an object or sound, the best approach is to stay calm and act like it's nothing. The been-there-seen-that attitude gives your puppy far more reassurance than bending over and soothing them, and it encourages them to look and bond to you as their authority on everything life-related.

Knowing when to pick them up — and when not to

Some puppies relish the comfort of being held in someone's arms. Many small breeds love the reassurance of being held tightly by someone larger whom they trust. But, like kids, no puppy wants to be held all the time. Pick up your puppy only when they're calm and restful. If your puppy squirms to be let down, don't take it personally. There's a time to hold and a time to let go.

Handling the heart hold

When holding a puppy, keep their spine to the ceiling and belly to the floor: This is a great mantra for kids and grown-ups alike. I refer to the proper way to hold a puppy as the *heart hold*, where you embrace the puppy sideways so that your hearts are pressed together, holding their hips and shoulder joints snug to your body.

Puppies don't like to have their legs dangling, and many puppies feel scared when flipped on their back. If your puppy appears to be uncomfortable in your arms, they are. Ask your veterinarian or another professional how to best lift, carry, and hold your puppy if you need guidance. By holding your puppy securely, they'll sense your loving power, which helps them bond to you.

TIP

If you have a small or young puppy, don't hesitate to lift them into a heart hold whenever they're meeting a new dog. If you're certain that the dog or other puppy is safe and can be trusted not to attack your puppy, kneel down and let the bigger dog smell your puppy thoroughly. If a helper is present, ask them to hold your puppy while you pet and playfully engage the other dog. You're letting your puppy witness your courage firsthand. In the moment, or over time, your puppy will grow more confident greeting other dogs and learn that sniffing is the proper way to say hello — at least if you're a dog.

Chapter 8

Including Everyone in Team Puppy

Bringing up a well-rounded puppy isn't a 1-person job, even if you live alone. However, if you're surrounded by family members or friends, striking a balance between consistency and cooperation takes some effort. You soon find out that sometimes your puppy is easier to train than your partner, kids, or roommate. If you're living near other people — whether in a subdivision, an apartment complex, or a busy urban neighborhood — incorporating your newbie may be tricky too. You'll quickly discover just who is a puppy lover and who isn't. Another paramount goal is finding the right outside help — from a veterinarian and dog walker to a fun, informative puppy teacher. In this chapter, you discover how to pull together Team Puppy to help raise a happy, well-behaved dog.

Welcoming the Help of Family and Friends

If I were asked to boil down family life with a new puppy to a single all-important concept, it would be this: Be consistent. It won't matter what your rules are and whether your puppy is off the furniture or not or given organic bones to chew or old shoes as long as everyone is on the same page.

One area that causes manic confusion is at the front door. If one person welcomes the rowdy puppy, while another gets mad, and still another tries to redirect their attention to a toy, the puppy will not have a clear vision on the proper greeting etiquette in your home.

If you can give your puppy one gift, let it be this: Gather your family around and decide on a few ground rules, such as whether you'll let your puppy do any of the activities in this list:

Eat from the table	Yes	No
Jump up for greetings	Yes	No
Sleep on the bed	Yes	No
Rest on the furniture	Yes	No
Ring a bell to go outside	Yes	No
Chew clothing or household objects	Yes	No
Go to daycare	Yes	No
Visit the dog park	Yes	No

WARNING

Though the answers to some of these questions might seem obvious to you, everyone is different and may not see it your way. Have the discussions up front and away from the puppy to avoid in-the-moment aggravations.

Encouraging Positive Interactions between Kids and Pups

One hallmark of my childhood was my dog, Shawbee, who was a husky-shepherd mix. She was my constant companion, waiting for me at the bus stop, hanging outside the church while I took ballet lessons, and sharing my ice cream cone on a hot summer day.

Today, kids are often overstimulated at a young age, and they have less time to hang out with dogs. Riding bikes and running around are often limited to parks where dogs aren't allowed. To boot, young puppies and young kids don't always hit it off. In some circumstances, the puppy views the child as another puppy to bite and bully. At other times, a child becomes jealous of the attention the new addition is getting, which leads to sibling rivalry between the child and the puppy. But as the ringleader in your household, you can help your kids and puppy hit it off and have a rewarding relationship.

With time, patience, understanding, and the guidance I provide in this section, you can teach your kids to interact with the puppy in practical ways and coach your puppy to respect their human siblings.

Short, fun lessons and groovy games

Kids like to help and be involved, but training exercises can bore them to tears. Face it: To a 5-year-old, mud wrestling for two hours is more exciting than a 2-minute "Follow" lesson. Training exercises are just no fun, and the phrase "It's your responsibility to feed Roxy" has a negative spin. The good news is that your kids get involved when the routines are upbeat and creative.

Before you teach the kids how best to play and teach the puppy, buy or make treat cups (see Chapter 5) and fill them with a trail mix of some tasty treats or mealtime kibbles. If your kids are crafty, have them decorate the cups with markers or stickers. When that's taken care of, have them try out three quick kid–safe games they can play with the puppy:

>> **Multi-toy toss**. Perch a child (or two) on a kitchen counter or have the kids stand on the opposite side of the gate, with five or more of the puppy's favorite toys. Have the kids say "Wait" as they hold the toy in front of the puppy, but have them hold off tossing until the puppy is still. Urge a tossing phrase like "Go get your toy!" Don't worry about fetching at this point. When your puppy grabs the toy, have the kids pull out another and call the puppy over to start the process all over again.

>> **Run-run-stop.** Play this game with your kid or kids until your puppy shows good impulse control — not jumping or nipping, in other words. Begin by standing with your puppy and child in the free-play area or outdoors. Give your child the treat cup, have them shake it as they call the pup's name, and then have them run just five steps away from the puppy. After a short run the child turns and holds out their arm like a traffic cop, saying "Stop" in a strong voice. The moment your puppy stops and holds still they should drop a treat at their feet, saying "Find it!"

If the puppy jumps or nips, either place a freedom line on your puppy so that you can interfere by stepping on it or have the child cover their eyes with their hands (the peek-a-boo solution described in Chapter 15), or, if the puppy scares them, lift or place the child out of reach. (If your child is too young to manage this game on their own, recruit them as your special helper as you play it for them.)

>> **Hide-n-seek.** Give your kid (or kids) a treat cup and ask them to hide around the corner or a piece of furniture. Have them wait to shake the cup and then have them call their puppy the moment you say the child's name. When your child is out of sight, ask your puppy "Where's Sophie?"— at which point Sophie should call your puppy as she shakes the treat cup. If your puppy is confused, go with them to find the child. Start with easy finds before moving outside or attempting more challenging hides.

For more fun ideas, flip to Chapter 20.

Don't leave young children alone with a puppy: Both species are mastering impulse control and can hurt each other unintentionally.

When rowdy play ends the fun

If you have kids, I'm sure you've already faced reality: They're not always angels! Kids can run hot and cold: One minute they encourage play with their puppy, and the next they're shouting that the puppy is hurting them. Neither species is all that sensible, and you'll have to step in more often than not.

My favorite phrase, whether you're raising kids or puppies, is this: You're the one on the park bench; they're the ones on the rollercoaster. In other words, when either the kid or the puppy is getting wild, you need to remain calm. Yelling at either puppy or child will upset the balancing act between them even more.

Here are some quick phrases and kid-safe moves I use with families in my private practice. They get life back on course as quickly as their wacky energy spirals out of control. Bottom line? Though kids and puppies love to play, their interactions can become scary to kids when the puppy starts nipping in fun.

>> **Alligator Island:** Designate a countertop in your free-play zone as Alligator Island. Lift the kids onto the counter or tell them to hop up there for safety. After they're safe on the island, they should ignore the pup until they're calm or, if they want to continue playing, toss toys once the puppy stands or sits calmly on all four paws.

>> **See you later:** As long as your kid and puppy are still working out the rules of play, make sure there's an easy exit over the gate or out the door. Use a phrase like "Bye-bye" or "See you later" as you leave quickly anytime your puppy is jumping or nipping.

>> **Treat cup redirect:** Puppies as young as 8 weeks old can learn the connection between hearing the treat cup shake and getting a reward. Teach the kids to toss treats on the floor and say "Find it" instead of directly handing the puppy the treat. Place treat cups in strategic locations and teach kids to use them to redirect the puppy when they become rowdy.

REMEMBER

Treats tossed on the floor teach puppies to look down when they're anticipating a reward.

TIP

Set up situations that your pup can expect to encounter to teach them how to handle themselves — such as the kids' running frenzies, snack time, or floor-level gaming. Redirect your puppy's focus away from the kids, using techniques like the counter condition skills and desensitization techniques detailed in Chapter 15. If your puppy can't detach from the kids' fun, use a freedom line and a choice of compassion wear (see Chapter 5) so that choking their neck doesn't intensify their frenzy. With a leash and the right training techniques, you can remedy many everyday occurrences between kids and puppies — behavior like mouthing and nipping, food grabbing, and chasing. (Chapter 15 provides more details on training to overcome these and other daily hassles.)

Getting Help with Shaping Good Manners from Day One

A puppy's early learning takes place primarily through cause-and-effect. If they get any attention (good or bad) or a reward when they do X (X can be just about anything — sitting or jumping or playing with a toy or whining or pottying in the right place on the carpet), they'll do it again.

Because early lessons are the most significant, I've outlined crib notes in the hope of helping you motivate your family and friends' participation.

Following early steps for house-training

Your goal with house-training aligns with your puppy's impulse to leave their living space to go potty. Because your puppy needs to relieve themselves after eating or drinking, resting, playing, or enduring long bouts of isolation, take them to an assigned spot in either a private and papered corner of your home or outdoors 10 to 20 feet from the door. Set a route to the bathroom area, and use words and gestures to guide your puppy each time you escort them. The important thing is to develop a routine. Here's one I can recommend

1. **Take the puppy from the crate to the designated bathroom spot, saying "Go to the papers," or "Outside."**

2. **Wait to give the pup attention until they're pottying in the right place.**

3. **Say "Get busy" as they potty, either poop or pee.**

4. **Greet, play with, or walk the puppy after they're done.**

TIP

In preparation for the inevitable "accidents," set up cleaning stations in strategic places, equipped with paper towels and house-soiling spray.

Redirecting jumping

All puppies are enthusiastic about their relationships and naturally try to get "up close and personal" whenever it's time for a proper greeting. That means they instinctively want to jump up and engage in some face-to-face contact, just like Great-Aunt Ernestine used to do. If one of your human friends or relations is eager for a kiss, ask them to wait until your puppy is on all four paws before coming down to their level. Here are other tips and creative ways to elicit help in teaching your puppy the 4-paw rule.

» Teach your helpers that your puppy will repeat whatever gets the attention of the humans around them. Ask them to place their hands over their faces, as though they're playing peekaboo, and wait until the puppy settles on four paws to greet, pat, or play with them.

» Place treat cups around your home in strategic locations. Show family members how to shake the cup to encourage your puppy's attention, but ask them to withhold the treat until your puppy is standing calmly on all four paws.

» Put toy baskets around the house and by the front door. Encourage everyone to direct your puppy to "Get your toy" throughout the day and when people arrive or they're getting excited.

Instilling good chewing habits

Puppies, like kids, like to keep busy. Kids play with their hands, puppies with their mouths. If you don't have toys for the kids, they'll make do — with your things.

If you don't give puppies toys to chew on, they'll settle for whatever they can find. If you'd rather they chew on their toys and not on your running shoes, I recommend the following strategies:

» Place puppy baskets around the house at your puppy's level. Ask everyone to direct your puppy to the basket, by saying "Go get your bone!" Gather the toys and put them back when the puppy is done playing.

» Choose a few different words for different toys — like "toy," "ball," and "bone." Encourage everyone to name the object as they toss it. Soon your puppy will be able to identify up to five different toys.

» Ask everyone to direct or redirect your puppy to their toys if they seem bored or is grabbing at items that aren't theirs.

» Have a spray deterrents (like bitter apple) around the house to spray objects or furnishings that your puppy may show an interest in chewing. Remind everyone to spray the item, not the puppy.

Displaying mealtime manners

Designate a routine for family mealtimes and share it with everyone. A puppy can either go back in the crate with a tasty chew or settle in their comfort station. If needed, a family member or friend can sit on the leash to keep your puppy from wandering or getting into trouble.

REMEMBER

A puppy can't sit still if they have a pressing need. Make sure your puppy has been fed, has gone potty, and has grown tired before expecting them to chill while you eat.

Discouraging nipping

Nipping puppies are generally overstimulated, needy, or tired. Show everyone the Needs chart from Chapter 6 (Table 6-2) and encourage consistent words and routines. If your puppy is nipping, remind everyone to

» **Review the puppy's needs.** A lack of sleep creates mania, so make sure your puppy rests 4 to 6 hours every day in addition to 10 to 12 hours at night. Avoid pushing, shouting and discipling your puppy face to face, because your puppy will see your theatrics as confrontational play. Instead, review which need might be distracting them.

> » **Avoid prolonged or assertively staring at you puppy when you address them.** Either of these actions may be interpreted as confrontational play, making rowdy problems worse, not better. If the puppy cannot be redirected to a toy, stop touching them. To an excited young puppy, touch excites interactive play.

If your puppy is still nipping and acting wild with older pets or kids, have them drag an indoor freedom line or leash. Also, consider the compassion wear head collar. (Read about it in Chapter 5.) This compassion wear enables anyone to take calm control without startling or interveneing with the puppy physcially.

Any physical or verbal intervention with a young puppy is perceived as play — adding to the puppy's idea of fun, not helping to calm them down.

Enlisting Outside Help

I'm sure you've heard the phrase "It takes a village to raise a child." Well, the same holds true for a puppy. Take time to surround yourself with a happy clan of outside helpers, and be sure to keep their contact info close at hand because you'll lean on these people more than you think. This section gives you an idea of who needs to make up your clan.

A movement is afloat to change the way professionals handle and think about their beloved dogs (and cats). Known as the Fear Free Initiative, this progressive movement was founded and is organized by "America's veterinarian," Marty Becker, with the goal of promoting a force-free, respectful manner of treating and managing dogs and positively conditioning puppies. Although the initial focus was on revolutionizing modern veterinarian treatment and hospital design, the Fear Free Initiative has grown into a certification hub for other pet care professions, including groomers, daycare, and training facilities. Fear Free even educates and certifies dog loving homes! To find out more about Marty Becker's Fear Free Initiative, log on to https://fearfreepets.com.

Your veterinarian

Think of your dog's veterinarian as being on par with your doctor or your child's pediatrician. Medical knowledge is essential, but a good bedside manner is the cherry on top of the sundae. Speak with the receptionists and bring in your pup for a cheerful social call before their initial visit. Talk to the doctor like they're a neighbor. Do you feel comfortable sharing all your canine concerns with them?

If you're unsure of which veterinarian to use, ask around. You can narrow your search by asking your friends and family whom they use and why.

TIP

Puppies can be quite impulsive — they often swallow things that look edible before even considering whether they are. So, at your puppy's first veterinary visit, ask the doctor for a recommended method for inducing vomiting. You should also find out the poison-control hotline number and always keep it on your phone in case of an emergency. Seek out a 24-hour emergency veterinary hospital in your area as well. Keep the hospital's number by or on your phone. Accidents can happen during off hours, so have a plan.

Dog walker

REMEMBER

Whether your life demands consistent hours away from home or circumstance steps in to temporarily rearrange your schedule, knowing a dog walker can make the difference between a happy puppy and a stressed-out one. Puppies are like human babies in that they have a strong need dependency. Even though an adult dog can hold their bladder until you get home or can survive until a late meal, your puppy may well eat the walls of your house if you get stuck in traffic. A reliable dog walker can be a godsend in times like these.

Ask around and interview a couple of dog walkers before you need one. Planning ahead of time makes handling crises that much easier. When considering dog walkers, remember that reputation counts, as does your puppy's reaction, so be sure to ask for references and allow your puppy to consider the candidate. Tail-wagging and kisses are equivalent to double-thumbs-up.

WARNING

Because anyone can hang out a shingle and claim to be a dog walker, look for walkers who are insured and certified with a known dog-walking group. These days you can use popular online sites, like www.rover.com/ to find a dog walker — a site that can be especially useful when traveling with your pet. Get references, no matter who you choose!

Puppy trainer

Puppy training techniques vary considerably. More and more trainers are suggesting 100 percent positive reinforcement and are coaching their clients to address their puppies only when they are doing everything right. Sometimes that can feel impossible for us human, but you can't go wrong with this approach. I support positive reinforcement trainers wholeheartedly.

Over the years, I've developed my philosophy, which has a slightly different slant. My goal is to teach my clients how to live happily with their puppy by developing systems and routines that their puppy can both identify with, count-on, and enjoy. Instead of commanding a puppy to obey, I teach puppies to identify words much like I would teach a foreigner English as a second language. When a puppy recognizes words like Place, Come, and Get Your Toy, it's easy to help them manage their day. People training is a big part of my program too: I teach my human clients the importance of sitting or kneeling to pet or handle their puppy instead of bending over them, creating calming station for their puppy in the rooms they share, and playing with their puppy to strengthen their bond. Consistent rituals, like food sleep and potty rituals, can make all the difference in having a puppy who feels calm and one that is anxious and out of sorts. In my world, training is as much for the people as the puppy. At the end of the day, puppies need to learn where to go and what to do in a range of situations: "Sit" as a matter of saying please, "Come" to mean that you're standing together, and "Get your bone" and "Go to your place" as a way to offer comfort when your puppy is fretting or alone.

WARNING

Some trainers follow the traditional alpha-dog methods — ones that assert we have God-like authority over our dogs and that dogs should listen to us robotically or bear our fury — were used decades ago and popularized by some celebrity trainers. They use physical discipline and often bully their clients' puppies with threatening mannerisms and battery-operated shock or vibrating collars. I never encourage these methods. Although a puppy may stop a behavior—who wouldn't freeze if shocked or threatened by a virtual stranger? — their cooperation comes at too high a cost to their joy and well-being. Fearful puppies may behave because puppies, like kids, are easily intimidated, but the majority mature to become manic or defensive dogs. Please avoid trainers suggesting any of these techniques.

Ways to Get Help

Sometimes you just need a kind professional to sort out just how best to raise your puppy to be the dog you want them to be. Puppies are frustrating — I get that. They're like children in their curiosity, energy, and desire for adventure. Raising a puppy is hard work, but your efforts will be rewarded! This section covers ways to get help with your puppy if you need it. Select your professional carefully, by reviewing their credentials as selectively as you would for a child.

Group Training

A group training program is worth its weight in dog biscuits. Social time mixed with structure and training blend for an experience that's fun for everyone involved. Look for a program that targets the size and age of your puppy, welcomes families (if you have one you want to bring along), and one that limits enrollment to four to eight puppies. The teacher who is teaching the class is important, too — make sure you can talk with them should you have a specific question and that they are tuned in to your individual puppy. As I always say, there is something nice about every person and puppy I meet — find someone who likes you both! You're undergoing training as much or more than your puppy: You should look forward to class, too.

REMEMBER

Puppies are impulsive and excitable. Find a class whose teacher takes excitability in stride and teaches with rewards and encouragement — and who doesn't single out anyone's puppy as problematic or perfect. All puppies are who they are, and the goal of the school is to find the magic in each student.

Free play is the time during a kindergarten class when the puppies get to race about and get to know the other puppies and people in the classroom.

Private trainer

If your situation has grown dire or desperate or you have the impulse and funds to hire a private puppy trainer to help you raise your pup, finding a positive coach to guide you can make quite a difference.

I've been teaching dogs and people for over 30 years, and although I could quit to devote myself to writing, making media appearances, and speaking in public, I wouldn't dream of it. I *love* helping people and families understand and live happily with puppies!

I've seen dog training techniques change and evolve a lot over the years. Starting in 1986, I was one of only two professional dog trainers in Westchester County, New York, where I still live. Now there's a trainer in every neighborhood, and though just about anyone can get a "certification" online, no licensing or accrediting organization can help you identify a qualified professional.

So, where do you begin when searching for a dog training professional? And how can you tell whether the person you've hired is right for you and your dog? Start by imagining your puppy as a toddler standing in front of a grown-up who doesn't speak the same language. These large people are talking, gesturing, smiling, frowning, and maybe yelling — *whoa*. What do these people want me to do?

That's how your dog feels — like a fur-clad 2-year-old in a foreign land. A good dog trainer is like a nursery school teacher and a sympathetic translator rolled into one. Keep looking — you're sure to find someone who has devoted their life to helping other people learn how to communicate and teach their puppies effectively.

Dog training even has franchises — just like a McDonald's restaurant. Anyone with capital can invest and call themselves a dog trainer. Sure, most people get into dog training because they love dogs, but it takes more than just a savvy marketing plan to help people and dogs communicate effectively.

Digital puppy trainer

A great option for busy families and professionals is digital dog training. With the advent of real-time nanny cams, your puppy's behavior can be recorded, shared, and discussed without the trainer having to experience it firsthand. Generally, more cost-effective sessions can be organized online or over the phone that cover topics from how to choose the right dog or puppy to problem-solving and training issues.

The benefits are tremendous: I've been doing digital sessions globally with great success for years, offering fresh insight on a whole range of questions and frustrations. It's also a cost-effective and quick way for someone considering private help to test the waters. Before choosing a digital dog trainer, consider their reputation and certifications.

Groomer

Groomers have a tough job, so I give them a lot of credit. Many dogs backpedal before they even reach the door. Many growl when approached, and a few may even need to be muzzled. Grooming is often a thankless job. You can greatly shape your puppy's opinion of the groomer by exercising your puppy before bringing them in, keeping them combed between visits (to keep painful knots at bay), and introducing them to the groomer's handling techniques from early puppyhood.

When deciding on a groomer, review their qualifications and certifications. Visit each facility ahead of time and ask to see where the dogs are stationed while they're waiting their turn or drying. What vibes do you get from each place? Do the dogs who are already there seem happy or stressed? Is it clean and *almost* odor free? Would you want to get a haircut there if you were a dog?

Watch the groomer's handling techniques. Is the person empathetic — do they speak gently or harshly to your dog? Though a groomer may need to be firm with your dog to keep them still during the process, they shouldn't be cruel or abusive.

If the idea of wrangling your puppy into a groomer doesn't get your tail wagging, you should realize that some groomers will come to your home, either using your bathing facilities or arriving in a full-service grooming van. Some of my clients use this service and are happy with it. Consider what you and your dog would prefer.

Doggie daycare

I love the concept of daycare for your dog, especially if you work all day, but there are good daycare centers and poorly managed daycare centers. Pick yours wisely; visit ahead of time or watch a live feed online to determine how the day will go.

Do the dogs enjoy playing with one another? Are they supervised? Do you notice one dog picking on or frightening the other dogs (bullying, canine style)? All dogs should enjoy attending daycare — the last thing you want is for your dog to learn bad habits from other dogs.

TIP

Ask the staff the following questions:

>> How are the dogs and puppies grouped? Small dogs should not be intermingled with large ones. High-energy dogs should not be paired with older, quieter, or physically compromised dogs. Ask what type of dogs the facility would pair your puppy with.

>> What does the staff do when a dogfight breaks out?

>> Who is the veterinarian on staff? If the vet is offsite, where is the office located?

>> Does the pet center kennel overnight?

>> What contingency plans are in place if you're delayed and can't pick up your pet on time?

>> Does the pet center offer auxiliary services, such as grooming, training, medical care, or medicating, if need be?

Bear in mind that your puppy may be exhausted after their visit to daycare. If training, walking, and bonding are high on your priority list, plan these events for another day. Your puppy may be blissfully brain-dead when they get home.

WARNING

Puppies, like kids, pick up both good and bad habits from their friends. If you notice your puppy roughhousing or being uncharacteristically defiant, ask to meet the dogs they play with. If their playmates are rubbing off bad energy, you may consider asking whether your puppy can be placed in another group. Or, consider taking a break from daycare until your puppy is more mature, because an older puppy or dog is less likely to acquire bad habits.

Dog park

Dog parks are fine places for dogs and dog lovers, but wait until your puppy is at least 7 months old before joining in on the fun. Until reaching their adolescence, your puppy will be annoyingly persistent, and though most dogs recognize the smell and gestures of young puppies, some don't. The risk at a dog park is that your puppy will annoy an undersocialized-though-free-ranging dog or dogs to the point of distraction and get attacked by one or more of them. My opinion? It's way too risky to chance.

Before bringing your puberty-age puppy to a dog park, check the place out. Though each dog park is organized differently, a properly run park should have a list of rules — usually posted at the entrance — to ensure that everyone enjoys their time at the park.

Some days will be perfect — your dog will meet nice friends, you'll bond with the other pup parents, and your dog will sleep like a log when you get home. Other days, the bullies will be running the park, no one will laugh at your jokes, and your dog will throw up in the car. That's okay. Just leave. And always leave — right away — if any dog (maybe even yours) is being aggressive. Though it's rare, serious dogfights have erupted at dog parks.

TIP

Bring a supply of food rewards and favorite toys with you to the park. Offer one whenever your dog returns to you. Your dog may be well behaved at home, but the freedom and fun of a dog park will test their listening skills.

TIP

Most parks have poop bags and water available, but it's always wise to bring your own supply.

Living in a Neighborhood

"It's a beautiful day in the neighborhood . . ." until, of course, you hear the constant serenade of a barking dog. I love my neighborhood dearly, but one quiet summer day, my neighbors left for the beach and tied their 8-month-old beagle (bless her little soul) out in the yard. That day, I swore I'd move to Barbados. However, the annoying barking was pitiful — poor Betsy the beagle was lonely, frantic for her family's return. I went over after 3 hours to console her and found that her water dish was empty. I gave her a fresh bowl and a chew bone, which kept her busy the rest of the afternoon.

There's a lot to keep in mind when trying to be a good dog neighbor, and fortunately, this section can help. If you're new to puppyhood, it helps to know the basics: Fortunately, it isn't too tricky. Here are the top five rules to being a good puppy neighbor:

>> **Scoop the poop.** Make a habit of cleaning up your puppy's elimination the moment they go to the bathroom. Aside from the obvious sanitation element, when your puppy is praised and sees you picking up their mess in the right location, they're more likely to go there again.

>> **Select the pooping place.** Teach your puppy to potty near your front door whether you live in an apartment, flat, or house. Though it's tempting to want to walk your puppy as far from your home as possible, you wouldn't potty-train a kid by sending them to the neighbors' bathroom, right? Because dogs mark their boundaries (also known as their *territory*), make sure your puppy learns where their property begins and ends. If you let them potty around the 'hood, as they mature they may become more reactive or excitable on leash as puppies identify their territory by scent marking. If your puppy is the reactive type, they'll likely be more reactive in the house as well, alerting when others pass your window.

>> **Be mindful of barking.** Waking up to a barking dog or puppy is no fun. Avoid letting your puppy out before 7 a.m. and after 9 p.m., or talk to your neighbor if you're worried that the barking might be bothering their peace of mind.

REMEMBER

Barking puppies are not happy puppies. If yours is barking uncontrollably, consider their state: Could chewing a bone, engaging in some interactive play, or experiencing the pleasure of your company calm their worries?

>> **Condition your puppy to everyday noises.** Most puppies alert to unfamiliar sights and sounds by barking, either in alarm or as a defense mechanism. Barking can develop into a bothersome routine if you don't get a quick, calm, and steady handle on it; see Chapter 15 for tips. Do your part in puppyhood to limit the startle reactions in your puppy by conditioning them to everyday noises — ranging from visits from delivery people to sounds just beyond the wall to neighbors passing by the front window. To do this, simply place treat cups in strategic locations so that when you hear a familiar noise or either you see or the puppy sees something beyond reach, you can quickly grasp the cup, shake it, and redirect your puppy to a chew toy or fun activity. Remember to move back and away from the center of the distraction. For more help on this issue, flip ahead to Chapter 15 and read up on curbing the barking habit.

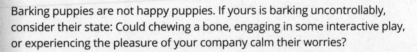
TIP

When leaving your puppy, put on some gentle music to drown out incoming sounds, dim the lights and close the blinds to block activity, and leave them with a satisfying chew toy.

If you leave your puppy outdoors, provide them with access to a shaded area and plenty of fresh water. If you're expecting inclement weather, don't leave your puppy alone outside. Go with them to their potty area and bring them directly back inside after they're done.

WARNING

If your puppy suffers from separation anxiety, they will suffer more if crated. Flip to that section in Chapter 16 for more tips on helping them cope when left alone.

Until your puppy is 5 or 6 months old, use a freedom line to play with them in your yard or an open park: Young puppies react strongly to being pulled or held in one place, and forcing them to remain tethered to you can cause fear and, later, explosive leash reactivity. As your puppy is maturing, you may begin to walk them around the neighborhood, but make every effort to teach them considerate walking skills.

Start by selecting a piece of compassion wear (either a front clip or head harness) to begin with, rather than affix your puppy to a neck collar and take them on a drag.

Take five to seven short walks (no more than 5 minutes apiece) inside your home, teaching your puppy their first walking words: Follow-Wait-Find-It.

>> **Follow**: This word directs your puppy to follow your lead! Project your voice in the direction you want your puppy to follow and stop every few steps initially (gradually lengthening the steps you take) to stop your puppy as directed below.

>> **Wait:** This word teaches your puppy to stop, look, and listen to you. To teach it, stop suddenly, and quickly direct your puppy to Find It as outlined below. If your puppy doesn't stay with you, hold a treat to their nose to get their attention, then say "wait" as you more gradually bring your pace to a halt.

>> **Find It:** As you come to a stop bring a treat to the floor by the side of your left shoe. As you do, say "Find it!" As your puppy gets the rhythm of the sequence lesson, you may drop the treat by your foot, so you eliminate the posture of bending down to get their attention.

Practice Follow-Wait-Find-It outside, first in short practice walks around the yard, and then on short walks, and then progress to longer excursions. If your puppy seems unsure of a sight or distraction, veer away from it rather than soothe your puppy (which would only reinforce their fear), and then play Find It and jolly them along. For more tips on walking, flip to an age-appropriate chapter in Part 3.

REMEMBER

Never approach a dog you don't know. Though the puppy parent may insist that the dog is friendly, you just don't know how the dog will react to a stranger. If you meet someone who is walking a friendly-looking puppy of a similar age, first ask whether you can approach to say hi. Respect the parent's decision whatever it is and don't take offense: The puppy may be sick or the person preoccupied or in a hurry.

WARNING

Teach walking skills on a 6-foot leash. Avoid using a retractable leash until you and your puppy have the hang of walking together. Never use retractable leashes near roadways or crowds — too dangerous.

situations

» Introducing your puppy to strangers, wild animals, noises, and interesting objects

» Handling life's many changes

» Taking your puppy into the world beyond your front door

Chapter 9

Socializing Puppy

Your puppy is born to be social — that's the good news. If introduced to people and places during their socialization period, they'll grow into a dog who can handle just about anything. Even though some of your early excursions may be restricted until your puppy is fully inoculated, make every effort to expose your puppy to a variety of situations and people so that they'll be more comfortable with situations new and unknown throughout their life. You can invite people into your home (asking them to remove their shoes and wash their hands) or take your puppy out in a carrying case or crate to get a handle on all the sights and sounds they'll experience in their lifetime.

The not-so-good news is this: If you miss this early window — this golden opportunity to get your puppy out in the world when they're young (before four months is ideal) — you could be sentencing your puppy to a lifetime of unknowns if you don't get a move on quickly. Older puppies who haven't been socialized to take unfamiliar sounds and people in stride often go into a metaphoric tailspin and become dogs who are wary or defensive of new experiences for the rest of their lives. Being a scaredy-cat is no life for a dog, so devote the time early on (or hire a professional to do it for you) to get your pup acclimated to everything they will encounter throughout their life, from objects and people to noises and other animals.

All puppies need someone to look up to: Like kids, they're eaily intimidated when they're little. Though they idolize their birth mama, that attachment will transfer to you, and just like that, your puppy will be watching your interpretation of new people and experiences for guidance on how to react. This is the ideal bonding experience if you cop a been-there-done-that attitude. Stay calm, be confident (even if you have to pretend), and use lots of rewards to help your puppy see that life is nothing to fret over.

If your puppy is older than 16 weeks, don't despair. Even though they have passed their ideal impression window, they're still open to your example when they get overwhelmed or excited. A noticeably defensive or wary reaction simply indicates that your puppy has no conscious memory of such an occurrence and isn't sure how to act. In these circumstances, your reactions to both the situation and the puppy are important.

Wondering how to handle your puppy during this formative time? This chapter is here to help.

JUST FOR
FUN

My favorite puppy quote is, to paraphrase Frederick Douglas, "It's easier to build strong puppies than to repair broken dogs."

Recognizing the Critical Stages of Your Puppy's Social Calendar

Socializing your puppy to all of life's surprises is just as important as training them during the first year. Though they may behave perfectly in your living room, if they fall to pieces when you hit the road, you won't be able to take them anywhere. And your puppy has so much more in store for them than the usual distractions and people in your backyard. Exposing your puppy to different animals, weather situations, objects, noises, and places will encourage them to accept anything new throughout their life.

Puppies, like children, go through developmental stages, and each stage brings with it a new perspective. In the earliest stages, everything is new, and your puppy's trust in you is innocent and faithful. This is the ideal time to get started. As long as you don't react to a new stimulation, your puppy won't, either — they'll get conditioned to new noises, sights, and people, often without pause or hesitation.

As your puppy grows up, they'll become less inhibited about how to act and will need persuading to stay focused on you. (Think food and fun here.) Here's a list of puppyhood developmental stages; socialization ideally starts in the first days and weeks they're born.

Birth to seven weeks

The first seven weeks of a puppy's life are tremendously important. Think of it as their earliest impression period. Sure, they're born blind and deaf (puppies' eyes and ears open within four weeks of age) and can't even potty without their mother's stimulation, but at least their body is aware of temperature and motion. Devoted breeders start stimulating their puppies with a gentle touch from day one to prepare their pups for their eventual lives with people.

After five weeks of containment, puppies explode into their first socialization period and learn from their mother and littermates what most kids pick up in kindergarten: In doggie terms, they learn about biting gently (what the pros call *bite inhibition*), respecting authority, and playing with an object to self-soothe. Unless you love a challenge (and I do mean a *challenge*), only adopt a puppy who has spent seven to eight weeks with their mother and littermates.

Seven weeks to 16 weeks

Seven to 16 weeks is the period when your puppy's brain grows, also called the *critical socialization* period, and for a good reason: Your puppy is creating mental pathways, learning routines, and developing habits that can last a lifetime; this is also the stage when your puppy will encode all the sights and sounds they will experience in their lifetime. That's good if you expose them to lots of stuff, but not so good if you're busy or you lose track of these most important weeks for your puppy. I'll go over just how to socialize your puppy and tweak your response for different reactions (hyper, fearful, or defensive) later in this chapter, but suffice it to say that if you have a puppy, the time to start exposing them to just about everything is *now*.

WARNING

Beware of the fear-impression periods, which last about two to three weeks. During this time, a puppy becomes easily startled by unfamiliar noises, sights, or overly reactive people. If your puppy has a dramatic reaction (runs back, drops their tail, or freezes), do one of three things:

» Remove or lift your puppy if the situation is truly dangerous (when a dog is threatening them, for example).

» Calmly allow your puppy to sit under your legs or stand behind you as you or a helper explore the situation with a dose of healthy curiosity.

» Just stay calm (during a thunderstorm, for example).

The idea here is that you should be the one modeling confidence, so be confident.

Sixteen weeks to six months

The sixteen weeks to six months stage happens during the body's rapid growth period. Though your puppy is far less impressionable than when they were younger, you nevertheless still have time to pack in some socialization outings to ensure that they can comfortably contend with all the unknowns of this world. Puppies older than 16 weeks become purposeful and confident and may look at times like they've never even heard a human speak, even if training was started early. Adolescents are never pretty, no matter the species. At this stage, they start losing their puppy teeth and begin expanding like they're on growth hormones — hence the term "growing phase."

Six months to one year

A puppy who is past the critical socialization window of six months, may have a more pronounced reaction to new situations, especially if they have no similar experience in their memory bank. But all is not lost: Studies show that puppies can learn new things after their prime socialization period, though it takes more exposure and practice. For example, an older puppy who hasn't navigated a staircase or hardwood floor may be terrified at the prospect. How you handle such a situation determines their future attitude. Help is just pages away.

Maturity

As far as socialization goes, maturity is like a funnel: It's right side up until about four or months old, at which time it inverts. Though an upside-down funnel can still be conditioned to new experiences, it takes more time and exposure.

TIP

Physical maturity happens at different rates for different dogs. Smaller dogs have it all wrapped up by about a year; larger dogs can take as long as two years. Emotional maturity happens around age 3.

Focusing on Your Puppy

New experiences are always stressful, no matter what the species; I'm sure you can relate. As you socialize your puppy, a good way to tell if a specific social experience (like seeing a vacuum, walking near roadways or meeting the postman for the first time) is overwhelming for your puppy is to notice when they stop engaging with you or taking treats. If they stop either activity for more than three seconds, you're too close to the distraction: this is what I call being in their red zone. When this is the case, double the separation between you and the distraction until you find that sweet spot where your puppy can experience new people or distractions and yet still play or eat: Mark that as a starting point with any new distraction that startles your puppy. Gradually move closer to it until your puppy is fully conditioned to being around it. And how will you know? Your puppy will eat and play with you!

As you're socializing to stuff, whether at home (also known as the *den*) or in the yard (also known as the puppy's *territory*) or the world beyond, your puppy may suddenly go from eating or playing with you happily to freezing in fear or alert. This reaction is what I call a *first-time fear*. It's normal. Each of these reactions is an opportunity to condition your puppy to the situation, as suggested in the pages ahead.

TIP

Though you may have to wait until your puppy is inoculated to go on field trips — flip to Chapter 19 for a typical inoculation schedule — you can still bring the world to your doorstep by asking family and friends to help you condition your puppy to different people and everyday distractions.

Even if your puppy is too young to walk in town, you can carry them with you in a sling or carrying bag. It's all part of safely socializing them to the hustle and bustle of your block or town. Help your puppy view an outing as a positive event by creating a cozy nest in their carrying case and rewarding them with favorite chews and treats. Excursions should last no more than 10 to 20 minutes, depending on your puppy's comfort level — and less time if they're stressed. Then when your veterinarian gives you the green light to socialize on the leash, you'll be ready to go, go, go!

TIP

From the moment your puppy comes home, they'll be socializing to life as you know it. Enlist a helper to do things like open an umbrella, drop a pot, run the mixer or vacuum as you sit on the floor, feeding and playing with your puppy. Most puppies startle to unfamiliar sounds, but if you act like they're nothing, your puppy will condition to the distraction almost immediately. Keep in mind that, as long as they start to recover within three seconds, you're fine; if it takes longer than that, repeat the distraction but at twice the distance from you and the pup.

Your puppy's personality

Puppies are as unique as snowflakes and, like children, are born with distinctive personalities. Knowing your puppy's type helps you to support their reactions so that you can better teach them how to cope with whatever life throws their way.

Can you identify your puppy's type from the options in the following list? If you're unsure how to read your puppy's body cues, flip to Chapter 6 for guidance.

>> **Active:** This interactive, gregarious puppy meets life with unyielding enthusiasm. You can bet that this puppy, celebrating every new possibility, will always meet the world head-on.

>> **Cautious:** This puppy hesitates before approaching anything unfamiliar. They may freeze, race behind your legs (or try to climb up them), or try another way to escape the situation.

>> **Defensive:** A defensive pup is wary of new situations and people, staring, analyzing, and often avoiding new people and situations. As they mature, they often vocalize a warning or throaty growl, and may approach (and then quickly back away from) whatever's triggering the reaction.

>> **Calm:** This type of pup reacts calmly and is patiently observant and has a relaxed body posture and mild-to-friendly curiosity level.

Puppies, like people, show clear signs of stress that are easy to read once you know what to look for: If your puppy stares, vocalizes (barks or growls), lunges, or jumps at the distraction, they're beyond coping. The pros would say that a puppy doing any of these things was being triggered. Help is just a page or two away.

TIP

Regardless of their age, your puppy's ability to stay calm and remember their manners around people will be determined by your responses to their behavior, their experiences, and their breed influences. Even a protective breed can be a model citizen if introduced to lots of people in lots of different places. On the flip side, a cautious puppy, if pressed to cope with unfamiliar situations too quickly, will become reactionary (in fear) and may develop an aggressive streak as they mature.

Setting your socialization goals

Is your goal to have a calm, well-mannered dog? If so, remember that the best lessons in life will come from *you* and are learned at home. When introducing or greeting your puppy, only acknowledge them or let them out of an enclosure if they're on all four paws and calm enough to stand still or sit for attention. When socializing them to other places, animals, or things, only approach when they have settled down enough to listen to you and are able to model your easygoing, been-there-done-that attitude.

Though I'll address just how to socialize your puppy in the next section, use the check-off chart in Table 9-1 to course the socialization schedule.

TABLE 9-1:   Keeping Track of Your Pup's Progress

Distraction	Calm Reaction	Excitable Response	Cautious Reaction	Fearful Response	My Response
People					
Weather events					
Loud noises					
People (male)					
People (female)					
Uniforms					
Children					
Babies					
Farm/wildlife					
Other dogs					
Cats					
Strange objects					
Unfamiliar footing (tile, ice, grates, decks)					

TIP

One of the all-time great dog training people is Dr. Ian Dunbar. As a veterinarian, he has devoted his life to promoting the value of off-leash puppy classes and personality socialization reform. He suggests that puppies be introduced to 100 new people in the first three months of life, stating that, if you can't go out, have puppy parties and invite a variety of people.

Choosing your words wisely

As you introduce your puppy to an array of new experiences, each person, place, and thing will have a unique look and smell. At first, your puppy, like most, may hesitate or overreact when experiencing something unpredicted or strange. Like a stressed child, your pup's unsure how to act and needs your directions so that they don't mature into a dog that reacts fearfully time and again to specific people, places, or sounds.

Before you head out with your puppy on a walk arround the neighborhood, practice the words in the list below in a quiet area of your home before using them around distractions. (For help with leash training, flip to the age–specific training tips in Chapters 10 through 13.):

>> **Find It:** Toss treats on the floor at your feet and play the Find It game detailed in Chapter 20. Your puppy will learn this game fast. When socializing your puppy to new things, use savory treats to entice their interest.

>> **Say Hello:** This cue will calm all greeting interactions. Because puppies view face-to-face greetings as invitations to play rough or act just plain confrontational, teach your puppy a new greeting style called the *welcoming curve.* As you say the cue word *hello,* lure your puppy to stand sideways instead of straight into you. Now pet them shoulder to tail instead on top of their head. Use "Say hello" as you greet admirers and see how your puppy adjusts their posture (instead of jumping) to ease the moment.

>> **Under:** Puppies like to crawl under things: It helps them feel secure. Direct your puppy under your legs as you sit on a couch or chair. If you can't find anything to sit on, crouch down and let your puppy curve in the crook of your legs.

>> Back: When something or someone startles your puppy, they will often run behind you. Let them. Rather than console them, courageously face the distraction; reward your puppy for following your lead. If your puppy freezes or reacts instead of turning to you for assurance, teach "back" at home. Lure your puppy behind your body as you say "back," rewarding them the moment they sit comfortably behind your heel.

WARNING

Do not force a cautious puppy to face their fear by lifting or pushing them toward something they have moved away from. Explore or greet the person yourself, and then reward your puppy for coming forward on their own.

>> **Follow-Wait-Find It:** These walking words teach your puppy to focus on you in unfamiliar places. Teach this medley in a quiet room at home, reviewing the lesson in Chapter 11 before practicing on a leash. "Follow" instructs your puppy to walk with you, "wait" to stop, and "find it" to come back to your side to discover a treat placed carefully by your left foot. More on this move in Chapter 11!

>> **To Your Place:** Bring a mat or blanket from home when socializing your puppy to new places. As detailed in Chapter 5, all puppies identify with calming stations — take your pup's mat to help them feel secure no matter where you go.

As you're exposing your puppy to new situations and surroundings, take note of their body posture. (See Chapter 6.) If they're reacting with extreme fear, excitement, or aggression, you're too close to the distraction. Increase the distance until your puppy can relax. Slowly move closer as you condition them to focus on you no matter what's going on.

Many of the useful techniques described in this book, such as teaching your dog to lay under a table or your legs, as well as all the sequence lessons, are shown on my website, www.sarahsayspets.com,. Check it out.

Remembering the three T's: Tips, tools, and techniques

Most young puppies under 12 weeks old will look to your reaction in all-new situations. If you're nervous, they'll pick up on that. If you get excited, uncomfortable, or edgy, they'll likely follow suit. Expose your puppy to new experiences under controlled circumstances so that you'll be centered and prepared to set the right example and deal with your puppy's reaction. Here's a list of tools, tips, and techniques to help you with all your socializing adventures:

» **Treat cups:** Condition your puppy to the sound of a treat cup. Purchase or create a treat cup as described in Chapter 5, and then shake it and reward them until they make a connection between the sound and the snack. Play games with the treat cup, including the run-run-stop game described in Chapter 7, and the sit-to-say-please game, where you teach your puppy to sit before offering a reward. once they learn to sit hearing the cup shake, offer the cup to visitors and admirers.

» **Compassion wear:** When socializing with your puppy, avoid restraining neckwear and back-clip harnesses that may stress them by making them feel trapped. Though you definitely need to leash your puppy near traffic and populated areas, if your puppy is a puller (and most are), consider a head collar or front-clip harness (also known as *compassion wear* and detailed in Chapter 5). Both eliminate your puppy's ability to pull against the leash as you guide them through unfamiliar situations.

» **Leash:** Condition your puppy to a light leash or freedom line, and keep these items on them when they're meeting new people. Leash control should feel similar to holding a child's hand rather than holding on for dear life. if it doesn't feel that way, follow the steps in Chapter 10 or consider finding a professional to give you some tips.

» **Toy basket:** Place toy baskets filled with three to five toys and bones near doors, enclosures, and played areas. Tell your puppy to "get your toy" as you walk to the basket and play with them. Now include the toys in your greeting ritual and ask anyone coming through the door to do the same. It's best to start with family and work your way up to delivery people or strangers.

» **Comfort station:** Create a comfort station in each room where you spend time or entertain others with comfortable bedding and chews. Whenever possible, bring the bedding with you when socializing, traveling, or taking your puppy to the doctor. It's their security blanket.

>> **Targeting signal:** Teach your puppy a targeting cue as described in Chapter 5, using either your hand or, if your puppy is cautious, an extendable target like a soup spoon or store-bought targeting bop. When you teach it as a fun game, you can use the target to direct your puppy to new objects or unfamiliar people.

>> **Target disc:** These discs, as described in Chapter 5, can also be used to settle your puppy when you're away from home. By teaching your puppy to stand in a specific location on a specific disc their focus will shift from the environment to concentrating on the task at hand!

Socializing Your Puppy, No Matter Their Age or Experiences

Yes, it's easier to socialize a young puppy when they're still unfamiliar with life and will naturally look to you for a clue on how to act. This can be a tremendously fun, adventurous, and explosive learning stage for both you and your puppy.

Does this mean you should just throw in the towel if you've adopted an older puppy or are reading this book after missing this window? Heavens, no. You'll still have a lot of influence over your puppy's interpretation of the situation, though less than if they were just a baby. For example, an older puppy who hasn't navigated a staircase or hardwood floor may be terrified at the prospect. How you handle such a situation determines their future attitude. If a situation is avoided (rather than dealt with as I suggest), a puppy will mature into a dog who is permanently leery of stairs or whatever the phobia is throughout their lives. You don't want that.

No matter their age, take notice of your puppy's reaction to new experiences: Watch their ears, eyes, tail, and posture and note their reaction. Using the descriptions found in Chapter 6, see if you can determine whether your puppy is excitable, cautious, or defensive. The next few sections spell out how you should deal with each puppy type.

Settling your excitable puppy

Excitable puppies have little fear and want to explore everything and meet everyone. Your goal is to successfully help them learn to redirect their excitement. Here are three techniques to deal with their enthusiasm:

>> **Redirect their attention.** Try using a toy, a special savory chew, or a treat cup.

>> **Limit their upward mobility.** Without applying any pressure, place your thumb under their chin and gently loop it over their collar with your fingers pointing straight down between their front legs; what I call the *thumb brace*. (See Figure 9-1.) Scratch their chest, and reward and pet them for staying on all four paws.

>> **Help them adopt an alternative greeting style:** They might grab a toy and dash around like mad or flip over on their back for a belly rub, also known as "belly up!"

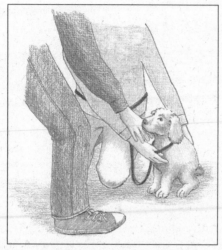

FIGURE 9-1:
Gently brace your puppy if they're jumpy when greeting people.

REMEMBER

All puppies repeat behavior that wins them attention — they don't care whether the interaction is negative or positive. As even a glance or light touch may be all that's needed to guarantee a repeat performance, avoid pushing or verbal admonishments. Give your reactionary puppy an example of calm in every situation — your future depends on it.

Coping with a fearful reaction

A fearful puppy needs a guardian and protector to step up and direct them: Here's your curtain call. Avoid the temptation to bend and soothe your puppy, because they may consider your reaction as modeling their behavior. Instead, adopt a been-there-done-that attitude, acting courageous and calm. Approach whatever distraction has rattled your puppy and — when possible — pretend to sniff it curiously. As your puppy overcomes their initial reaction, use treats to reward their baby steps. Continue to expose them to whatever the new distraction is for three to five minutes each day until they absorb the distraction as blasé.

WARNING

Commit now to socializing the paws off a fearful-type puppy. However, remember that it may take many outings to mellow their caution to the point that they'll become more pleasant to have around.

Don't lift your puppy or coddle them if they have a fearful reaction. Your lowered body posture and high-pitched tone convey the message that you're afraid, too. Let your puppy move out of the situation that's overwhelming them, and then kneel and pet them with full strokes. Breathe deeply and stay calm: Your composure will be reassuring.

WEATHER EVENTS AND SOUNDS IN THE NIGHT

Your puppy's first thunderstorm or fireworks celebration may be a memorable event. The best thing you can do is act like it's nothing — petting or soothing when your puppy is in a state of panic may model their fear, creating a panic reaction instead of what may initially have been just a normal caution response. Rather than model fear by crouching low, talking in a voice that sounds more like whining than confident reassurance, and staring at them in intense concern (your puppy may startle to being stared at this time), stay calm, use familiar directions, and keep your puppy with you. Here's a helpful list of things to do when your puppy is unsettled by life's unavoidable events:

- **Use a leash in tandem with compassion wear.** If your puppy has already developed a fearful reaction to storms, use a leash affixed to your choice of compassion wear (see Chapter 5) to guide them through each episode rather than let them hide or run about in a state of panic.

- **Set a good example.** Put on soothing music and stay calm as you read or relax as if nothing is happening. If your puppy will eat, chew, or play with you, that's a good sign: Offer them the opportunity.

  By staying calm and just reading a book or doing another low-key activity, you're setting an example of how to act in a storm.

- **Use a sound recording.** If a specific sound is unsettling to your puppy, record it or see whether you can find a sound machine that has the sound prerecorded. Play it at gradually increasing volumes while your puppy is playing or eating. If they are still startled by the noise, lower the volume and play it in a distant room.

  If your puppy's reactions don't improve, speak to your veterinarian about medication.

Any attention given to a puppy reinforces their reaction, which is fine *if and only if* your puppy is calm. Other responses need redirection. Read on to find out how.

Chilling out a defensive reaction

A defensive puppy takes life a little too seriously. Socializing them is necessary to calm their intensity. Teach your puppy the terms Back and Under, as encouraged earlier in this chapter, to mean "stay behind me" and "follow my example." Look to the coming age-appropriate training chapters to work on Find It and other treat-cup games, as well as the directions To Your Place, Bone, Stay, and Follow. Over time, your pup's resolve will melt.

WARNING

If your puppy displays an early defensive reaction (before they're 14 weeks old), take it seriously. If the tips in this book don't lessen your puppy's intensity, hire a professional. The onset of adolescence, with the release of adult hormones, will intensify any aggression that's at the root of their defensive reactions, so you need to deal with this behavior immediately.

Adapting to Life Changes

Change is a part of life. Even though many changes are for the best, all changes are stressful — and not just for humans. Puppies experience stress, too. The difference between their tension and ours is how they display it. Sure, I may pack on some extra pounds when I'm feeling anxious, but I don't destroy the couch; your puppy may, though. And if you discipline an anxious pup, they'll become more stressed and destroy other items — perhaps your rug or the bed. Is this a sign of spite? No, never: puppies live in the moment and in moment's like these your puppy is just confused and worried, and they need your help to adjust. Other signs of stress are aggression, barking, hyperactivity, and extreme withdrawal. In this section, I advise you on how to ease your puppy's stress when facing a move, when your household is coping with a death, or when adding a new family member to the home.

Moving to a new home

Moving is one of life's most stressful changes. First, the financial decisions may bring about more theatrical conversations than you have on an average day. Then you have the packing, shipping, and traveling back and forth. When the big day finally arrives, you've reached a new peak of exhaustion. If you have to move, my heart aches for you, but it bleeds for your developing puppy. Chaos often sends their routine into a tailspin. During this change, you may notice your puppy resorting to early puppy behavior: They may become hyper, demand attention, nip, jump, or chew. Forgive them and vow to help them cope.

Try to include your puppy in your preparations, giving them bones to chew while you're busy boxing up your life. If you're traveling to your new home, bring familiar objects such as dog beds, bones, and toys to make them feel connected to your new home before you move in. Also, use familiar words, schedules, and routines from day one. If you keep your day-to-day habits the same, your puppy will adapt in no time.

REMEMBER

The first time you leave your puppy in your new home, they may stress out, resulting in destructive chewing or excessive barking. Confine your puppy in a small room or familiar pen or crate with your old shirts and a favorite chew toy; dim the lights and leave on comforting, familiar music. Don't discipline your puppy if they demolish something. Your corrections only increase anxiety. If you return home to scenes of destruction, ignore them and clean up the area later when your puppy is occupied.

WARNING

Don't let your puppy off-leash in your new yard unless it's fenced in; they'll be disoriented for a few weeks and may get lost if they wander off. Instead, let them explore their new surroundings on a reactable leash or freedom line, provided you're a safe distance from all roadways. As your puppy appears more comfortable in their new surroundings, introduce fun games as outlined in Chapter 20.

REMEMBERING YOUR PUPPY'S NEEDS DURING LIFE CHANGES

Whether family or friends call on you unexpectedly or your life takes an unexpected turn, your daily demands as a puppy parent will continue. Here are some tips that can help you and your pup through this confusing time:

- **Buy new chew toys.** Buy lots of them — chewing is a self-soothing exercise for your puppy.

- **Enlist the help of friends or neighbors.** Have volunteers come and walk the puppy in the morning and afternoon when you're unable to do so.

- **Set an alarm.** Set an alarm on your phone to alert you at mealtimes so that you don't forget.

- **Set aside some daily bonding time.** Take a break five to ten minutes a couple of times per day for bonding, some playful training, a hike, or even just a snuggle. Keep saying the words your puppy may already know, like *sit, stay,* and *come* so that they don't get rusty.

And baby makes three: Expanding your family

Whether you're giving birth or adopting a child, your puppy will notice the shifting dynamic when someone new comes to live with them. All family additions generally add up to less attention for a puppy. With some forethought and cooperation, you can reverse the inevitable and show your puppy that this new addition is a plus for everyone.

Preparing your pup for the new arrival

REMEMBER

A new baby in the house can be one of the coolest changes of a lifetime — for people, that is. Puppies, on the other hand, can get the short end of the stick. Less attention, weird smells, and less exercise often result in puppies acting out from restlessness or a lack of structure. To ensure that your 4-legged pal doesn't feel left out, start planning for the new arrival.

Imagine the baby has moved in. They're a cute little creature who's just weeks old. Your parenting instincts are in full throttle. Now enters your beloved puppy. Are they used to lounging on the furniture or jumping up for attention? Do they order you to give them a back rub by pawing, barking, or nudging you? Can you see the problem that's developing there? They won't stop this behavior just because you're holding a newborn. If you shout at them or isolate them suddenly, they may grow leery and jealous of your new fancy. Fortunately, you can take a few steps ahead of time to ensure that nobody gets left in the doghouse:

>> **As early as possible, socialize your puppy with small children.** Use treat cups as described in Chapter 5 to help your puppy associate kids with fun and food. Toss treats down, saying "Find it" as you cast them to the floor; this helps to ensure that your puppy stays focused on your hands and looks down instead of up when kids are around. Stay calm while the kiddies visit, but keep your dog on a leash if you're uneasy. Dogs are telepathic, so any nervous emotions come across loud and clear.

>> **Take your puppy to a playground.** Keep your puppy on a 6-foot lead and play Find It games as you socialize them to the sound and activity of children. If your puppy is relaxed and calm when admirers approach you, offer them an open treat container and ask them to toss the treat down as though they were feeding chickens. If you're puppy jumps uncontrollably, try using the *thumb brace* technique mentioned early in the chapter or flip to Chapter 15 for other tips on settling down an excited puppy or building confidence in a fearful one to ensure that your puppy doesn't stare at or jump on anyone. Retreat if your pup is cautious or defensive. (See Chapter 6 for descriptions and illustrations of the kinds of body language you should look out for when it comes to fearful or defensive pups.)

WARNING

If your puppy shows any signs of aggression, call a professional. Your reaction can make the problem worse. Petting or soothing reinforces the behavior, and disciplining make your puppy feel more threatened.

» **Walk through your daily routine with a smelly stuffed doll.** If you know someone with a baby, ask to borrow a blanket to accustom your puppy to the smell. Wrap a baby doll in the blanket, allowing your puppy to sniff its feet as you say *gentle.* When changing your baby (both the doll and the real thing), practice the directions Wait, Go to Your Place, and Stay. See Chapter 11 for more on teaching your puppy these words.

» **Set new-furniture rules.** I think it best not to keep your puppy on the furniture around a new baby, but if you wait to spring this rule on your pup after the baby's home, the puppy may feel confused or anxious. Keep a short freedom line on your puppy, and if they hop on the furniture, gently guide them off, reminding them to Go to Your Place. Remember that shouting or shoving them off is interactive and suggestive of a game.

» **Help your puppy get used to all the new equipment.** With baby comes a lot of new stuff — big stuff like strollers and rockers and loungers as well as little enticing chewables, like pacifiers and rattles. Bring all these items in well before your baby arrives; then use Find It to positively familiarize your puppy with each one, and Leave It (as taught in Chapter 11) to distinguish between what belongs to your puppy and what doesn't.

» **Establish an exercise schedule for your puppy.** Make one that is realistic with your new responsibilities. Mornings may be rough, so help your puppy look forward to afternoon romps instead.

» **Establish a comfort station (see Chapter 5).** Place it in or just outside your baby's room and get your pup accustomed to settling there. Teach them Go to Your Place as described in Chapter 11; if they're properly leash trained, you can secure them on a 3-foot tether with a chewing toy if they seem restless.

» **Watch your words.** If the phrases you use for baby and dog are too similar, your pup may get hyped up at the wrong time or be utterly confused. ("Why are you looking at the newbie instead of me!") Change phrases like "What a good girl!" to "What a great puppy!"

» **Help your puppy get used to being ignored sometimes.** Yes, I want you to ignore your puppy completely. You can break it up into two 30-minute or three 20-minute segments, but get your puppy accustomed to life without your doting. If your puppy can get your attention wherever and whenever he wants it, he'll be upset when you're focused on the baby.

REMEMBER

» **Ease off confrontational games.** No more tug-of-war or wrestling, and eliminate all in-home chasing matches. Play games outside and teach your puppy calm household manners. If he's a tugaholic, practice the release Give, covered in Chapter 11.

>> **Consider how your child's future toys may compare to your puppy's favorites**. Reconsider your puppy's toys, if necessary, way in advance as you teach your puppy the phrase Go get Your Toy. Keep these objects in an accessible basket or on your puppy's bed. Discourage chewing.

>> **Condition them to erratic handling, such as touching, poking, and hair-pulling.** Babies and small children like to grab and pull, and your puppy may be startled if the baby's tug is the first one they experience. Feed them a savory or lickable treat as you gently condition them to your mimicking of a baby's touch. Say *gentle* as you do this, and repeat this phrase when it happens in real time. Don't forget to make some baby sounds, too, for the full effect.

Bringing baby home

The day will come. Your baby will arrive, and your life will never be the same. To help your puppy adjust, follow these suggestions:

>> **Ask the nurse if you can bring home an infant blanket from the nursery.** It may seem like a strange request, but I'm sure yours won't be the first. Ask your partner to let your puppy sniff these items, placing them in normal spots like the nursery and kitchen so that your puppy conditions to the new smell.

>> **Brush up on obedience lessons while mom's in the hospital.** Puppies love structure and the attention showered on them during training sessions. The brush-up will be a good base for the weeks ahead, when life gets more unpredictable and stressful.

REMEMBER

>> **Hire a dog walker if the house is empty.** Isolation is stressful for puppies.

>> **Plan baby's homecoming.** Keep your puppy on-leash and let them welcome the baby, too.

>> **Harness wild puppy energy:** If your puppy's too boisterous, offer them a special savory chew or busy toy, as described in Chapter 5, and gradually reintroduce them back into the circle around baby. Spread some butter on a serving spoon and use it to lure your puppy some distance away until they have calmed.

TIP

The butter trick also works as you establish a bond between your baby and your puppy when the puppy settles down. Dab some butter on your baby's foot or booty and say *kisses.* (See Figure 9-2.)

WARNING

If your dog growls at the baby, call in a professional to assess the situation.

FIGURE 9-2:
Teach your puppy to focus on your baby's feet, not face, by dabbing butter on their feet or booties.

Traveling with Your Puppy

People love to travel. We love to see new sites, taste new foods, and meet interesting people. We pore over travel sites and pick places we know we'll enjoy. We pull out our calendars and create itineraries: Leave on Friday, home on Tuesday. For the most part, we know what's coming and where we're going.

Your puppy? Not so much. Depending on your dog's level of socialization, breed, and temperament, travel can be quite stressful. Car rides are fun for many dogs, but a 10-hour marathon drive may test their mettle. And if you think airplane seats are uncomfortable, try flying in the cargo hold.

Consider your destination. Will your hosts welcome your dog? Yes, they said "bring everybody," but confirm in advance that this means your dog. Not everyone puts dogs in the same category as kids.

Know your dog. Are they adventurous or more of a homebody? Are they easily distracted by a favorite toy, or do new scents and sounds send them into a frenzy? Do they walk companionably on a leash, or do they need a little work in that department?

If you've confirmed the dog-friendliness of your destination and your dog is socialized and ready for a trip, pack carefully to ensure a comfortable journey. Bring as many homey things as you can — beds, crates, toys, bowls, and leashes. Pack a list of your dog's familiar words and routines. Dogs are much happier when surrounded by things they recognize. If your hosts have dogs, introduce them to yours in a neutral location (preferably outdoors to avoid territorial disputes). Let both dogs drag long leashes to allow natural interaction while maintaining your ability to intervene if needed.

REMEMBER

If your dog stays behind, try not to feel guilty. He will be content with a stable routine and delighted when you get home. Keep in mind that the aggravations of travel that frustrate humans may overwhelm your dog and create a situation that makes you wish you had all stayed home.

Taking your puppy on a plane

I'm leery of planes, so you can imagine how neurotic I get thinking of a dog in the belly of one of those steel babies. I'd avoid taking any pet on a plane if I didn't have to. Sometimes air travel is unavoidable, however, so follow these tips to make flying easier on everyone:

>> **Condition your puppy to the air travel carrier or kennel long in advance.** Check out the section on crate training in Chapter 7 and follow those instructions as many weeks in advance as you're able to plan it.

>> **When possible, plan direct flights in the evening or early morning.** Ground temperatures are cooler then. (Heat-induced suffocation is the biggest risk in airline travel.)

>> **Make your puppy's reservation when you make your own.** Planes accept only so many four-legged passengers.

If you can't fly direct, book a flight with a layover that's long enough for you to reunite with your puppy. Take them out for a stretch, drink, potty break, and hug.

REMEMBER

>> **Obtain health certificates and proof of vaccination.** Airlines require them for all dogs, so you need to get them from your veterinarian and forward a copy to the airline immediately. Carry one with you on the day of the flight, too, in case any questions arise about your dog's clearance to travel.

>> **Write the flight info on top of the traveling crate.** Using 1/2-inch letters, write the flight's destination, including your name and the name, address, and phone number of the person or place you're visiting.

>> **Avoid feeding your puppy within six hours of the trip so that he's pooped out—literally—before being crated for the trip.**

>> **Prepare the crate for takeoff.** Add light bedding and paper (taped down) in one end to absorb mistakes. Affix kennel bowls inside the crate. Freeze water in one so that your puppy can have a drink while in flight.

>> **If your puppy is a champion chewer, evaluate whether to nix the bedding.** Some puppies are so stressed by air travel that they'd chew the shirt off your back if you were sitting next to them. If you suspect that your puppy will be distressed, ask your veterinarian for a sedative.

Road trip! Traveling by car

I've never owned a puppy or dog who didn't love a road trip. I know some dogs have less-than-enjoyable experiences, but even they can be transformed with some patient car conditioning.

Following safety rules for the road

Puppies do best with structure in the car. Always take them to the same passenger door or hatch, saying the phrase *to the car* as you go and while directing them into a crate or cozy nest decorated with bedding and bones. If the routines are not organized, your puppy may feel restless and ill-at-ease, which can lead to a cascade of problems, the least of which is pacing, whining and barking at everything that moves.

For any road trip, make sure your puppy is secured in some fashion. Here are a few options:

>> **Put your pup in a crate during road trips.** Buy a strong, wire-mesh type (for good air circulation) that is sized for your puppy's weight and breed. Line the bottom with a mat, cloth, or similar bedding to provide a surface that they can sink their paws into while you're driving.

>> **Secure your puppy with a seat belt.** Give your puppy their area in the back seat for short jaunts. Secure a doggie-style attachment to the seat belt and decorate the area with a mat and toys to keep them comfortable and occupied during the drive.

>> **Erect a sturdy barrier.** Barriers enclose your puppy in the back compartment of a wagon or sports utility vehicle.

TIP

The Center for Pet Safety rates different items, such as toys, bones, and car safety harnesses. Check out the site before you buy any of these items: www.centerforpetsafety.org.

Taking a few precautions

Cars can be a dangerous place for dogs, so you must take certain precautions:

>> **Never** leave your puppy in the car on a warm day. Even with the windows down, your car will bake like an oven, leaving your puppy uncomfortable — or dead. Nothing is worth that.

>> **Keep an extra set of keys on hand.** If you must leave your puppy, keep the engine running with the air conditioning on full blast and lock the doors. Keep the second set of keys with you so that you can get back into the car.

>> **Think careful, not cool.** While driving, keep windows cracked but not wide open. Some people think that letting a dog hang their head out the window is cool, but it's dangerous. Dogs can get hurled from the car in an accident or have debris fly into their eyes, causing permanent damage.

Guidelines for long trips

Are you planning a long journey? The following guidelines can help ensure that both you and your puppy get through the trip with minimal hassle:

>> **Keep your pup's diet and feeding times consistent.** A change can upset their system, and that's one discomfort you can easily avoid.

>> **Avoid traveling in extreme heat unless you have a good air-conditioning system.** If you're in extreme heat, plan to travel at night or early in the morning.

>> **Keep your puppy on a leash at *every* pit stop.** When traveling, a puppy's homing device shuts down. If he wanders off or gets momentarily distracted, he may have trouble finding their way back to you. Traffic is also a danger, so be safe, not sorry.

3

Training with a Positive Spin

Chapter **10**

Taking Baby Steps: 8 Weeks to 14 Weeks

Many people picture bringing a puppy home during the "adorable" stage, between 8 and 14 weeks, and professionals do claim that it's the best age to bond with a puppy. Though I agree that it's an impressionable time, the truth is that you can bond with a puppy (or a dog, for that matter) at any age. It's fun to watch a puppy morph through each developmental stage, but puppies are a lot of work, too; this chapter helps you get a focus on just what's in store.

TECHNICAL STUFF

Some breeders offer their puppy buyers what's known as *imprinting foster care* after a puppy separates from their litter at seven or eight weeks old. This service involves paying someone else to house-train, socialize, and teach your puppy for weeks to months, depending on the arrangement. I've seen this work well for some of my clients and not so well for others: Much depends on who's doing the foster care. The choice is up to you.

Understanding Your Puppy's Mindset

Before giving birth to my first child, I anticipated snuggly cuddles and long, lingering morning gazes — the two of us blissfully smothered in mutual adoration. Little did I know. The first months were in fact a blur of late-night crying jags, poopy diapers, and wishing that someone had prepared me for the labor involved in parenting. If you're a new puppy owner or you're preparing to bring home a puppy, let me help you out: At the stage between 8 and 14 weeks, your puppy is all about getting familiar with their surroundings and routines. Don't expect too much from them. Even though a puppy at this age is capable of learning, their brain won't finish developing until they're 14 weeks old.

So, what can you really expect? First and foremost, puppies at this stage need *tons* of sleep: between 16 and 18 hours of quiet time. If you're tempted to overstimulate your young puppy, don't do it. Your puppy will end up acting like a colicky baby who is chronically sleep deprived. How can you tell? Puppies who need sleep act fidgety, pushy, and *mouthy*. Unless they get the right kind of sleep, overtired puppies develop into restless dogs — and you don't want that.

Nor do you want to start off on the wrong foot when it comes to socializing your puppy. The most important lessons at this stage involve associating words with specific routines. Luckily for you, these lessons aren't hard to teach. If you stay consistent, the associations should develop naturally as you tend to your puppy's everyday needs. I outline just how to tackle this task in the following sections, so put the high-intensity exercise and training lessons on the back burner for now. If you're disappointed that your puppy won't be running that fancy doggy parkour obstacle course just yet, try not to be — there's still a lot of fun to be had at this stage.

REMEMBER

All puppies are programmed to look to their family's body language and postures for clues on how to act, as I discuss in Chapter 6. Your first goal is to teach your puppy to listen for direction by outlining lessons similar to teaching a foreigner a new language. Using a say-n-show format, you'll say words that tie into where you're going or what your puppy is doing. When you pair words with action, your puppy will learn to listen for direction in no time.

Taking Care of Your Puppy's Basic Needs

Like a human baby, your puppy is paying attention to you *all the time*, absorbing everything going on around them at a rate never to be equaled again in their lifetime. Young and impressionable, they look to others to learn how to handle new situations. But they can't understand what you're teaching them until they learn to identify the meaning of certain words. After all, training isn't an exercise in domination or control; it's teaching English to your puppy so that you share a common language.

Taking care of your puppy at this stage can be a little repetitive: it's a continuous string of sleep-potty-eat-drink-potty-play-potty-sleep-potty — and then rinse and repeat. Bonding during this stage occurs as you calmly and routinely take care of these basic needs: Yes, those needs in fact involve eating, drinking, pottying, sleeping, and playing. Help your puppy learn their first words by teaching them where to go and what to do when all their needs are pressing. Your puppy desperately wants to know, "Where do I go when I am thirsty, hungry, or tired or need to potty?"

REMEMBER

Your puppy at this stage needs lots of potty breaks because their bladder muscles don't fully develop until four to five months of age. For more on house-training your puppy, flip to Chapter 14.

With consistent routines, schedules, and word cues, your puppy will start indicating their needs by initiating the routines you've shown them! (For printable puppy schedules, visit my website at SarahSaysPets.com.

In Table 10-1, I list five important routines your puppy should know at this stage, pairing each one with a word cue to help them link each routine with a specific action.

TABLE 10-1: Teaching Your Puppy English by Using Routines

Word Cue	Routine
Outside or *papers* and *get busy*	Designate a footpath to your puppy's bathroom area. Guide them to this area as you repeat a direction like *Outside* or *Papers*. Say *Get busy* as they potty.
In your room	Say this direction as you calmly lead your puppy into their crate or quiet room to rest. If they hesitate, guide them with food lures or favorite toys. Settle them in with a busy toy or chew to help them self-soothe. Avoid dragging them, pleading, feeling guilty, or getting cross.
Mealtime	Each time you feed your puppy — whether by hand, bowl, or feeding toy — identify the activity with a word and routinely go to the same area to get their food. If they jump or bark, stop and walk away. Only feed a *calm* puppy.
Water	Keep your puppy's water dish in the same area. Have them hold still before lowering the bowl.
Toy or *ball*	Help your puppy identify their belongings by keeping their toys and bones in one area. Identify each object as you play with it.

Making Learning Fun

Your puppy will learn more quickly if training is incorporated into everyday habits and playtime. Use their name and directions like *Sit* and *Find it* as you share treats and food and play with toys. Your number-one routine will be to teach them where to go to the bathroom, as I discuss in Chapter 14.

REMEMBER

Forget discipline at this stage because your pup is just too young to understand it. You succeed only in frightening them and eroding your relationship — and that's not good.

Teaching the Find It game

This game is easy and fun and you'll use it forever. Take a few kibbles, as outlined in Chapter 20, and drop them at your feet (gently at first), saying *Find it*. It's that simple. How many repetitions does it take to teach your puppy this cue? With each Find It treat-drop, they're one step closer to learning this all-important word game.

I talk about Find It a lot in this book, but that's because it has tons of important uses, from calling your puppy to your side or teaching them to play with the children without jumping or nipping to conditioning them to look down when cars, cats, cyclists, and critters pass. You can also use Find It to keep greetings with strangers on an even keel and teach cooperative leash walking skills.

TIP

Use Find It when feeding your puppy. Toss one kibble at a time (a great game for children) as you encourage the 4-paw rule as detailed later, in the section "Helping your puppy learn the 4-paw rule," or toss a few handfuls down for meal-time fun.

Saying your puppy's name

Treat cups (see Chapter 5) help your puppy learn their name quickly. If your puppy has yet to associate the sound of the cup shaking with receiving a food treat, practice shaking and rewarding until they do. Now make multiple cups and spread them around for easy access. When you're ready to have your puppy learn their name, follow this 3-step process:

1. **Shake the cup and say the puppy's name simultaneously.**

2. **Repeat until you get a quick response each time you call.**

    Use this trick everywhere you spend time so your puppy will alert each time you call out.

3. **Call out their name first, immediately followed by a shake of the cup.**

   Once your puppy is alerting to their name and no cup is immediately necessary, begin Step 3.

4. **Call out the puppy's name and progressively extend the time you shake the cup.**

   Go from 1 second later to 2, 3, and 4 seconds later until you see that your puppy has learned their name. Gradually phase out shaking the cup, but continue rewarding your puppy with play, praise, and other rewards, like letting them play.

TIP

Pick a short name or nickname and say it anytime you're offering your puppy positive rewards, like treats, toys, or attention.

Learning Sit

Teaching your puppy to sit is like teaching a child to say *please*. You can't teach your puppy to literally say *please*, but you can get them to use a gesture to say that they want something. If you consistently direct your puppy to sit before offering them anything they perceive as positive, they'll sit when they want something just as readily as most dogs jump. Here are some situations where you want your puppy to say *please*:

>> When receiving meals, treats, or water

>> Before a ball toss or toy offering

>> Before doors open to let them in or out

>> Whenever they want an item on the counter or tabletop

>> Before car entrances and exits

>> During all greetings

>> During introductions to children and older people

TIP

Make sure your puppy doesn't generalize a learned routine, like Sit, to one spot, such as their place or your kitchen. Practice new routines in a variety of different places and around various people and situations.

Learning Come

Teach your puppy that the word *Come* means you're together, not apart. Eventually, it will bring your puppy running from afar, but initially *Come* should reflect touch, reassurance, and rewards, not separation and frustration. Here's how to do it:

1. Hold a treat in one hand. Hold the other hand open, palm out, 2 to 3 inches from your puppy's nose. The instant your puppy touches their nose to your palm, say *Come* and drop the reward from the other hand, saying *Find it!*

    Your puppy will quickly associate touching your palm with both the word *Come* and the reward.

2. Continue the hand gesture and saying *Come* in different areas around your home and outdoors so that your puppy learns to respond to both your signal and the word.

3. Practice flashing your hand without saying the word *come*, rewarding your puppy for touching your hand by saying *Find it* and dropping a treat on the ground at your feet.

4. Practice saying *come* as you step back three steps, using rewards to lure your puppy to follow you. Increase the distance, as you step back two steps at a time, from 3-to-5-to-7 and so on. Flash your palm and reward your puppy the moment they nose you.

TIP

Use a portion of your puppy's meals to work on Come every day. You will continue the lesson in the next few chapters, using a building block approach: Practice inside, outside, and when socializing your puppy away from home.

Give

Most puppies enjoy playing with toys, but they won't understand the concept of sharing for a while. To help your puppy along, play the following game. Try it first with your puppy on a leash and with some treats or a clicker in your pocket. Take your puppy into a small, quiet room with a favorite ball or squeak toy and then follow these steps:

1. Kneel on the floor and praise your puppy happily for a minute before you bring out the toy.

2. When you bring out the toy, toss it in the air (and catch it) to encourage their interest and then give it a short toss.

3. If they take the toy, let them keep it for a while.

    You want them to feel that you're not there to challenge them for it.

4. Bring out the treats (and clicker, if you're using that method). When you offer your puppy a treat, they will spit out the toy. As they do, say *Give* and either click-and-treat or simply treat as you praise them. Do not take the toy away from them. The goal is to teach your puppy that "Give" means "spit it out."

This action highlights your good intentions to play and not steal.

TIP

You can use a treat cup to encourage sharing. When your puppy has an object or a toy, shake the cup enthusiastically and say *Give* when they do.

Practice these directions in the confines of a small room for five days, and then bring the direction into normally populated areas. Phase out the treats gradually. If your intention is to toss the toy, take it after they spit it out and toss it immediately. Praise them with an exclamation like this: "Good boy — let's play!"

Associating words to everyday routines

Earlier in this chapter, I tell you about the importance of associating words with everyday routines; Table 10-1 gives some examples of phrases to use. The list of words you can use to identify your routines is endless, however. For example, you can teach your puppy the names of each room in your house, if you want to, or the name of each and every toy.

REMEMBER

Whatever phrase you choose, teach your puppy using the say-n-show format: Say the word and do the action. Reward your puppy for following along. Don't stare and repeat directions over and over and over again, because your puppy may feel threatened and freeze up.

Here are three more phrases I highly recommend teaching to your puppy:

>> **Inside/Outside:** Teach your puppy how to navigate in and out of your home (also known as their den) by saying these words as you go inside or outside. Use treat cups and toys as you guide them by saying the word. Look at, reward, and praise their cooperation.

>> **Car:** Say *Car* each time you take your puppy to the car. As soon as they're able to walk on their own, use treats or a toy to guide them, and then toss the rewards in the vehicle and say *Find it* as you help your puppy in.

>> **Family names:** If you live with family or friends, teach your puppy everyone's names as you identify who's entering their free play area. Say *Daddy's home; Lizzy's coming down.*

Helping your puppy learn the 4-paw rule

I insist on the 4-paw rule when dealing with pups and often advocate its use in this book. It's especially important to impress on puppies at this stage the importance of the rule. Your puppy's first lessons simply *must* include not jumping for treats, toys, or attention. Using the 4-paw rule (no notice or greeting or reward unless all four paws are on the floor) is easy at this stage. Every time your puppy jumps up at the gate to get attention or jumps during greetings, stop dead in your tracks and cover your face with your hands — a technique I refer to as the *peeka-boo solution.* (The idea here is to ostentatiously deny them the attention they seek.) If they jump for treats or toys, lift them out of reach. In all these situations, wait until your puppy is on all four paws to give them what they want.

Walking the stairs

Stairs can be a formidable obstacle for puppies. Some small breeds are just too little to tackle the stairs, so they must be carried up and down at this age. (Don't worry: In time, they'll be scampering up and down like the big dogs do.) Some larger-breed puppies, although big enough to use stairs, are afraid because their depth perception is only begjinning to develop around eight weeks of age.

TIP

If you have a puppy with stair phobia, help them walk the stairs, by wrapping your hands around their ribs and guiding them down slowly. A helper can crouch down to their level and shake a treat cup to cheer them on.

Helping your puppy identify their place

In Chapter 7, I talk about how you should set up your puppy's free-play area. Start teaching your puppy their "place" ASAP — by putting a washable mat in a corner and arranging their toys and bowls nearby it. Teach your puppy the word *Place* by waving a toy or shaking a treat cup as you guide them to their area. Reward them after they have all four paws on the mat — good puppy! Should your puppy go on their mat on their own, keep treats handy to reward them.

Teaching your puppy to ring a bell

In Chapter 14, I talk about how you can teach your puppy to ring a bell when they need to go outside to potty. The fact is, though, that your puppy can learn to ring a bell to get whatever they want. Hang one by the water dish to ensure that they stay hydrated, and by the doors so that they can alert you whenever they need to potty or want to come back inside. Tap the bell gently with your fingers just before you fill the water bowl or open the door — soon, your puppy will catch on and ring it, too.

TIP

If your puppy doesn't catch on to the bell ringing within two weeks, dab the bell with a spreadable treat. Walk your puppy to the door as normal, but just before opening the door, offer the bell to investigate. Once your puppy touches it, praise them and proceed with the routine.

Leash and collar associations

Young puppies have strong oppositional reflexes (something I call *entrapment panic*) if they feel caught against their will in any way. It's a survival instinct that may play out if you insist on forcibly walking your young puppy on a tight leash. If you do, they may buck, freeze up, bite through the leash, or yelp as though they were caught in a bear trap. Worst of all, when forced to yield to a leash, a puppy grows up instinctively pulling in an attempt to break free, and will bolt given the opportunity.

It's okay to place a lightweight collar or harness on your puppy soon after you get them home. If they're like most puppies, they'll fuss at first by scratching at their neck or rolling on the floor. If they do, condition their cooperation by placing it on before meals or for 20-minute intervals while you play Find It or toss favorite toys. Does your puppy run from you or back up when you approach to place their collar/harness on them? If so, kneel or pick them up first, use a spreadable treat or crumbly treat that you can place on the ground, and then place the item from behind your puppy.

REMEMBER

Puppies grow fast, so keep an eye on the collar size and loosen it when necessary.

When your puppy is accustomed to the collar, attach a light 4-foot freedom line to the buckle and let them drag that around as you play Find It, shake their treat cup, and toss toys. After a day or two, pick up the leash and follow behind them. Continue to play Find It and play with toys, as they get used to having you following along at the end of their leash. Once that's happening with ease, start to call your puppy's name and encourage them to follow you.

Do any number of foolish things to pique your puppy's interest. When they start following you, reward them by placing the treats on the floor and saying "Find It-Follow."

TIP

If your puppy actively resists following you, don't run over to them; doing that reinforces the resistance. Instead, wave rewards or lower yourself to the floor while you praise them.

Conditioning Your Puppy to Be Handled

Throughout your puppy's life, they'll be prodded, pinched, and probed for good (though unclear to them) reasons. To get your puppy used to all of life's surprises, practice the handling exercises in this section early and often. No one would wish a cut on a puppy's paw, a burn from an electrical cord, or a double ear infection, but these things do happen, and it helps to get your puppy prepared. (I talk more about health concerns and emergency issues in the chapters in Part 5.)

Playing doggie-doctor

Here's a handling tip your veterinarian will love: Once a day, take out some savory food bits or a spreadable treat, and — while your puppy is cheerfully eating — play doggie-doctor. Use household objects to pretend with or scare up a toy doctor's kit as you gently give your puppy make-believe shots, look in their ears and eyes, probe their belly, and so on. Mimic all the things they'll experience during their wellness visits and mirror the actions you will take if your puppy gets sick.

TIP

If possible, schedule a tour of your chosen animal hospital before your puppy's first appointment, to help them make a positive association to both the place and the people.

Touching paws

Though you may never have given your puppy's paws much thought, their feet are essential to every interaction. Handle and touch your puppy's paws daily to ensure that future nail clipping, routine check-ups (for thorns or cuts after adventuring), and any future medical care their paws might need is a non-issue.

Remembering the Importance of Early Socialization

A brand-new puppy is easy to condition and socialize because they're unsure of themselves and how best to react to new situations. Most puppies look to their people to direct and translate new situations. How you greet and interact with people from all walks of life are their greatest examples.

When welcoming new visitors, allow your puppy to approach them on their terms rather than thrust them forward or lift them excitedly. If your puppy is unsure, let them hang back, and encourage your visitors to wait for them to approach them.

Of course, the best lesson in appropriate greeting manners comes from you. Mom was right again when she said, "Good manners start at home." When greeting your puppy, be casual. Even though you may be beside yourself with delight, stay calm and interact with your puppy only when they're calm, too.

TIP

As the weeks pass, your puppy will feel more a part of your household and be more interactive when new situations arise. If your puppy begins to jump or mouth you or your company, kneel next to them and *brace* them by clipping your thumb gently under their collar. (See Chapter 9 for an illustration.) Steady them on all four paws whether you're greeting them or someone is approaching you. Give the command *Say hello* as you or the admirer offer pats or treats.

TIP

If your puppy is fearful or tense, ask the person to shake a treat cup and treat them so that they shape a new and more positive outlook. Also, ask the person to approach them from the side or to kneel. Straight on, the head-to-head greeting can easily overwhelm a nervous puppy, who'll interpret the approach as threatening.

For more tips and tricks on socializing, flip to Chapter 9.

When You're Feeling Frustrated

Already getting frustrated with your puppy's behavior? You're not alone. Before you leash, er, *lash* out, however, remember that your puppy isn't capable of translating your anger into a meaningful lesson. Your reactions only teach them to be wary of your moods, something that makes their behavior worse by the hour. Studies show that puppies who fear retaliation chew and nip more, and often misbehave when their people are out of the room or not watching them. You have a long life with your puppy: if you're having trouble with an issue, please refer to the appropriate areas of Part 4. (Flip to the table of contents or the index for guidance.)

Chapter **11**

Teaching Your Preadolescent Puppy: 14 Weeks to 6 Months

All good honeymoons must come to an end, and in the realm of puppy parenting, most end during the preadolescent phase. It's not a pretty time, no matter the species. During this stage, puppies are beginning to recognize what behaviors get your attention, what games seem to last the longest (and not necessarily the games you want to play), and who's organizing the day-to-day interactions — in their eyes, it may not be you. Even though your puppy may act pretty confident during this phase, they still need direction from you. The advice in this chapter can help you guide your puppy successfully through their preadolescence.

Understanding Your Puppy's Mindset

Puppies emerge from their sleepy, early brain-growth phase with eagerness and enthusiasm for all of life's many adventures. Your efforts will boil down to helping your puppy understand where to go and what to do in every situation. Say you're sitting at the table or texting a friend or welcoming a visitor or waiting your turn at the vet's office: Where should your puppy go and what should they do? How about when they're bored or hungry or wants to play? If you don't direct them, they'll test out all the typical preadolescent shenanigans, including jumping, nipping, barking, and grabbing-'n'-going. It can be an utter nightmare.

Fortunately, this chapter provides a happy alternative to this type of nightmare. If you follow my advice here, you'll end up surviving — and maybe even enjoying — your puppy's preadolescence. With my tried-and-true sequencing approach, you'll be able to introduce your puppy to three cues at a time. You'll then be able to use those words to help your puppy understand where to go and what to do in every situation.

REMEMBER

As you're training your puppy and introducing new words into their vocabulary, make it fun. Your puppy will cherish their time with you, and lessons that help them identify words and end with rewards build a positive team spirit.

Conditioning good habits

Because your preadolescent puppy has neither the attention span nor impulse control of a 7-month-old dog, the lessons in this chapter are tailored to meet your puppy's capacities at the 14-weeks-to-6-months stage. Taken altogether, they allow your puppy to be successful, mastering each direction before you start applying it to their daily routine — similar to letting children master their addition skills in school before asking them to balance your checkbook.

TIP

Puppies, like kids, love plunging into group activities. The behavior they repeat is determined by what gets your attention, so focus only on the routines you want your puppy to repeat. Is your puppy over on their mat, chewing a bone? Stand up — quick! Race over and reward them for doing just that.

Practicing your lessons

I suggest that you practice each of the lessons outlined in this chapter twice daily for five to ten minutes per lesson (shorter lessons for younger puppies). As you practice, you may notice that your puppy picks up some directions faster than others. Don't be too surprised. That's how training usually goes. After all, think of what you're accomplishing: You're teaching another species your language. My advice is to be patient throughout the many phases because puppies learn best from an understanding teacher.

TIP

During the 14-weeks-to-6-months stage, continue sleep training (as detailed in Chapters 6 and 10) and organizing your puppy's time in the house, by either containing them in their free-play area, supervising them while dragging a freedom line or leash, or introducing them to all areas of your home on a walkabout. (More about walkabouts later in this chapter.) As they grow more comfortable with your surroundings, rather than burst out of their confinement and barrel through your home — grabbing every roll of toilet paper, stuffed animal, or sock they find in their way — you may gradually trust them with more freedom. Don't rush it, though. If they do well for the most part but falls apart when company arrives, put them on the leash whenever you have visitors.

Taking Care of Your Puppy's Basic Needs

At this stage, your puppy should feel pretty confident in knowing where to go to get their basic needs met (eat, drink, sleep, potty, and play). If you've not outlined these routines, review the Needs Chart (Table 6-2) from Chapter 6 and the tips in Chapter 10. During preadolescence, however, your puppy will be far more interested in how they fit into the fabric of your everyday life. If you don't tell them where to go and what to do, they will turn your life upside down by making their own set of rules — and that's a nightmare I wouldn't wish on anybody.

Making Learning Fun

As your puppy is developing, both physically and mentally, you need to start teaching the following useful directions: Follow, Sit, Down, Stand Still, Stay, and Come. Though you may have already started some of these lessons, continue reinforcing them throughout your puppy's development. Build your lessons around their regular nap times (in the middle of the day), and don't forget to intersperse the lessons with plenty of play and socialization.

REMEMBER

As you're teaching your puppy the meaning of different words, remember that they will respond to the sound of your voice, not the actual sense of the words. Say each cue word clearly, in a strong but nonthreatening voice.

Play training

The very best way to turn your puppy on to listening and learning from you is to use your words during the day as you play and care for all your puppy's needs. Because playtime is every puppy's top priority during this stage, the following list highlights which directions to use during each game. (To find instructions on how to play a particular game, flip to Chapter 20.)

>> **Can't Catch Me:** Use your puppy's name to attract their attention as you're running away from them, and use the directions Wait and Find It when you stop abruptly to reward them. If your puppy jumps up, lift the treat high above their head until they are standing securely on all four paws.

>> **Get Your Toy:** When playing with your puppy's toys, gather multiples so that you are never caught focusing on just one. Toss one toy, saying "Get Your Toy" and cheering your puppy on if they run after the toy. If your puppy returns to you, pair the cue "Bring" with their delivery, but don't reach out or immediately demand that they fork it over to you: Remember, puppies like kids need to learn how to share! If you can inspire their sharing the toy by offering a treat or baiting them with a new toy so they spit out the one they're holding, say *Give* as they spit it out.

>> **Belly Up:** Anytime your puppy naturally lies down, say *Down*. Use Belly Up whenever your puppy rolls on their back to get a scratch.

>> **Roll Over:** If you have a roly-poly puppy, say *Down* and *Roll Over* to get them comfortable with both positions.

Helping your puppy slow down

If there's one thing young puppies lack, it's impulse control. If you're like most parents, you may feel overwhelmed and discouraged during your puppy's transformation from a sleepy baby that everyone couldn't wait to cuddle to the preadolescent state — the puppy everyone avoids. To control their exuberance, or to help your puppy should a sudden noise or activity startle them, get a handle on these lessons as soon as you're able.

Stay

Your puppy's ability to hold still for any length of time depends on their age as well as on how you introduce this lesson. At first, keep the lessons short and completely food-centered as you practice in a low-commotion environment. Work with your puppy off-leash or on a light freedom line if they're easily distracted. Practice at a time when they are neither exhausted nor ready for play — it's what I call the *sweet spot of ideal focus.* (All I can say is that you'll know it when you find it.) Read the steps in the following sections, and visualize the exercise before getting started.

HAND SIGNALS CAN HELP YOUR PUPPY FOCUS

All puppies are born posturing, and they focus quickly on learning by way of signs and gestures. Though you'll want to teach your puppy to listen for your direction, using signals to reinforce your words can speed the learning along. As a bonus? A puppy who learns to read signals may watch you more attentively.

Direct your signals just above your puppy's nose or muzzle. Here are the signals you use in this chapter:

- **Sit:** Point your finger as you swing your right arm from your puppy's nose to your face (as if you were scooping their attention toward you) and say *Sit.*

- **Down:** Point to the ground directly between your puppy's paws.

- **Stand:** Position your flat palm parallel to the floor.

- **Stay:** Flatten your palm like a paddle. Flash it quickly in front of your puppy's nose and say *Stay.*

- **Okay:** Point your finger and swing your right arm out from your puppy's nose as you step forward. Say *Okay* to tell them *Job well done!*

- **Come:** Your open palm signals your puppy to come close to you. When calling your puppy from a distance, raise your arm straight above you and wave your hand (a move that I call the *human exclamation point*) as you say *Come.* If they're coming too quickly, hold your arm in front of you like an air traffic controller and then draw your finger up to your nose (like the Sit signal) to encourage them to stop, sit, and check in with you.

- **Wait:** Slice the air directly above your puppy's face with your flat palm.

- **Good Dog:** To reassure, praise, and calm your puppy, pat your heart with your open palm and say *Good dog.* To encourage enthusiasm or to release your dog from a long stay, throw one arm or two above your head.

TIP

Practice Stay on a carpet or nonskid mat so your puppy has a good grip.

STAY, STEP 1

1. Count out 25 dry food pellets (if your puppy enjoys them), or break up as many morsels of a soft treat needed to get to 25.

2. Direct your puppy to *Sit,* reward them with the first morsel, and then instruct *Stay* with a flash of your hand. (See Figure 11-1.)

3. Within one to two seconds, reward your puppy with another morsel. Repeat *Stay,* pause one to two seconds, and reward again.

4. Continue to remind *Stay* and reward your puppy every second or two for three or four rounds before releasing them with *Go Free!*

Reward your puppy with morsels and attention only when they're in the Sit-Stay position. Ignore them after they get up. Wait 10 to 15 seconds to call them over to start the next Sit-Stay sequence.

5. Repeat this Stay lesson — all food-motivated at this point — until they consume the treats you've set aside.

Illustration by Robert Golinello

FIGURE 11-1:
A flash of your hand tells your puppy to stay.

TIP

You'll notice that your puppy is catching on when they keep holding their Stay position even after you release them. If this happens, praise them and give them another treat.

After three days of short, consistently reinforced Stay lessons, practice for three more days but lengthen the duration of Stay from 1 or 2 seconds to 3 or 4 seconds, and then progress to 5- or 6-second Stay sequences. Follow the preceding steps, practicing in low-distraction rooms (the rooms may vary) on nonslippery surfaces.

STAY, STEP 2

Your next goal is to wean your puppy off the repetitive reward pattern by introducing a variable reinforcement schedule — one that has no identifiable pattern. Borrowing from the psychology of casino gambling, where erratic rewards are used to hook their patrons, this same inconsistent schedule will also excite your puppy's participation.

Following the same five steps outlined in the preceding section, your puppy will enter into a new phase of learning when you step away from the second-by-second reward loop and instead begin varying the time intervals between each treat. Here's one example:

Stay – Pause 2 seconds – Reward

Stay – Pause 4 seconds – Reward

Stay – Pause 1 second – Reward

Stay – Pause 6 seconds – Reward-and-Release Go Free!

Now vary the second interval between each Stay — and don't worry about keeping track, because the whole goal is not to develop an identifiable pattern. After your puppy shows self-control, extend the intervals from 2 to 6 seconds to 2 to 10 seconds to 2 to 15 seconds and so on.

Many puppies learn the magic of holding still along the way. They often default to sitting still and just patiently waiting, watching you. Reward that action!

Don't rush this direction. Take your time and use encouragement to ensure that your puppy has a rock-solid Stay throughout their lives.

If your puppy has zero interest in food and you've exhausted all effort to find something tasty enough to excite their interest (I've used hot dogs, bacon grease, and various dried animal parts), find something else to reward them. A happy voice or a special toy might work.

STAY, STEP 3

After you're both more confident with Stay, begin to increase the level of distraction your puppy can tolerate — practice in the kids' computer room, for example, or in the kitchen before mealtimes. If your puppy is having difficulty holding still when other people are present, go back to rewarding short interval stays every 2 to 4 seconds before building up to their previous average.

Incrementally include Stay lessons in real-life situations such as around the cat, the kids' activities, and even when greeting new people.

Preadolescent Stay lessons should be all about self-control around distractions. I tell you how to work on long-distance Stay (where you leave your puppy's side) in Chapter 12.

Leave It

The term *Leave It* tells your puppy that whatever they're approaching is off limits. You can teach this lesson in two ways. Use both methods to help your puppy understand that whatever they're tempted by is best to avoid.

LEAVE IT, METHOD 1

Find a spray or oil that many dogs find repulsive, such as a bitter-tasting spray deterrent found in most pet stores. (Vinegar works as well.) Before introducing your puppy to the odor, douse a tissue or paper towel with it and discreetly drop it on the floor.

As your puppy approaches the lure, say *Leave It* to warn them off. When they back away, kneel to play, reward, or pet them lovingly.

Now use the scent to deter your puppy from chewing household objects or nipping your body or clothing. Continue to say *Leave It* when your puppy approaches objects that you prefer them to leave alone.

LEAVE IT, METHOD 2

The second part of the Leave It lesson initially involves two treats: a high-value, preferably smelly treat and a low-quality kibble or biscuit, with each broken into small pieces. Using a leash is optional. Follow these steps:

1. Call your puppy into a quiet room.

2. Ask them to *Sit* on your left side.

3. Holding the low-quality treat in your right hand, turn to hold it down at your puppy's level (about 8 to 12 inches from their nose) as you say *Leave It* in a firm-though-nonthreatening voice.

4. If your puppy lunges for the treat anyway (and most will), snap your hand shut over the treat like a clam and wait until your puppy pauses from even a split second to toss the more savory treat at their feet, saying *Find It!*

5. Repeat this sequence several times in each session. Soon your puppy will know that when you say Leave It, they should resist the impulse to grab whatever is directly in front of them and look to you for a better option.

   After your puppy has mastered this step and can resist food even when it's in front of them, you may begin to hold the low-value kibble lower to the ground (where it will be more tempting) or increase the value of the food you're presenting to them.

LEAVE IT IN THE REAL WORLD

Though it takes some time and practice to get your puppy to the point of leaving a cat or critter alone in the middle of high chase, you should start to use this direction around household distractions after they have the ability to contain their impulse around their food. Use Leave It if your puppy looks on the counter or when Auntie Grace drops their handbag or a visitor tells you that they're afraid of dogs.

REMEMBER

Leave It isn't an admonishment — it's a direction that teaches your puppy self-control.

Teaching your puppy Stop, Look, and Listen (also known as Wait)

Your puppy needs to learn one word that rises above all others when it comes to getting them to stop dead in their tracks no matter where they are or what they're doing. If you play your training cards right, your puppy will learn this word as an exhilarating game of Stop and Go. Begin with this fun off-leash exercise:

1. Use your puppy's meal kibble, or break favorite snacks into bite-size bits.

2. Go into a quiet room, calling your puppy to your side.

3. Holding a treat between your thumb and index finger, bring it to your puppy's nose.

4. Before giving them the treat, call their name and take three to five steps forward so that they follow you.

5. Stop abruptly, with your treat hand at their nose.

6. Use a word like *Yes* or *Good* to mark the moment (or use a clicker, if you have one).

7. Release the treat, saying *Find It*.

8. Continue to step and stop, taking the game to other locations and even practicing outside after your puppy is catching on.

Now test it out during playtime and as you give treats. Hold a treat or toy in front of your puppy and instruct *Wait*. If they leap for it, lift it out of reach. Do not lower the toy again until they are standing or sitting calmly. Repeat *Wait*. If they hold still with the reward two feet above their head, drop it quickly for a quick game of Find It.

Use Wait to teach your puppy self-control at doorways and during playtime as well as to teach them to check in with you periodically during walks or outings. Rewarding their cooperation with treats and toys — especially when they're first learning this direction — ensures a lifetime of cooperation.

Because your doorway is the center of a lot of actifvity, it's a good place to start teaching your puppy self-control:

1. With your puppy on their leash and collar or harness, walk to the door.

2. Plan on either shaking your puppy's treat cup or using a toy to reward them when you say *Wait.*

3. The moment they alert to the word, release the toy or treat and say *Good Puppy.*

4. Repeat these steps, but this time when you say *Wait,* open the door a small crack.

5. If they lunge, hold the leash steady, waiting until they stop pulling to reward them.

6. Gradually open the door until you're able to open it fully wide without your puppy lunging.

Include Wait on your outings to instruct your puppy to stop in place. With your puppy on their freedom line, periodically (no more than once every five minutes and as needed) say *Wait* and then step on or pick up the leash. Release your puppy to *Go Free* the moment they pause without struggling.

REMEMBER

Wait differs from Stay in that it's a momentary pause that can be used to instill polite manners at doors, stairs, and thresholds, as well as used in everyday conversation. With a home full of pets and people, Wait is one word we use a lot.

The Sequencing Method

Teaching your puppy new words and routines can be fast and fun when using the sequencing method, which introduces three interlaced behaviors at once instead of just one at a time. Why three? Well, one is too few, and two is predictable — your puppy will naturally vacillate between the two behaviors without concentrating on what you're saying — but three is the perfect challenge. Watch as your puppy slows their reactions to tune in to what you're saying so that they can get it right.

Practice one sequence per 5-minute lesson, and no more than two different sequences each day. Once your puppy is showing an understanding of words, you may bring the sequence out of lesson time and begin to use them in your daily interactions.

Organize your lessons in a quiet room or area. Treats are essential, so bring those along too — or a toy, if your puppy prefers it. The leash is purely optional at this stage.

Sit-Down-Stand

I call the Sit-Down-Stand word cues the A-B-Cs of puppy training. You and your puppy will have fun learning this quick sequence.

Initially, practice luring your puppy one behavior at a time. Remember to practice after a potty-and-play routine when your puppy is neither too sleepy nor too worked up to focus on learning something new.

When doing Sit-Down-Stand, avoid ramming your puppy into position with your free hand. At best, you'll get them there, although they won't learn to do it for themselves; at worst, you'll frighten them and they'll grow more cautious during lesson time.

Follow these steps:

1. **Sit**: Hold the treat from your puppy's nose, bringing it to a point directly above their ears. As they sit, say *Sit*.

2. **Down:** Hold the treat from your puppy's nose, drawing it straight down to a spot directly between their paws. When they lie down, say *Down*. (See Figure 11-2.)

3. **Stand:** Hold the treat from your puppy's nose, drawing it out in a line directly in front of their eye, or if they are lying down, draw it at a slightly upward angle in front of their face. (See Figure 11-3)

Your puppy may have an easier time learning one skill than another: That's common. Or, you may feel like you're not able to move your puppy from one position to another without physically pushing them along with your free hand. Ideally, give your puppy time (sometimes it takes 30 seconds) to move into each position on their own. After the lightbulb goes off — this position works to get the treat — they will more quickly assume it the next time around. If you need to see this sequence in action, tune into my YouTube channel at www.sarahsayspets.com.

FIGURE 11-2:
Lure Down with
treats and toys

Illustration by Robert Golinello

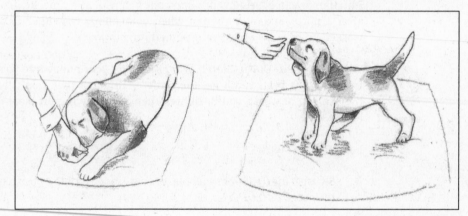

FIGURE 11-3:
Lure Stand with
treats and toys.

Illustration by Robert Golinello

After your puppy has gotten each of the separate positions correct, sequence them together in random order. Gradually increase the number of behaviors they can complete per each reward — and time them, if you're competitive, to see how many behaviors they can nail per 15-second interval.

Follow-Wait-Find-It

Place your puppy on their leash or freedom line and get their attention with a treat cup or toy or by holding out a tasty food treat. Walk forward in a straight line, saying *Follow* as you do. If your puppy jumps ahead or on you, stop and lift the reward out of their reach. Start again when they calm down. After three to five steps, say *Wait* as you come to a stop. When they stop and look to you, drop the treat on the floor at your feet and say *Find it.*

After you've established your walking rhythm, extend the steps between pauses. Begin around the room and then proceed into other areas of the house, as described in the "Instilling Household Manners" section, later in this chapter.

If your puppy swings out in front of you, walk along a wall and hold the reward behind your thigh. If they continue to jump at you, ask a helper to hold the line loosely and to tug it downward should your puppy leap up.

Come-Sit-Lean-In or Belly Up

Come is one of the first directions all puppies should know. Though I introduce it in Chapter 10, it bears repeating that Come should be taught as a cue that means you are together, not apart. During this preadolescent stage, practice Come as a sequence with other words to help your puppy understand that Come is a direction that leads to interactive fun. Here's how:

1. Break treats into bits, and pocket or carry a treat cup while practicing this lesson.

2. Call your puppy's name as you step backward or run from their side. (Keep the distance short initially — fewer than five paces.)

3. As you stop, direct your puppy to *Sit,* and then reward them.

   As your puppy learns this skill, your new goal will be to help them understand that Come ends with full hands-on interaction, ensuring that future Comes end up with your puppy at your side.

   To do this, choose one of their petting poses — either Belly Up or Lean In (leaning into your legs).

4. Say *Come,* and after your puppy comes and sits, kneel and lure them into a Belly Up or Lean In pose.

5. Mix it up, pairing Come with either Sit, Lean In, or Belly Up.

Think of the Come direction as the human phrase equivalent of "Huddle," and encourage your puppy with that level of confidence. Convey that Come invites reconnection and that togetherness is the safest, most wonderful place to be.

Over-Under-Through

**JUST FOR
FUN**

Whether you have kids around or you're a kid at heart, the Over–Under–Through sequence is just plain fun. It also helps to teach your puppy self–control whenever people are sitting at their level:

1. **Get a handful of treats and sit on the floor with your legs side-by-side and extended out in front of you.**

2. **Hold a treat in front of your puppy's nose and lure them over your outstretched legs as you say *Over*.**

   If two legs are unsurmountable, separate your legs, letting your puppy tackle one at a time.

3. **Bend your legs to create a tunnel beneath them: Lure your puppy under your legs as you say *Under*, rewarding them for crawling under your legs.**

4. **Bend one leg (if your puppy will fit) over the other to create a modified tunnel combination, saying *Through* as you lure your puppy through the "tunnel" with a treat.**

5. **Mix it up and reward your puppy at various points along the way.**

REMEMBER

When you see good behavior that you want to reward, be careful how you mark the moment. Saying *Good Dog!* repetitively in a high-pitched tone may create so much excitement that your puppy may abandon their good behavior for something more recreational, such as nipping or jumping. Instead of lots of verbal praise, if you're using a clicker, click before you treat. (See Chapter 5 for more on clickers.) If you're not using a clicker, use a sharp, marking word like *Yes* or *Good* to highlight the exact behavior you want your puppy to repeat.

Instilling Household Manners

Turning your young puppy free in your home, even if they've been doing well with their potty training, is a big mistake. They'll misbehave and you'll end up paying for it — in more ways than one. Unsupervised, a puppy can rearrange your closets, eat garbage, and chew on the chairs.

If your end game is to teach your puppy how to be free in your home, however, this is an ideal time to get started.

Leading daily walkabouts

Once or twice a day, lead your puppy through your home on-leash. Though anyone in your immediate circle of friends and family may guide your puppy, let common sense prevail. Do not tether them to children younger than 12 or secure a rambunctious dog to an unsteady person.

Following are some suggestions when touring your home:

>> **Keep the walkabouts short and upbeat.** Direct with the familiar words Follow, Wait, Sit, Place, and Leave It that you've been teaching them and reward their cooperation with treats and praise.

>> **Speak directions clearly, and enunciate syllables.** Also, give directions only once; repeated directions sound drastically different from single directions. (Consider the indecipherable "Sitsitsitcomeonpleasesitdown.")

>> **If you're sitting, arrange a place for your puppy and settle them with a chew.** If they can settle down, keep them with you.

When your puppy gets into a routine in your home, you can test their self-control and cooperation by letting them drag a freedom leash as described in Chapter 5. Use your words and signals to direct them, guide them to their stations if you want them to be still, and pick up the lead if they get rambunctious or needs reminding.

Establishing a special place in the rooms you share

All puppies love to follow their families, and, when given a choice, yours will always want to be near you. Too much isolation is a bad thing because a puppy gleans their personality from group reflection. When possible, teach your puppy their special place in each of the rooms you share so that they can hang with you wherever you are in your home. If your puppy is still working on their house-training or instigates mayhem when given too much freedom, either walk them on a leash or tether them, as shown in Figure 11-4.

WARNING

Your puppy must be fully comfortable on a leash and at least 12 weeks old before you begin tethering them. Until this age, most puppies feel frantically trapped on a leash and need more sleep than active training. Before then, supervision, crate time, and safe-room freedom are best.

FIGURE 11-4:
Tether when you can supervise and teach Stay.

REMEMBER

Determining how long you can keep your puppy tethered to their special place depends on their age and mental state at the time. A sleepyhead of any age can handle an hour or more, and an older pup can handle more extended periods. The best gauge is your puppy's behavior — always keep them tethered near you and be aware of their signals. If your pup has been resting by you for an hour and suddenly stands up and starts acting restless, they probably need to go to their potty spot. If your puppy chews on a bone for 15 minutes and then starts acting like a jumping bean, they're likely experiencing an energy spurt and needs time for a little play.

When creating tethers for your puppy, follow these steps:

1. **Select a station area in each room you share — perhaps a spot near the couch in the TV room but away from the table in the dining room.**

WARNING

    Puppies fidget, so make sure the station is away from stairs, electrical cords and outlets, and other entanglements.

2. **Set up the area with a comfy mat and your puppy's favorite chew toy.**

    Doing so helps them identify their special place — their comfort station. Think of the comfort station in human terms: When you go into your living room, don't you have a favorite couch or chair?

3. **Identify an immovable, sturdy, and secure object near the comfort station where you can secure the puppy's leash. (Refer to Figure 11-1, where the leash is hooked around a table leg.)**

    If you have nothing to secure the lead to, screw an eye hook into the wall and clip the leash through it.

FOR THE PUPPIES WHO LOVE TO CRAWL UNDERFOOT

Some puppies like to get in the way. Blocking you attracts your attention, but it can be dangerous if you trip or step on your pup. Whenever your puppy trips you up, gets on the wrong side of the leash, leans, or gets in your way, say "Excuse

Eventually, your puppy will go to their station naturally. Initially, though, you must secure them at the station until they learn to enjoy their special place.

WARNING

Some puppies panic when initially tethered. If you're concerned about your pup, arrange their place nearby and sit on the leash rather than tether it to an immovable object. Encourage bone chewing and begin to leave their side only when they're sleeping. They'll soon get the hang of it.

TIP

If your puppy is a leash chewer, you may find them chewing their tethering leashes — it's a common frustration. To circumvent the issue, purchase light-weight chain leashes for tethering times.

Mealtime manners

Teaching your puppy polite manners around food — for their meals *and* yours — is a must-do task. And it's a whole lot easier when everyone is following the same routine.

For your puppy's mealtimes, they need to learn to sit and wait as you prepare their food. If they won't cooperate — jumping or barking at you in anticipation — you have a few choices:

>> Push the food bowl back and ignore your puppy completely, putting their food down only after they have settled down.

>> If your puppy gets set off by the routine, break the routine into parts and teach your puppy to sit and wait for each step, giving them handfuls of the meal or a reward for each successful step. If they act up, push the food out of reach and walk away. Resume this mealtime-manners game in 5 or 10 minutes.

>> If your puppy still jumps or barks as you're in the throes of final preparations, have them drag a leash before you begin. If they become overexcited, step on the leash using the techniques I outline in Chapter 15.

For your own mealtimes, designate a station area four to six feet from the table where your puppy can sit or play while you and your family are eating. If you've already encouraged interruptions, you can be sure that they won't stay put initially, so tether them there, as described earlier in this chapter. If they're still having trouble relaxing, exercise and play with them just before you eat, and set aside a special chew or toy that comes out only when meals are served.

REMEMBER

Looking at your puppy invites them to the feast. To encourage civility, ignore them while you eat. I know that it seems cold-hearted, but in the end, you're teaching them that this is the time to snooze or catch up on some undisturbed chewing.

Handling Run-Throughs

During your puppy's preadolescence, their adult teeth will emerge and their hair will begin to grow and fill in; it's a happy time and a sad one, when many of their infant puppy characteristics fade away. Though Chapter 17 addresses grooming tips and techniques, I thought I should stress at least once in this chapter the importance of conditioning your puppy to their grooming tools *now* — the sooner you get started, the more they will link their sprucing to food and fun.

Here are three tools to introduce your puppy to. Use favorite chews, spreadable treats, and high-value food rewards to get your puppy acclimated to their use:

>> **Toothbrush:** Organize a routine around the tooth-brushing event to build excitement for the activity. I always brush each of our dog's teeth separately in the small downstairs bathroom to build up eagerness for each turn.

Sandwich a dab of safely formulated doggie paste between your chosen brush and a high-value food treat. Say *Pearly Whites* as you extend the brush to your puppy. After they alert to the routine, continue to play the game for a few more days, slowly diminishing the size of the food treat. Ask a partner to steady your puppy's head by holding a treat to their nose as you get them comfortable having the brush rotated in their mouth.

>> **Nail and hair clippers:** This is an excellent time to get your puppy used to the sound of any future clipping tools you or your groomer will use in your puppy's lifetime. It bears repeating that preadolescent puppies are more receptive to noises as well as to any handling or unfamiliar physical interactions than at any other time in their lives. Pairing handling with positive outcomes becomes forever lodged in the area of their brain labeled It Must Be Okay Just Because It Leads to Something Good.

Here's how the pairing works:

1. **Take whatever tool you'll use (a nail clipper, for example).**

2. **Present it to your puppy to sniff.**

3. **Remove the tool and reward your puppy.**

4. **Repeat Step 3, but this time open and shut the clipper one time. Remove it and reward your puppy.**

5. **Continue to expose your puppy, open and shut the clipper a time or two, and reward them only after you've removed the clipper from sight until they are relaxed about the activity.**

   Repeat this activity with the other grooming tools.

» **Grooming brushes:** Whatever your puppy's coat type, assemble the brushes, shedding blades, or combs you'll need during this stage. Condition your puppy to their presence as outlined with the clipper, but extend the practice to gently touching their coat. Remember to reward them after you remove the object. Gradually comb through their coat, removing the object often to reward their cooperation.

TIP

Your puppy "sees" the world through their sense of smell, so let them sniff everything that comes near their body. They have to have a good sniff to feel comfortable with their surroundings.

Chapter **12**

Surviving Puberty: 6 to 9 Months

During your puppy's teenage months, you'll witness their emotional awakening — it's a time when their adult hormones let loose and external distractions interrupt everyday routines. If you know your dog's breed or mix, this is also the time when many specific traits emerge: Terriers grow more vigilant; protective breeds, more territorial; retrievers and herders, more obsessive with their passions.

If you've established good habits, they'll stick, although at times you may think your puppy has forgotten every lesson you've ever taught them. Trust me: No hostile or domineering impulses are taking over your puppy's brain. It's just that teenage puppies, like maturing kids, blossom into early adulthood with a lot on their minds. As I stress throughout this book — and even more so at this particular stage in your puppy's life — keep your cool. Sure, your puppy may act like a stranger at times, but they still identify with you and adore you most of all. This chapter will help you appreciate your puppy's changing priorities and coach them through this awkward time. Together, you'll not only discover how to survive this time but also how to thrive with everyone's dignity intact.

TIP

Starting the training process with an older puppy? Flip to Chapter 11 to learn the early lessons you missed.

Understanding Your Puppy's Mindset at This Age

At the teenage stage, your puppy's world is being shaped by two conflicting forces: the desire to please you and the desire for some independence. Don't take it personally. Your efforts to follow through with your directions will assure your puppy that you mean what you say and will result in their respect, regardless of whether they feel like listening at any given moment. Build on the lessons I sketch out in Chapter 11, and, before you know it, you'll survive the worst of it when it comes to bringing up puppy. Here are a few rules to help you through this stage:

>> **Remain calm.** Don't let your puppy see that you're angry or frustrated.

>> **Make sure your puppy doesn't ignore you.** If your puppy blows off your direction, often as if they hadn't even heard it, calmly repeat the direction and reinforce your expectations. If your puppy is off-leash and ignores or defies a direction, ignore them and withdraw from the situation, provided they're in a safe enclosure. When possible, take the treat cup and pretend to eat from it, refusing to share or even acknowledge the puppy that just moments ago blew you off.

A graceful retreat isn't a failure.

REMEMBER

>> **Raise your puppy's consciousness.** Teach your puppy the concept of Nope. For more details on developing their awareness, see the later section "Teaching your puppy the concept of Nope."

Conditioning Good Habits

If you began training during one of the early stages of puppyhood, many of your training habits are likely set already; if not, refer to the relevant conditioning sections of Chapters 10 and 11 to bring your puppy up to speed. Puberty, which happens during the teenage stage, results in the release of adult dog hormones that dramatically shape and modify your puppy's mannerisms. Many parents report what you'll experience: a cheerfully cooperative puppy suddenly blowing you off; a get-along-with-everyone puppy terrorizing the new pooch at the dog park; and what in the world do you call that thing they're doing on the couch cushions — a pelvic thrust? Oh, the things you have to look forward to.

Before your puppy strays too far off course, make a list of all the good puppy manners you expect from your darling and share it with friends and family. Insist on following through with expectations, and refuse to settle for any new ideas, lest friends and family develop their own set of rules. Here's a mock list — you should use it to clarify for everyone reading it what you want your puppy to do in each situation — and don't be afraid to remind them.

>> **Approaching a door, at home, or on the road:** Puppy must sit, coming in and going out.

>> **Greeting:** Puppy should grab a toy from the basket and only be greeted after they've calmed down enough to sit or roll on their back

>> **Mealtime manners:** Puppy must sit and wait for puppy food and also lie on a mat with a bone during your meals.

>> **After-hours TV/computer:** Puppy should lie on a mat and chew a toy.

>> **Greeting other dogs and people while on a leash.** Puppy must sit at your side before approaching.

Dealing with canine backtalk

Somewhere during the teenage stage, your puppy will give you The Look — the one that says they know what you want but they're not going to obey immediately. Maybe your puppy's look will say, "In a minute!" or "Have we met?" Or maybe your puppy will give you the equivalent of a teenage eye roll. But you'll get The Look someday, so prepare yourself. Acting out is a part of growing up.

So, how should you deal with your puppy when they don't want to listen to one of your many directions? Well, number one, don't sweat the small stuff. If you get mad over a minor infraction like your teenage puppy blowing you off, life's going to get a lot worse for you. Don't yell, chase, hit, or isolate your puppy, either — those techniques won't buy their long-term cooperation.

As you work with your puppy during this stage, remember that they're the one going through puberty right now, not you. (Whew!) Life is hard and confusing for them now; they're easily distracted. Sometimes all it takes is a gentle reminder; at other times, maybe you need two or three. No matter how often t has to occur, calmly insist on what puppy needs to do with stationary directions like Sit, Stay, and Down.

REMEMBER

Try not to be angry if your puppy willfully ignores a direction. You still know best what has to happen next. Calmly repeat yourself even if your puppy is distracted, insisting that listening to you is a requirement, not an option.

One particular situation needs a firm hand — handling a runaway puppy. If your puppy is off-leash in an unconfined area and you feel that you must go to them, walk at an angle to a point ten feet away from where they're standing. If you have treats or a treat cup, make a big fuss about eating the treats yourself. (Your puppy has no idea that you won't actually do it.) Avoid walking straight at your puppy as they may interpret your direct approach as a game. If your puppy approaches you, calmly cast treats on the ground or floor and play Find It. Then calmly hold their collar or attach a leash.

After you have your puppy back on-leash, review the lesson they ignored, and practice on-leash lessons for five or ten minutes every day for one week. Reminders are often all they need.

TIP

If your puppy continues to ignore a stationary command like Sit or Down, review that one as well.

Teaching your puppy the concept of No

Many puppy parents dole out No as if it were their puppy's middle name. More often than not, though, people use the word No inconsistently, which tends to leave puppies baffled about its meaning. It should mean Leave It or Stop — an instructional cue, not a discipline per se. You don't want your puppy to ever see you as a venting machine. You're the one who is too cool to blow your lid. If you want your puppy to respond appropriately to this type of cue, avoid the following mistakes:

>> **Shouting it:** Shouting to a puppy sounds like barking. Would barking excite a situation or calm it down?

>> **Using it with your puppies' name:** In fact, many puppies think No is the second half of their name: "Buddy, no!" "Molly, no!" You should use your puppy's name only when you're happy, not angry.

>> **Saying it after the action has occurred:** If I yelled at you after you ate a bowl of soup, would you understand that I was upset at you for opening the can? Said at the wrong time, No communicates nothing.

>> **Repeating it:** "No, no, no" sounds different than a one-word direction.

The purpose of teaching your puppy to stop doing what they're doing is to help you weigh in when you're giving your puppy direction around distractions. Maybe you'll need to use it when you're calling your puppy from another group of dogs — or when you walk by a big pile of animal scat. Since No is used frequently, we'll use a softer version, Nope, through the training lessons in the following sections.

Taking Care of Your Puppy's Basic Needs

Your puppy will get pretty creative as they mature, testing out new behaviors and revisiting a few old habits before they're all grown up. Though a whiny, couch-cozying, slipper-chewing, garbage-grabbing puppy can look completely inno-cent, and it's hard to resist laughing the first time your puppy streaks by with that roll of toilet paper unfurling behind them, if you let anything slide twice, your puppy may have a new habit in the making. Decide early on what your puppy needs in order to feel included and satisfied in each situation (a bone, a mat, a 15-minute game of Toss after a nap), and insist on only the behavior you've outlined.

Sleeping out of the crate

Though your puppy may still need up to six hours of daytime rest in their crate, they may like sleeping on their calming station (see Chapter 5) as well. Test it out by gating the crate room area, placing the rest mat outside the crate, and leaving the crate open for nap times. Can the puppy sleep as well outside of the crate? If they can, you may begin phasing out the crate for afternoon nap times.

You may want to continue crating your puppy at night, though the choice is up to you. If you want to have your puppy sleep crate-free, tether your pup with a light leash to your bed or another immovable object, as fully described in Chapter 11.

WARNING

Teenage puppies are still growing and need lots of replenishing sleep. If your puppy is restless or fidgety outside of their crate, go back to schedulling naps in their enclosure.

Phasing out the midday meal

Most puppies start phasing out a meal on their own. If yours does not, you can wean them off their midday meal during this stage over a 6-day period using the following strategy: Cut one-fourth of the meal for one day, one-half for days 2 and 3, three-fourths by days 4 and 5, and then phase out the meal altogether.

Learning to hold it

By this stage, your puppy has bladder control. Urge them to stay in their crate 15 to 30 minutes longer each morning by waking them up with a bone or food-stuffed hollow toy, until they're content sleeping in until your ideal target time.

THE DIFFERENCE BETWEEN A LURE, A REWARD, AND A BRIBE

There's a big difference between the following three concepts — especially in your dog's eyes:

- **Lure:** Lures are generally a value food reward or a favorite toy used to guide a puppy through an action. A word cue can be attached to the action, which a puppy will learn over time.

- **Reward:** Anything that a puppy values (freedom, a toy or bone, playtime, release from a crate or car) may be used to reward them for listening or responding to a signal.

- **Bribe:** Bribes (generally, food) are used to cajole after a puppy has ignored a direction.

Though lures are good for early training and rewards for good behavior can be given at any time, bribes are a big no-no unless you want a puppy who listens only when you're waving a big piece of chicken in your hand.

Making Learning Fun

As your puppy moves from preadolescent puppy lessons into the next phase of their learning, you'll notice a few new things — namely, that your puppy is processing a lot more information than just "them" and "you." Suddenly, that other dog barking in the distance has a crucial message that needs translation and often an immediate response, the vehicles zooming by take a form that elicits their developing predatory impulses, and, when given a choice, they'd often rather stay at the dog park than come home with you.

The good news is that your puppy will still excite to their old word cues if you keep the lessons fresh, and may work even harder to please you if you come up with new fun routines. Bring your lessons out into the real world, phase out your treat dependency, and engage your puppy's focus by rewarding them with anything they consider positive, from playing with their dog friends to a swim in the lake.

Stay, continued

Stay is a direction best left unrushed. I introduce it in Chapter 11 using treats and toys. Although you should continue to use Stay to encourage self-control around food and games, bring this lesson into your everyday interactions, challenging your puppy's focus as you add more distance and distractions to each exercise.

Here are a few rules to follow when teaching the Stay direction:

REMEMBER

>> **No staring.** Avoid staring at your puppy when they're holding a Stay. It's too daunting for them.

>> **Stand tall.** When you bend down, you can look threatening to your puppy or as if you want to play.

>> **Stay close to your puppy when you start.** You should have about six inches from toe to paw. Creating too much distance too soon can be confusing for your pup.

>> **Hold the lead directly above your puppy's head.** Do this initially for each exercise. That way, if they confuse Stay with Go, you're there to steady them in place.

>> **Vary the pause time.** When you return to your puppy's side at the end of each exercise, vary the length of time you pause before you release them with "Okay!" This variation prevents their "reading" the pattern and encourages them to keep a more watchful eye on your whereabouts.

>> **Resist petting.** Hold off until you finish the entire lesson. Praise is better — do that with your voice. Too much petting ruins their concentration.

Practice the simple sequence in the following steps twice a day until your puppy is feeling mighty fine about their accomplishments.

To prepare for your first lesson, follow these steps:

1. **Take your leashed puppy into a quiet room.**

   No TV. No kids. No cats. Just you two.

2. **Fold the leash in your left hand and hold it directly above their head, so that it's taut (but not tight) at hip level.**

3. **Position your puppy behind your heels.**

Now you're ready to teach your puppy their first lesson. Repeat the following steps four to six times — depending on the intensity of each exercise:

1. **Instruct "Sit" and align your puppy with your ankles.**

2. **Instruct "Stay" as you flash your hand in front of your puppy's nose. Remove the hand signal and pause for five seconds.**

3. Instruct "Okay" as you swing your arm forward and step out of position.

4. Again, instruct "Sit-Stay." This time, pivot to face away from your puppy and pause ten seconds. Return to the starting point and release with "Okay!"

5. Back to the start position again, instruct "Stay." Pivot in front of your puppy. Pause. Now march in place to create a physical distraction that will teach your puppy how to contain themselves.

   Yes, I said *march!* March slowly at first, like you're sleepwalking. After your puppy holds still for that, gradually increase your physical motions.

6. Instruct "Stay" and pivot and pause. Then try jumping and waving your arms.

   Go slowly at first. You want to ease into your mania. Then make some noise.

7. Pivot, pause, and then make the sound of your favorite barnyard animal while looking away from your puppy. Then turn back, pause, and release.

REMEMBER

   I've said it before, but it bears repeating a thousand times: No staring into your puppy's eyes, because dogs view prolonged glares as confrontational, not instructional. Instead, keep looking over their head.

8. From your starting position, instruct "Stay," pivot in front, and pause for 30 seconds.

   Stand up tall, relax your shoulders, and keep the leash above your puppy's head (taut not tight) just in case they're tempted to break.

9. When the time is up, return to their side, pause, and release with "Okay!"

   "Good pup!" Only use verbal praise between exercise as petting can excite your puppy's playful nature!

REMEMBER

Some puppies have a reduced attention span and initially may not be able to hold still for long. Check to ensure that you're following protocol: Did you start with the early Stay lessons outlined in Chapter 11? Are you standing right in front of them as you increase distractions? Are you keeping the leash above their head to enforce their control? Are you introducing this direction in a discrete location? Too many distractions make it impossible to concentrate. If you think your puppy may have to go potty, take them on a quick potty run. If they're fidgeting, bring them back to a Sit and either make the sequence shorter or stand closer to your puppy.

When your puppy can hold still for 15 seconds, you're ready to increase the three *D*s:

>> **Distraction:** Step up your march, add a new aerobics twist, walk full circle around your puppy, and chant like a chimp. Can you do all these crazy things without tempting your puppy to move?

REMEMBER

Are you wondering why you're jumping around and making noise while your puppy is expected to stay? Eventually, your puppy will have to concentrate while confronted with motion and sound distractions, so you're helping them get accustomed to temptations.

>> **Duration:** Stretch your 30-second standstill to two minutes.

>> **Distance:** Move out one foot at a time. When you're successful, reintroduce distractions gradually and increase the duration.

As you progress, you may try securing the leash to an immovable object and increasing your distance or practicing Stay at the door or while a friend opens the door or while you ring the bell. Gradually introduce Stay to challenge your puppy's self-control. When they can handle all that, the two of you should feel like pros.

Cooperative leash skills

Your puppy's lust for adventuring will expand a lot during the teenage period, as will their taste in friends both on-leash and off. As they become more mindfully aware of life around them, it's the perfect time to work on their leash-walking skills. Because an unruly leash-walking dog can be one of life's biggest nightmares, work twice a day on shaping cooperative walking skills (using your choice of compassion wear as detailed in Chapter 5) to ensure that you and your puppies walking together are nothing short of a dream.

Follow, no pull

Teaching your puppy to walk calmly with you on a leash is a bit of an art form. Because leash pulling is so common that it could practically qualify as an Olympic sport (all dogs pull against resistance, no matter their age or size), teaching your puppy not to pull takes effort. Here's what you have to do:

1. After playing with your puppy for 10 to 15 minutes (preferably off-leash), secure them on their compassion wear collar or harness (see Chapter 5) and a 4-to-6-foot walking leash, and guide them to your left side. (See Figure 12-1.)

2. Place a handful of food rewards in your pocket (no fewer than 25 small treats).

3. Walk in a familiar area outside, saying "Follow me."

4. If, after three to five paces, your puppy is walking with you, stop as you say "Wait," and then reward them by placing a treat next to your left foot.

5. Walk in a counterclockwise circle with your puppy on the inside as you extend the distance you move together. Gradually lengthen the steps you take before each pause.

Practice five circles twice a day.

FIGURE 12-1:
Be cheerful and upbeat when teaching your puppy to walk at your side.

If you have a puller, don't tug, yank, or jerk them back: Most interpret your sudden surges as Game On and pull a lot harder. The best thing to do is to stop. Relax your arm straight on the leash and think of your elbow as a hinge. Rock it back slightly to offer the slightest give and hold your puppy in place until they stop pulling. The very moment your puppy stops pulling, looks back to you, or sits in place, mark the moment with a happy exclamation like "Good" (or use a clicker, if you have one) and place their food reward by your left foot.

TIP

Is your puppy too strong for you to manage? Consider a conditioning harness or head collar, mentioned in Chapter 5. You can hold the leash behind your back with both hands. This position transfers the strain of the leash from your arms to the trunk of your body. If your puppy hacks or strains harder, however, call a professional for assistance. If you persist, you may do damage to their airway.

TIP

To help perfect the leash move, practice without the leash. Relax your arms at your side, and let them swing back and forth from your elbow. Now imagine that I'm holding my hand behind your back. Slap my hand without doing more than flexing your triceps muscle with a slight bend of your elbow. Now pick up the leash. Pretend that my hand is there and that you're trying to hit it.

Changing your pace

As your puppy follows more willingly, play the pace-change game to keep them interested. Holding your leash hand steady, move faster by trotting. Then slow your pace by lengthening your stride. Make sure you change gears smoothly, and indicate the change by saying "Click-click" or "Shh." Remember, your puppy's a canine, not a Porsche.

Doing an about-face

After you have your puppy walking to your rhythm, you're ready to teach them the turns. Walking at a reasonable speed, say "Follow" and pivot to the right. To help your puppy keep up, slow down as you turn. Click your tongue, bend your knees, or slap your leg to keep them with you. Walk six paces, stop and position the Sit, and then hug your puppy for a job well done.

REMEMBER

Avoid pulling the puppy through the turn. That's no fun for them.

Taking Follow into the real world

You'll know you're ready to practice the Follow direction in everyday situations when your puppy responds without pressure on their collar. One obvious place to use the Follow direction is on your walks. If your puppy's young or just beginning to learn, practice Follow for one-fourth of your walk. Increase the distance over the next month until your puppy is always walking at your side.

WARNING

Stay calm if things get out of hand when you're out in public. If you yell, "Follow, follow, follow!" and jerk your poor puppy back and forth, they'll get more excited. If you have this problem, determine whether you're asking too much too soon and check to see whether you're using the right collar. (See Chapter 5.) Maybe your puppy needs to exercise more before you practice in public.

Greeting dogs and people

As you're walking, you will pass other dogs and people. Though it's okay to let your puppy greet some dogs and some people, they should not greet everyone. You need to be the one to judge whom to approach. Dog people are easy to identify: They look lovingly on your puppy as if just one pat will make their whole day. If you have the time, ask your puppy to Wait and Sit. Only after you have them settled should you allow them to go and greet a new person.

If you see another dog, well, that's another matter. You need to make super-sure that any dog you approach has good leash manners and is dog-friendly. Unless you know the dog, you may not be able to tell; in this case, it's better to teach your puppy the phrase *not now*, speeding up as you pass the other dog and discouraging your puppy from making any direct eye contact with passing dogs.

If you know an oncoming dog and want to stop to allow some on-leash interaction, you may certainly do so. Ask your puppy to Wait and Sit, however, before releasing them to greet.

WARNING

Allowing your puppy to drag you over to greet another dog is foolish and unsafe. Leashes modify a dog's natural posture, making them look confrontational even when they're anything but; also if your puppy were to break free from the leash, they would impulsively take off, putting themselves and others in danger!

Distance control

Chapter 11 stresses the fun to be had learning the meaning of lots of different words, from Come to Sit, Down, and Follow. Using a sequence lesson format, Chapter 11 also shows you how to teach three words simultaneously and how to vary the order of the words you use in order to perfect your puppy's listening skills. This chapter asks you to put their understanding to the test by using their words out in the real world and teaching them to listen, no matter the distance between you.

Wait

Continue using the Wait direction to catch your puppy's attention at doorways, cars, or stairs or before entering an area of high stimulation (for example, the veterinarian's office, a room full of children, or a dog training class). This directive tells your puppy to stop, look to you, and listen for another instruction. If you're successfully using this direction in these situations, begin to practice it on your walks, and then at a distance:

On a leash

1. **Stop in your tracks as you direct** "Wait."

2. **Hold the leash securely if your pup doesn't stop with you.**

3. **Release with** "Okay."

On a freedom line

1. **Position yourself next to the line, initially ten inches behind your puppy's tail.**

2. **Say** "Wait" **in a clear, strong voice.**

3. If your puppy stops and checks in, mark the moment with a clicker or a word like "Good," and then immediately release your puppy with "Go Free" to continue exploring.

4. If they cannot process Wait from this distance, step on the line. When they are brought to a stop, wait for them to check in, then respond as though they stopped on their own. Mark the moment they look to you with a click or *Good!* then release with "Go Free".

5. Repeat the steps, this time furthering the distance in Step 1.

Come

The goal when you say "Come" is to have your puppy return and reconnect with you. Each time you say this direction, pat, treat, or otherwise handle your puppy so that they learn that "Come" means "togetherness and interaction." As you gradually instruct them to come from a greater distance, they'll want to close the gap.

Chapter 11 has all you need to know in order to teach your puppy Come. Continue to practice this lesson (review, if necessary) throughout the day whenever you have something positive to share — a pat, a treat, a toy, or even dinner. Make sure your puppy's first associations in this direction are warm and welcoming.

Going for control from short distances

Before you can teach your pup to come from a distance, they must understand that "Come" means togetherness. After they understand, you're ready to go for distance control, using a freedom line or retractable leash. (See Chapter 5 for info on leashes.)

TIP Practice this exercise in a quiet room and keep your lesson short and upbeat.

To teach distance control, make sure your pup is wearing a long lead and then follow these steps:

1. Practice three regular Sit-Stays, finishing each by returning to your puppy's side and releasing them with "Okay!"

2. Leave your puppy in a Stay position and walk to the end of the leash.

3. Pause. (Vary the duration each time.)

4. Call "[Name], come!" in a directional tone. Signal it by raising an arm straight above you and waving (the human exclamation point!).

5. As soon as you issue the direction, scurry backward and reel in the leash.

6. When your pup gets near your feet, bring your finger up to your eyes.

7. Encourage eye contact by standing or kneeling and making kissing sounds.

8. Pet their head or belly as you reward them with positive love and interaction.

9. Release them with "Okay" and always remember to praise your good puppy.

TIP

Practice Come three times per session. That's all. More than that is stressful for your pup.

Building focus by throwing in distractions

If your puppy gets excited when they hear "Come," you're doing a good job. Now you can start encouraging focus around everyday distractions and increasing the distance from which you call them. Use the leash, freedom line, or retractable leash. Instead of putting your puppy from a Sit-Stay, wait for them to get distracted. Stand behind them and call "[Name], come!" If they don't look to you, tug the leash and use rewards and praise to entice them. You may also run away from them a short distance before turning and welcoming them into your arms.

If you're having trouble getting your puppy's attention around distractions, you're not alone. Keep practicing, but start in a lower distraction area so that you can build your puppy's success rate — and yours, too.

Come do's and don'ts

Here are a few things to remember when teaching the Come direction:

TIP

» **Do use it sparingly.** When you overuse Come, dogs stop paying attention.

When your puppy understands the direction, avoid using it all the time. Say it infrequently and make it extremely rewarding. (Don't forget about the other directions you have in your arsenal: Inside for coming indoors, Let's Go for following after you, and Follow for staying at your side.)

» **Do use a different direction to bring your puppy inside.** Coming in from outdoors is a big drag for your pup, no more fun than being left alone or ignored. Using the Come direction when you want to bring your pup inside makes it a negative direction. Instead, pick a direction like Inside. Start using it on-lead when bringing your puppy into the house. Quickly offer a treat or ball toss.

And here's a list of don'ts — be sure to follow them:

>> **Don't chase your puppy if they don't respond.** Practice on-lead for now or use a long line to give them more freedom to explore.

>> **Don't call for negative interaction.** Do you have to brush, bathe, or isolate your puppy? If so, don't use Come. Also, avoid using it when you're angry. You'll only freak your puppy out.

>> **Don't repeatedly call or discipline your puppy when they run away.** I know the frustration of marching around in the middle of a cold, wet, rainy night looking for your puppy, but if you call or discipline your puppy, you're only teaching them to run from you.

>> **Don't discipline your puppy when they return to you.** They won't come back so quickly the next time.

REMEMBER

Taking Nope outside

Once your puppy recognizes that the word "Nope" means stop whatever their doing, you can begin to practice it around distractions. Use it on your walks and when adventuring on the freedom line. If, say, you instruct Follow and your puppy sticks their head in a bush, say "Nope," tug the line, and then remind them again to Follow. If you call your puppy on the freedom line and they give you one of the Looks — the In-a-Minute look, for example — say "Nope," tug the line, and call them again — remembering to look to the ground or call them as you run in the other direction!

Sit

Continue to reinforce all your puppy's manners by using Sit throughout the day and in a variety of situations, from greetings to an automatic response when your puppy wants a toy, pat, or meal. This direction is the human phrase equivalent of saying "please." Give the direction once in a clear, strong voice. If your puppy ignores you, don't be afraid to walk closer to them and say it again. Sit is not optional.

Quick Downs

Continue to work on the Down direction even in situations where lying down might be the furthest thing from your puppy's mind. The Down pose forces relax-ation, which your puppy may not want so much as need throughout their day. Initially use food to urge your puppy's cooperation in distracting areas, slowly phasing out rewards as your puppy is more reliably listening to you. For tips on learning this cue, flip to the sequencing section of Chapter 11.

When your puppy begins cooperating, use Down for everything, such as before treating (hold the treat to the ground and direct Down) and before dinner (cover the bowl with your hand and, as you put it down, say "Down").

Leave It

To teach your puppy Leave It at a distance and out in the real world, set up six to ten different situations — a maximum of one or two for each day, as this lesson is stressful. Work inside before you set up an outdoor distraction.

Indoors, put your puppy on their leash and have someone secretly place a tissue or another temptation on the floor in a neighboring room. (This is your prop.) Follow these steps and pay attention to timing:

1. **Put your puppy on their collar/harness, and then bring them to your side and casually walk toward the prop.**

2. **The second your puppy alerts to the prop, say "Leave it" in a strong, calm voice as you side step to the right of the object.**

   Your puppy has a built-in antenna system: their ears. If their ears perk up in the direction of the prop, they're alerting to it. When teaching Leave It, watch your puppy's ears. Say "Leave it" the moment your puppy notices the temptation, issuing a quick leash tug if they continue to eye it.

3. **Now, the fun part: Scold at the prop — point at it, tap it with your toe, and say "Bad, bad tissue!", similar to telling a toddler that the stove is hot. Do not, however, look at your puppy.**

   By warning the puppy with Leave It and correcting the object, your puppy will fear the object — not you.

4. **Step back from the prop and remind puppy to Leave it as you walk on. Direct your puppy to a toy or reward them with treats and attention after you've moved away from the bad, bad tissue.**

5. **Walk by the prop several times to ensure that your puppy got the message.**

Give

Give (also known as "Kindly release what's in your mouth now") is a vitally important direction to get at a distance. Parents can instruct a puppy to give a toy to the kids even from across the yard, and puppies can be encouraged to release things even from afar.

To get this distance control down, work your puppy on their freedom line and practice during playtime:

1. **Get multiples of an identical toy, like a tennis ball.**

2. **Toss one for your dog**

3. **When they have the ball, show them that you have the same one.**

4. **Instead of reaching for the toy in their mouth, shake and bounce your toy as you wait for the puppy to release the one they're holding.**

5. **As they are releasing the object, say "Give," as you toss the copy.**

Now practice inside when your puppy is holding a toy or a bone:

1. **Stand three to ten feet from your puppy when they're holding or playing with a toy or chewing a bone.**

2. **Show them a food reward, and then say "Give."**

3. **The moment they release, say "Find it!" as you toss the food bit over to the left so they need to get up to get it.**

You can choose to toss the toy for them or just let them resume chewing.

Socializing in the World Beyond

Life is very different for a puppy once their hormones start flowing: It's a fact of life. Personal space becomes an issue, and so does sexual status, whether or not you choose to neuter them (which, hopefully, you will — see Chapter 17). Though there won't be any #MeToo movement in the dog world any time soon, the days of your puppy's innocent groveling, chin-licking exuberance, greet-anything-that-moves-and-hope-they-like-me activities are long behind them. In their place come many of the adult mannerisms that will stick with them throughout their lifetime. Fortunately, you still have some influence on how they will get along with other people and with dogs. This section tells you what you need to know.

Off-leash dog play

Your puppy will not only feel different during this stage of maturity — but will also smell different. Of course, you and I might not notice, but other dogs are another story. It's a time of heavy sniffing — your puppy will be like a debutant at the new ball of life.

Though it's an exciting time to be a puppy, it's also a very impressionable time. Surround your puppy with fair-minded, well-socialized companions. (Age matters less than comfortable social skills here; experience with a variety of dogs is ideal to ensure that your puppy is comfortable with all dogs.) When introducing your puppy to a new dog off-leash, approach the other dog and engage with them to show your puppy your comfort level with the new dog.

It may take up to ten minutes for two unfamiliar dogs to find common ground, especially if they're dissimilar in age or size. You can facilitate interaction with a toy or by running around like another dog, to whom they may both give chase. If your puppy overwhelms a new companion, separate them before the other dog lashes out.

Interactive words

Keep the following words at the ready when encounters occur:

>> **Gentle:** Use a word like *gentle* as you facilitate interactions with your off-leash puppy. When it's said in a calming voice, you may use soft touches to separate your puppy if you feel they're playing too rough.

>> **Away:** This word directs your puppy away from a dog, especially when that dog's body cues are communicating that they have had enough interaction for one day (averted eyes, tail, and posture down, with lip curling or a growling sound).

Use your puppy's favorite treats or treat cup to call them over to you and away from the other dog. Though you should never overuse this direction, practice calling them two or three times and, when possible, letting them return to the fun immediately so that Come isn't perceived as a dead end.

>> **Sit:** Every three to five minutes, interrupt your puppy's play and instruct Sit to ensure that, friend or no friend, they always check in with you.

Chapter **13**

Striving for Off-Lead Control: 9 Months to 1 Year

When I was growing up, the understanding was that dogs aged seven years to every human year: It was simple math that I loved to practice on just about every dog I met. Since then, however, the equations have gotten a little more complicated. It turns out that puppies mature a lot during their first couple of years and then slow down considerably as they grow older. A quick search online (type "age equivalents in dogs") will show the lifespan of a dog and their age equivalent, which varies even more, depending on your puppy's size. Suffice it to say that simple math won't help you here.

The good news for you is that all the drama of your puppy's growth and emotional development should pass in a year instead of the decades it takes human kids to grow up. If you've done your work together as outlined in the other training chapters of Part 3, you'll be able to communicate with your puppy using the words they know and routines that should be habituated by this stage. If you're jumping into the book here, flip back to Chapters 10 and 11 to start your lessons off on the right paw!

Understanding Your Puppy's Mindset at This Age

Magic happens if you routinely train your puppy through the various stages of learning. In addition to watching your puppy's awareness grow, you will witness habits take form. Your puppy sits at the door because that's what they've always done; they ring a bell when they need to potty, because that's just the order of events, they drop the ball, fetch a toy when greeting, whip their head around when you call because it's, well, that's just how life works. It's how it's always been.

Training the Off-Lead Dog

You can't overestimate the pleasure of living with a well-trained dog. In Chapters 10 and 11, I cover the first steps of training for puppies. Start there and master those exercises before you begin the ones described below.

Whether your goal is to have your puppy off-lead around the home or to be responsive when you're on a hike at a park (check the rules to ensure that you're allowed to take your dog off-leash in a public area), the most considered question is, "How will I know when my puppy and I are ready for off-lead-control training?" Well, there's no magic age or season or day; readiness is something you gauge by experience. If you practice giving these directions and your pup shows signs of stress (such as licking their lips, hyperactivity, nipping or roughly jumping at you, chewing on their freedom lines), they've given you a signal to lower your expectations for now. Puppies show readiness with concentrated eye contact and responsiveness that's quick and cooperative. A puppy has their timetable for preparedness: Off-lead work requires impulse control that emerges anytime between the ages of 6 and 18 months. Read on to get started.

Getting mentally prepared for off-lead control

Training off the leash requires that both you and your puppy be mentally prepared for the challenges you'll face. Get your game face on, and then prepare your pup.

Psyching yourself up

To have off-lead control, you must be confident that your puppy will listen. If you're a bundle of nerves when you let go of the leash, your puppy will know it and will become anxious and unresponsive. Puppies, like people, are drawn to confidence, so you need to act with authority and self-assurance even if you have to fake it.

As you work toward off-lead control, don't get too bold too quickly. When the leash disappears, both you and your puppy will feel a little disoriented. Praise, rewards, and confident direction will keep your puppy's attention focused on you. If you begin to chase them or repeat yourself, your puppy will make their own decisions, and if at that moment they don't want to Come and they're free to run, you may be standing there helpless. Off-lead control means continually reading and rereading your puppy — especially in the beginning — and being aware that your puppy is also learning about you. To have control, you must look like a confident parent so that your dog can trust your judgment.

REMEMBER

To further your mental preparation, keep these three suggestions in mind:

>> **Stay cool.** Frustration makes you look foolish. As you work toward off-lead control, your puppy may act confused and unresponsive because your guidance is gone. You used to give the direction and guide them with the lead. Now you don't, and it feels awkward to them. Whatever your pup's reaction, stay cool. Any attempts at discipline add to their confusion. Jazz up your body language and use some pep talks to encourage them to stay focused on whatever you're doing.

>> **Stay focused.** You want your puppy to grow up thinking their activities revolves around whatever you're doing, not the other way around. If your puppy can turn your day upside down by stealing a sock from the laundry basket, or toilet paper from the bathroom, or muffins off the counter, then you're the one living in the dog house! Sure, most puppies will try to get all the attention by doing things that get you riled up, but aim to be a calm voice of reason and redirection. Work in a confined area or let your puppy drag a freedom line so that you can ignore or redirect your puppy when they act up.

>> **Allow one step back for two steps forward.** Your puppy is responding beautifully off-lead . . . until someone rings the doorbell, a chipmunk runs across the driveway, or another dog comes trotting past the gate. Then everything they've learned goes out the window and you're back to being ignored. Let me tell you a secret: Off-lead control takes time. If your puppy is good but is still having trouble in a stimulating situation, review on-lead exercises in distracting environments. (See Chapter 12.) Using a freedom line helps control the situation and at the same time conditions more appropriate behavior.

Getting your puppy's mind in the game

So, what goes into making your pup mentally ready? Maturity serves your off-lead goals well. As your puppy passes into doghood, you'll note calm predictability. Wanderlust and mischief will have most likely lost their thrill. Your dog's joy will manifest itself in silent teamwork and shared activities. The stages your puppy follows to maturity aren't so different from the ages and stages of a child growing into adulthood.

TIP

Consider your puppy's breed instincts when working toward off-lead reliability. For example, a terrier, who was bred to follow their hunting instincts independently, is far less impressed with your direction than a Shetland sheepdog, who lives for the camaraderie and guidance of a shepherd. Hounds and Nordic breeds are other pups who must be monitored closely because their instincts can override your direction. Do some research to discover whether your puppy's breed was bred to work in concert with people or to work independently. Independent thinkers may need more persuasion to focus. (A clicker and some food can work wonders.) With an independent thinker, understand that 100 percent reliability may not be a realistic goal.

Buying the Right Equipment — and Using It Correctly

As you work toward off-lead obedience, you'll practice exercises that extend your control over greater and greater distances. Before you start, however, you should round up the following items (each of which is discussed in more detail later in this section):

» **Retractable leash:** The retractable leash is invaluable for advanced work — the longer, the better.

» **Indoor freedom line:** This item is a light, 4-foot leash worn around the house.

» **Finger lead:** This lead, shown in Figure 13-1, should be long enough to gently guide but short enough not to distract your dog (1 to 6 inches is a common length).

» **Tether-n-train:** This type of leash, with a clip on each end (see Figure 13-2) teaches your pup to walk beside you. You can also use this leash outside to tether your puppy to an immovable object (such as a tree or bench) to practice distance Stay directions. See the later section "_Tether and Train_" for more details.

FIGURE 13-1:
Bridge to off-lead cooperation with a short leash that you can use to gently direct your puppy to your side.

Illustration by Barbara Frake

>> **Outdoor freedom line:** Purchase or make a light 25- to 50-foot line to allow your puppy some freedom while you retain control.

>> **Walking freedom line:** This light 5-foot line can be used to teach your puppy to walk at your side. It also suffices for an indoor dragging leash if your puppy acts up when given too much freedom.

FIGURE 13-2:
Tethering helps teach your puppy to Stay outside.

Illustration by Robert Golinello

TIP

Attach any dragging lines you use to your puppy's buckle collar or harness — never to a head collar or choking collar.

REMEMBER

Off-lead puppies don't develop overnight. Training is a step-by-step process. Use your new equipment to increase your puppy's focus, but don't get itchy fingers. Just because they behave well on their retractable leash one day doesn't mean they're ready for an off-lead romp the next. Take your time. Even though I explain how to train with each piece of equipment separately, you can use them interchangeably to vary your puppy's routine to keep them interested, engaged, and on their toes!

A retractable leash

A retractable leash is an excellent tool for distance training when you're working alone in an open environment. However, that's the only time I ever recommend its use as it gets easily tangled around objects, people, and other pets. This lead allows your pup limited freedom to explore while enabling you to enforce directions the moment you give them. You can use the retractable leash as a training tool to reinforce the following directions:

>> **[Name].** Call your puppy's name enthusiastically. If they look at you, praise them. That's all that's required — just a glance. If they ignore you, you need to either turn and run away from them or tug the leash and then then look at the ground, acting as though you're calling them for a good reason. Praise them after you have their attention.

>> **Wait.** Use Wait to get your puppy to check in with you during walks. Begin when your puppy is 3 feet in front of you and then extend to 6 feet, 8 feet, 12 feet, 16 feet, and 26 feet in front of you. If your puppy passes the line you have set and continues forward, press the Stop button and remind your puppy: "Wait."

>> **Stay.** "Stay" and "Wait" differ in two ways: duration and your focus. Wait says stop, look, and listen for my next direction, Stay says relax you're going to be here a while. To bone up on Stay, using your retractable leash increase your distance incrementally. (To accustom your puppy to the pull of the retractable leash, pivot in front of them and slide the leash out a few times.)

>> **Follow.** Use this direction to call your puppy back to your side. Call their name and then direct "Follow" as you slap your leg. Praise your puppy as they respond, and then walk a short distance before you stop to release them: "Go Free!"

>> **Nope.** Whenever your puppy's focusing on something they shouldn't be concentrating on, say "Leave it" and then redirect them with a familiar direction. Immediately refocus their attention with a toy, a stick, or another direction.

An indoor freedom line

Use an indoor freedom line to keep an eye on your puppy during high distraction times like kids' homecomings or parties. Stand by the line and give a direction (Sit, Down, Wait, or Come). If your pup is too preoccupied, you may need to go back a step and lure them into position with food or a favorite toy. Your puppy may have generalized that "sit" and "down" only count in the kitchen alone. Once you've practiced this new out-of-lesson format, phase off luring, lest you become treat dependent. Now if your puppy looks at you, walk closer to their side and repeat the direction. For example, if you give the direction, Down, and your puppy gives you a blank stare, step on the line to stop them, and then repeat both the word cue and the associated hand signal. (For more on hand signals, see Chapter 11.) It's not uncommon to give the directions two or three times when you move from on-leash to off-leash directions. Your patience can help them overcome their off-leash confusion. Praise your dog when they're cooperating.

A short lead

After your puppy has proven to be reliable on the freedom line, use a short lead to reinforce your stationary directions: Sit, Stay, Down, Wait, Follow, and Come. (Refer to Chapters 11 and 12 for more on these directions.) The short lead adds weight to their collar, reminding them of the security of on-lead direction as well as giving you the ability to guide them calmly if they get confused.

In addition to using the short lead around the house, do one of their standard lessons once a day. Bring your puppy into a quiet room and practice a simple directional routine. Initially hold the short lead, but then drop it after you've warmed up. Slap your leg and use hand signals and peppy body language to encourage your dog's focus.

The Tether-n-Train

When using a leash with clips on both ends (what I call the Tether-n-Train), you use the end clip to secure the leash to a tree so that you can work on distance and out-of-sight Sit and Down-Stay directions. Follow these training steps:

1. Warm up with five minutes of regular on-lead practice.

2. Stop your puppy next to a tree or another stable object you can secure the leash to (as shown in Figure 13-3).

3. Keep your hands free.

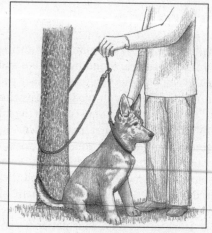

FIGURE 13-3:
Secure your
puppy to a tree or
another
immovable object
to begin
practicing
distance
commands.

Illustration by Barbara Frake

4. **After you direct your puppy to "Stay," walk ten feet away.**

Extend your distance as they gain control. Run your fingers through your hair and swing your arms gently back and forth to emphasize that the leash is out of your hands.

5. **As your puppy improves, practice a Sit-Stay and duck out of sight, practice Down from a Sit-Stay, or practice a distance Down-Stay.**

REMEMBER

If your puppy disobeys, determine whether their response is motivated by anxiety, confusion, or disrespect. If they're confused or anxious, their posture will shrink, their tail will lower, and both their eyes and ears will flicker distressfully. Don't issue a correction: Doing so may only create more stress when you're separated. Calmly return to their side and reposition them gently. Repeat the exercise at close range. If its disrespect, review your role and review earlier lessons to build your partnership.

TIP

If your puppy gets overexcited or breaks from the position when you return, try the walking-in-backward trick. Holding a distance Stay is hard work — many dogs feel stressed when they can't see you and pop up when you finally return. If this sounds like your situation, walk back to your puppy backward. Wait until you've released your puppy from a stay to make eye contact and praise them!

A freedom line

I introduce the freedom line in Chapter 5, and it's a staple for off-leash practice. Attach your puppy to a 25- to 50-foot freedom line and let them roam free as you keep a watchful eye on them. I generally leave the leash dragging, though if you're concerned that your puppy will run off quickly, you can secure the end of it. Engage your puppy by playing with a stick or ball and investigate your surroundings together. Avoid giving too many commands. Just hang out and enjoy some free time with your pup. Every five minutes, position yourself near the line and give an enthusiastic but clear direction.

REMEMBER

If you're issuing a stationary direction, such as Sit, Wait, or Down, stop abruptly as you signal and direct them simultaneously. If you're issuing a motion direction, such as Come or Follow, run backward as you encourage your puppy toward you. If they race over, help them in the proper position and give them a big hug. If your puppy ignores you, quickly step on the line, as shown in Figure 13-4, and say "Nope." (Don't scream; speak sternly.) Redirect and position your dog and praise them enthusiastically. End the session with a favorite game.

FIGURE 13-4:
Use a freedom line to work on distance cooperation outside.

Illustration by Barbara Frake

TIP

Does your puppy love mealtime? As often as you can, pack their meal into a fanny pack, treat cup or baggie and take them out on their freedom line. Every time they check in with you, say "Come" and give them a handful of kibbles. Now the command Come and your reconnection is associated with praise and food — what could be better than that?

Gauging Your Pup's Reactions

When practicing various exercises, you may notice that your puppy is in one of two camps: the excitable explorer camp or the more timid and clingy camp.

Neither is preferable; they are what they are. Both warrant gauging whether your goal is to enjoy this time together. A radically excitable puppy finds it difficult to focus when distractions mount and will likely dart away if not taught better impulse control. On the other hand, a puppy who is nervous when you're out of sight won't enjoy the splendor of an off-lead stroll and may react inappropriately to passersby. Keeping your puppy focused on you, regardless of their personality or the situation, is the key to happy off-lead experiences.

Training an excitable explorer

Some puppies can't get enough of life! Social, curious, and outgoing, excitable explorer puppies race about, trying to take in every new stimulus. Before practicing an off-lead exercise with your excitable explorer, tire them out a bit. Play games (indoors or out) that don't require strict conformity to detail. Soda Bottle Soccer and Two-Toy Toss (see Chapter 20) are wonderful options. At first, practice your lessons before your puppy's meals, using either their kibbles or special treats to enhance their focus and cooperation. A clicker (flip to Chapter 5) can often add a spark to lessons as well. If your puppy is too excited to respond, practice on-lead for half the lesson or return to the basics for a few more weeks.

Guiding a more timid pup

If your dog is cautious, they'll be less inclined to romp when you unclip the leash. Their tail may immediately attach itself to their underside, their ears may pin back, and their eyes may dart around, looking for a familiar place to hide.

REMEMBER

Don't soothe your timid pup. Act with confidence as though nothing has changed — this reaction will impress your puppy. Until now, their leash has served the same purpose as a child's security blanket: It created a sense of safety until the moment it disappeared. The goal is to help your puppy have faith in your presence and your direction. Try the following tips to get your pup to have faith in your direction:

>> Increase your use of visual hand signals.

>> Use a treat cup or a click-and-treat combination (provided that the sound of the clicker doesn't startle your puppy) to alert your puppy and reward their cooperation.

>> Respond in ways that pique their curiosity, such as playing with a stick or toy or showing mock interest in a scent.

>> Instead of simply unclipping the freedom Line, shorten it by slowly snipping away at it, one inch at a time. Some puppies like the feel of the leash and prefer it to running "naked!"

Do you know that your puppy can read you as well as — or maybe even better than — you can read them? If your timing is off by a hair or your mind is drifting, they'll notice and may modify their cooperation. If you feel that your puppy's testing you, you may be on to something, but their resistance is caused less by disrespect than by their interest in learning the rules of this new off-lead game. Practice the lesson only when you can be mindful to detail, and use a freedom line to prevent any mishaps. In case your puppy becomes genuinely out of control, have a few backup plans, such as running to the car, faking a tremendous accident, or shaking a treat cup. Be positive when reunited so that your puppy doesn't lose faith in your reconnection.

Getting the Emergency "Down" Down Pat

Chapters 11 and 12 cover the standard Down direction, but for off-lead safety you need to take it a step further with the *emergency* Down direction. The emergency Down is a high-octane version of the Down direction that'll have your puppy hitting the dirt mid-pace. It can be a real lifesaver. I used it to stop one of my puppies who broke their Stay to greet my husband, who was walking home across a busy street.

REMEMBER

In the beginning, your puppy may be a little confused, so be patient and positive throughout their training sessions. Don't start practicing this exercise until your puppy has mastered the Down direction. (See Chapter 11.) To teach your pup the emergency Down, follow these steps:

1. **Stand next to your unsuspecting puppy.**

2. **Suddenly direct "Down" in an urgent tone as you kneel or bend and point toward the ground, as shown in Figure** 13-5.

   Use the type of tone you'd use if a loved one were about to walk off a cliff.

3. **Tap the ground and repeat Down if they look confused.**

4. **Act like you're being bombed, too, by kneeling next to your pup.**

If your puppy needs a food lure initially, go ahead and use one, but phase off within five repetitions to avoid treat dependence. Soon, your puppy will catch on. After they do, begin extending your distance from them as you direct "Down" in your most urgent tone.

FIGURE 13-5:
The emergency
Down can save
your dog's life.

Illustration by Robert Golinello

It's true — the emergency Down really does save lives. Once I was leaving my training classes with my husky, Kyia, when a tennis ball slipped loose and started rolling toward the road. Kyia, the sweet thing, wanted to help and ran innocently to collect it. In a panic, I shouted "Down!" and she dropped like a rock. What a good girl!

WARNING

The emergency Down exercise is very stressful. Limit your practice to one out-of-the-blue emergency Down sequence a day.

Knowing When to Trust Your Pup and Other FAQs about Off-Lead Training

WARNING

Before I address frequently asked questions about off-lead training (OLT) let me warn you: It takes only one mistake to lose your puppy. Many things can happen: your puppy may get confused, or see a friend, or see a squirrel, child, or cat. Many young dogs test their people's reactions by turning into an instant comedian and bounding away from you just for fun. So practice all initial training in an enclosed area. Keep the situation safe until they're both mature and reliable. It is never wise to walk a dog near a roadway off leash: don't do it, no matter how confident you are in your puppy's reliability.

You may be wondering many things about OLT at this point. Here's a list of questions that I'm asked most often:

>> **When will I know I can trust my dog off-lead?** You should feel it. This road is never smooth in the beginning; some days you get a quick and happy response; other days feel more like your first lessons together. Stay cool, though — frustration is a sign of weakness, and you can quickly lose your dog's respect. You'll gradually notice your dog's hesitation diminish. They'll respond happily and without consideration, and you'll get a fluid feeling that they enjoy being near you and listening to you. Until this point, keep your puppy in an enclosed area or dragging a freedom line as you practice so that if they start to act cocky, you can retreat immediately. And don't hesitate to go back to the freedom line or on-lead exercises for a quick review.

>> **I get so frustrated when my puppy ignores me that I sometimes feel like hitting them. Is it ever okay to hit them?** Feeling like hitting is fine. Hitting them isn't. If you hit your dog, you erode your relationship and diminish their off-lead trust. If you're really angry, walk away calmly. Remember, a graceful retreat is not a failure.

>> **My puppy breaks every time I leave them in a Stay on their retractable leash. What can I do?** Make sure they're okay with the pull of the leash-pivot in front of them, and then walk forward and — because they may respond to the tug of the leash — remind them to stay. Then increase your distance slowly. For example, if your puppy gets up every time you walk out 15 feet, practice at 10 feet for a week, and then at 11 feet and 12 feet, and so on.

>> **Sometimes my dog crouches and barks at me. How can I make them stop?** Don't look at them. They're trying to turn all your hard work into a game. Ignore them until their antics subside. Work on-lead at short distances if they're uncooperative.

>> **Don't the lines get caught around trees and doors?** Yes, they do. Clip all lines to the buckle collar and never leave your puppy unsupervised.

>> **When I place my puppy on the short lead, I can't get near them. Should I give it up?** You need to work on your freedom line for another week or so. When you try the short lead again, put it on *with* the freedom line and correct them by stepping on it when they dart away.

DOG-TO-DOG GREETINGS

If you meet up with an off-lead dog, stay calm. Tensions can get misconstrued, prompting two otherwise peaceful dogs to tussle. Here's what to expect:

- **Normal greeting:** When meeting for the first time, it's normal for dogs to posture considerably, which may include raised hackles or a raised tail or jumping, pawing, growling, staring, or mouthing. When two dogs meet in an open space, they'll generally race at an angle to one another and circle, assessing who should organize the interaction. After they've established their roles, the dogs will get along unless human interference stresses the situation.

- **Abnormal greeting:** Dogs don't charge directly at one another unless they're preparing to fight. A face-to-face, chest-to-chest, direct-eye-contact approach is friendly only if you're a person — dogs view it as an attack. Dogs generally attack one another only if they're defending their young or protecting their territory. When this type of confrontation occurs, the only hope may be for the other dog to lie still in complete submission or turn and run away, which may or may not happen. If you have any control over the outcome, leave immediately.

Out and About

A well-behaved dog is a welcome social guest, a plus at parades and picnics, and an added fan at after-school sporting events. The pleasures of having a well-mannered puppy who matures into a wonderful, responsive dog are undeniable! So, why does the world have so many ill-mannered dogs — dogs who jump and bark at the door, have accidents, and chew their families' belongings? The answer is straightforward and simple: because no one took the time to teach them how to behave — inside their home or out. Don't worry: I won't let that happen to you!

The key to etiquette training is to set your goals and share them with family and friends — and even with strangers who interact with your pup. Think of this last training chapter of Part 3 as sending your puppy off to Miss Sarah's School of Dog Etiquette, which is a short-term course with long-term freedoms and rewards.

REMEMBER

To develop the all-important canine consciousness, you must do two things:

» Decide what you want when you give a direction.

» Follow through — if your expectations are unclear, your puppy's reaction will be, too.

Following five key rules

When debuting that almost-grown puppy of yours, follow these five essential rules:

1. **Make sure your puppy is familiar and comfortable with the setting before you attempt to introduce them to anyone.** Don't greet people your first day out.

2. **Before each introduction, insist that your puppy stand still at your side.** Gently hold still or bring them back to your side and instruct "Wait."

3. **Tell admirers "We're in training."** This statement will help them respect your efforts and contain their excitement (hopefully).

4. **Stay more focused on your puppy than on the admirer.** Insist that your puppy use good manners before you let them approach a new dog or person.

5. **Put faith in your knowledge.** Just because everyone has advice doesn't mean they're right. "I don't mind if they jump" doesn't hold water. *You* mind if they jump, so don't give in.

Under and back: Helpful commands when you're out and about

Have you ever marveled at the sight of a dog lying patiently under the table or their human's legs? It's calming on all fronts because the dog is at peace knowing that the person is safe and in charge. Fortunately for you, it couldn't be easier to teach your pup this skill.

Under

Your puppy wants to rely on someone who has a better idea of what's going on in the world; dogs are just not equipped to understand our society and the oh-so-very-long list of dangers that abound. Whether resting at home, with company, or in town at a cafe, your pup will feel most secure when tucked safely under your legs. (See Figure 13-6.)

To get this result, teach your pup the Under command, which calms them and helps them feel secure in social situations:

1. **Sit on the edge of a chair with your legs bent in front of you.**

2. **Wave a treat to lure your puppy.**

3. **Lead them under your legs and say "Under," rewarding them and petting them with soothing, loving strokes.**

4. **Direct your puppy to Stay and give them a bone to chew or toy to play with.**

Illustration by Robert Golinello

Back

Another direction, Back, teaches your puppy to back up and get behind your feet. This direction is ideal for outings and social greetings, where their enthusiasm may override their focus. To bait them with a treat, draw it back directly under their chin and guide their body behind you.

Introducing Your Pup to People

Meeting people doesn't have to be a hair-raising experience. If your puppy is good on the leash, knows their directions, and is friendly, you have what you need to introduce your pooch to strangers.

REMEMBER

Before you venture into the social scene, though, read over the following disclosures. If any of these possibilities applies to you, follow my specific instructions and skip the rest of this section:

» **If your puppy is aggressive:** If your puppy is having aggression problems, the only person you should introduce your puppy to for now is a trainer or behaviorist with a specialty in aggression rehabilitation. How do you find such an expert? Ask your veterinarian. It's better to be safe than sued.

» **If your puppy is nervous:** If you notice your puppy getting nervous or tense around unfamiliar people, join a class or work under private supervision. Don't push the issue alone.

Introducing the wild one

How you handle introducing your puppy depends on none other than your puppy. If your puppy is overly enthusiastic and wild, you need to tame their expressiveness. Keeping them focused on you is the key.

TIP

Ask people to wait until your wild one is calm before they approach. Enforce a Sit-Stay at your side. Use treats to toss on the ground (playing Find It) so that your puppy learns a new habit when greeting people — looking down instead of leaping up. Use the term Say Hello (see Chapter 10) to encourage your puppy to lean into people versus approaching them head-on. Remind your puppy to Stay and don't let up on your vigil until the person is gone. Whew! What a workout.

Introducing the scaredy-cat

When introducing a scaredy-cat, ask the greeter to wait until you and your puppy are in position. Teach your puppy the Back command, as outlined earlier in this chapter, to let them know you're in charge, and place them in a Sit-Stay. Kneel at their side and, if you can muster a free hand, take the person's hand. Let your puppy sniff the two together. If they won't keep their head up, lift it for them as you gently rub their chest.

TIP

If your puppy is a little cautious when people approach, before you start, place some treats in your pocket (or, if your puppy likes peanut butter, bring some along) and play Find It, tossing the treats down as the admirer approaches you.

Entering Buildings Peacefully

Pick a building that you plan to visit with your puppy, such as the veterinarian's office, the pet shop, or your kids' school. Your puppy's behavior in those buildings depends on their self-control when entering the building. If your puppy's wild, bursting through the door and scanning the room to see who they might jump on first, you're doomed. Instead, follow these steps.

After you've selected a building, approach it with your puppy on-leash and follow these steps:

1. **Bring your puppy to your side as you exit the car.**

   As your puppy exits the car, gather their leash and call their name. Kneel down, say "Shh" to calm them and play "Find It" to get your puppy focused on you.

2. **Pause before you open the door and direct "Wait."**

3. **Don't open the door until they're settled enough to be sitting patiently.**

   Pause again until your puppy is calm.

4. **Say "Okay" as you lead them through the door.**

5. After you're inside, direct your puppy under your legs or onto a mat positioned at your side and encourage them to Settle.

6. **Give them a bone to help them displace their excitement.**

TIP

Some dogs are nervous when they enter new buildings. If your puppy is, bring them to your side and show confidence. Bring high-value treats and play Find It as you walk to the building from your car. After you get to where you are going, place your mat by your feet and direct them to their "Place." If you'll have to wait, consider a high value chew to entertain your puppy.

Making Friends: Introducing Your Pup to Other Dogs

A well-socialized puppy makes friends wherever they can. Meeting other dogs and puppies will top their list of priorities. However, you need to teach them impulse control or else they may dart headlong into traffic or rush an unfriendly candidate.

Gaining control when encountering other dogs

Before you rush up to every dog you see, stop and ask yourself whether the dog is friendly and the people are open to greeting. If you think they are, gain control of your puppy to ensure that the interaction goes smoothly. Do not approach dogs who are barking, jumping, or out of control: This type of dog is overwhelming to both dogs and people.

Before approaching a friendly, well-mannered dog, gain control of the situation by following these steps:

1. **If your puppy acts excited, bring them Back and encourage them to Wait.**

2. **Ask the person to wait to approach you until after your puppy has calmed down.**

3. **After you have your puppy under control, you can permit a greeting by saying, "Okay, go play."**

4. **When playtime is over, instruct your puppy to Follow and move on.**

5. **Use rewards and praise to encourage them to leave the other dog alone and focus on you.**

6. **Keep working on it.**

Getting your puppy in control around new dogs and people can take a while.

Enjoying puppy play dates

Puppies love playdates as much as kids do! If your friend or neighbor has a dog-friendly dog or another puppy and you want to get the dogs together to play, try to organize a first meeting at a neutral location, such as an empty playground or field. (Doing so prevents territorial reactions.) When possible, give both dogs freedom to interact on a freedom line (see Chapter 5), because choking up on a short leash can prompt containment aggression.

When they first meet, you may see some rough interaction in the form of play, or you may witness dominance displays such as growling, mouthing, and mounting. Don't freak out or choke up on your lead. This behavior is natural, and your interference often prompts a fight. Stay calm, but observe closely. The dogs must determine a hierarchy. After that's accomplished, they'll play and have fun on their own. If you're certain that a fight has begun, separate them with the leashes. Don't handle fighting dogs.

WARNING

If you're approached by an off-lead dog, don't hesitate, don't look at the dog, and don't let your puppy look at the dog. Just walk quickly away from the area. Discourage any confrontational attempts your puppy makes. Both of you should avoid eye contact. An off-lead dog defends their territory. However, if you leave without confrontation, they'll stop the chase immediately to harbor their fighting reserves for a more threatening foe.

HOW TO IMPRESS YOUR VET

I'll let you in on a secret: Veterinarians love a well-behaved dog. It makes their job a lot easier. To impress your vet, follow these steps:

1. Bring your puppy's favorite chew toy in case you have to wait, because your puppy will probably be excited or afraid.

2. Take charge the moment your puppy hops out of the car. Direct "Follow" as you walk to the door and "Wait" after you get there.

3. If you must wait to see the vet, direct your puppy under your legs ("Under") or at your side ("Back to me") on a mat. Give them a bone to chew and tell them to "Stay."

4. Instruct "Wait" at the threshold of the examination room to keep them calm and focused.

5. Place your puppy's mat on the examination table to calm them, which, in turn, pleases the doctor.

Some puppies aren't wild about receptionists and aren't too impressed by the veterinarian, either. Set up a practice run and ask the receptionist to meet you outside with your puppy's treat cup. (See Chapter 11.) Ask the person to avoid making eye contact with your puppy. If your puppy is tense, avoid confrontation. If your puppy wants to approach, have the receptionist reward them with treats.

4
Conditioning Good Manners in Your Puppy

Understanding naughty behavior from your puppy's perspective.

Discovering how to redirect chewing, jumping, and nipping into positive routines.

Housetraining lessons everyone can master — including your puppy!

Understanding and reassuring the anxious dog

Helping your aggressive dog feel more safe and in control.

Learning how to manage and redirect socially unacceptable behavior.

Chapter 14

House-Training for Success

Fortunately, there are a lot of similarities between toilet training a kid and house-training a puppy. Both like to leave their living spaces to potty and prioritize privacy. By using many of the same techniques, like scheduling activities and feeding schedules, you'll teach your puppy to go to an area of your choosing on an absorbent surface of your choice to potty. With a plan and a heavy dose of patience, house-training your puppy is just a matter of time.

TIP

When possible, plan your puppy's homecoming around your vacation time. This initial bonding-and-training period is an ideal way to kick off your life together!

If house-training worries you, this chapter will help. Even though it's a project that requires consistency and cooperation, it is, by all means, doable. Lay out a plan before the homecoming, if possible, or, if your puppy's still having accidents, try this fresh approach. In this chapter, I'll establish ground rules and a schedule you can apply no matter where your puppy is in the house-training process.

REMEMBER

Stay positive! Your attitude will make or break this process. A proactive and positive approach will ease your puppy's misunderstanding. If you let frustration creep in, however, your tension will stress your puppy out: Corrections teach your puppy to avoid you when they need to potty, both inside and out.

Picking Your Puppy's Potty Place

The first step in house-training your puppy is to choose the elimination area. Your goal is to teach them to leave their living spaces to go to the bathroom, so decide whether you want that place to be indoors or outdoors. Papers should be neatly arranged in the far corner of a room or pen, away from food and water dishes and gradually shimmied to an out-of-the-way bathroom or mudroom where your adult dog will go for privacy. Outdoors, choose the surface first: Do you want your puppy going on mulch, grass, or pavement, for example? Once that's decided, choose or create a place by putting down, say, mulch — initially just 10 to 20 feet from the door to help your puppy stay focused on the goal of your outings. Take your puppy to the toilet area on a 6-foot leash and wait until they potty to pet, play, or walk them.

REMEMBER

Because eliminating puts puppies in a vulnerable position, privacy is best. Choose a spot that is discrete, whether indoors or outdoors. Like people, dogs don't like to potty out in the open, nor should they get in the habit of wandering about to find their ideal elimination spot.

Although I find training a dog to go outside makes the most long-term sense, city people often have to start out with paper training until their puppy has received their vaccines. You may also want to choose paper training over taking your dog outside if you have a small dog or an indoor lifestyle. Whatever you choose, many of the same rules apply:

>> Consistently use the same bathroom spot (inside or out).

>> Say a word or phrase — such as "Go outside" or "Papers" — when you lead your puppy to the area.

>> After you bring your pup to the area, ignore them until they eliminate.

>> While your puppy is eliminating, say a word or phrase such as "Get busy."

>> Don't use the potty place or papers for play or interaction.

CROSS-TRAINING: GOING INSIDE AND OUTSIDE TO POTTY

You may wonder whether you can *cross-train:* Have your puppy pee inside when the paper is present but go outside when it's not. This scenario is ideal for working parents or for zones that are hit with extreme weather patterns. (House-training a husky in the middle of winter may not present problems, but getting your teacup Chihuahua to piddle in subzero frost just isn't going to happen.)

This cross-training option is slightly more challenging for your pup to comprehend, but any routine can be learned as long as you're consistent. Just be clear on your expectations — that they potty on paper when you're out of the house or during inclement weather and outside at all other times. Here are some suggestions for cross-training:

- Establish a routine for going outside when you're home and in all but extreme weather.

- Get your puppy to ring a bell to alert you when they need to go (see the section "Helping Your Pup Communicate Their Need to Go," later in this chapter), and routinely take them to a predetermined spot near the door or exit.

- When you're not home, secure your puppy in a small room or playpen with papers or pads. Calmly remove the pads when you return home, clean them in front of your puppy to reinforce eliminating in the right place, and then return to business as usual. Keep your puppy confined near you if they try to venture off to potty elsewhere in the house.

- During inclement weather, place the papers down in a distant room in your home — preferably, in the garage, mudroom, or hallway or by the exit door. As you approach the area, call "Papers!" and lay them down.

Establishing a Routine

In Chapter 6, you find out that puppies have five basic needs: to eat, drink, sleep, play, and eliminate. Fortunately, all these needs have a predictable pattern. Your puppy will need to go outside or to their papers to potty after they eat a meal, drink, or wake up from a nap or during long sessions of chewing or playing.

Even though my suggestion that you take your puppy outdoors after each activity sounds like a lot, a very young puppy can't control their impulses. However, establishing a routine early on can cement their understanding of "holding it" until they reach their potty place.

Following general guidelines

Your puppy will catch on quickly if you're consistent with a house-training routine. After you've selected the potty area (discussed in the earlier section "Picking Your Puppy's Potty Place"), follow these guidelines:

- » **Take your puppy to potty with a cue.** Routine is important, so consistently take your puppy to potty after they come out of their crate, wake up from a nap, or finish playing, chewing, eating, or drinking. (Times vary, depending on the age of your puppy.) Say a word cue like "Papers" or "Outside" as you walk to the specified area. Try to use the same route each time so that your puppy gets used to the routine. (See Figure 14-1 for an example.)

REMEMBER

- » **Stay calm.** With puppies, it's important that you always remain neutral as you navigate them to their potty area. Overexcited greetings or delight may promptly shift their focus to play instead of pottying. Withhold your attention until after pottying to motivate their cooperation, and keep it calm to avoid riling up your puppy. Keep your puppy focused on the routine of getting to their area and going to the bathroom before you greet, reward, or play with them. All good things come to puppies who potty!

- » **Keep still.** When you arrive at the potty spot, either place your puppy in a pen or keep them on a leash. Hold off on letting your puppy play or wander until they have done their business. Stay near your home or apartment until your puppy has finished their eliminations: Remember, a human parent would never toilet-train a child by sending theirs to the neighbors to potty.

TIP

  If you have a small dog or young puppy, encourage them to walk themselves to the area. It's all about muscle memory — they need to navigate to the area so that they'll remember where to go. If they're struggling with stairs, flip to Chapter 10 for a quick lesson on stair navigation.

- » **Potty cue!** While your puppy is positioning themselves to eliminate, use a direction like "Get busy" so that they learn to go when directed to do so. After a month of saying this phrase as your puppy is beginning to pee or poop, they should go when prompted.

- » **Consider a potty marker.** Some people find success using treats to reward house-training, while others find that their puppy soon learns to go more frequently to get more rewards. To test whether food rewards will speed up the process, use a word or sound marker to highlight the moments your puppy poops or pees. Wait until they're almost finished to click (see Chapter 5) or say "Yes." Follow each marker with a food reward.

- » **Rewards for going.** After your puppy is done eliminating, greet, praise, and walk them as usual. Good girl!

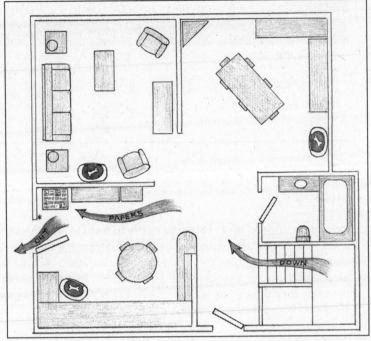

FIGURE 14-1:
Follow the same
path to your
puppy's potty
area because
consistency
breeds
understanding.

Illustration by Barbara Frake

TIP

If your puppy doesn't eliminate within 5 minutes, either carry, crate, leash, or otherwise confine them for 5 to 15 minutes before trying again. This step prevents an accident and helps your puppy build the bladder muscles they need to hold it. Whining, nipping, and frenzied activity are all signs that they may need a potty break.

Getting on a potty-time schedule

Just how many potty breaks does your puppy need per day? Well, that depends. Young puppies (younger than 12 weeks) may need to go outside every hour or two. Older puppies can hold out quite a bit longer.

Use the general guidelines in Table 14-1 for your puppy.

Based on this table, you need to set up a daily house-training schedule. If you're home during the day, follow the plan shown in Table 14-2. If you're out during the day, follow the schedule shown in Table 14-3. As you go through this schedule, you may remember what I mention in Chapter 6: Dogs are *crepuscular* — most awake at dawn and dusk and restful during the rest of the day. Your puppy may need to go outside every 30 minutes to an hour in the early morning (depending on their eating, drinking, and playing routines) and then only once or twice during the stretch between 9 a.m. and 4 p.m. All puppies are different — keep a log to help you recognize patterns.

TABLE 14-1:

Potty Break Requirements According to Puppy's Age

Puppy's Age	Number of Potty Breaks a Day
6 to 14 weeks	8 to 10
14 to 20 weeks	6 to 8
20 to 30 weeks	4 to 6
30 weeks to adulthood	3 to 4

Note: In Tables 14-2 and 14-3, the italicized events may not be necessary as your puppy matures.

REMEMBER

A puppy younger than 12 weeks has little to no bladder control, so you'll be taking them out quite frequently during the daytime. Occasional accidents are not uncommon during this time, so don't be discouraged. (See the section "Quick Tips for Handling and Avoiding Accidents," later in this chapter.) As your puppy matures, they'll have the bladder control to hold it as well as the awareness to let you know when they need to go potty.

Dogs of all ages need interaction between the times listed in the tables, so remember that playtimes are extremely important throughout the day. If you work outside the home, try to come home for lunch or hire a dog walker to split up your dog's day.

TABLE 14-2:

House-Training Schedule for Stay-at-Home Owners

Time of Day	House-Training Action
Wake up	Go outside immediately
Breakfast time (7:30 a.m.)	Go outside after breakfast*
Late morning (11:00 a.m.)	*Go outside*
Lunchtime (11:15 a.m.)	*Go outside after eating**
Midafternoon (2:30 p.m.)	Go outside
Predinner	Go outside
Dinnertime (4:30 p.m.)	Go outside after dinner*
7:30 p.m.	Remove water
Evening (7:30 p.m.)	*Go outside*
Before bed	Go outside
Middle of the night	Go outside

Most puppies need to eliminate after isolation; if you find your puppy uninterested in a meal, take them outside for a quick bathroom run before each feeding.

TABLE 14-3:

House-Training Schedule for Go-to-Work Owners

Time of Day	House-Training Action
Wake up	Go outside
Breakfast time (7:30 a.m.)	Go outside after breakfast
Lunch break feeding and walk	Go outside
Midafternoon	*Young puppies must go outside*
Arrival home	Go outside
Dinnertime (4 to 6 p.m.)	Go outside after dinner
7:30 p.m.	Remove water
Before bed	Go outside
Middle of the night	*Go outside*

REMEMBER

A puppy cannot hold their bladder all day — few dogs can, either. If you have to leave for more than four hours, either drop your puppy off at a daycare center, hire a dog walker to stop in at midday, or create a space that allows for a good stretch as well as a place to potty. Though your puppy might be confused at first by your expectation that they potty inside on paper and outside when you're with them, they will adjust to the routine as long as you're consistent.

WARNING

If you find that your puppy can't hold their urine — they're even going in their crate or when stationed — they may have developed a urinary tract infection. If you think this is the case, take a sample of your puppy's urine to your veterinarian for testing. To collect a sample from your pup, take a plastic container outside and catch a spray of morning urine by holding it under your puppy as they go. Either race over and drop it off at your veterinarian's office within an hour or refrigerate it for preservation.

Being consistent

Consistency is the number-one concept of a good house-training routine. Help your family and helpers learn the program by drawing or copying Figure 14-1 and highlighting these points:

>> Where to take your puppy to potty

>> When to take them to potty

>> What signs your puppy might give, from pacing to quick exits or frantic nipping rituals right before they poop or pee

>> Your route to the potty area, including any sound cues, such as a word or ringing a bell

>> Your catchphrases, like Outside and Get Busy

Helping Your Pup Communicate Their Need to Go

A young puppy's needs are confusing. A baby will cry when needs are not met. Puppies, on the other hand, do other things to signal their need confusion, such as fidgeting, nipping, racing away, or whining. I've found that nipping is the most common reaction — think of it as a healthy way to reach out for your help. Even though you teach them a better signal down the road, for now be mindful that a young puppy's nips may highlight their need to potty. Rather than disciplinie a baby puppy, direct them "Outside!" or to their "Papers!"

To help your puppy learn to give you a more appropriate signal, consider these suggestions:

>> **Ring a bell or chime.** Secure a bell or chime at your puppy's nose level, raising it as they grow. (See Figure 14-2.) Tap the bell just before you go on a bathroom run. If your puppy has access to the door, hang it there so that the sound always indicates an open door. Otherwise, start by hanging it next to the gate, stairway, or banister that encloses their free-play area. Ring the bell for them or with them for a week. If they don't catch on, discreetly smear butter or cheese on the bell first thing in the morning. When your puppy touches the bell, open the door — voilà.

>> **Bark near their area.** If your puppy is a barker, teach them to bark on cue. As you approach the exit area for a potty outing (door, gate, whatever), encourage them to Speak (see Chapter 16). When they do, praise them lavishly, and on you go outside. Good puppy!

As soon as you have the routine down pat (after a week or when your puppy is older than 12 weeks), encourage your puppy to signal you that they need to go out. Rather than chant "Outside," lead your puppy to the door and wait for a sign that they need to go outside. If they're a subtle signaler, call them to you and pump them up: "What is it? Outside? Good dog!" Show them the bell and then let them out. Repeat the process in rooms farther and farther from the door or their papers, running enthusiastically to the door with them and leading them to their spot on a leash.

FIGURE 14-2:
Teaching your puppy to ring a bell when they need to go out is easier than you think.

Illustration by Robert Golinello

Gradually phase out the bathroom escort by letting the leash drop on your way to the potty area. As they learn the drill, start stopping three-quarters of the way there, and then halfway, and then let them go it alone.

SPECIAL CONFINEMENT ISSUES FOR CRATE SOILERS

Shelter or pet store pups often have a handicap when it comes to crate training. After all, they had no choice in that early impressionable time away from Mom. Though a mother dog in an ideal setting would teach their pups to move far away from their sleeping areas to go potty, shelter and pet store puppies often potty, sleep, and eat within the same enclosure.

If your puppy is having a problem with soiling in their sleeping area, the crate may not be the best option for house-training, because it symbolizes a potty area. At night, a young puppy can sleep at your bedside in a large, open-topped box or secured on a leash to your bedside (after they're leash trained and comfortable with daytime stations). If they still can't seem to keep their areas separate, you may need to gate a bathroom and leave papers down. During the day, keep your puppy with you or confine them in a small room, taking them outside or to the papers as often as your schedule will allow (ideally, within a half-hour to 2-hour period). Take them to the same area, over and over, following the routine described throughout this chapter. Having another dog eliminate in this area is helpful because the scent can give your puppy the right idea.

Quick Tips for Handling and Avoiding Accidents

Accidents do happen, and some puppies will have more than others, so knowing how to handle the situation is the key to limiting their frequency. Here are my quick tips:

» Limit their freedom to a small confinement area. If your puppy is eliminating in little-used corners of your house, they may have too much freedom. Puppies are den animals. Most young or untrained adolescents won't soil the area right around them, but if they can race upstairs or into an adjacent room outside their "den," they're more than happy to relieve themselves there.

Keep your puppy confined in a crate or on a training tether (available online), or use a generic leash to serve the same purpose. A training tether leash can be quickly modified to secure to your waist or to an immovable object in the room you share. Designate an area in each location with a mat and chews so that your puppy can easily occupy themselves if you're busy.

TIP

Before letting your puppy run willy-nilly through all the rooms in your home, review Chapter 11 for tips on a more gradually integrated approach, one that I call *walkabout*.

» **Clean up accidents privately.** If your puppy eliminates in an unacceptable place, don't let them see you clean up their mess. Doing so may signal fun with paper towels or a nurturing acceptance — after all, their mom did lick up their messes — that will encourage a repeat performance. Calmly place your puppy in another room or with a family member as you clean it up.

» **Neutralize the odor.** Your puppy has a very sensitive sniffer. They automatically return to areas where their smell is concentrated. Use a pet store formula or a 50-50 mixture of water and vinegar to remove the scent.

REMEMBER

» **Know when corrections count.** If you catch your puppy in the process of eliminating in the house, startle them just a little. (Shouting and running at your puppy is way too scary.) Clap your hands as you say, "Ep, ep, ep!" After you've interrupted your pup, relax your posture and calmly direct them to the elimination area as if nothing happened. When they're done, praise your pup for finishing.

» **Know when disciplinary actions don't count.** As much as you want to think your pup is human, they aren't. Your frustration and anger toward your puppy make you look foolish. I've heard this claim: "My puppy knows what they did was wrong — you should see the look of guilt on their face." But the truth is, your puppy doesn't understand the world in the same way you do. Though all dogs recognize our frustration, they can't dial it back to what prompted their wrongdoings. Sure, you can frighten a puppy into looking guilty, but scaring them won't teach them anything — except to be leery of you.

If you catch your pup soiling someplace other than in their designated area, you can interrupt the process, but lay off all other corrections.

» **Maintain a stable diet.** Avoid changing dog food brands, unless your veterinarian directs you to do so. Your puppy doesn't digest food the way you do: Their intestine is small and unable to process and absorb a varied diet. If you must change food, do it slowly, shifting 25% every three days until you have 100% of the new food.

» **If your puppy is pooping in the house, lay off constant food treats.** If you sporadically give food in any form throughout the day, their elimination habits may be random.

» **Watch the water intake.** Puppies, especially young ones, drink water excessively if they're bored or nervous. If your pup is having house-training problems, monitor their water intake. Provide water or ice cubes (which absorb faster into their system than water) during mealtimes, just before an outing, and when they pant or go to their bowl.

BE A GOOD DOG OWNER: PICK IT UP!

Regardless of where you live, pick up after your puppy. Stools attract bugs and worms, and stepping in dog poop is gross. Do your part — after all, in the city and many suburbs, cleaning up after your dog is the law. Retail scoopers are available at pet stores, or you can do what I do:

1. Place your hand in a plastic bag.

2. Clasp the mess with your bagged hand.

3. Turn the bag inside out.

Because bags are easy to carry on walks, you should never have an excuse for not cleaning up after your pooch.

Chapter **15**

Conquering Common Frustrations

When a client calls complaining of everyday hassles — like a chewed slipper or puppies who jump or nip a lot — I pinch myself and smile. Though I respect their frustration, each of these behaviors is a sign of healthy development. Of course, no one likes having chewed carpets, pricked fingers, or company that hides from your puppy when you open the door, but resolving this list of typical dog frustrations is straightforward and pretty simple, compared with more severe aggravations like leash reactivity, separation anxiety, and aggression. If these issues have you down, flip to Chapter 16 for more specific tips and tricks. For now, let me help you understand, empathize with, and create solutions for a host of common puppy problems.

Understanding What Shapes Your Puppy's Routines

Whatever frustrations top your list, know this: You are not alone. There isn't a problem in this chapter that hasn't been had by just about every puppy parent at one time or another. Many solutions are common sense, with remedies that are so obvious you will wonder why you didn't think of them yourself. As you address each frustration, follow this 3-step solution:

1. **Be proactive**.

Your puppy loves your attention and will repeat anything to get it — even if it's negative.

2. **Tell your puppy what to do.**

Your puppy is more interested in knowing what to do than being scolded for what not to do.

3. **Address the frustration.**

Only after you've taught your puppy what they *should* do can you address the frustration with a remarkably easy, parental-sounding redirection: Don't do that — do this! Other forms of discipline are often viewed by your puppy as confrontational play. Instead of calming your puppy during everyday interactions, your puppy will grow up doing bothersome things just to feel included. As I point out in Chapter 6, even negative attention (shouting, shoving, glaring) excites a puppy.

Fortunately, help is just ahead. You will learn how to encourage different routines, like chewing their objects instead of your furnishings, sitting for attention instead of jumping, and grabbing a bone when they're excited instead of little Casey's ponytail. The choice of how your puppy behaves is really up to you.

Shaping and Redirecting Behavior

Your puppy's misbehavior exists only in your mind. From their perspective, whatever they're doing — sock stealing, counter cruising, nipping, digging, barking, or engaging in impulsive greeting rituals — has value and is often just plain fun. Before you can phase out one behavior, consider what you'd rather they do instead. We will explore your options together.

Talking the talk

After you're an official puppy parent, your eyes and ears will perk up to any nearby conversation, article, tip, or controversy about dogs. Sometimes you'll hear unfamiliar terms — every field has its own jargon. To get you up to speed, here are some definitions of common terms used by dog professionals and dog lovers alike (for more examples or videos of these terms in action, visit my site, SarahSaysPets. com, or use that site's Contact button to message me with your question):

» **Block:** Blocking breaks the eye contact between your puppy and a distraction, be it a muffin on the counter or another dog. Place an object or your body in your puppy's line of vision to calm any reaction.

» **Condition:** The idea here is to create an association between what's going on in the environment and your puppy's reaction to it. Ideally, you'll condition your puppy to stimulations they'll experience throughout their life. Sometimes your puppy will condition involuntary (known as *classical conditioning*), as in their response to the sound of a treat or food bag, and at other times you can condition voluntary responses, like teaching your puppy to sit when they see you holding a toy or food reward. Though you can use conditioning to train your dog chosen habits like sitting instead of jumping, your puppy can also condition bad habits just as quickly.

» **Counter-condition:** Dogs can be taught new behaviors and routines to counter another habit, like lying down or returning to your side when they see another dog on a leash, or sitting or fetching a toy when they hear a doorbell.

» **Desensitize:** Desensitization involves gradually exposing your puppy to stimulations, like a noise or dog, that otherwise bring about a strong startle response until they've conditioned to its presence without reaction.

» **Extinguish:** This references a way to bring an end to behavior by simply ignoring it. When a puppy barks for attention you can ignore it until the behavior is extinguished.

» **Habituate:** This term refers to the gradual exposure to a former overstimulating situation until your puppy can redirect or cope with the situation more calmly. A good example is a puppy who is reactive to vacuums being gradually habituated to them.

» **Mimic:** Recent studies show that dogs, like people and other primates, are capable of both emotional and behavioral copycat behavior, also known as *mimicking*. You could use mimicking to encourage calmness in situations where your puppy is excited or use cheerfulness if your puppy is cautious of a new dog or person. You can also use mimicry to teach your puppy the meaning of new words like "Upstairs" or "Outside."

» **Plan proactively:** The real difference between a trainer and a person who needs to hire a trainer is that trainers are proactive planners who understand behavior problems without needing to see them in action. Proactive training involves teaching your puppy what to do rather than waiting until your puppy is misbehaving to call attention to the wrong behavior.

» **Punishment:** Anything that discourages a behavior is known as a punishment. Positive punishment *adds* something that your puppy will want to avoid, like a shock or a shove (although most positive punishments scare your puppy and result in other undesirable behavior, like chewing, self-mutilation, or avoidance). Negative punishment *removes* something when an action happens, like lifting a treat out of reach when your puppy jumps.

>> **Redirect:** Redirection involves changing your puppy's focus from one activity to another activity. By associating words such as their name and phrases like Go Get Your Toy or Can't Catch Me (see Chapter 20) with a fun activity, you can redirect your puppy when they're feeling cautious, defensive, or excited, for example when greeting or chasing.

>> **Reactive responses:** Reactive responses happen in response to bad behavior. Many people (including many ineffective trainers) wait until bad behavior occurs to direct or interfere with a puppy's behavior. Instead of resulting in understanding, reactive responses create a negative behavior loop that strains the relationship between puppy and parent and leads to other annoying rituals like pacing, barking, and self-mutilation.

WARNING

Avoid anyone who tells you to use battery-operated collars that deliver shocks as a training strategy for your dog — and remember that these collars are illegal in many European countries.

>> **Reinforce:** Anything that encourages a behavior to occur is considered to be reinforcing the behavior. Certain positive reinforcements provide something rewarding to your puppy, like a reward for sitting for treats and toys — ensuring that they'll repeat the response. On the other hand, negative reinforcements remove a positive aspect, such as covering your face each time your puppy jumps or paws for attention. (Puppies crave face-to-face contact and will adjust their behavior if it is denied them.)

>> **Socialize:** This process involves getting your puppy used to the different sights, sounds, and stimulations they'll be exposed to throughout their life. A puppy who isn't well socialized will have strong, often paralyzing reactions to unfamiliar things.

>> **Trigger:** Anything that stimulates a strong reaction in your puppy is commonly called a trigger. Some sounds or sights or situations will trigger fear, hyperreactivity, or defensiveness in a puppy. Keep track of what triggers your puppy, and work to socialize them to the situation until they're comfortable with it.

Stopping the chewing frenzy

Chewing is a puppy thing. It's nothing personal. Puppies don't know a stick from a table leg or a doll's head from a chestnut. Just like kids, pups are curious about the world around them, and they love to explore. Kids use their hands to explore, and puppies use their mouths.

Additionally, pups between 3½ and 11 months old are teething and growing: They start out with a tiny, adorable head filled with 28 little baby teeth, and within a year they end up with a big head filled with 42 adult chompers. During this time, your puppy may chew on the furniture, the walls, or your favorite shoes to alleviate discomfort. To ward off possible destruction, supply (and encourage the use of) appropriate chew toys. Get spray deterrents to make your valuables taste bad. In addition, be patient and use some of the tried-and-true techniques described in this subsection to teach your puppy what to chew instead of what not to.

Be proactive

Having objects scattered all over the floor can confuse your puppy, who may think that everything on the ground belongs in their mouth. Instead, organize a calming station in the rooms you share and place a couple of bones and toys on it or near it in a toy basket. Teach your puppy the phrase Go Get Your Toy (or Bone), by saying it each time they look bored or it's clear they want to play. Reward your puppy with time, play, or food bits.

TIP

Designate one favorite toy to offer during greetings. Pull it out whenever you're coming in or visitors arrive, and keep a replica by the crate to offer whenever you're greeting your puppy there. Wait to greet your puppy until they either settle down or grab the toy playfully. Not sure what to use as a greeting object? I use a tennis ball for one of my doggies and a hollow bone stuffed with peanut butter for another. See what your puppy likes best and use that!

USING SPRAY DETERRENTS

Spray deterrent can be very useful if you find one that works. Any odor or bitter-tasting fluid can be dabbed or sprayed onto the surface to discourage your puppy from mouthing it. Certain store-bought products or household products (like vinegar or diluted oils) may do the trick. If you notice your puppy chewing on the furniture surrounding their station, coat everything except their bed and bone. Also, if your puppy is chewing household items such as wires or phone cords, say "EP, ep" as you discreetly spray the article. Before you leave the scene, redirect your puppy to their chew toy.

Discovering why corrections backfire

When one puppy steals another puppy's toy or bone, the object's value increases. The same is true if your puppy grabs something you'd rather they didn't and you race over to them or chase them to get it back. Instead of teaching the puppy to avoid whatever they've just grabbed, you've just communicated "Prize envy!" In other words, they'll consider that whatever they have is valuable because you're challenging them to get it back. If you make a fuss after they grab it, your puppy thinks, "Wow, what a great prize — everybody wants to take it from me!"

REMEMBER

Avoid disciplining after the fact, too; your puppy won't understand you. And remember, yelling is barking to a puppy, so they'll bark back or grow fearful of you or interpret your aggression as an invitation to play rough. To create a flowing, happy relationship with your puppy, set up situations so that you can catch their thought process and redirect their focus to a more appropriate toy.

Tell your puppy what to do

To your puppy, everything is a treasure — whether or not you agree. Too often, when you're chasing or admonishing a puppy for taking something, the puppy learns the wrong message — that you'll stop everything to get the particular thing back . . . so they take it again and again and again. The solution is just as easy — here's how you do it:

1. **Start with making a treat cup.**

Making a treat cup is easy; refer to Chapter 5 for specific instructions. If your puppy hasn't made the connection on what a treat cup is, shake the container and offer them treats until they associate the sound with getting a treat.

2. **Spread treat cups all over your home.**

Keep the sound consistent and familiar by using the same kind of cup in every room.

3. **Each time they chew or play with a toy (yours or their item), approach with a treat cup and toss treats on the ground as you say "Find it."**

When your puppy drops the object, say "Give" as they release it.

4. **If the object is a bone, just let them go back to chewing it.**

Don't touch it or take it away if you don't have to.

5. **If the object is a toy, toss it and continue playing for several minutes to highlight the bonus of playing together.**

6. **If the object is one of your belongings, pick it up and put it out of reach.**

7. **Calmly redirect them to their toys and play with them if you have a few minutes.**

I can hear you already: "Doesn't treating encourage the behavior?" Even though this technique doesn't discourage your puppy's mischief, it does encourage them to share their treasures, which can save you a lot in replacement fees. A delivery system is better than a destruction crew.

TIP

If your puppy has learned to run away from you with objects, place them on a 4-foot freedom line in the house, and then step on the line as you shake the cup and follow the new routine of tossing treats on the floor and encouraging them to Grab-n-Show. After they understand that your approach isn't threatening, the next time your puppy grabs something you don't want them to have, find a treat cup, shake it, and call them over. Say "Give" as you offer a treat. Praise them when they release the object and help them find a chew toy. You can say "Where's your toy?" to encourage them.

Address the frustration

How you shape your puppy's understanding of what to chew and what not to depends on their age. Puppies younger than 16 weeks are like babies: self-absorbed and floating from one need state to another. They sleep, they eat, and they poop. Sure, they pick things up, but they're not aware of any value or consequence. An older puppy, however, begins to seek things out to get your attention or to relieve physical growing pains. How you deal with your puppy depends on their age.

Puppies younger than six months

A puppy younger than 16 weeks is too young to comprehend your frustration. Sure, when you yell or grab them, they may look guilty, but I've got news for you: You're only terrifying them. Think about it: The very person they look to for reassurance is chasing them down, wild-gorilla style. Pretty scary, no?

REMEMBER

Your puppy's mouth is equivalent to your hands: If your puppy is restless, or nervous, they chew. Young puppies live moment to moment just doing whatever comes naturally. They can't remember what they did two seconds ago, so all interruptions are translated as confrontational — by the very person they love. And if that weren't bad enough, guess what an overcorrected, nervous, fearful puppy grows up doing to relieve their tension? Right — they chew!

Fortunately, I can introduce you to a better way. The following system works for puppies at any age, but it's especially important to teach a young puppy good chewing habits:

>> **Create a playroom:** Place a mat down to rest on and a collection of their toys and chew items. Keep it clean, with no other temptations around. Spend time together teaching them to identify toys and chews by name.

>> **Take a walkabout:** These are planned "walks" round and about your home; use them to condition your puppy where to go to find their place, toys and chews in each room you share. Guide your puppy on a leash, and show them their places in various rooms in the house. (You can learn more

> » **EP, ep:** If your puppy shows interest in grasping an inappropriate object, tug their leash toward you and say "EP, ep," and then quickly redirect your puppy to your side with a quick Find It game or to their place and toys.
>
> » **Share rewards:** Use a treat cup to reward sharing, as outlined in the section "Tell your puppy what to do," earlier in this chapter.

Puppies older than six months

As your puppy matures, you'll be better able to impress upon them the difference between their belongings and those objects that are off limits. That said, if you come upon destruction after the fact, you *have* to let it go. After-the-fact corrections are ineffective and damaging to your relationship because your puppy will grow anxious of your sudden (and to them, anyway, unexplainable) outburst. On the flip side, correcting the thought process and then *shaming the object of interest* helps teach your puppy what to avoid. And, when done correctly, this method puts the negative focus outside your relationship, allowing you to maintain your loving connection.

SHAMING THE OBJECT, NO THE PUPPY

Review the Leave It instruction, as taught in Chapter 11. Then set up a situation with something your puppy's obsessed with — tissues, shoes, a Barbie doll, or whatever else strikes their fancy — and follow these steps:

1. **The Set-Up.**

   While your puppy's resting in another room, set the object in the middle of the floor.

2. **The On-Leash Walk-By.**

   Bring your puppy to the object on their leash.

3. **The Alert.**

   Though a casual glance or sniff is okay, racing or grabbing the item is not. If they're intent on a snatch (ears and eyes focused, leaning away from you and toward the item), guide them back (using a high value treat if you need too) and say "Leave it."

4. **Bad Sock! (or Chicken, Counter, or Garbage, and so on).**

   Calmly lean down, pick up the object, and shame it woefully — bad, bad sock! — without looking at your puppy. (See Figure 15-1.)

   You read that right: Get upset with the object, not at your puppy. You're doing the puppy version of telling a child the stove is hot — the focus isn't on the child's being bad but on the fact that the object is unsafe for them.

Don't even look at your puppy as you mouth off to the naughty thing. Your neighbors may think you need to be committed, but your puppy will love you for it.

5. **Walk by the object again.**

   If your puppy walks by without lunging, keep them focused. Your reminder to Leave it combined with a treat or toy should convince them to ignore the chastened object like the plague (See Figure 15-2.) If they don't ignore it, consider their age; they may be too impulsive to absorb this lesson (wait a month and Your puppy repeat this sequence after they turn six months), or you may be looking at them, or perhaps your timing is off. Say "Leave it" as your puppy approaches the item, and then scold the item, not your puppy.

Illustration by Robert Golinello

Avoid practicing off-lead. If you can't stabilize your puppy, they're more likely to dance about, snatching at the object and then darting away from you, turning this lesson into a game of bait and chase.

Use the Leave it to catch your puppy in the thought process. If your puppy already has an object in their mouth, you're too late. Stay very calm at this point and focus on teaching your puppy to share their finds instead of coveting them as described above.

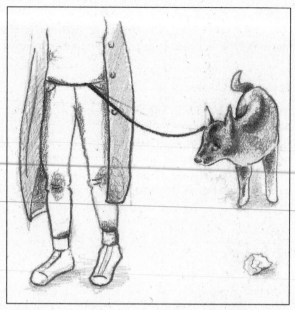

FIGURE 15-2: "What sock?" If you scold an object, your puppy then avoids it.

Illustration by Robert Golinello

Grabbing, tugging and chasing, oh my!

Puppies, being puppies, are bound to chase and grab at things. If the item is a ball or squeak toy, you don't have a problem. But if it's the children, cats, or your clothing, well, that's an issue. Your new goal is to teach the puppy what's acceptable to grab, pull, and tug at and what's off limits.

TIP

In Chapter 20, I point out that the teaching Tug and Give simultaneously is critical to developing your puppy's understanding of when it's okay to tug on items and when the items have to be released. You may want to check out that chapter before trying out this section's strategies in your day-to-day interactions with your pup.

Ending the bathrobe assault

If your puppy is a clothing grabber or a scarf puller or a hair band snatcher, you'll need to make it crystal-clear that worn objects are off limits. Purchase or make a dog play pole that you can bounce about like a fishing rod as you encourage your puppy to Go Get Your Toy and play Tug-Tug-Give (described in Chapter 20) with their toy. Then fill a small spray bottle with a distasteful spray deterrent and carry it with you when you suspect an assault. Don't look at your puppy or turn and face them when they jump after your clothes, as they'll interpret your actions as rough play or confrontational. Without looking at your puppy or responding impulsively, spray your clothing discreetly while your puppy is instigating this interaction and continue walking.

If the clothes-grabbing problem persists, get help now. It can mature into adult aggression — no joke.

Calming the child-, cat-, and critter-chaser

Kids and critters running around the yard, apartment, or house are a big temptation to your puppy. If you were a puppy, you'd be stimulated to chase them, too. Because you can't teach kids and critters to freeze on cue, you need to help your puppy control their impulses. Follow the 3 step program mentioned earlier in this chapter, as it works well here, too.

1. Be proactive.

Get ready for action by putting your puppy on their leash and training collar or harness — ideally, around mealtime so that you can use their food to engage in the following lesson (feeding their food in portions or by hand). Now have your kids role-play — ask them to race around the room and engage in exciting mock play in front of you and your puppy as if you and the puppy weren't there. (Remind them not to look at the puppy.)

2. Tell your puppy what to do.

Engage your puppy by luring a lesson (first outlined in Chapters 10) or by playing Find It or another favorite game from Chapter 20.

3. Address the frustration.

Anytime your puppy looks, leans, or lunges at the children, either step between them (block) or move in the opposite direction as you redirect them to another diversionary game or activity (refer to Step 2).

After you've calmed your puppy indoors, repeat this same routine outdoors until they can be together without setting each other off. Refer to the kids-and-puppy section of Chapter 8 for more tips on peacefully raising your kids and puppy together.

For safety reasons, never leave the puppy and children unattended. Remind the children of the differences between dogs and other kids — namely, that dogs don't like being hugged, because it makes them feel trapped and threatened and they only stare directly at each other when inviting rough play or a fight. Because kids have poor memories, grown-ups have to be around to remind them.

Grounding the joyous jumper

If your puppy could get their paws on some magic device that conveyed them through the world at eye level to humans, they'd never jump again. There'd be no need — they'd be face-to-face with their pack members, seeing what they see and doing whatever they do— bonding, hanging on the couch, checking on the pancakes, or slapping a big, friendly wet one right on Aunt Sally's kisser.

Of course, puppies can't live their life at that height, so your puppy takes to jumping. They jump to greet, explore, and join you in places where you'd rather they not. When you correct them — nudge them off the couch or attempt to repel their 2-legged embrace, they translate your physical interaction as playful, exciting, and interactive. You're encouraging them with your attention.

Be proactive

Puppies who jump need to learn the *4-paw rule,* which means that they don't get what they want until all four paws are on the floor. For your puppy to understand that the 4-paw rule applies everywhere and with everyone, consistency is a must, so use one of the creative ways spelled out in this chapter to involve your friends and family. Soon you'll realize that your puppy isn't the most difficult one to train.

TIP

Place toy baskets by key excitement points, like entranceways and your puppy's crate so that, when greetings arise, you can direct your puppy to grab their toy or bone first, as I discuss in Chapter 8.

Tell your puppy what to do

All puppies want you down on their level. If they can't figure how to get you down, they'll come up. Though you may feel frustrated at the moment, any pushing or shoving only encourages more jumping, as most perceive physical corrections as confrontational play. A better solution is to counter-condition your puppy by teaching an alternative behavior, such as the ones in this list:

>> **Sit:** Teach your puppy to sit when they hear the doorbell, the word *hello,* or the sound of a treat cup shaking. Flip to Chapter 10 for tips on teaching Sit.

>> **Belly Up:** If your puppy likes a belly rub (most do), pair calming rubs with the words "Belly Up!" After a week or so of pairing the word with the action, say "Belly Up!" during greetings.

>> **Go Get Your Toy:** Each time you enter the house or play with your puppy, pair a word to the action of getting a toy. If you have a basket of toys by the door or greeting area, direct your puppy to Go Get Your Toy each time there's a meet-and-greet.

>> **Dance:** Some little dogs are obsessed with hopping around on their hind legs, especially when they're happy. If this sounds like your baby, teach them to Dance on cue by holding a treat or toy above their head a full arm's length from your body. Now do the same thing at the door. There's only one rule — no physical contact.

>> **Go to Your Place:** In Chapter 7, I talk about the calming value of giving your puppy a comforting place in all the rooms you share. Having a place by the door is helpful, too: Send your puppy there for greetings and also after they come in from muddy or wet walks.

TIP

To learn how to teach your puppy these directions, flip to the age-appropriate sections of Part 3 for instructions.

Address the frustration

To address the frustration at the moment, you need self-control. Remember: Any attention — negative or positive — given to your puppy at the moment will only encourage more jumping, not less. After you get hold of yourself, try these strategies:

>> **The peekaboo solution:** The most effective solution for an attention jumper is to do the exact opposite of what they're hoping for: It's what I call the peekaboo solution. (See Figure 15-3.) The pros would say that we're solving the problem by extinguishing it. Consider this: If I kept bugging you to play Monopoly and you didn't look up once, I'd go elsewhere for fun. After your puppy stops jumping, encourage them by saying "Sit" or "Go get your toy!" and then give them attention for that.

>> **Block:** This solution often takes puppies by surprise. Do it gently and without any engagement with your eyes or torso. As your puppy jumps, calmly move your leg or torso into the space their body occupies so that they're bumped slightly off balance. Even if they try to jump a couple of times, keep moving your leg into their space. When they pause to consider the incident, instruct "Sit" and praise them.

>> **Reverse yo-yo:** If your puppy's a real jumper, keep a lead (at least 4' long) attached to their collar. When they jump, either step on the leash so that it's short enough to get them only a few inches off the ground but no higher, or gently pull your puppy sideways. Continue to ignore them as if they weren't there, giving no eye contact, body language, or verbal corrections until they've settled enough to sit calmly.

>> **Spray away:** Also effective when it comes to discouraging eager jumpers is to spray a bitter-tasting deterrent (lemon juice-water, vinegar-water at a 50% mix, or a marketed taste deterrent) between your bodies. Avoid spraying your puppy in the face; spray your clothing instead to create a vapor boundary between you. After your puppy pulls away, refocus their energy to a toy or game.

FIGURE 15-3:
Cover your eyes
when your puppy
jumps for
attention.

Illustration by Robert Golinello

I want to see what's on the counter, too!

Counter-cruising is a common habit — after all, you spend an awful lot of time moving stuff around on them. Blatant corrections are perceived as prize envy — that you're coveting whatever's up there. If your corrections are too pronounced and threatening, you may encourage sneaky behavior such as counter-cruising behind your back. Even though you think your puppy's grabbing out of spite, they're not.

REMEMBER

The reason your puppy snatches things off the countertops when your back is turned or you leave the room is that — obviously — they want to avoid being challenged by you. Basically, they're thinking, "Whatever is on the counter must be great, so I'd better grab it when all backs are turned, or else I'll have to give it up."

Follow these steps to get a handle on this issue (a puppy must be six months old to understand this sequence):

1. **Place a tempting item on the counter and bring your puppy into the room on-leash.**

2. **The instant your puppy looks up to sniff the counter, calmly pull back on the leash and say "Leave it." Next, shame the counter in an admonishing tone, "Shame on the counter!"**

3. **Continue to work in the kitchen, reminding your puppy to leave it when they look at the countertop then redirecting them to their place and their toy or chew.**

If your puppy's already stolen something off the counter, try not to be upset. To retrieve the object, call your puppy to you and calmly exchange the item for a treat or toy. Yelling or shoving your puppy after they're already in possession of something will only reinforce their behavior, ensure they counter-cruise when your back is turned, and guarantee a repeat performance.

TIP

If mealtimes are too distracting for your puppy, tether them while you cook. (See Chapter 11 for advice on tethering.)

That couch sure looks comfy

There are people who really don't see any issue with dogs being on the furniture. If you count yourself among them, you have my permission to skip this section. However, some people invite young puppies on the furniture only to regret it during adolescence when they use the furnishings as a parkour course. If you have a puppy and you don't want them on your furniture permanently, or you want them to come up by permission only, do yourself a favor and discourage the behavior until they're eight months old. You can still snuggle anytime, but it's better to slide down to the floor so that you're making the choice to come down to their level, versus bringing them up to you.

When a client doesn't want the puppy on the furniture, or they want their puppy only to come up when they say it's okay, I teach a technique I call *level-training*. It's especially important if a puppy struggles with house-training (puppies are more likely to pee on absorbent surfaces), chewing or impulse control. Hopping on the couch and standing eye to eye gives many puppies the impression that it's playtime. A better approach is to have your puppy stay on their place, looking up to you with parental reverence. As your puppy matures, you can *permission-train* them, as detailed later in this section.

Training puppies to stay at floor level

Already got a couch hugger? The habit's not too difficult to break as long as you're consistent. Follow these steps to level-train your young pup:

1. **Be proactive.**

   Be fair — set up a calming station nearby to help your puppy feel welcome and directed when you're relaxing on the furniture.

2. **Teach them what to do.**

Tell your puppy to "Go to Your Place" when you approach their area and direct them to a bone or ball each time you approach the area. Reward them with treats and attention whenever they go into the area on their own.

3. **Redirect.**

If your puppy places a paw or two on your leg or cushion, catch their impulse early and calmly remind them to Go to Your Place. Have plenty of toys and bones for them to play with, and give them lots of attention once they're settled down.

Permission training: Allowing older puppies on the furniture

I enjoy cuddling with my dogs on the couch and sometimes even on the bed — especially when I'm sick. However, each of my dogs was taught to come up only when given permission. Sound confusing? It isn't. Your puppy can learn anything if your rules are consistent.

WARNING

Wait until your puppy is at least eight months old to introduce the concept of permission. Until this point, you should keep your puppy on the floor so that they don't assume the cushions are theirs and don't see you as a puppy.

Follow these steps to teach your puppy to join you on the furniture when they're invited:

1. **Be proactive.**

Give your puppy a place in all the rooms you share. Teach them to go to bed when you say "Place" by following the steps in Chapter 7. Then teach them the meaning of Off.

2. **Teach your puppy to join you on permission.**

Tap the cushion and instruct "UP, up."

They might freeze and look confused; if they do, guide them up.

3. **Tell them what to do**

After 5 to 15 minutes, direct them to their place and to their toy or bone.

4. **Redirect.**

If your puppy jumps up without permission, calmly guide them to their comfort station and direct them to their objects. It often takes some repetition, just like teaching young kids to sit at the table. When you'd like to invite your puppy up, bring them to the furniture and ask them to "Sit" and "Wait."

Sitting and looking to you is how your puppy should learn to ask permission to join you. When they do tap your lap or the furniture and say UP, up to invite your puppy to join you on the furniture (See Figure 15-4).

FIGURE 15-4:
Teach your puppy
to say "please"
by sitting!

Illustration by Robert Golinello

REMEMBER

If your puppy gets hyper on the furniture, they're too young to contain the excitement of being on your level. Wait a couple of months before reintroducing permission training.

Controlling Mouthing and Nipping

Mouthing and nipping are two different issues. *Mouthing* is an oral activity, where your puppy will gently grasp your hand or arm in their mouth; it's more of a communication skill to convey need or confusion or to inspire playful interaction. *Nipping*, on the other hand, is a more direct communication, inviting rough play or signaling tantrum-like behavior resulting in overstimulation or lack of sleep. Nipping with intent to harm is a more concerning issue and may be a sign of resource guarding or another form of aggression: Speak to your veterinarian or consider outside help. (For more on how to deal with aggression, flip to Chapter 16.)

Mouthing

All puppies mouth — it's what they do. Getting nipped with those sharp little needle teeth can hurt, but consider this: Before your puppy came home with you, mouthing is just what they did all day long. They mouthed their mama, they mouthed their littermates, and they put their mouth on everything they could reach. Bringing them home is a real culture shock, and suddenly being expected *not* to mouth is a confusing lesson. Here are some tips to make it easy and fun:

>> **Be proactive.**

- *Teach gentle:* Instead of teaching your puppy not to mouth you (a losing proposition), teach your puppy to mouth you gently. Relax your hand in your puppy's mouth and say "Gentle" as long as they're doing just that.

- *Teach kisses:* Whenever your puppy licks you, say "Kisses" and praise them warmly. Encourage licking by slathering your hands with a frozen stick of butter. Yum! With the butter treat, they'll gladly lick your hand instead of mouthing it.

- *Teach YOUCH:* When your puppy bites down too hard (which will happen), make a big sudden to-do like you're hurt, which may not be so hard to pretend, after all. Shout "YOUCH" dramatically, and watch your puppy's reaction. Some take it to heart, recognizing your pain threshold, and return to gentle mouthing. Other puppies find your theatrics hysterically funny and get even more excited. If your puppy is the latter, don't try this again, because it'll only make matters worse.

>> **Redirect:** Puppies generally mouth because they want to be with you. If you substitute a toy for flesh, stay with your puppy as you encourage them to engage in a chew. You can also try these strategies:

- *Check your puppy's needs chart:* Needy puppies (hungry or thirsty; tired or wound up; potty-ready) get mouthy.

- *Play games.* Choose chasing games with multiple toys or a play pole.

- *Pet your puppy soothingly.* Use long strokes, which has a soothing effect on puppies.

TIP

Mouthing generally slows after your puppy's milk teeth fall out, around four to five months old. If mouthing continues, you can extinguish it by withholding your attention when your puppy nips softly. Keep your hand still, because withdrawing it is an invitation to play and nip harder. Encourage kisses and give them attention when the lick your hand instead.

Nipping

Sometimes a puppy can go from mouthing gently to nipping: They're two very different behaviors. Mouthing is loving, nipping is bossy — and it smarts. A nipping puppy isn't a bad puppy. They're just pushy — and because you're the one who let them get away with being pushy in the first place (although I'm sure it wasn't your intention), you're the only one who can get them to stop.

Your puppy might nip you from behind to demand your attention. A puppy might nip in play or when chewing a bone or resting and they don't want to be bothered.

Physical corrections get interpreted as confrontational play, so they can cause a puppy to escalate their mouthing to nipping as a defensive reaction.

If you have children, please flip to Chapter 8 for more tips on raising them together.

Discouraging nipping follows the same pattern of the other behavior modification strategies I've mentioned:

>> **Be proactive.**

Consider whether your puppy might be overtired (one of the leading causes of early-onset aggression) or under-exercised. Both situations can cause very similar reactions.

Write down all the situations that trigger your puppy's nipping — for example, when they're resting or chewing a bone or you're talking on the phone.

Consider using a compassion-wear head harness. These collars automatically correct a lot of behaviors, like nipping, because of their calming effect. As outlined in Chapter 5, the pressure of these collars on the nose and behind the ear allows you to gently guide your puppy and enables you to calmly break their staring when they're getting reactive.

>> **Redirect.**

Reconsider the types of games you play with your nippy puppy. Though they may love aggressive, physical games like tug-of-war and wrestling, until they learn oral impulse control and soft-mouthing-only rules, play games that keep them at a distance, like Soda Bottle Soccer, Find It, and Play Pole Fun. (For instructions on these game alternatives, see Chapter 20.)

Sit-for-everything training will give your puppy a whole new perspective. Instead of being pushy, they will wait on your every direction: To your puppy, life is a game. You want to be the one to teach them what comes next. Have your puppy sit for everything, and use treats, toys, or even their meals (feeding them kibble by kibble or spooning out the food, if you have the time) as you walk around asking them to Sit by the stairs, in the hallway, and by the door. Getting bored with just sitting? Work on Down and Stand and Come — see Chapters 10–14 for instructions.

Leave a leash on your puppy so that you have something to direct them with — and so that you can avoid physical confrontation. Use a long line outdoors and a drag lead indoors (when your puppy is enjoying free rein of the house) to enable easy guiding.

» Cause and effect reactions.

Remember with your puppy, any attention — negative or positive — will be interpreted as confrontational play and make the nippy behavior more intense and frequent. That said, when it occurs, do the following:

- *Give yourself a timeout.* Separate from your puppy; Don't scold your puppy as you walk away or isolate them in their crate, free play area or pen.

- *Seek higher ground.* When the kids and the puppy are playing and the puppy is getting too wild, teach the kids to escape to Alligator Island. Say what? Flip back to Chapter 8 for a full explanation of this game, but in short any countertop can be used as an island! Have the kids ignore your puppy completely, until they are calmly standing or sitting on all four paws. If the puppy continues to jump, tell the kids to cover their faces with their eyes. Once your puppy is settled, the kids can toss toys or treats at a safe distance!

- *Spray away.* If your puppy persists, try spritzing yourself with bitter apple spray or putting a leash on your puppy so that you can guide them off your body part instead of leaping out of their way.

Purchase several small spray misters to place around your home for handy access. Discreetly hold them in your hand as you spray whatever object your puppy is nipping — clothing, furniture, or body part.

Never stare at your pup while you spritz or spray them. Doing so turns an unpleasant result into a confrontational interaction.

If your interactions and discouragement don't calm your puppy's reactivity, find a professional to help you rehabilitate them. Some mouthy puppies grow into dogs who use aggression to get their point across.

Chapter **16**

Addressing Extreme Reactions — On and Off the Leash

As your puppy matures into adolescence, they start taking life far more seriously. They notice things and respond to unusual sights and sounds. Your pup is now fully aware of comings and goings — yours and everyone else's. They grow bored with the same old stuff and worrisome when alone. Without your understanding and direction, or if unfairly disciplined for what are, to your puppy, completely normal reactions to life's uncertainties, their reactive behavior will get worse and not better.

In this chapter, you'll learn how to respond and redirect the behaviors that concern or aggravate you — like digging, barking, aggression, leash reactivity, and other anxious behavior (especially when left alone). Keep in mind, though, that changing your puppy's behavior is less about them and more about how you handle their reactions to everyday situations. Hyperassertive or soothing approaches generally backfire because they're more interactive than instructional.

If you read along and analyze just what might be causing your puppy's reaction, you can tweak your response. *Remember:* Everything depends on what you do at the moment. If you react to a barking, lurching, digging, mounting, or grazing puppy with the wrong kind of intervention, you're guaranteed a repeat performance. If instead you counter-condition, desensitize, or redirect them (more on those terms in a bit), you can guide your puppy to a behavior that's more chill or socially acceptable, like chewing on a bone, sitting still and watching you, or fetching. Are you wondering, "What can I do to redirect my puppy to a new skill or to alleviate my puppy's stress completely?" Read on to figure out the answer.

Recognizing What Aggression Is and What It Isn't

Dogs display several different types of aggression. Understanding what may be developing enables you to react appropriately. This section identifies the various types of aggression and gives some advice on how to hold it in check.

WARNING

The following descriptions and suggestions don't take the place of professional attention if your puppy is showing aggression. Aggression becomes more serious as puppies mature and lose their puppyhood inhibitions.

WARNING

Never approach an aggressive dog, and do not face them straight on — those movements are perceived as challenging. If you get into an encounter with an aggressive dog, don't run away in a frantic panic: Many dogs view this behavior as prey-like and may chase and bite you. When possible, drop your head and close your eyes — and don't move. After a dog sniffs you over and accepts your non-threatening posture, they'll likely retreat. If you need to move away, back away slowly and *do not* make eye contact with the dog.

Dominant aggression

Do you have an interactive pup under your roof who steals clothing for fun, barks for attention, leans against you in new environments or around strangers, or successfully solicits attention whenever the mood strikes? Giving constant attention and dedication to their motion conveys the notion that you're the one being trained! When you do finally assert yourself, a dog who is prone to use aggression to resolve conflicts may use it when you change gears and try suddenly to control them. To regain control, follow these tips, for starters:

>> **Feed them half or more of their food by hand.** Teach them the sequence lessons outlined in Chapter 11, and insist that your puppy mind you to be fed. Practice two to five lessons each day (from five to ten minutes each), and during those lessons use every direction they know.

>> **Say "Excuse me" when your puppy blocks your path.** (I first mention this tip in Chapter 11.) Shuffle through them with your feet, or calmly walk through them if they're standing in your way.

>> **Ignore all their attempts to get your attention.** Some of these attention-getting behaviors include barking, pawing, head-butting, and whining. Use the peekaboo solution I describe in Chapter 15.

>> **Don't stare at your puppy.** Unless you're exchanging loving glances when you're both relaxing, dominance stares-downs can be threatening to young puppies.

WARNING

If your puppy growls during any of these efforts, such as when getting them to move out of your way, don't push it. Stop everything until you get professional help. Your problem is serious.

Resource guarding aggression (object guarding)

A puppy who shows aggression while eating, sleeping, grooming, or being medicated by a family member, stranger, or dog professional (veterinarian or groomer) is showing *resource guarding*. This type of aggression is usually tied in with dominant, territorial, or idiopathic aggression.

REMEMBER

If you see this type of behavior from your puppy, don't freak out, hit them, or scream. These reactions only reinforce their defensive notion that you've come to steal their prize or assert yourself.

The prevention and remedy for this problem are to help your pup accept you as less threatening. Don't make a power struggle over whatever object they're guarding. Follow these steps to train your puppy to let you into their personal space and near their favorite items (such as a food bowl at mealtime). Although I reference a food dish, you should also practice this exercise with a favorite toy or bone:

1. **Condition your puppy to a positive sound, such as a shaking treat cup or a clicker.**

   Always follow the sound with a food reward. (Chapter 5 describes using these training aids.)

   Practice this step three times a day. Continue until your puppy connects the sound with a reward, and then go on to the next step.

2. **Once a day, while your puppy is eating a meal or chewing on a bone, approach them with the treat cup and reward them, at first, by tossing a treat at their feet and saying "Find it." Do not reach down or take the food or object away.**

3. **Next, approach your puppy and kneel or crouch so that you are able to toss the treat into their bowl while they are eating or between their paws.**

WARNING

   If your puppy tenses up or growl as you approach them during a meal, stop and seek professional advice immediately. Your puppy is too close to what's known as a biting threshold and may bite anyone who stands too close them. Don't let your puppy become another dog-bite statistic.

4. **When your pup is comfortable with your kneeling and tossing a treat into their bowl or by their feet, try letting them take the reward from your hand.**

WARNING

Dogs notice fear. If you're afraid, your puppy knows it and will be suspicious. If you're fearful of your puppy, call a professional immediately.

REMEMBER

I can't guarantee that you won't get bitten in the process of training a puppy who shows resource guaring aggression, so you be the judge. Proceed only to the point that your puppy seems happy and comfortable with your interactions. If they tense up or lay their head over their possessions or growl, call in a professional trainer for help. One session can provide all the enlightenment you need.

Territorial aggression

Dogs who act aggressively when strangers approach their homes are territorial. This problem is commonly encouraged when

>> **Delivery people approach and leave the home territory:** Because the puppy thinks that they were successful in "driving the people away," their defensiveness is reinforced.

>> **The owners are home and react to a territorial response by yelling or physical handling:** In this situation, the dog perceives the owners' heightened response as attention, which reinforces their response.

>> **A dog is allowed to react aggressively in a car or tethered outside:** When a dog acts defensively in these situations, they're warning all intruders to stay away. Because they do, they consider themselves victorious, which reinforces their territorial aggression.

>> **Dogs are isolated during greetings or visits:** These isolated dogs may develop what I call *frustrated territorial aggression* (FTA), which isn't a good thing. In a normal group of dogs, all the dogs are allowed to "sniff-greet" a newbie. Isolation frustrates this normal process and encourages an aggressive response the next time the doorbell rings.

TIP

Another territorial behavior is *marking* (or peeing) all over the house. It differs from house-training accidents in that the "marks" are tiny squirts of urine made in deliberate areas, such as the outer walls or highly trafficked paths. See Chapter 14 for tips on resolving this issue, and use them in combination with the other techniques for resolving territorial aggression.

To make associations to visitors more positive, try the following tips:

>> **Use a treat cup or clicker to help your puppy associate outsiders with a positive reward.** If your puppy is relaxed enough to take a treat, ask the visitor to cast a handful of treats on the floor and play Find It.

>> **If your puppy barks or acts hyper, stay calm.** Shouting or other demonstrative corrections add more negative energy to an already tense situation. Stay calm and use a leash to direct your puppy "Back" and behind you. Focus your puppy on a bone or toy until they've calmed down, and then introduce them when the situation is appropriate.

TIP

If your situation is already out of hand, purchase a *head collar* (described in Chapter 5) and leash or station your puppy during arrivals. This collar reduces the negative restraint around the neck and places the puppy's body in a submissive posture.

Handling an aggressive dog on a chain collar is like holding an angry man's arms behind their back. It creates fury. Using a head collar or front-clip harness (what is collectively called *compassion wear*) reduces this tension and communicates structure and discipline passively.

REMEMBER

Although guarding and herding breeds are genetically prone to territorial aggression, this behavior can be found in any breed. So, if your puppy is threatening anyone, get help immediately. A territorial puppy, no matter the breed, almost always turns into a dangerous dog.

Protective aggression

Does your puppy feel threatened when unfamiliar dogs or people approach? Even outside their territory, do they react aggressively when anyone approaches? If so, they may think it's their job to defend themselves against the unknown. You must teach them to look to you when their life feels overwhelming.

Many dogs develop a protective relationship when their owners are too relaxed during a walk, as in talking on their cellphone and paying little attention to where they're going and who they're with — namely, their puppy. If you want a well-mannered puppy, take an active role in the walk to ensure that they walk respectfully at your side. Otherwise, your dog will roam in front or drag you along and then act aggressively when they encounter unknown situations, people, or other animals.

To correct protective aggression, you must identify what your puppy's triggers are (seeing or hearing people at the front door, through the window, or on the street, for example,) and then train and work with your puppy to keep them below their breaking point. Meanwhile, find a treat or toy and reward them until they make a more positive association to the trigger. Here are some other tips you may find helpful:

>> **Use compassion wear — either a front-clip harness or a head collar.** These teaching tools control your puppy passively with very little pressure. Neck collars cause oppositional reflex — a drag on your puppy's neck that makes them feel more frustration, not less.

>> **Train yourself and your puppy.** Remember, dog training is like teaching English as a second language: it will require a lot of patience and understanding on your part! Teach your puppy to look to you for the best ideas on how to behave!

>> **Call a professional if you need help.** Is your puppy giving you no respect? Get help before things get too out of hand.

Predatory aggression

Predatory aggression is an instinctive behavior from pre-domestication, when dogs still had to hunt for survival. Most dogs still possess a chasing instinct. Even though breeders have suppressed the drive to kill in most breeds, some dogs instinctively chase and, in some instances, catch what they're after.

If you have a chaser on your hands, rehabilitating them is quite a project. Instincts hold powerful sway over behavior. Focused play gives a chaser an outlet, but you need to redirect their impulses with other animals or children to discourage interactive chasing rituals. For focused predatory games, see Chapter 20; to correct your puppy's impulses with kids, see the discussion of chasing behavior in Chapter 15.

Fear-induced aggression

Every litter has its shy puppies. These mama's boys or girls depend on their mom's wisdom for safety. After these pups move into human homes, they continue to be needy. Their timidity, which surfaces in new situations, may turn into overwhelming fear if you don't give them proper direction and support. A puppy in this situation may react aggressively during adolescence.

Although shyness is a temperamental trait, a puppy's reactivity can be toned down through routine socialization and exposure to specific stimulations. Discover what motivates this puppy — food, toys, or loving attention — and use it to help your puppy react in a more positive fashion to distressing situations.

REMEMBER

If your puppy shows the early signs of fear when you have company (such as flight, approach-avoid, or protective barking from behind your legs or furniture), you need to be understanding and patient. You can't correct a fearful puppy; doing so only increases their fear. Use favorite rewards (play Find It and other favorite games) to counter-condition a happy reaction to life's unexpected occurrences.

A large part of the problem is that the puppy isn't sure who has control over the situation. To help prevent this problem, you must begin training to teach your puppy to look to you for directions on how to manage unpredictable situations, like someone coming over or meeting a dog on a walk. You must get in the habit of looking at life from your puppy's perspective and ensure that you remember to give your puppy directions when they're feeling unsure of themselves or a situation.

Calming your highly sensitive and fearfully reactive puppy can be unnerving for everyone—most of all your puppy! Stay calm and use familiar words and routines. Here is a list of suggestions:

>> **Encourage everyone to ignore your puppy until the puppy approaches them.** Ask people meeting your dog for the first time to shake a treat cup, click and treat, or extend a tasteful snack.

REMEMBER

When people back away from a threatening puppy, the puppy receives the message that aggression works.

>> **Remember the phrase *hip-to-head* when introducing your puppy.** Because face-to-face greetings with humans can seem confrontational to puppies, teach your puppy to stand next to visitors to greet them (as I describe in the Say Hello exercise in Chapter 10).

>> **Use your puppy's treat cup or a clicker and treats to encourage a more positive association to unfamiliar situations and people.**

>> If your puppy feels comforted by being leashed, keep them leashed when you expect company. When you greet the people, let your puppy hold back. Act cheerful and welcoming to set a good example; consider playing Find It around the visitor's feet if your puppy will participate. Wait to introduce your puppy and give them attention after they're relaxed with the new situation.

TIP

If you can't make progress and decide to seek out a professional for help, find one who uses a soft and positive approach. Threatening this type of dog often creates more fear.

Dog-to-dog aggression

Aggression between dogs occurs when they perceive their territories as overlapping (which can happen anywhere because some dogs think that their territory is extensive) or when a hierarchical struggle takes place in a multidog household. This type of aggression is often exaggerated by well-meaning owners who scream or pull back when their puppies show aggression. Such a reaction only adds to the tension.

OVERLAPPING TERRITORY DISPUTES

Overlapping-territory disputes usually result from a lack of early socialization or from having a neighbor dog who is tense and reactive. If your pup has limited socialization, you must assess how serious it is. A puppy class may be the perfect solution. You, as an owner, need to show your puppy how to act with their species — the best way to do that may be surrounding your puppy with other friendly puppies.

In my puppy kindergarten classes, I allow ten minutes of off-lead play, which allows the puppies to socialize with each other and with other people. Socializing your puppy at a young age ensures that they learn to greet, play, and interact naturally with other puppies and grow into a dog who's less reactive to the sight of their species.

If your puppy is showing territorial aggression — barking frantically at the periphery of your home or yard or unable to calm down with visitors — seek professional help. Unchecked, this behavior becomes far worse as a puppy matures and can lead to all-out aggression.

HIERARCHICAL DISPUTES

Whenever a home has two or more dogs, the dogs develop a hierarchical relationship. Dogs and puppies need to work out patterns of relating to toys, to food, to passageways, and attention. Though you may expect one dog to control in all areas, the patterns can fluctuate, and the rules can change for each situation. For example, one pup may be a zealot for squeak toys but less intense about the eating ritual.

More damage is done when owners try to interfere with the dogs' established interactions. Though you don't want to let dogs escalate their reactions, you should not try to equalize every interaction, either. If you sense your puppies/dogs are overreactive, place them on leashes and separate them calmly when the situation is intensifying beyond your comfort level, or tiffs last more than 5 seconds. Ask the dogs to sit, redirect their attention to an object, or encourage them to take rough play outdoors if you have a yard enclosure.

If your dogs are fighting routinely, find a professional to help you sort it out.

Idiopathic aggression

I very rarely come across idiopathic aggression, but it does exist. Most, although not all, puppies with this problem are the result of poor breeding from a puppy mill. Idiopathic aggression is identified by erratic or fearful aggression responses in atypical situations, and these traits are seen at a very young age. Idiopathic aggression falls into two general categories:

>> **Erratic viciousness:** At unpredictable intervals, a puppy in this category growls fiercely from their belly. This behavior may happen when the puppy's owner passes the food bowl, approaches when they're chewing a toy, or even walks past them. At other times, the dog is perfectly sweet.

>> **Fear-biting:** A puppy in this category shows dramatic fear or a startled bite response to nonthreatening situations such as turning a page of the newspaper or the sudden movement of an arm. These puppies, who are known as *fear biters,* may also act extremely confused or threatened when strangers approach.

Many well-educated dog people use the term *fear biter* incorrectly. They don't realize the big difference between a puppy who bites out of fear and a fear biter. A puppy who bites because they're afraid feels trapped or threatened for a good cause; a fear biter may suddenly fly off the wall and attack you when you turn a page in a book. Don't automatically assume the worst if someone labels your dog with this term.

REMEMBER

Don't panic if your puppy occasionally growls at you or barks at the mail carrier. A lot of puppies growl when protecting a food dish or toy, and the guarding instinct is strong in many breeds. You can cure or control these behavioral problems with proper training. Even many biters can be rehabilitated. Dogs with psychotic aggression display *severe* aggression — bared teeth, hard eyes, a growl that begins in the belly, and a bite response you'd expect from a trained police dog. These personality disturbances are seen very early, usually by four months of age.

Idiopathic aggression is both frightening and tragic because nothing can be done to alter the dog's development. Unfortunately, their fate was sealed by the people who ran the puppy mill they came from or who bred them irresponsibly, and it's often the result of extreme early stress or inbreeding. In my career, I've seen only a handful of idiopathic puppies, and all were purchased from unknown or suspicious breeders. If you suspect that your puppy is displaying erratic viciousness or fear-biting, speak to your breeder and veterinarian immediately and call a specialist to analyze the situation.

DETERMINING HOW SERIOUS THE PROBLEM IS

To determine how serious the aggressive behavior is, you need to consider the following factors:

- **Breed:** Do you have a more instinctively driven dog — a sled dog, terrier, or guarding breed? These breeds have a greater propensity toward reactive responses like aggression when they feel threatened, because they're not genetically programmed to look to people for interpretation. Breeds from the Herding and Sporting groups are genetically programmed to look to people for direction, so seeing a 17-week-old Golden Retriever, known for its passive nature, growling over their dish is more alarming than seeing a protective dog growl over their possessions. Neither dog should growl, but a growling Golden indicates that you may have a deeper problem than just a breed-inherent trait.

  Research the breed. Recognize your pup's personality. Understanding their natural inclinations and working through them at the earliest age possible can help you prevent problems.

- **Age:** A very young puppy should not show serious signs of protecting food and toys. Though an occasional play growl is normal, hard stares and belly growls are causes for concern; consult with a professional to determine how you ought to handle your situation. As your puppy matures, their hormones will release, and they may begin to use more assertive reactions (like jumping up, growling, or nipping) to communicate. Though normal, this is still cause for concern. A puppy who challenges people is showing a sharp lack of social inhibition that can lead to a lifetime pattern of confrontation. Call a professional for your puppy if the pattern of aggression escalates or continues.

- **Temperament:** Aggression is an emotional reaction when an animal is frustrated or fearful. All puppies determine early whether you're giving direction or taking it. If you're not considered authoritative, your puppy will take charge of their own life. As they grow, they become more mindful of sounds and stimulation and may often use defensive displays like barking or aggression to keep their space (your household) under tight surveillance. Of course, passive puppies can show a similar type of aggression. When a passive puppy is neglected or untrained, they may assume self-protective behavior in reaction to changes.

- **Early play patterns:** If you bring up your puppy on games of rough wrestling and tug-of-war, they may become aggressive during adolescence. These challenge games can set the stage for larger confrontations, especially if the puppy's training is ignored.

- **Corrective techniques:** If a young puppy is subjected to heavy-handed corrections early in their life, they learn self-control through fear, not through understanding. For example, if you slap your puppy for grabbing a sock, they may grab the sock less often when they're with you, but they'll be more protective of the sock after it's obtained (known as *possession aggression*).

If you have a puppy who shows aggression when resting, keep them off your bed or couch. You may not think it's a big deal, but an aggressive dog thinks that these high sleeping grounds are their right to be defended, not a privilege. If you can't keep them off your bed, crate or station them nearby. (See Chapter 11 for stationing tips.) If they growl as you attempt to relocate them, call a pro.

Silencing Your Barking (or Whining) Puppy

Most puppies are pretty quiet until they're five to seven months old, when their grown-up hormones start flowing, so don't be giddy if your 3-month old puppy doesn't make a peep. Start these tips early on to prevent a lifelong barking habit, and remember that puppies sound off for a lot of reasons — primarily because they're excited or stimulated but also because they're just plain bored.

The first step in teaching your puppy not to bark is to recognize the impossibility of that statement. Puppies bark like kids talk, and though some are quieter than others, that's all relative. Here's a more realistic goal:

1. Condition your puppy to everyday sounds.

2. Socialize your puppy to the people and places that they'll meet and see throughout their lifetime.

3. Teach more appropriate self-soothing activities to help your puppy cope with slow days or times when they'll be alone.

4. Teach your puppy to quiet down on cue.

REMEMBER

A chronic barker is a real headache. How you handle your puppy, especially as they're initially testing their vocalizations, will dictate how much barking you'll hear over the next decade-plus. Your reactions should depend on what's prompting them to bark in the first place, and the following sections address the different possibilities.

Conditioning your puppy to everyday sounds

Puppies have remarkably acute hearing and will alert to any sound they hear within earshot of their den (also known as your home). Barking is their way of alerting you to something that's approaching. This trait was a key part of the dog-human bond that's not as necessary as it used to be. One way to help your puppy condition to everyday noises so that they'll be less likely to alert to everything they see or hear is to condition and desensitize them using food and fun. For example, to prevent your puppy from barking every time someone comes to the door or walks by, have treats and toys at the ready and use them to distract your puppy. Soon your puppy will recognize the noise as part of their daily routine, whereas yelling at them for barking will reinforce that something scary was going down.

TIP

Make recordings of everyday sounds like the doorbell, the garage door opening, the elevator, or footsteps in the hallway — whatever might or does alert your puppy. Play these recordings at low volume to desensitize your puppy to the sound while playing or feeding your puppy so that they're accustomed to the noise and associate each with good things!

REMEMBER

The cardinal sin when rehabilitating a barker is yelling. When you yell, your puppy thinks you're barking too, which leads to — you guessed it — more barking. To solve your problem, stay cool and follow the advice in this section.

Socializing your puppy early on

In Chapter 9, I talk about the importance of socializing your puppy and how to do it. Nothing could be more critical in helping your puppy feel safe in your home (which in turn leads to less alert–barking) than socializing them to everyday routines and people. Use treats and happy talk when introducing your puppy to your daily cast of characters, from your neighbors and friends to delivery people of every persuasion (postal, pizza, and beyond!). Here is a hit list of other essential socialization scenarios:

» **Anyone or anything approaching your car:** Condition your puppy to see people and other animals approach or pass the car while you're driving *and* when you're parked. Use treats or chews or busy toys, and have people — like gas and fast food attendants and children — toss treats into the car when they approach to speak with you.

» **Delivery people, dog walkers, and yard workers:** These helpers are staples in our lives and come in all shapes and sizes. Ask them to pay the puppy toll each time they visit, tossing a super prize to your puppy each time they enter — a handful of high-value treats, a busy toy stuffed with a super-savory treat, or a tasty chew set aside for special occasions.

» **Plumbers, carpenters, construction workers, and so on:** Whether you invite working folks in to fix up your home (which I recommend you do if at all possible, just to socialize your puppy) or visit with some in the neighborhood, socialize your puppy to the whirring and the banging and the other (sometimes random yet familiar) noises of manual labor.

» **Neighbors (both kids and grown-ups):** Whether you live in the city or the suburbs, you'll be surrounded by neighbors who sound, look, and act differently than you do. Get your puppy used to everyone by holding a puppy party as soon as you're able. Ask whether you can bring your puppy over to watch the children play. Knowing that your puppy won't be alert-barking every time they hear a ball bounce or see a bike go by should be encouragement enough to get started early!

» **Neighborhood dogs and cats:** Introduce your puppy to neighborhood dogs and cats as early as you're able to. Because they'll spend their entire lives separated in a zoo-like existence, it's far better that they exchange friendly barks, greetings, and get-togethers for occasional romps than it is for them to establish a defensive relationship.

Busy puppy, quiet puppy

Puppies bark when they're bored and have nothing else going on. They bark to get a rise out of you or to communicate with another pet or the barking dog down the hall or across the street. Your immediate goal, whether it's preventing barking or redirecting an already formed habit, is to find another way for your puppy to self-soothe. One tried-and-tested method is to provide your puppy with busy toys and feeding tubes — hollowed-out bones or plastic, chewable container toys — that your puppy will have to chew and work on to get their food. I realize that might sound cruel to you, but dogs are programmed to hunt, and after a few days of working fervently to get their food from a chewable feeding tube, the activity will be a more pleasant and exhausting habit than barking their head off — so much so that habitual chewing will take the place of chronic barking!

Developing your puppy's Off switch

To teach your puppy how to settle down on cue, teach them what you expect them to do when you say "Shhh."

To develop your puppy's understanding of "Shhh," practice the following seps two or three times a day for a week, independently of any real-life barking situation:

1. Take a handful of your puppy's food or favorite treats and call them over to you.

2. Line the treats on the counter, in sight but out of reach.

3. As you turn to face your puppy, say "Shhh" as you lure them into a sitting position.

4. If they jump or whine or — heaven forbid — jump *at you,* lift the treat above your head and wait until they're sitting quietly and looking at you to reward them with it.

5. To reward them, say "Find it" and toss the treat on the ground by their paws.

    This step focuses them on the floor and away from other goings-on.

6. Practice three to five repetitions, and then move to a new spot and repeat the activity.

Read the barking scenarios in the following section to see how best to handle your puppy in the moment.

Barking at e-v-e-r-y-thing

Does your puppy alert at everything they see and hear? If so, nothing will go unnoticed at your home — bikers, the neighborhood kids, or lively creatures passing through your yard. Practice the conditioning and socializing steps in the previous section, "Developing your puppy's Off switch," and provide lots of busy toys to ensure that the next decade is peaceful and *quiet*. Here are some additional tips:

>> **Avoid leaving your puppy alone outdoors for long periods.** Unsupervised confinement often breeds boredom and territorial behavior. Put those two together and you're likely to end up with a barkaholic.

>> **Block off areas that your puppy uses, or might use, as lookout posts, such as the front yard or a living room couch or windowsill.** If they're a night guard, crate them or secure them on a lead in your room at night, giving them three feet of freedom — just enough to lie comfortably on their bed.

>> **Remember that screaming at your puppy is translated into barking.** When you yell, you're reinforcing the barking and supporting your puppy's role as border patrol. Anytime you see or hear your puppy start to perk up, call them back to you using a treat cup or a dragging leash (refer to Chapter 5) if they won't focus. Say "Shhh" and ensure quiet as instructed in the previous section before rewarding them.

WARNING

Don't' buy battery-operated barking collars. Aside from being outlawed for cruelty in many countries, they're virtually ineffective. Even the products that claim to be cruelty-free often misfire; all types leave your dog, at best, confused or scared, and, at worst, savvy to when it's on, when it's off, and when the battery has gone kaput.

Barking for attention or protest

Most puppies test their barking prowess around four to six months of age, in the form of bratty barking. They bark when you're focused on something else: the dishes, computer, or dinner table, for example. Prepare yourself: The first bark is always the most precious, but believe me: The barking-for-attention gag loses its glow fast. If you respond to a barking puppy, you end up with, at best, a barking dog or worse — a dog with separation stress. Take charge of this situation before it becomes an all-out habit. Here are some tips:

>> **Be proactive.** Give your puppy lots of tasty chews and food-stuffed hollow toys to keep them busy. Keep to the schedule laid out in Chapter 6, making sure you've given your puppy not only a tiring play romp but a midday nap too. A tired puppy is a yappy puppy.

>> **Focus on good behavior.** Reconnect warmly to your puppy whenever they're chewing a toy, exploring calmly, or resting on their bed. Give them a sense of how to get your attention positively.

>> **Ignore the barking if you can, and never yell.** Your puppy translates shouting as — you guessed it — more barking. Earplugs help.

>> **Interfere without attention.** If you must address the barkfest, do so discreetly by entering the zone without eye contact or notice. Generally speaking, being in the same space will calm any fussing, but regardless, wait until your puppy has settled to leash them up for a walkabout, or place them in their crate or a quiet room with a bone to redirect their angst.

Discouraging Mounting

Puppies mount for a whole host of reasons, and none of them is wrong or bad. Mounting, which is gender neutral, generally starts around five to seven months of age. Puppies mount because it feels good, new, and different — it's a fun way for them to self-soothe. And yes, boys will mount things as a general response to their surging sex hormones, but this is only one of many situations that cause this behavior. Female dogs mount, too: In this respect, mounting is used to displace tension or test rank. So, don't go off the deep end if your puppy — male or female — is scaling your pillows, your leg, or your neighbor's Chihuahua.

If mounting is all-consuming, you can dial it back with one or more of these techniques:

>> **Calm interference:** Leave freedom lines on your puppy indoors (4-foot) and outdoors (25-foot) to enable gentle interference, as described in Chapter 5.

>> **Counter-conditioning:** If you notice your puppy's stimulation rising, stop and play a high-energy game, like fetching a toy or playing tug.

>> **Redirection:** If your puppy starts mounting, call them away from their focus and redirect them to a different activity, like practicing a trick or chewing a bone.

>> **Blocking:** Stand between your puppy and the center of their momentary affection. Pair your blocking with redirection and positive reinforcement lessons, using treats, toys, and attention.

>> **Noting the triggers:** Try to take note of the events that trigger the mounting, and begin a training regimen so that you're able to direct your puppy at these times. Puppies are a lot like kids: They need the structure of socialization and lessons to instill civility.

WARNING

If your puppy reacts aggressively at any point during these steps, terminate the corrections and seek professional help. Your puppy may act out because they perceive the situation as a power struggle: Ask yourself, are you staring at your puppy? Your puppy may observe your reaction as a confrontation.

Getting Control of the Digging

Digging occurs for a multitude of reasons: It's a great way to cool off or alleviate isolation stress or boredom, but it can also be a predatory reaction to sensing underground critters or (for many creatures) just plain fun.

You either have a digger or you don't. If your puppy realizes that digging is a great pastime or a satisfying self-soothing behavior, it can be tough to redirect. A good approach is to be proactive, teaching your puppy alternative self-soothing activities, like chewing and searching for food in a hollow bone, toy, or puzzle feeder and creating a Go Dig spot whenever your puppy feels the need to dig.

REMEMBER

You'll be hard-pressed to teach your puppy not to dig, but you can coach them where to dig when the impulse strikes them! Here's how:

1. Pick one area where your puppy can dig to their heart's content, whether that spot is around your house or in a park (if you live in an apartment or a condo). You can also buy your pup a sandbox to give their digging some satisfaction.

2. Bring toys and treats to hide when you model how to dig by digging yourself in front of your puppy. Don't forget the garden gloves!

3. Go to your puppy's digging area with them every day, instructing "Go dig!"

4. Have a dig-fest. Dig with your puppy and cheer them on.

5. If you catch your puppy digging somewhere they shouldn't be, call out to them and redirect them to their spot with the cue words "Go dig!"

REMEMBER

Spraying your puppy with a hose or setting mousetraps is cruel, and I don't encourage those correction techniques. A more humane method that works is to place a couple of piles of your puppy's stool (provided they don't like it) in the hole with a dose of oregano oil or red-pepper flakes before covering it up.

TIP

Are you a gardener? Well, if you are and you let your puppy watch your garden, guess what? That's right — monkey see, monkey do. I suggest that you place your puppy indoors when you garden. It's just too tempting for them after seeing you dig in one area all day. Remember, dig together *only* at your puppy's designated digging spot.

Remedying Leash Resistance

Whether your puppy is a puller or just stops dead in their tracks, the result is a no-win situation for everyone involved, where walking your puppy ends up being stressful and their social skills suffer. What's a puppy parent to do?! In this section, I tell you how to overcome leash resistance.

The first and most important question is how old is your puppy? Young puppies (younger than four or five months old) don't like to stray too far from their den — also known as your home. Positive outings should be short to begin with and should be shaped with food. You can use your puppy's meal to motivate them to stay with you.

To start teaching your puppy to walk with you, follow these steps:

1. Let your puppy drag their leash around inside the house or apartment to get them used to having it on.

2. Teach them to follow your lead by shaking your treat cup or luring them with a treat or toy. Gradually extend the distance between each reinforcement.

3. Begin to lift the leash and use it to guide your puppy through familiar rooms in your home.

4. If they resist you, simply kneel in front of them (still facing forward) and tap the ground with your finger while you shake the treat cup or clap your hands to urge them along. Reward them as soon as they reach you!

5. Using a head collar or front-clip harness, use incentives to urge them to walk with you. Don't tug or drag your puppy, because they will resist following you even more.

The lunge-and-drag

If your puppy pulls you when you put them on the leash, you have a no-win situation on your hands. The more you pull back, the harder your puppy will dig in their heels, and no matter how strong you think you are, you're fighting a battle that you're never going to win. Keep these concepts in mind:

>> **Oppositional reflex rules the walk.** Your puppy isn't dumb! When your puppy pulls away from your iron grip, they're responding to an instinct called *oppositional reflex*. If I caught you by the shirt sleeve and began pulling you down the road, you'd pull back too.

>> **Posture sends a message.** Leash strain puts your puppy's body into a compromised and confrontational pose, making other dogs and people nervous when they see your dog approaching. This creates a vicious cycle

because the dogs who view your dog automatically assume that they're aggressive and act defensively, which may then trigger your otherwise friendly puppy to be scared or reactive.

» **A relaxed hold on the leash:** Almost any puppy would be happier if you'd keep the leash relatively loose on walks, but that doesn't happen by magic — someone has to train a puppy how to manage it.

So, do you want to teach your puppy how to walk on a loose leash? I thought you'd never ask:

1. Work in your home first, then your neighborhood or yard. Gather treats or food. Hold a 6-foot leash in your hand or secure it to your waist.

2. Instruct "Wait" before you start moving, and drop treats at your feet and say "Find it."

3. Step forward and walk three to five steps. If your puppy pulls, stop.

4. Wait until your puppy stops pulling (which may take a few minutes). The moment they do, click or mark the moment with a word like "Good." Then reward your puppy by saying "Find It" and dropping the treat at your feet.

5. Continue this exercise for days until your puppy stops and looks back to you when you stop. Gradually lengthen your steps, and add a turn.

6. Walk in a straight line. (See Figure 16-1a.) If your puppy races ahead get their attention by clapping your thigh or calling their name and then turn around and walk in the opposite direction. (See Figure 16-1b.)

7. Verbally praise your puppy for catching up to you ("Good puppy!"). Repeat these turnabouts until your dog is predictably focusing on you.

FIGURE 16-1: Walk forward, turning as your puppy pulls, and then praise them as they catch up.

a

b

Illustration by Robert Golinello

Mule wannabes

If your puppy plops down on the sidewalk and refuses to walk with you (don't you love walking a mule?), try to avoid the turn-and-face routine, remember not to drag them, and try never, ever, to pick them up! These actions reward their resistance. You also don't want to acknowledge your puppy's resistance with coddling, or else you'll create a dog who is plagued by learned helplessness. Coddling won't teach them how to follow along.

Here are my top three favorite tips:

>> **Plop down wherever you are.** You read that right! Kneel or plop down and pretend to find something fascinating on the ground. When your puppy saunters over, act truly happy and surprised and reward them.

>> **Use your puppy's treat cup effectively (preferably filled with your puppy's meal or high-value treats).** Shake the cup as you take gradually more steps between each reward. Say "Find it" and drop the treats by your foot each time.

>> **Liven up the walk:** Tie your puppy's favorite toy on a rope or bring their play pole out and turn the outing into a chase-and-grab walk until they're more comfortable being both on a leash and away from their den.

Redirecting Your Little Grazer.

Some puppies eat the strangest things, from grass to crayons to socks. Should this worry you? Well, yes, a little. Swallowing a nondigestible object, should it get stuck in their intestines, can be life-threatening, requiring surgery to remove (which is in itself a trauma). What can you do to prevent your puppy from swallowing anything within reach? Here are six helpful tips:

>> **Don't sweat the small stuff.** If your puppy is grazing on grass, sticks, and pebbles, you need to be mindful, but don't go bonkers. Any hyper reactions will only draw more attention to your puppy's activity, making them more likely to graze again. Instead, teach them the puppy version of Leave It (see Chapter 11), and take toys and treats with you on your outings. If you toss, drag, or play with treats and toys on your walks, your puppy will be less likely to search for random mouthables.

>> **To a puppy, any attention is good attention.** If you focus on your puppy when they're mouthing, running away from you, or eating an unacceptable item, your body language and actions are saying "prize envy!" Your puppy will likely grab more things or, worse, grab the forbidden items only when you're not looking.

REMEMBER

>> **Litter the yard.** First place balls and toys and other distractions around the yard, or string up ropes for your puppy to grab and tug. When you go out together, direct your puppy to these activities and play together.

>> **Teach Bring**. Your puppy can learn fetching games early on; use multiple toys when they're young so that you're always seen as having the better toy.

>> **Never chase or grab objects from your puppy.** Puppies love a chase — they always feel in control, even if it ends up in your favor. Chasing a puppy may lead to gulping the evidence the moment they perceive your interest in taking their prize.

>> **Keep the house clean.** The surest way to prevent your puppy from grabbing non-digestible items is to keep them out of reach. That's easier said than done, for sure, but way less costly than an operation.

WARNING

Some puppies love squeak toys; others gut them. If your puppy tears or ingests objects, eliminate those types of toys or bones from their toy box. Find toys that your puppy enjoys playing with and that are durable to stand up to their ideas of fun.

Surviving Isolation Stress and Separation Anxiety

Puppies hate separation. If they had their way, they'd follow you to the ends of the earth. But, alas, they can't. Puppies suffering from FOBA (fear of being alone) have varying degrees of separation stress. Although few puppies start with full-blown separation anxiety, many unfortunately end up there. To ensure that your puppy learns to cope with isolation, learn the three levels of isolation issues, in growing severity, so that you can analyze your puppy's reactions and deal with the symptoms before they get out of hand.

Isolation anxiety

Many puppies feel isolation anxiety. They may whine or bark when you leave them alone or isolated in a crate, especially during the first few minutes. These puppies may begin to cling to you when you're home, nudge, lean in, or paw for reassurance, sometimes just seconds after you've stopped petting them. Many prefer accompaniment when going outside or into another room. What you may think is bonding can quickly evolve into a more serious attachment disorder if confidence-building measures are not taken. (See the later section "Helping a puppy with isolation issues.").

TIP

If your puppy is stressing when left in a crate, especially in the first days of separating from their litter, consider a Snuggle Puppy toy, as described in Chapter 5, to give them a sense of comfort when you can't be near them.

Isolation distress

One level above anxiety is *distress,* defined as a growing sense of anxiety when left alone, including hyper-excitement when you're preparing to go as well as when you come back. You may notice a change in your reaction to your puppy's behavior as well — from adoration to feeling guilty or resentful.

Puppies who are distressed often eliminate or chew destructively when left alone. Never, and I say *never* — repeat, NEVER — discipline a puppy after the fact, especially if you suspect distress. Your corrections will be paired with the separation, making each separation from you all the more stressful. At that pace, your puppy is at risk of going from a puppy who isn't crazy about departures, but can nevertheless cope, to one with full-blown separation anxiety.

REMEMBER

Puppies who turn your separations into high drama don't love you more or less than the puppies who can rest calmly in a crate while you're gone. Because your comings and goings are a part of everyday life, focus on conditioning your puppy to be alone using the steps listed in the later section "Helping a puppy with isolation issues."

Separation anxiety

Properly defined, true *separation anxiety* reflects a full-blown panic state every time a dog or puppy is left alone — a state that's soothed only when one of their loved ones is present. Symptoms include a pronounced reaction to anything that hints of departure — from simple readying routines like dressing, bathroom routines, or even the sound of the car keys — to chewing, clawing, barking, pottying, stress pacing, window escaping, and frenzied greeting rituals when reunited. Although a discussion of true separation anxiety is well beyond the scope of this book, if you suspect that your puppy is far gone, reach out to the woman who has become the separation anxiety guru here in the states, Malena DeMartini. Her books, lectures, and personalized digital lessons are spot-on: Check her out in print and online at https://malenademartini.com.

WARNING

Puppies with separation anxiety cannot be easily isolated when you can't be home. These dogs grow increasingly frantic in the crate, pacing, whining, and attempting to escape to the point of doing physical harm to the paws or mouth or entire body.

Your veterinarian may recommend a veterinarian behaviorist to help you analyze your puppy's condition and prescribe medication to alleviate their separation anxiety. These drugs can be true lifesavers, helping your puppy feel relief as you work through the steps listed in the next section.

Helping a puppy with isolation issues

Sometimes, puppies who stress when isolated and those who are just restless and poorly socialized to household etiquette share many of the same symptoms — so how do you know the difference, and what can you do to help? Generally, though not always, puppies who show separation stress fall into one of two personality types (see the following list) and consistently repeat behaviors when left alone, whereas hyper or frustrated puppies cycle through good days and bad, depending on their age and their daily sleep-and-exercise routines:

>> **Passive puppy:** This puppy is sweet but undirected and needy. No matter the amount of affection you offer, it never seems to be enough. What they need in order to feel more secure in their world is more direction, not more attention, but because they're not getting it, they impulsively check in with you, time and time again.

   Their constant interaction speaks volumes: Their constant vigil to get attention is a sign of their insecurity: "Do you love me? It's been seven seconds; do you still love me?" Although your puppy adores you, what they need most is the direction to help them organize their behavior in your home. Without guidance, this type of puppy is prone to a virtual panic attack when left alone in the house.

>> **Assertive puppy**: Left to their own devices, confident and bossy puppies like to organize the household activity, so they need to learn their manners and be trained to listen to their people. Headstrong, they're often unimpressed by you — until, that is, you leave the den (your home) and they're trapped inside. When that happens, frustration anxiety sets in.

Separation anxiety demands a multipronged solution that involves training and, often, medication when their self-soothing and calming reactions are interrupted. If you need help with training, get it. In the meantime, here are some tips:

>> **Don't waste your energy on correcting your puppy after the fact.** You'll only make your problems *much* worse. Your corrections get linked to your arrival, adding another reason for your puppy to stress while you're out.

>> **Think of it this way: When you leave your home, you're trapping your puppy inside.** They can't get out if they want to — and they will want to. Puppies (like people) want to explore sights and sounds. Your puppy cannot snack, hop online, or text a friend either, so the best choice is to teach your

puppy to rest or chew while you're out. Left to their own devices and given more freedom than they can manage, they will get nasty and frustrated, which leads to barking, chewing (items as well as themselves), and marking.

>> **Up the play and training routines to build your puppy's confidence.** Play and training go together — use words including Sit, Down, Place, Find It, Come, and Stay before you toss your puppy's toys and offer food or treats. Work on tethering stays around the house. Take your puppy out for random adventures and play-train your puppy while you spend time together. These word directions and reassurances will help steady their nerves when you're gone. (For more on training strategies, see the age-appropriate training chapter for your puppy in Part 3 of this book.)

>> **Learn to earn.** Teach your puppy how to earn more attention by performing simple, fun routines. Make a list of possibilities, like Get Your Toy, Sit and Stay for ten seconds, or Find It games. Although giving your puppy attention whenever and however they ask for it might seem natural to you, just ask yourself what your puppy will do when you're not there to satisfy their attention itch the second they have it?

>> **Create steady come-and-go patterns.** Leave your puppy alone a lot, even if it's just to go to the bathroom or answer the door. Sure, your puppy will fuss — most do — but don't pay a lot of attention to it. If they follow you to the bathroom or gate, say "Stay" and block their following with your leg. If your puppy whines or barks while you're gone, that's their issue; ignore them until they've calmed down. That means no eye contact, petting, or nurturing until they're self-soothing or coping. Gradually and mindfully increase your departure lengths from 30 seconds to a minute to two minutes and then to five minutes to ten minutes. (For more on practicing departures, see the Stay exercises in Chapter 13.)

>> **Establish a leave-alone routine.** Keep in mind that dogs are by their nature calm, restful animals. *Crepuscular* (versus *diurnal* or *nocturnal*) means that they rest 75 percent of the day and are most awake at dawn and dusk. To create sleeping patterns in keeping with their natural rhythm and to reduce the separating stress they feel, follow a few calming routines:

- *Drown the silence.* Puppies don't like silence: It often makes them antsy and unnerved as they're left to interpret every noise they hear. Leave on reggae or soft rock, or buy specially composed dog music to mask the sounds of silence.

- *Create a den vibe.* Ideally, leave your puppy in a darkened room, like a mudroom, kitchen or bedroom, pulling the blinds and playing gentling music to drown out noise and encourage your puppy to rest while you're out. Crates or small pens are good for puppies who'll also be working on strengthening their bladder muscles.

- *Condition your puppy to rest while you're home.* Use the sleep schedule outlined in Chapter 7 to establish resting and feeding times, and use your puppy's crate for both, especially if your puppy is reluctant to settle during those times.

- *Leave your puppy a favorite chew toy.* Rub the toy between your palms so that it smells like you.

Knowing how long is too long

If you routinely go out for long stretches, either come home every three hours or hire someone to take your puppy out. Though it's okay to leave your puppy for two separate 3-hour blocks of time in a row, any more may result in crate accidents or, worse, your puppy may develop isolation anxiety. If long departures are the norm, consider a pen, an enclosed room, or daycare. (See Chapter 8 for more on daycare.)

TIP

Don't give in to "pet me" solicitations. The petting-on-demand ritual makes being alone even more difficult. Going from lots of attention to no attention at all is too sharp a contrast for a pup. When they're alone, your puppy longs for companionship. Because watching the soaps or chewing fingernails isn't an option for them, they instead may devour your couch.

TIP

If your puppy is prone to destruction when you leave, make them a party bag: Put a selection of treats, toys, and chewies in a brown paper lunch bag, crumple it closed, and place it in the middle of the floor just as you walk out the door. Even though it won't resolve their anxiety, the party bag will give them something to focus on for the first few minutes after your departure, which is when most of the tension happens.

Dealing with a Stimulated Tinkler

Do you have a tinkler — a puppy who pees when they're overexcited or (on the flip side) scared or submissive? It isn't uncommon, and it goes away faster if you follow the formula outlined next. Most puppies grow out of this stage within weeks or months.

REMEMBER

Tinkling isn't a conscious act — puppies do it because they're overexcited or anxious. As a dog-to-dog interaction, pee is a signal of respect and awe. Discipline only makes the problem worse.

If tinkling has become part of the greeting ritual, ignore your pup until they're calm, see if you can take them out or get them to focus on a toy or treat-led game. If your puppy is in the crate, ignore them until they've calmed down, and then walk backward (with your back facing your puppy) into their crate space, open the latch — still without making any eye contact — and direct your puppy to their potty area. Wait until they're playing with a toy or focusing on a treat to greet them calmly.

TIP

To reassure your puppy that your gaze is loving, pair your glances with food and favorite objects.

REMEMBER

Kneel to pet them rather than lean over. Review Chapter 6 to recall how your posture affects your puppy's behavior.

Here's are a few more tips to help your stimulated tinkler, especially if it happens with visitors:

>> **Ask any person who excites or concerns your puppy to ignore them unless the puppy approaches them.** Give them a stash of high-value treats, and encourage them to dole them out by tossing them on the floor and playing Find It.

>> **As the interactions at the door and with select people become less stimulating, see if you can approach the puppy without an incident.** Begin to engage the puppy at the moment while continuing to avoid eye contact or directly facing your puppy, which may feel more like a confrontation than comfort.

>> **Does the tinkling happen when your puppy is overexcited or frustrated? See if you can calm down.** If you're too hyper, they get scared; if you're too frustrated or angry, they also get nervous. It's just the way some puppies are: They know when you're out of control.

>> **Disciplinary actions are ineffective and make matters much worse.** Forgive your puppy now — they don't understand why you're mad.

REMEMBER

Use treat cups and favorite objects to engage your puppy when they're nervous or excited. Ask a guest to shake treats from a cup and to kneel versus bending over to pet your puppy.

TIP

Whether you soothe or admonish them, your attention reinforces the moment's mood, whether that's excitement or fear. Stay calm no matter what's going on, and focus your puppy on an object or a food-led activity.

5

Creating a Wellness Plan

Chapter **17**

Maintaining Healthy Habits

To keep your puppy healthy and injury free, prevention is worth a pound of cure. The good news: You're in charge of your puppy's health and well-being. Taking a proactive role in your puppy's health can prevent a lot of disease and heartache. One way to accomplish this task is to keep your puppy well-fed, active, and clean.

Fifty years ago, humans knew little of their own nutritional needs, let alone the needs of their dogs or puppies. Commercialized dog food wasn't even commonplace until the early 1970s. Nowadays, you may feel the need for Chemistry 101 to decipher the label on your puppy's food. This chapter helps explain the mystery surrounding puppy food. When you're finished reading this chapter, you can answer the questions you weren't sure who to ask.

Paying attention to your puppy's overall health doesn't stop there! Maintaining their outer appearance not only makes your puppy look and feel good but also helps you discover any ailments before they become serious. Grooming — including brushing, nail clipping, haircuts, and, yes, even dental care — are just some of the ways to keep your puppy in tip-top shape. I'll help you figure out just how to keep track of your puppy's needs while teaching you how to help them enjoy all your prods and pokes! Of course, the other way to stay on top of your pup's good health is to make sure you join forces with a caring vet who can help your puppy grow into a healthy adult dog.

And then this chapter keeps on giving: In it, you'll learn how to incorporate diet, fun, and fitness into your daily routine — and what age-appropriate activity you can do with your puppy. I also cover everything from how to gussy up your puppy to how to prevent illness through daily maintenance.

REMEMBER

A healthy puppy is a happy puppy, which, for you, means less chewing, more cooperation, consistent potty habits, and a calmer attitude overall.

Puppy Nutrition 101: Your Puppy's Changing Dietary Needs

Feeding your puppy the wrong diet affects their health and their behavior. The wrong diet can increase your puppy's susceptibility to disease, infection, and, possibly, nervous/aggressive disorders.

You have a myriad of choices about what to feed your pup: store-bought or home-made, premium brand or run-of-the-mill, wet or dry. When nearly every brand on the market claims to be the best, how do you decide? Don't worry. I've done some investigative reporting to get the scoop on just what makes one puppy food different from the rest. Here I explain the ingredients in plain English and then help you decide what the best diet options are for you and your puppy.

REMEMBER

As your puppy ages, they'll need a different balance of nutrition to keep them healthy. Like humans, older dogs need less protein and fewer calories.

Comparing different types of food

Deciding what to feed your puppy is a major to-do these days. Though all dog food manufacturers are sworn to meet your puppy's nutritional needs, the amount of food you'll need to give your puppy in order to meet their minimum daily require-ment (or MDR) differs greatly: a fact that matters if you're the one holding the poop bag. The ingredients they use, how they mix it, and even the tricks they use to make it palatable to your precious puppy are what set one diet apart from another. Some pet food companies take great care to use top-of-the-line ingredi-ents that most dogs can easily digest; other companies do not.

How do you know if the diet you've chosen suits your puppy? Ask these questions: Do they enjoy eating? How are their poops — firm and regular? Is their coat shiny and their nose slightly moist? Those are all good signs. Another significant sign is their weight and growth rate: It's important not to overfeed your puppy, because it throws the nutrients in a well-balanced diet out of whack. Excessive weight or rapid growth spurts, which can be encouraged by overfeeding, can put pressure on their developing joints, bones, and muscles, causing skeletal pressure that may haunt their adulthood.

TIP

One way to judge your puppy's weight is to feel their spine and rib cage: Though you should be able to feel the last three ribs, their shoulder blades, and their spine, neither element should be protruding.

Looking at your puppy's food options

There are key differences you need to know about before you can decide which food type is right for your puppy:

>> **Dry food (kibble)** is cheaper and more convenient, but it has more preservatives and is less appealing to dogs. Dry kibble requires processing to blend the various ingredients, and its cereal-like consistency is unlike anything a dog would be attracted to in the wild. Dry food uses lots of chemical preservatives to keep it fresh and prolong its shelf life. When you hear in the news of dry food being recalled, most cases are because the fat in kibbles has turned rancid and deadly.

>> **Wet (canned) food** often uses fewer preservatives (due to airtight packaging) and carbohydrates, and is generally more palatable to dogs. But it's more expensive, and it can grow bacteria and become contaminated relatively quickly, so you shouldn't leave it out for more than an hour. For dogs with sensitive digestive systems or allergies, wet food can make a huge difference. Canned food also retains more water and uses less cereal-type grains than dry food, which can also dramatically affect your puppy's processing because few dogs would nosh on rice or wheat stalks if allowed to scavenge for food. The soft, gushy consistency of wet food, as well as its pungent meaty odor, is often more attractive to both dogs and owners.

>> **Raw food** is another option to consider when choosing food for your puppy. A *raw-food diet* is exactly like what it sounds: a mixture of raw meat, uncooked bones (often pulverized), veggies, fruits, and a few other raw ingredients that strive to mirror the foods a dog/puppy would eat in the wild. Specialty pet stores sell premade raw-food diets, or you can research how to make well-formulated meals right in your kitchen. (Of course, safe storage and careful handling are musts when handling any raw food, so remember to wash those hands!)

>> **Freeze-dried food** is still considered raw food. Should you choose to rehydrate it for your pup, it will have much the same allure as any other unprocessed diet. As the name suggests, the ingredients have been dried at a low temperature until all the moisture is removed, which eliminates the need for chemical preservatives. This is good news if your baby has a sensitive, processed-food-rejecting, allergy-prone stomach.

TIP

Though freeze-dried food can be quite costly, it crumbles nicely and serves well as a high-value treat or topping for a dry food option. With just a touch of water, it can be mashed into a nice gravy topping!

>> **Home-cooked food** is an increasingly popular option for feeding dogs of all ages and sizes. Home cooking, like commercial food, allows for a lot of variation, from the types of meats you choose to the extra additives that meet the requirements for vitamins, minerals, and carbohydrates. If your puppy is prone to allergies or has a highly sensitive digestive system, you may want to consider this option seriously. You may end up spending as much or more at the veterinarian and on medication as you would on a high-end diet.

If you're considering going this route, make sure you think it through carefully. While feeding your puppy a well-balanced and nutritious diet has many pros, it is a time commitment, especially if you have a special-needs puppy who requires more protein to support their development. Followed responsibly, the home diet can be modified for your puppy's age, breed distinctions, and individual needs. If you need help with your homemade formula, check out *The Holistic Guide for a Healthy Dog,* by Wendy Volhard and Kerry Brown (Wiley). Your recipe may call for some tinkering until you get a formula that best suits your puppy's everyday needs.

REMEMBER

When buying any dry or wet food, try to get human-grade ingredients (ingredients safe for human consumption). Read the label before you buy. Low-end foods often use by-products, discarded meats, and additives to enhance the smell and color. Although the wet food may look okay for your plate, low-end foods can wreak havoc on a dog's overall health.

Evaluating essential ingredients

Broken down, aren't all dog foods the same? I'm afraid not. The only real similarity is in the percentage of components required to meet a dog's daily allowance, which is determined by the Association of American Feed Control Officials (AAFCO). Foods must contain six essential elements: protein, fat, carbohydrates, vitamins, minerals, and water. These elements make up the minimum daily requirement. But that's where the similarities end.

Even though the requirement is set by law, each company can choose whatever ingredients it wants to fill that requirement. For example, some foods include soy to meet the daily protein requirement, whereas other foods include meat or other animal protein. What's the big difference between soy and meat? Your puppy will have to eat about four times as much soy to reach their MDR of protein than meat: which amounts to about four times as many calories and one ginormous pile of poop! For dogs, animal protein beats soy hands down.

When searching for the right dog food, pay close attention to your dog's digestion. Foods with low-quality ingredients aren't absorbed as well and can give your dog loose stools. Good food should help your puppy produce two to four compact, inoffensive-smelling stools a day.

The following sections discuss each of the essential components in dog food and compare how the various grades of food meet these requirements.

Proteins (recommended 21 to 26 percent of the food)

Puppies need protein for their growth and development and their immune system — more so when they're in their growing phases. Your puppy's food should be between 21 and 26 percent protein in makeup. (You can find out how much is in the food by looking at the label on the back of the packaging.)

The need for protein changes throughout your puppy's life. Whenever they experience a temperature change or any kind of emotional stress, their system demands a certain amount of protein. When stress occurs, your puppy uses more protein (and therefore relies on you to feed them more protein). If your puppy leads a more sedentary existence or you've restricted exercise due to a recommendation or injury, speak to your veterinarian about reducing the ratio of protein in your puppy's diet.

More protein isn't always better. High-protein diets are used for show or working dogs. If you have a sworn couch potato or a dog who must spend hours alone, feeding them a high-protein diet (which, broken down, equals energy) makes them jittery and hyper.

The source of the protein determines the quality of the dog food. When you read the label, you see one or more protein sources: meat, animal, or grain protein. Here's the translation:

>> **Meat protein:** Meat protein consists of organ meat or muscle meat. This type of protein is the closest to human quality and is superior to other protein sources.

>> **Animal by-products:** Animal by-products consist of any part of the animal that contains protein — hair, hooves, lips, and eyelashes are included in this group.

>> **Vegetable or grain proteins:** Anything that includes the word *gluten* can be translated to mean a hard-to-digest, low-quality vegetable protein that is inexpensive for the manufacturer to produce. Vegetable and grain proteins are typically soy or corn-based, which are hard to digest, and your puppy will have to eat more food to get their MDR. If that isn't bad enough, some puppies are allergic to grains found in dog food. The most common allergies are to corn, wheat, and soy. Certain grains also may contain fertilizer residue, which can cause an allergic reaction. If your pup refuses to eat their food or if their digestion seems abnormal in any way, consult your veterinarian and bring along the labels from your puppy's food to help the vet identify any possible aggravating ingredients.

Make sure you provide your pup with a diet that contains more animal protein than vegetable protein by picking food that has two or more animal sources of protein listed in the first five ingredients.

Carbohydrates (30 to 70 percent of the food)

Puppies get energy and dietary fiber from carbohydrates. Sources of carbohydrates in dog food vary dependent on the food: Lower-quality foods use less expensive and more readily available ingredients from corn or wheat; higher-quality foods use rice, barley, and oats. The total amount of carbs should equal about 42 percent of the food.

Understanding the digestive system of your puppy is important because not all carbohydrate digestion is the same: Foods high in carbs can cause digestive problems in dogs, such as bloating, upset stomach, constipation, and too much stool. If you notice these symptoms regularly in your puppy, speak to your veterinarian and consider a dietary change

If your pup inhales their food, slow them down. Either buy a slow feeder or place a too-large to-swallow rock at the bottom of their food bowl to create an eatable obstacle course.

Fats and preservatives (15 to 20 percent of the food)

The fat in the diet gives your puppy stable, even-tempered energy. Also, fat keeps your puppy's skin and coat healthy, mobilizes digestion, and stabilizes temperature — keeping them warm when it's cold and cool when it's warm. Look for foods that are 15 to 20 percent fats and preservatives.

Sources of usable fats include chicken fats, sunflower or canola oil, fish oil, and lactose-free dairy products. I say *lactose-free* dairy products because after a puppy loses their baby teeth, they lose the enzyme needed to process the milk chemical lactose. Even though a dog doesn't know the difference between lactose and lactose-free, their stomach sure does — lactose in dogs produces gas and loose stool.

Here are some tidbits to keep in mind when researching fats in your puppy's diet:

>> Many food companies have begun adding tallow fat to meet the minimum daily requirement. Used in the production of candles, this fat is inexpensive and indigestible. When a brand claims a "new formula," make sure the change doesn't include this unusable ingredient.

>> Supplementing fat in your puppy's diet is often unnecessary. However, if your vet encourages you to increase fat content, use pressed safflower oil drizzled over their meal, approximately one teaspoon for small dogs and one table-spoon for large dogs. This oil has a high concentration of linoleic acid and is least likely to cause an allergic reaction.

TECHNICAL STUFF

Although animal fat is an important part of your dog's diet, it's the one ingredient that can go bad shortly after manufacturing. For this reason, all dog food contains preservatives. Preservatives can be natural or artificial, and whereas artificial is certainly cheaper (a cost difference that's passed on to the consumer), it's often dangerous to your pet's health. Watch out for the following artificial preservatives:

>> **Rendered fat**: We're talking boiled-down animal byproducts in order to create saturated fats.

>> **Propylene glycol:** This preservative is banned by the FDA in cat food for its toxicity level but still used in dog foods

>> **Butylated hydroxyanisole (BHA) and butylated hydroxytoluene (BHT):** These two preservatives are suspected carcinogens.

Safer, natural preservatives include vitamin C or E (which show up on the label as tocopherol or ascorbate).

Vitamins (1 percent of the food)

Vitamins are organic additives that the body requires to unlock nutrients from food, and they help the body use energy. Dogs need to ingest vitamins with food to digest properly.

Vitamins come in two types:

>> **Fat soluble:** These vitamins, which include vitamins A, D, E, and K, are stored in fatty tissue and the liver.

>> **Water soluble:** These vitamins, which include vitamins B and C, are flushed through the body daily — either used up or excreted.

Look for foods that have these vitamins listed and speak to your veterinarian if you're tempted to give your puppy a multivitamin supplement. It's often unnecessary with most foods because a proper balance of vitamins is required by the FDA.

MAKING SURE YOUR PUP GETS ENOUGH H_2O

Did you know that your dog can live three weeks without food but will die within days without water? Water is necessary for all digestive processes as well as temperature regulation and nutrient absorption. Water acts as a transportation medium, shipping things between organs and out the body.

How much water your pup needs has been relatively boiled down to 1¼ cup per ten pounds of body weight, but that does depend on the intensity of their physical activities and the type of food they eat. Whereas canned food is composed of 75 percent water, lowering the amount of additional water necessary for optimal health, dry food contains only 10 percent moisture. Regardless of how and when you offer your puppy water, recognize that panting is equivalent to a person sweating — a sure sign that your puppy needs a drink!

If you're using water from the faucet, have it tested (or test it yourself) to ensure that it's free of harmful contaminants. Faucet water has been known to contain bacteria, viruses, lead, gasoline, radioactive gases, and carcinogenic industrial components that can cause chronic health problems. Department stores such as Walmart carry inexpensive water-testing kits that measure hardness, chlorine, pH, nitrate, and iron levels. If you find your water high in chemicals, consider a water softener or store-bought filter to filter the water you and your pets drink.

Some foods have a long list of vitamins. Keep in mind that only 1 percent of the food should be sourced from vitamins. Though the list may look impressive, less is more.

Minerals (1 percent of the food)

Minerals are a lot like their vitamin cohorts. They help the body in its normal daily functions, like circulation, energy production, and cell regeneration. By law, the FDA mandates that foods have a balanced supply; if you're concerned about it, know that over supplementation can be harmful to your puppy's development and health. Speak to your veterinarian if you have more specific questions.

Interpreting food labels to get more bang for your buck

When considering diets for your puppy, remember that each food is monitored by the AAFCO and must meet specific nutritional standards. How each food arrives at those standards is what you need to evaluate.

To pick the right food for your dog, you need to figure out how to read ingredient labels. You also have to consider your puppy. Formulas that agree with one puppy don't necessarily agree with another.

Figure 17-1 illustrates how the ingredient labels differ between lower-quality and high-quality food. Note the ingredients to stay away from.

Take a minute to read the ingredients listed in Figure 17-1. Compare the protein and carbohydrate sources, and then focus on fats — *animal fat* is a generic term for a class of inexpensive fats. Chicken fat and sunflower oil are better alternatives. Again, if you're unsure, ask your vet for advice.

REMEMBER

Some people would say that the high-quality foods cost more, but that's arguable. Consider that you have to feed your puppy more to get the daily requirements; when you factor in the health concerns, you may end up saving more money in the long term by feeding your puppy a healthier diet. And if that doesn't win you over, just remember the idiom "What goes in must come out!" A healthy diet truly does affect your puppy's health, saving you loads in the long run as you get to enjoy your life together.

Lower Quality

INGREDIENTS: CORN, SOYBEAN MEAL, GROUND WHEAT FLOUR, BEEF AND BONE MEAL, ANIMAL FAT (BHA AND CITRIC ACID USED AS PRESERVATIVES), CORN SYRUP, WHEAT MIDDLINGS, WATER SUFFICIENT FOR PROCESSING, ANIMAL DIGEST, DRIED CHEDDAR CHEESE, PROPYLENE GLYCOL, SALT, HYDROCHLORIC ACID, POTASSIUM CHLORIDE, CARAMEL COLOR, SORBIC ACID (PRESERVATIVE), SODIUM CARBONATE, CHOLINE CHLORIDE, MINERALS (FERROUS SULFATE, ZINC OXIDE, MANGANOUS OXIDE, COPPER SULFATE, CALCIUM IODATE, SODIUM SELENITE), VITAMINS (VITAMIN E SUPPLEMENT, NIACIN SUPPLEMENT, VITAMIN D SUPPLEMENT, D-CALCIUM, PANTOTHENATE, RIBOFLAVIN SUPPLEMENT, PYRIDOXINE HYDROCHLORIDE, THIAMINE MONONITRATE, VITAMIN D3 SUPPLEMENT, FOLIC ACID, BIOTIN VITAMIN B12 SUPPLEMENT), CALCIUM SULFATE, TITANIUM DIOXIDE, RED 40, YELLOW 6, YELLOW 5, BHA (PRESERVATIVE), DL-METHIONINE, ADO3.392

High Quality

INGREDIENTS: DEBONED CHICKEN, CHICKEN MEAL, WHOLE GROUND BROWN RICE, WHOLE GROUND BARLEY, OATMEAL, RYE, WHOLE POTATOES, TOMATO POMACE (NATURAL SOURCE OF LYCOPENE), CHICKEN FAT (PRESERVED WITH NATURAL MIXED TOCOPHEROLIS), NATURAL CHICKEN FLAVOR, WHOLE CARROTS, WHOLE SWEET POTATOES, BLUEBERRIES, CRANBERRIES, FLAXSEED, BARLEY GRASS, DRIED PARSLEY, ALFALFA MEAL, KELP MEAL, TAURINE, L-CARNITINE, L-LYSINE, GLUCOSAMINE HYDROCHLORIDE, YUCCA SCHIDIGERA EXTRACT, GREEN TEA EXTRACT, TURMERIC, GARLIC, SUNFLOWER OIL (NATURAL SOURCE OF OMEGA 6 FATTY ACIDS), FRUCTOOLIGOSACCHARIDES, MONOOLIGOSACCHARIDES, DRIED CHICORY ROOT, BLACK MALTED BARLEY, OIL OF ROSEMARY, VITAMIN D3 SUPPLEMENT, BETA CAROTENE, CALCIUM ASCORBATE (SOURCE OF VITAMIN C), VITAMIN B12 SUPPLEMENT, NIACIN (VITAMIN B3), CALCIUM PANTOTHENATE (VITAMIN B5), RIBOFLAVIN (VITAMIN B2), PYRIDOXINE HYDROCHLORIDE (VITAMIN B6), THIAMINE HYDROCHLORIDE (VITAMIN B1), FOLIC ACID, BIOTIN, CHOLINE CHLORIDE, CALCIUM PHOSPHATE, ZINC AMINO ACID COMPLEX (SOURCE OF CHELATED ZINC), IRON AMINO ACID COMPLEX (SOURCE OF CHELATED IRON), COPPER AMINO ACID COMPLEX (SOURCE OF CHELATED COPPER), MANGANESE AMINO ACID COMPLEX (SOURCE OF CHELATED MANGANESE), POTASSIUM AMINO ACID COMPLEX (SOURCE OF CHELATED POTASSIUM), COBALT PROTEINATE (SOURCE OF CHELATED COBALT), POTASSIUM CHLORIDE, SODIUM SELENITE, SALT, LACTOBACILLUS ACIDOPHILUS, BACILLUS SUBTILIS, BIFIDOBACTERIUM THERMOPHILUM, BIFIDOBACTERIUM LONGUM, ENTEROCOCCUS FAECIUM.

FIGURE 17-1: Label-by-label comparison of a commercial versus a holistic brand.

Understanding Food Allergies and Special Needs

All puppies are different. One formula just can't suit everyone. Find out as much as you can about the nutritional needs of your puppy by talking to your veterinarian, breeder, or educated pet-store professional to determine the diet that best suits your pup's needs, especially if you notice anything odd about your dog's behavior or digestion.

Pinpointing allergies to your food and theirs

Diet allergies are being diagnosed with increased frequency. Symptoms include itchy face and paws, vomiting, and diarrhea.

To detect what's causing an allergy, your vet may begin your puppy on a hypoallergenic diet. Hypoallergenic diets use novel protein and carbohydrate sources that your puppy hasn't been exposed to. The chosen protein (such as lamb, venison, rabbit, or fish) is usually one that isn't in other types of dog food; rice is often the carbohydrate of choice. (Your veterinarian can provide you with a specialized diet or ingredients to blend.) In addition, all flavored treats, chews, and medicines are eliminated. You then reintroduce familiar food groups one at a time to determine your puppy's allergies.

Accommodating special nutritional situations

If you have a large-breed puppy who's prone to grow quickly, don't be surprised if your breeder or veterinarian suggests feeding them adult food.

Some puppies have specific ailments, such as a sensitive stomach, that require a prescription diet. Your veterinarian can guide you in your selections and provide appropriate foods to keep your dog well.

Keeping Your Puppy Looking and Feeling Tip-Top

Regularly bathing and grooming your puppy not only establishes healthy habits, but it also means you're doing your part to ensure your puppy is a clean, fresh-smelling dog. Done right, these activities are also great bonding moments!

Attention to your puppy's outer appearance not only makes your puppy look and feel good but also helps you monitor your pup so that you can discover any ailments before they become serious. Of course, the other way to stay on top of your pup's good health is to make sure you join forces with a caring vet who can help your puppy grow into a healthy adult dog. For more on grooming as your pup grows up, check out *Dog Grooming For Dummies*, by Margaret H. Bonham (Wiley).

The one glaring way that your puppy differs from a child is that they're unable to articulate discomfort or dismay. When puppies feel pain, stress, or entrapment, they may withdraw, react defensively to touch, or vocalize loudly in the form of a whimper, yelp, or growl. It's your job to be their interpreter. Establishing routine daily checkups not only conditions your puppy to handling but also keeps you aware of anything that may be running amiss.

HIRING A GROOMER VERSUS DOING IT YOURSELF

Think you've got chutzpah to groom your puppy yourself? You just might, but before you start drawing the bathwater, consider all that's involved in keeping your puppy clean, brushed out, and coiffed.

- **Time and patience:** Depending on your puppy's coat type, the adult length, and whether their hair grows or sheds, getting into a routine of daily brushing and monthly or bimonthly bath times to keep your puppy free of knots and tangles is a must.

- **The right equipment:** Will your puppy need periodic clips? You'll need proper clippers and special scissors as well as a sedate puppy and a steady hand.

- **A groomer's precision:** And if all that fantabulous fur weren't enough, taking care of your puppy also requires nail, ear, and eye care. Read the following sections to see what's involved with those areas.

DIY: Making bath time lots of fun

I remember dog baths from back when I was a kid. I had a big husky–shepherd mix named Shawbee. To say she hated baths is an understatement: She would dig in her heels the minute we turned her down the hall. Restraining her in the tub was no picnic, either. Four hands had to be on her or else she was hall–bound, shaking suds as she ran down the stairs and out the door. It was quite entertaining for us kids.

To prevent your dog from bolting during bath time, make "Tub" an event! Teach the word as a direction, and practice tub exercises long before you need to bathe your puppy. The trick works so well that your puppy may start jumping into the tub on command. Use the following steps:

1. **Teach your puppy to run into the bathing zone without actually doing anything.**

    Say "Bath time!" and run to the area, either shaking the treat cup as you go or simply rewarding them with high-value treats or a lickable treat (peanut butter or a store-bought formula) when you arrive. Repeat this silly game until they're beating you to the area.

2. **"Puppify" your tub ahead of time.**

    Place a towel or rubber mat on the bottom of the tub or shower for traction, decorating the bathing area ahead of time with high-value treats or lockable mats and toys or chewies. You'll use your puppy's favorite items to help them associate pleasant thoughts with bathing

3. **Have some pre-water fun!**

   Help your puppy into your pre-puppifed (refer to Step 2) tub or shower, reward and play for two to three minutes, and then take them out. Repeat this step until your puppy looks forward to tub togetherness.

TIP

   Try this fun water game: Place a large mixing bowl in the tub for your puppy to sniff; as they're exploring, drop their favorite treat, toy, or bone into the water and say "Find it!"

   Remember that this is a pre-water step; the only thing in your tub should be a towel to stand on, a spreadable treat (like peanut butter) rubbed onto the sides at your puppy's nose level and some toys. This is a practice run! If they show stress or attempt to escape, use enticing treats or special toys to focus their attention, and use soothing, loving strokes to calm them down.

4. **Run the water as you're playing, but let it drain. (Don't fill the tub.)**

5. **After your puppy allows the water to run while they're in the tub, let the tub fill to hock (ankle) depth.**

   If your dog squirms, stop the water, sing softly, and offer some treats as you scratch their back lovingly.

6. **Proceed gradually until you're able to fill the tub and bathe them peacefully.**

I know these steps sound extensive, but think of it as one week's adventure. After all, it's a training exercise — and a relatively small effort for a lifetime of easy bathing.

Brushing made easy

Grooming can be a complete nightmare or a delightful, interactive time with your dog. Whether grooming is a chore or a treat is determined in puppyhood. Keep the first brushing episodes fun, and always end on a positive note by giving your pup a treat or their favorite toy.

TIP

The following suggestions can help make your puppy's first associations with grooming pleasant ones:

>> **Use a soft-bristle human or puppy brush.** You can eventually work toward using the brush of your choice, but at first, avoid wire-bristled brushes. Also keep in mind that as your puppy matures, they'll shed their puppy coat and

will require a more sophisticated brushing tool. To discover which brush is best for your pup's needs, speak to a groomer or pet-store professional.

>> **Spread peanut butter or a store-bought equivalent in your puppy's food bowl, or provide a delectable chew for distraction.** Show your puppy the seasoned bowl when they're in a quiet mood, and as they enjoy the diversion, softly draw the brush over their body.

If you follow the preceding suggestions, your puppy will take the experience in stride, and soon you'll both be looking forward to the time together.

WARNING

If your puppy growls fiercely at any point while you're brushing them, stop everything and call a professional right away.

Performing daily care and spot-checks

In addition to brushing, cleaning, and clipping, you want to do regular care and spot checks of your pup to ensure that their eyes, ears, nose, and mouth are healthy. Close inspection can identify potential issues before they become serious so that you can notify the vet.

In the following four sections, I've detailed more important cleaning and grooming pointers to help keep your pup smelling fresh, looking swag, and staying healthy.

Toothbrushes and dental care

Taking care of your puppy's teeth is not optional: The earlier you start, the sooner this habit will become a routine that you and your puppy will enjoy. Sure, dogs have more-concentrated saliva than humans do, and dogs who chew a lot are less prone to tartar buildup than humans are, but these forms of prevention don't take the place of dental care. Without a little help from friends (that means you and your veterinarian care team), poor dental hygiene can cause tooth decay, abscesses, periodontal disease, and tooth loss as well as heart, liver, and kidney disease, which are especially dangerous and costly in adulthood.

Follow these tips to keep your puppy's teeth healthy through their life:

>> **Include chewing bones or dry food in your puppy's diet.** The natural bacteria-cleansing elements in your puppy's saliva help clean your puppy's teeth and will continue to do so throughout their life. Making chewing (and buying) quality bones a lifelong obsession.

>> **Start brushing your puppy's teeth.** Use special dog toothpaste instead of human toothpaste because fluoride and dogs don't mix! To get your puppy used to brushing, find a paste they enjoy — they come in flavors — and then spend a few days letting your puppy get comfortable having the paste-coated head of the brush in their mouth, rewarding your puppy after 5-second stints. Gradually introduce gentle strokes downward from their gums into your daily routine. Initially, remove the brush every two strokes and offer your puppy a high value reward; each day add another stroke, removing the brush between and rewarding your puppy until they can tolerate a full cleaning.

TIP

If you have a young puppy, acquaint them with this procedure early on. Gently mirror the brushing action with your index finger, removing your hand and rewarding them with tasty treats.

>> **Make dental care part of a routine checkup!** Veterinarians have recently discovered that your puppy's lifelong health is dramatically affected by good dental hygiene; so much so that they've included dental checkups as part of your dog's overall yearly health analysis. As your dog gets older, you may opt for professional cleaning. To clean your dog's teeth, your veterinarian will need to scales each tooth separately and finish with polishing. Dogs generally need to be anesthetized for this procedure.

WARNING

Some puppies put up an enormous struggle when getting their teeth brushed. If your dog is averse to the brush, try using a plastic finger brush that loosely fits over your index finger instead, to ensure that you and your puppy get in the habit of cleaning their teeth regularly. If your dog growls at you, quit immediately and call a professional.

Nails

Long nails can force your puppy's foot out of position, causing strain, injury, or discomfort; if that weren't bad enough, long nails can crack or break if they catch on something, resulting in sustained injury and multiple trips to their doctor.

How do you know when your puppy needs a clip? If you can hear their nails on the floorboards, it's time for a trim. To keep your pup's nails healthy, you need to schedule a nail trip to a local groomer or veterinarian hospital, or go the DIY route about once a month.

TIP

You can trim your puppy's nails in two ways — with clippers or a file:

>> **Clippers:** You can choose from two types. The scissor type is considered best for larger dogs; the one that looks like a guillotine is best when clipping medium to small dogs. Many videos on YouTube are posted by manufacturers: Watch the videos and talk to your veterinarian before you consider the investment.

Take extreme care to avoid cutting into your puppy's quick (the tissue part of the nail). Aside from being excruciatingly painful, the cut will bleed for hours because the quick has lots of veins. To prevent excessive bleeding, purchase a clotting solution like styptic powder from your veterinarian. It works like magic.

>> **File:** A dog file is just sandpaper-like material on a stick or rotating tool (like a Dremel tool) that files your dog's nails rather than cuts them. (Filing prevents that "cut to the quick" business mentioned in the previous bullet.)

When clipping your puppy's nail, clip the very tip, just at the point it starts to curl. (See Figure 17-2.) You may notice that your pup's front nails grow faster than the hind ones due to the kind of surface they exercise on. If your dog has a dewclaw (a nail that rides high on the back or front paw), don't forget to trim it.

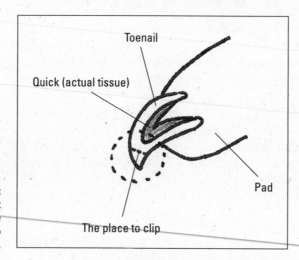

FIGURE 17-2: Clip the nail at the tip where the point starts to curl.

Whether clipping or filing your dog's nail, position yourself next to your dog, not front-facing (that position can appear confrontational and startling). Use treats and peanut butter to create a positive association with this activity.

If you're filing your dog's nails, ask a helper to pet your dog while you get familiar with using the tools. You should file off just the hook at the end of your dog's nail, the same portion you'd cut with the clipper. File in 5-second intervals, praising and treating your dog between intervals.

CONDITIONING PAW-FRIENDLY HANDLING

If you're reading this sidebar before you've had to cut your dog's nails, consider your-self blessed because you can prevent problems before they begin. To avoid having a clipper-phobic dog, make paw handling part of every positive interaction, from petting to treating, by following these steps:

1. **Initially, just handle your puppy's paws — nothing fancy.**

   Throughout the day, touch and handle your puppy's paws. Say "Good puppy!" then reward your puppy each time you've successfully held their paw for over 1 second. Have as much hand-on-paw contact as possible for a week or two. Perform no clipping at this step.

2. **Swipe some peanut butter (or a similar paste) across the refrigerator at your dog's eye level. As they lick, rub their paws with the clipper.**

   Don't cut the nails just yet. Open and shut the clippers to acquaint them with the sound.

3. **Gradually manipulate your puppy's paw to get them acquainted with having their paw held against their will for more than 3 seconds.**

   To do this, determine the best pose for you to clip your puppy's nails. Will you have them stand with their paw on your knee, or do you want them sitting while you hold their paw gently in one hand and clip with the other. I tell my clients to face in the same direction as their puppy, rather than facing them as many puppies view that pose as threatening.

4. **Practice this pose with your puppy — as if you were about to clip, but don't do it just yet.**

   Sit, hold their paw as you would for clipping, and after two seconds let go and reward them. Gradually increase the time, always rewarding them with a high value treat after they cooperate with the exercise.

   If your puppy holds nicely still for up to 4 seconds but starts to squirm after 6 sec-onds, don't reward the squirming. Dial it back to where your puppy was successful and reward that stage. Gradually — very gradually — inch back up to 6 seconds, even if you have to increase the hold one millisecond at a time!

5. **Once your puppy will sit still while you handle their paws for up to 10 seconds, try one cut — just one — by placing the edge of the clippers over the top of the nail and quickly squeezing the handle.**

   Clear nails are easier to cut as you can literally see where the pink quick of the tip begins. If your puppy has dark nails, you need to take extra precaution. You can ask your veterinarian or groomer to give you a lesson.

(continued)

(continued)

6. The next day, try two nails and then three.

Note: Don't correct your dog if they protest. Be understanding and slow down. Consider the alternative — filing instead of clipping. Again, nail clipping sounds like a major production, but in the long run, you'll be glad you took the time to do it right. Anyone who has cut their dog or frightened them by being too rough can tell you that having a clipper-phobic dog is a nightmare.

Eyes and ears

Soulful, sweet, comic — your puppy's eyes express it all. Keeping them healthy, bright, and clear is up to you. If you notice that your puppy's eyes are tearful, full of mucus, swollen, or itchy, see your veterinarian. Your puppy may be suffering from conjunctivitis (contagious to other dogs), a cold, an internal parasite, or an allergy.

Your puppy has a third eyelid. If you lift the lower lid carefully, you see a pinkish lid that closes independently. This lid protects your puppy's eye from dust and other particles that are picked up near the ground. This third lid can become infected, so note its healthy color and take your puppy to the veterinarian if you notice it becoming inflamed.

TIP

If your veterinarian prescribes eye medication, administer it carefully by swiping something tasty on the refrigerator (peanut butter or broth) at a 30-degree angle above your dog's eye level. Stand behind your dog or to their side and pull back the upper lid until you see the white of your dog's eye; then carefully drop in the medication.

Different dogs require different cleaning schedules, ranging from every couple of weeks to daily. As a general rule, floppy ears require more care than uprights because of limited air circulation. If you have a hairy-eared breed, you may be instructed to pluck the hair out of the way because excess hair can trap wax and make one big mess that cries out for parasites. Talk to your veterinarian or groomer for personal instructions. (Refer to Chapter 18 for information regarding ear mites.)

Follow this general advice for caring for your puppy's ears:

>> **Clean the outer ear flap.** Ask your veterinarian to recommend a commercial ear solution that helps prevent infection. Using a cotton ball soaked in the

solution, wipe the outer flap. Use caution when cleaning, because the ear is very tender and going in too deep can be painful. Repeat this process until the cotton comes up clean.

Don't use cotton swabs or poke into your puppy's ear canal. You can cause irreparable damage by doing so.

>> **Prevent water from entering the ear.** If you're bathing your pup, put a cotton ball in the opening ahead of time and wipe the ears out with a dry cotton ball when you're finished.

Ear infections are quite common. Signs of infection include a red or swollen ear, discharge, head shaking, ear itching, or bad odor. If you notice any of these symptoms, get your puppy to their doctor immediately. Left untreated, infections can cause fever, depression, irritability, and loss of balance. Your veterinarian may prescribe an ointment that you administer at home. Here's how to use it:

1. **Wait until your dog's a little sleepy.**

2. **Bring them to the refrigerator and swipe some peanut butter or broth at their eye level.**

3. **As they're licking the refrigerator, gently squeeze into their ear canal the amount of ointment specified by your veterinarian.**

4. **Massage their ear as you praise them warmly.**

Nose

You don't have to know much about the nose, though it is helpful for tipping you off to the fact that your puppy's not feeling well. A warm nose can be caused by elevated temperature. (See the nearby sidebar, "Taking your puppy's temperature.") However, weather conditions also can lead to dryness or fluctuation in body temperature. If you suspect that your puppy has a fever, touch their other body areas without fur (belly, paws, or the inside of their ears) or take their temperature. Did I mention that you have to do it rectally? What fun!

A dog's nose can become discolored. One potential cause is the sun. When your puppy hangs in the sun, protect their nose with sunblock with a sun protection factor of 45. Another reason a pup's nose may become discolored is an allergic reaction to a plastic food dish or household detergent. In such cases, use stainless steel bowls for your dog's dishes, and clean with environmentally safe products.

TAKING YOUR PUPPY'S TEMPERATURE

Here's a fun activity your whole family will enjoy. Okay, maybe not. With all the technological improvements of late, your puppy still has to endure the old thermometer-in-the-bottom style of preventive care. I recommend that you occupy their mouth with a tasty treat (peanut butter and treats top the list for my dog Whoopsie) while you dip a rectal thermometer in petroleum jelly and slide it in gently. The time varies by thermometer; read the instructions for use. Note that a resting dog's temperature is between 100.5 degrees and 102.5 degrees, which is much warmer than the normal 98.6 degrees for humans. A good idea is to take your puppy's temperature when they're well so that you can gauge an illness when symptoms show.

Taking Your Pup for Regular Checkups

Puppies, like kids, need vaccinations and regular checkups. Get out your appointment book and schedule regular visits to ensure that your puppy gets all the protection they need.

A puppy's first vaccines should be given as they're weaned off their mother's milk. Unless a puppy is orphaned, which would require more medical intervention, that usually means a puppy's first vaccine should begin at six weeks. If a series is recommended, follow-up shots are given two to three weeks later. These shots are called boosters. After the puppy reaches doghood, vaccines generally need to be given annually.

WARNING

When possible, spread out the vaccines so that your puppy isn't exposed to so many on the same day. This plan may cost you a little more in veterinarian visits, but in the long run, it may prevent your pup from having an adverse reaction.

Finding a veterinarian you see eye-to-eye with is truly important: You'll be together through thick and thin. Of course, it's a little different from finding a doctor for yourself — you need to make sure your puppy feels safe and happy going there, too. Here are the most important factors to consider:

>> **Knowledgeable doctors and staff:** Those days when scruff-shaking, pinning, and staring down dogs to achieve dominance were regarded as acceptable behavior are long gone. These techniques have been proven by veterinarian behaviorists to terrify dogs and ensure a fearful or defensive reaction. Any vet or vet staff member who tries to intimidate your pup with these forceful techniques or even a stare down should be avoided or educated. Although these practices still exist in some uneducated circles, they're flat-out wrong.

TIP

If necessary, educate staff on how you expect your puppy to be treated, and if they're less receptive, go elsewhere.

>> **A less-than-terrified reaction:** To ensure that your puppy enjoys their vet visits, find a facility that will let you make social calls, or, better yet, find a facility that offers puppy classes.

>> **Clean, organized, and friendly:** Make certain that the hospital you choose is well organized and clean. Ask to stay with your puppy during routine visits so that you can make sure their techniques are minimally forceful.

TECHNICAL STUFF

There are a few accreditations in the veterinarian world, including ones certified by the American Animal Hospital Association (AAHA) and Dr. Marty Becker's Fear Free organization. Though not required by the American Veterinary Medical Association (AVMA), the AAHA and Fear Free certify those hospitals that meet a set standard of practice. In the case of AAHA, they work to verify that facilities are thorough, sanitary, responsive, and safe. To be certified as a Fear Free practice, a facility must show that it focuses on the most recent scientific studies to alleviate their patients' stress while inspiring and educating force-free methods of care, training, and intervention.

Identifying and Remedying Allergies

Dogs with allergies suffer from swollen and itchy paws, itchy skin or gums, sneezing, and eczema. Some dogs even suffer a severe internal upset, like respiratory problems and digestive issues. The worst part is that dogs can't articulate what's wrong, so pinning down the culprit is difficult. Canine allergens come from many varied sources:

>> **Nature:** Trees, grass, weeds, house and garden plants, pollen, mold, dust, dander, feathers, fleas, and dust mites

>> **Household products:** Perfumes, prescription (as well as illegal) drugs, cleaning products, fabrics, insecticides, cedar chips, rubber, plastics, and cigarettes

>> **Food and food ingredients:** Beef, chicken, pork, corn, wheat, and soy

Although most puppies can tolerate most items, a puppy or an older dog who develops an allergy does suffer miserably. How can you tell that your puppy is having an allergic reaction to a substance or food? If your puppy develops an allergy, their body goes into overdrive trying to rid their system of whatever it is. If their skin comes in contact with an allergen, your puppy may develop a rash or spend their time scratching in an attempt to scrape off the offending molecules. If the allergen is inhaled, your puppy may develop a cough — or worse, bronchitis — to dispel the foreign substance. If your puppy eats something that doesn't agree with them, they may vomit or have diarrhea.

If you suspect that your dog has allergies and you're unable to isolate the allergen, talk to your veterinarian. Routine tests can determine what's bugging your puppy, then you may either eliminate the causing element or give your puppy medication to soothe the symptoms.

The most reliable method for testing food allergies is determined by tweaking your puppy's diet. After your veterinarian has prescribed a 12-week hypoallergenic diet, they will use one of the following tests to pinpoint the exact allergen:

Blood test: Your veterinarian may take a blood sample to determine an allergy: using either the RAST test (radioallergosorbent) or ELISA test (enzyme-linked immunosorbent assay). These tests are used primarily for airborne allergens, although they can test for food and fabric allergies (cotton or nylon, for example) in some cases.

Skin test: Quite similar to the way children are tested for allergies, your veterinarian will shave a patch of skin and inject various substances to judge your puppy's reaction.

To prevent possible allergic reactions, keep the following tips in mind:

» Use detergent soap designed for babies' diapers when washing your puppy's bedding.

» Check the various sprays (cleaning, insecticide, plant fertilizer) used in your home, yard, and garden. Don't use any products toxic to your pet. Plain white vinegar is a surprisingly effective pest control and cleaning agent. Imidacloprid and fipronil are also nontoxic, pet-friendly insecticides that do the job well.

» Don't overuse cleaning or parasite products. Flea sprays, powders, and dips can be toxic.

» Watch what you feed your puppy throughout their life. Many dogs have (or, over time, acquire) food allergies. If you suspect a food allergy, speak to your veterinarian. They will likely suggest a dietary change and may want to narrow your pup's diet fundamentally to pinpoint the cause.

Spaying or Neutering Your Puppy

One of the key ways you can prevent roaming, injury, certain types of cancer, and a variety of behavior problems is to spay or neuter your pet — not to mention doing your part to improve the horrific pet overpopulation problem that results in millions of dogs being needlessly killed every year. Close your eyes and consider that image.

You have two surgery choices for this procedure, both resulting in infertility requiring anesthesiology:

>> **Traditional:** In traditional surgeries, which use a knife and scalpel, the sex organs of male and female dogs are removed:

> *Male:* Testicles

> *Female:* Ovaries or both the ovaries and the uterus

> The traditional type of operation limits the heat cycles in female dogs and renders male dogs sterile. Recovery generally takes 5-14 days and often requires that your dog wear a cone (a head immobilizer) to prevent the dog from aggravating the incision.

>> **Laparoscopic (or keyhole):** During this procedure, the surgeon uses laser technology via a miniscule blade to make one or two small incisions. Following an internal camera, they make a cut to the tubes leading to the the reproduction organs. While it is the latest, highly technogical development in this veterinarian procedure and ensures a faster recovery time, this procedure is less widely used. Perhaps it's because the equipment is costly and the procedure requires a steady hand to handle a precision blade inside your dog reproductive zone, making the operation more risky, in some people's opinion, as well.

TECHNICAL STUFF

Many dog lovers request a gastropexy during their dog's spay or neuter procedure. It tackles a separate health concern: It staples the stomach down to prevent a fatal condition known as *bloat*, in which the stomach fills with gas and twists. (For more on bloat, check out Chapter 19.)

TIP

If you're not planning to breed your dog, do have your dog spayed or neutered. Hormonal drives can override all else, and an intact dog will try to escape the warm, safe perimeters of home to go out and look for a mate. Doing so can lead to catastrophe, but placing your dog under lock and key in the home can lead to great frustration, which can lead to destruction, chewing, and restless, chronic pacing and barking behavior. Spaying or neutering generally leads to a happier life for all involved.

I've loved every dog who lived under my roof, but none was intended for show or breeding, and consequently, all were either spayed or neutered. It didn't change their personalities, and they didn't get fat. Trust me: This alteration isn't like a lobotomy — it simply removes the need to scope out and fight for mates. Here's a list of other common arguments for alteration:

» Spaying prevents female dogs from going into heat and bleeding (twice a year for three weeks at a clip), which can be a mess for owners.

» An estimated 4 to 6 million dogs are euthanized in animal shelters each year. Don't add to the problem.

» Having your dog fixed reduces the chance of breast, ovarian, uterine, and cervical cancer in females and testicular cancer and prostate infection in males.

» Male dogs are less likely to mark your home or fight with other male dogs and are more likely to stay close to home when they're neutered.

REMEMBER

If you adopt your puppy from a shelter, you will be required to neuter them. Some shelters offer to do the procedure for you, and others direct you to a low-cost facility. Altering can cost anywhere from $50 to $550, depending on where you choose to have it done. When choosing a low-cost facility, be mindful to ask how they keep costs down, and use good judgment if the low cost means that they cut corners on medications and individual care for your puppy. If your puppy is comfortable at the veterinarian's office, you may request certain comforts to be provided pre- and post-surgery, such as their favorite blanket or calming music.

WHY NAPS ARE CRITICAL TO A HAPPY PUPPYHOOD

With puppies as with babies, there's a great saying worth posting to the refrigerator: Sleep creates sleep. I'd go so far as to say a puppy's sleep training, or the lack of it, keeps my phone ringing year after year. Here's the secret that most people don't know: Dogs are crepuscular. Before you look up that word, let me cut to the chase. People are *diurnal:* We're awake two-thirds of the day. Some animals are *nocturnal:* They're awake at night. Dogs are *crepuscular:* They're most awake at dawn and dusk, and they sleep for 75 percent of a 24-hour cycle. This is great news if you hop on the sleep training routines listed in Chapter 7, but it's bad news if you're already overstimulating your puppy with constant activity. If you've been duped into thinking that your dog needs entertainment when you can't be with them, you likely have a puppy who is chronically sleep deprived. And how will you know? They have trouble getting to sleep, they don't like being left alone, and they're very, *very* nippy. Flip to Chapter 6 for help — and get some sleep!

Playing for Fun and Fitness

When you bring a young puppy home, they have five needs: food, water, elimination, sleep, and play — also known as exercise. Yes, exercise is a need! Your puppy needs exercise to keep their system in balance. Make sure you incorporate exercise in your puppy's routine. Because a walk down the street can be frightening to a new puppy because of cars, big dogs, and other creatures, games (see Chapter 20) are the best way to tire them out.

REMEMBER

If your puppy were to live in the wild, they wouldn't be permitted to wander far from their territory until they reached six to seven months of age; it's a safety issue, tied to the release of adult dog hormones. Though I do encourage social jaunts to town, I do not recommend that my clients walk their puppies far from home — for many reasons, including their fear-impression periods (as discussed in Chapter 9) and their immature dog-to-dog greeting skills (discussed in Chapter 12).

Exercise outdoors does lead to a calmer dog indoors, but proper exercise is the key phrase. Proper exercise involves planning age- and size-appropriate activities and setting aside time to join in the fun. See Table 17-1 for guidelines on determining how much exercise and interaction your puppy needs.

TABLE 17-1:

Amount of Exercise Suggested for Different Energy Levels

Energy Level	Amount Needed	How Often
Very high	20 minutes to an hour	2 to 4 times daily
High	15 to 30 minutes	2 to 3 times daily
Medium	10 to 20 minutes	2 times daily
Low	5 to 10 minutes	1 to 2 times daily

If your puppy doesn't work off their energy outdoors, they'll work it off indoors. Along the same lines, if you don't run them, they may demolish your couch. No, it's not spite. It's just energy coupled with boredom.

REMEMBER

Puppies don't like to exercise alone. They need a companion to frolic and play with. Unless you have a couple of dogs, you need to exercise your puppy two to three times a day for 10 to 20 minutes, depending on their age and breed. Although this amount may sound like a lot, after you get into a groove, the exercise will be fun and a good bonding time for you and your puppy.

Although all puppy's need to move about, their energy level is fairly set. My golden mix could run for hours, while my German Shepherd Dog-mix poops out after about 20 minutes play. Check out Table 17-1 to determine how much exercise and play your puppy really needs!

WARNING

One common misconception about dogs is that leaving a dog outside all day is good for them. "They need fresh air" is not a valid argument. If you leave your puppy out all day, you end up with a neurotic creature who digs in the yard and barks until the neighbors complain. Why? Puppies need time with you, inside or outside — basically, wherever you are!

Chapter **18**

Identifying and Preventing Common Ailments

This chapter is a virtual encyclopedia of information about health problems and preventive care and vaccines. In this chapter, you'll find a list of many of the common ailments and a list of the more serious conditions that your puppy may suffer from, including diarrhea, bloat, and teething. If you're raising a purebred puppy or wondering about your mixed breed, a few discomforts are known to be hereditary, such as compacted anal glands and hip and elbow dysplasia. In life with dogs, as in life in general, it's better to be prepared!

In addition, this chapter teaches you all you'd ever need to know about parasites, those that feast on your pup's insides *and* on their skin. Oh, the joy! Thinking about any bug — flea, tick, or otherwise — nesting on or in my dog really gives me the creeps. External parasites live for blood — your dog's, to be precise, although some settle for a human snack if the mood strikes them. I describe all these suckers (pun intended) one at a time, later in this chapter.

First stop? Destination vaccination! A good rule of thumb: Prevention is truly worth a pound of cure.

Controlling Diseases with Vaccines

Many highly contagious bacteria and viruses can wreak havoc on a puppy's internal system, causing symptoms ranging from vomiting and diarrhea to seizures, fever, and loss of appetite. The good news? Many of these diseases are preventable with vaccinations. In this section, I detail the many vaccines that your veterinarian will recommend. Core vaccines are considered essential because the diseases they prevent are common and highly contagious — and have a mortality rate. Other vaccines may be a good idea too, depending on where you live and what your puppy is exposed to. Speak to your veterinarian about what they recommend.

TECHNICAL STUFF

When your puppy gets vaccinated, your vet injects *antigens,* or small amounts of the disease itself, into your puppy's vein or muscle. When the antigens are introduced, they act like a tiny army of invaders — two or three little disease soldiers. Instantly, your puppy's internal defenders — the good soldiers — set out to destroy the invaders. The good soldiers win easily because so few antigens are present. Most puppies can conquer the invaders without developing any symptoms. This internal battle of good-versus-evil helps your puppy develop a fleet of protectors called *antibodies.* These newly enlisted antibodies stand at the ready to shield your puppy if the disease reappears. The same holds true with human vaccines.

Core vaccines

Core vaccines prevent diseases that have a high mortality rate and are widespread in the United States. All puppies must get these vaccines or be at great risk of contracting and passing on deadly viruses. These inoculations are routinely given at 6, 12, and 16 weeks of age.

WARNING

Many people have concerns over giving too many vaccinations all at once. The worry is that a puppy's emerging immune system cannot tolerate or defend itself against multiple vaccines, so the puppy can get sick or even die when following a routine vaccination schedule. Though most puppies can and do tolerate the suggested formula, a few puppies cannot. These puppies get highly symptomatic, and — although it's extremely rare — they may die from an intolerance of vaccinations. If you're concerned about your puppy's sensitivity, speak to your veterinarian about spacing out the vaccines instead of giving them all at once.

Parvovirus-2

The highly contagious and often deadly viral disease parvovirus-2 affects the lining of a puppy's intestinal wall. Though puppies get a protective boost against this disease from their mother's milk, your puppy will need three additional vaccinations as well. Symptoms include vomiting, increasingly severe diarrhea (yellow to yellow-gray and then tinged with blood), and overall depression. Although there's no medical "cure," early supportive care is essential to a puppy's survival. Your veterinarian will recommend that you keep the puppy still and well-hydrated and offer you the option of leaving your puppy in their care until the worst symptoms have passed.

Distemper

Another potentially deadly virus, *distemper* is a respiratory disease that passes from pup to pup through airborne discharge from coughing or sneezing or bodily contact. Distemper is tricky to diagnose because the symptoms appear in stages. At first, a puppy may have a fever and loss of appetite, and then they may appear fine and healthy as the disease incubates for six to nine days. Stronger symptoms appear a week or more later, including eye and nose discharge, coughing, vomiting, diarrhea, walking and balance issues, and seizures. If the puppy is unable to fight off the disease, it often causes brain swelling and can lead to death.

Canine hepatitis (adenovirus type 1)

Canine hepatitis, a type of adenovirus, is a disease of the liver with symptoms similar to human hepatitis (though not transmittable to humans), and it can cause death. Symptoms include fever, an enlarged liver, and coughing. Passed through stools and urine, this highly contagious disease gets lodged in the tonsils and can cause respiratory tract illnesses as well.

Rabies

This deadly viral disease is transmitted through the saliva and bite wounds inflicted by infected animals. Rabid animals are often compelled to bite their victims, people included — sounds like a bad vampire movie, but you won't get a happy ending here. The disease enters the body, moves to the brain where it incubates for a month or two, and then causes disorientation, fever, personality changes (increased aggression and biting tendencies), and seizures. In its final stages, the infected animal enters a paralytic stage, can't move its head or neck, froths at the mouth (because it can't swallow), and dies a horrid, suffering death. Vaccinate your pet today!

Noncore vaccines

Noncore vaccines may be specific to a given geography (for example, a Lyme vaccine is important in areas where the tickborne disease is rampant) or may be considered optional if the effects of the disease aren't life-threatening. Speak to your veterinarian about these vaccines and decide which, if any, are essential for your puppy's health and well-being.

Bordetella

Bordetella is the classic kennel cough vaccine that's required by most dog facilities, from kennels to daycare and group training centers. Passed through feces and saliva, it's highly contagious (though nonfatal) and results in symptoms including a dry cough, loss of appetite, fever, and nasal discharge. In advanced stages, it can develop into pneumonia (detected by a chest X-ray). Though kennel cough has no medical cure, you can ease your puppy's suffering if you

>> Keep your puppy calm (because exercise triggers coughing spasms)

>> Moisten dry food to prevent rough kibble from aggravating their throat

>> Remove their collar when indoors

>> Offer time in a steamy bathroom or near a humidifier if the cough seems severe

Parainfluenza

Parainfluenza used to be limited to horses, but recently a strain of the virus has affected dogs as well. A more serious strain of kennel cough than *Bordetella,* this highly contagious virus has a higher mortality rate and is a concern in dog facilities. Depending on the severity of the case, antibiotics may be given.

Coronavirus

Coronavirus is a highly contagious virus that lodges in your puppy's intestinal tract and causes fever, loss of appetite, vomiting, and diarrhea. Passed through feces, it runs its course in two to ten days. Although it's not deadly, there is some debate about whether it lowers a puppy's resistance to other viruses, such as parvovirus. Routine vaccinations starting at six weeks prevent this disease. If it takes hold, lots of fluids help flush it out; in advanced stages, it requires medication to curtail symptoms, like diarrhea.

Leptospirosis

Leptospirosis, a bacterial disease, has not one but *eight* strains. Carried in the bloodstream, it can affect many internal organs but seems to do the most damage in the liver and kidneys. Both wild and domestic mammals can transmit the disease through contact with urine and stagnant water. Symptoms include vomiting, fever, weight loss, and overall pain and discomfort, and it's easy to diagnosis through a blood sample.

Treatment involves a round of penicillin or antibiotics to help your puppy rid their system of the bacteria. Left untreated, it can be fatal in puppies younger than six months. Speak to your veterinarian about the prevalence of leptospirosis in your area to find out whether the vaccine is a good idea for your pup.

Lyme disease

Lyme, a tickborne bacterial disease, attacks a puppy's nervous system and causes a whole host of ailments that should trigger suspicion, including lameness, swollen joints and lymph glands, loss of appetite, lethargy, and aggression. The odd thing about these symptoms is that they may appear and reappear suddenly, and the joint pain and swelling may shift overnight from one leg to another.

The medical treatment involves a series of antibiotics. Left untreated, Lyme disease may cause severe kidney disease that can lead to renal failure and death. If that's not bad enough, Lyme disease can also cause heart disease and nervous disorders in advanced stages. If you live in an area where Lyme disease is prevalent, talk to your veterinarian about this vaccine.

Giardia

Giardia, discussed in the section "Other internal critters," later in this chapter, can be found in open water where your puppy may pause innocently to quench their thirst, and it's contagious to other dogs and people. (Egad!) A vaccine is now available to build your puppy's resistance to giardia. Consider your lifestyle and speak to your veterinarian if you feel your puppy may be at risk.

Day-to-Day Health Concerns

Throughout your puppy's first year, you may witness a range of health conditions: One day they'll be zestful, determined, and confident, and the next day they may sleep late and show little interest in daily activities. After all, a lot is going on under the surface. Their bones are growing and their hormone levels are fluctuating, and their body is growing accustomed to all the little airborne particles their world has to offer, from pollens to pollution. So, how can you know when your puppy is actually suffering from a health problem?

To judge whether your puppy is just having an off day or something more serious is bothering them, take notice of your puppy's happy, feelin'-fine state so that you're better able to recognize changes in both their mood and bodily functions. By scheduling their needs (as described in Chapter 7), you can notice when they're off schedule, which may indicate a health problem. Make a note of what's different, from excessive sleep to refusal of food to changes in their poop. If the issue persists and you need to take your puppy to the veterinarian for a checkup, the vet will appreciate the detailed info that you can provide, because you know your puppy so well.

Teething

Like kids, puppies have a first set of 28 teeth, also known as *milk teeth*. After birth, the adult set of 42 teeth grow up in your puppy's gums and then, between the puppy's fourth and six months, begin to make their descent, shoving the baby teeth out of the way. The process is painful and affects some puppies more dramatically than others, bringing symptoms ranging from loose and watery stools to mopey behavior and loss of appetite to whining.

WARNING

Some milk teeth are stubborn — they hang on even as the adult teeth are making their appearance. Aside from causing terrible discomfort, the double-tooth scenario can affect the adult tooth's alignment or cause tooth decay. Routinely peek inside your puppy's mouth and speak to your veterinarian if this problem happens to your puppy.

Coughing

When your puppy coughs, they're trying to get rid of a foreign particle. The source can be anything from an allergen to pollution or a respiratory illness. If your puppy is coughing, consider whether environmental factors may be the cause and then try to avoid any likely suspects. If the cough erupts irregularly throughout the day or during physical exertion, it may be a sign of a viral infection. (The most common infection is caused by the *Bordetella* virus — the kennel cough virus — but luckily enough there's a vaccine that can render your pup immune to the disease.). In the most serious cases, a cough can signal heartworm or distemper, especially in young dogs who aren't fully vaccinated. If the cough lingers, make a note of any other symptoms and call the vet.

Lethargy

Your puppy is known for their enthusiasm, joy, and innocent excitement. If you notice *lethargy*, a sudden drop in your puppy's pep — for example, they can barely get up to greet you or show little enthusiasm for treats, walks, or adventures — it may indicate a more serious problem. Look for other signs, such as fever, diarrhea, and respiratory issues. If your dog's lack of energy persists for more than a day or two, call their doctor. Although many puppies may display these symptoms when they experience the sudden emergence of hormones, a drop in energy level is often the first sign of internal upset.

Diarrhea

Diarrhea is a common ailment in puppies, and when unaccompanied by other symptoms, it usually signals a reaction to dietary changes or stress (from the drama of a move or abandonment to even the simplest change in schedule). Many puppies have bouts of loose stools during their teething stage and after a vaccine as well; such symptoms generally pass in a day or so.

If the diarrhea occurs with other symptoms, which may include a fever or lack of enthusiasm or appetite, it may signal a more serious illness or infection. Keep a record of your dog's imbalance and see your veterinarian if the problem continues — or if the diarrhea goes from loose and foul smelling to bloody or mucus tinged.

Dry skin

There are lots of reasons your puppy might have a sudden scratch, and most often it's nothing to worry about. If your puppy starts to itch and itch and itch, however, especially in the same place, it might do you well to take note. Dry skin can signal an allergy, a cut or scrape, or a parasitic invasion (fleas, mites, roundworm, and the like). Occasionally, an itch can even signal something worse. If this symptom persists or if you notice something wonky on your dog's coat or skin, make an appointment with their veterinarian.

Constipation

Many young pups have an occasional bout of *constipation,* or trouble pooping. You can remedy it by giving them more to drink and adding a little fiber to the diet. Canned pumpkin, chopped veggies, or a little olive oil can work as a laxative.

If your puppy can't poop and the constipation is accompanied by a sudden drop in activity and a belly that is hard or painful to the touch, call your veterinarian immediately. Your puppy may have eaten something that is blocking their intestines, which is a serious problem.

Vomiting

Your puppy may vomit from time to time, especially if they're a speedy eater or they overeat or even when their belly is empty. (If your puppy is hungry, they may vomit up *bile,* a yellow, frothy liquid.) Help your puppy strike a balance with the right amount of foods fed at the right intervals, especially when they're young.

REMEMBER

Be especially mindful not to exercise your puppy right after eating. It can not only cause vomiting but also lead to a far more serious, life-threatening condition where the stomach twists and circulation is blocked, known as *bloat*. (More on bloat later in this chapter.)

Here's the big question with vomiting: Are other symptoms present, too? Make sure everything checks out: normal eating, bowel movements, and energy level. If you notice drooling, whining, or diarrhea in addition to vomiting, you have cause for concern. These symptoms can signal a host of ailments, from eating poisonous items to having parasitic infestations, food allergies, or life-threatening viral diseases such as distemper or parvovirus.

Gas

Here's a problem that stinks! Gas is created somewhere along the digestive tract and can have many causes:

>> **Ravenous eating or chewing:** Your pup may be taking in a lot of air, but, fortunately, this type of gas doesn't smell too bad.

TIP

Try to slow down their eating by feeding them in a specialized slow feeder or foraging mat — or do-it-yourself by placing a large rock in a feeding bowl. If you have multiple dogs, try isolating your puppy from them if the eating appears to be a competitive feast.

THINGS TO WORRY ABOUT

Where your puppy's health is concerned, it's always better to be safe than sorry. If anything causes a sudden and persistent shift in your puppy's personality and mood or if your gut just tells you to go to their veterinarian, *go!* No matter what someone else might tell you, if you sense that something isn't quite right with your puppy, then something is not quite right with your puppy. Your pup cannot voice their pain — so you're their one and only guardian.

Certain symptoms that your puppy has — such as appetite fluctuations, lethargy, diarrhea, vomiting or a persistent cough, inability to poop, chronic thirst/urination, insistent itching, or changes in stool — can indicate a serious problem. If your puppy shows dramatic symptoms of any of the conditions listed in the "Day-to-Day Health Concerns" section, call your vet immediately and make an appointment. This section is not intended to take the place of veterinarian care.

>> **The chew toy culprit:** If your puppy rips through one type of chew toy quickly, find a less destructible option.

>> **Eating certain foods:** An odd item in the diet can cause gas. Perhaps you changed the diet suddenly or the puppy has a sensitivity to the food you're feeding them — or your puppy may have gotten into something unusual.

>> **Suffering from a health problem:** Foul-smelling gas accompanied by either diarrhea or vomiting signals a more serious issue. When foreign bacteria make their home in your dog's intestine, it can cause disease and infection as well as gas. Call your veterinarian if your puppy has these symptoms.

Bloat

Bloat is a word that strikes fear into the heart of every dog owner. If you're blissfully unaware, bloat is a condition that causes the stomach to twist in on itself. Whether 180° or 360°, this torsion is immediately life-threatening because fluid cannot enter or exit and creates a buildup of pressure on the heart and lungs. Symptoms include a bloated belly, unsuccessful vomiting, foamy saliva, restlessness, panicking, and shallow breathing. Do not wait — shock and death follow rapidly. Get your dog to their veterinarian or, if it's after hours, to an emergency hospital.

Compacted anal glands

Near your dog's anus are two small anal glands that produce squirts known as *secretions.* This odor blast helps dogs identify one another and even provides such intimate stats as the dog's age and hormonal state. Each time your puppy poops, a small squirt of this liquid coats the stool. However, the anal glad can become compacted, and then your puppy has problems. Some puppies are more susceptible to gathering residual fecal matter in these glands, which become blocked and painful. If you see your dog scooting around dragging their bottom, it's a fairly sure sign the glands are compacted.

You can either learn to express these glands yourself (ask your veterinarian to show you) or let the vet do it for you. Unexpressed glands may become infected and require a cycle of antibiotics and, in worst case scenarios, a surgical procedure.

Limping

Puppies limp for lots of reasons. If it's a passing thing, don't worry yourself, but if it continues or worsens, here are some causes to consider:

>> **Thorn, sliver, or obstruction:** Your puppy's pads are similar to a tire: thick and resilient but always pressed to the ground. Run your finger gently over your puppy's pad to eliminate the possibility of an embedded foreign object.

>> **Rough play or overexertion:** Puppies grow throughout their first year: Bones, muscles, and tissues are prone to aches and pains, especially if your puppy enjoys roughhousing and tearing circles around the yard or dining room table. If your puppy comes up lame, a few day's rest and relaxation will usually improve their condition but if their condition worsens or doesn't improve, it could be a sign of a more serious issue.

>> **Lyme disease:** One symptom of this condition is joint pain and sporadic limping. If your puppy's aches and pains are coupled with lethargy, fever, increased water intake, and lack of appetite, schedule a trip to the veterinarian immediately.

Bugging Out: External Parasites

Gee whiz! It's a *whole section* devoted to parasites, diarrhea, and infections. Though making this chapter fun and entertaining may be an impossible task, it's important to keep the end goal in mind: If I can help your puppy remain parasite-free, your house, bed, and couch cushions clear of any disease-carrying organisms, and help you remain calm when your puppy isn't feeling 100 percent, I'll have done my job.

Fleas

Fleas are an age-old problem, and they're not going away anytime soon. They generally hang out in the lower portion of your puppy's body, behind the shoulder blades. Contrary to popular belief, fleas don't live on dogs — they only feed on them. Fleas live in carpets and grass, so treating the problem involves all-out war.

Talk to your veterinarian about safe options for treating your puppy. Your vet may recommend collars, uniquely formulated pills, oil pouches, or other products during flea season. (Be sure to use these remedies only as frequently as the label instructs.) These products repel fleas, but remember that fleas don't live on your dog so much as feast on them, so repelling fleas from your dog may result in their jumping on people. (The following section discusses removing fleas from your home and lawn.)

Don't spray, rub, or squeeze flea prevention products near your dog's face or bottom regions, because most products are toxic. Not all products are created equal. Pet stores sell many of the older flea-and-tick preventions that aren't as safe as some of the newer products.

If you want to deal with fleas in a pet- and human-safe way, you may want to look into nontoxic remedies. Some herbal sprays (home mixed or purchased) containing eucalyptus, lavender, and tea-tree oils may help with flea problems. You can also use a flea comb to remove the fleas from your puppy. (Then drown the fleas in a cup of soapy water.) To discover other non-toxic ways to prevent and remedy flea infestations, talk to your vet and visit dogster.com. (www.dogster.com/dog-health-care/home-remedies-for-fleas-on-dogs)

Ask your vet about flea tablets or prevention powder. Although these remedies don't take care of the fleas you have now, they do sterilize the fleas, putting a cramp in their reproductive cycles.

Ticks

A *tick* is another blood-sucking parasite. Like fleas, ticks prefer furry creatures, but they settle for humans in a pinch. Unfortunately, ticks are found all over the world, and some can carry bloodborne diseases. Unlike fleas, however, ticks prefer to navigate to the front portions of your dog's body, near their heart, and they prefer areas where the blood is located near the surface. (Think head and arteries.)

Ticks are remarkably tiny until they've filled up with blood — to find ticks on your pet, disguise your tick search as a massage session. Probing deep into your puppy's fur, feel for unusual, tiny bumps in your dog's coat.

Removing a tick

Ticks love to climb, so their favorite area is naturally around your puppy's head. Removing a tick is no picnic. When ticks feed, they insert barbs into the skin like fish hooks. If you try to pull out a tick, you end up with a headless, blood-filled sac, and your puppy ends up with a nasty bump on the head.

Removing ticks is easiest before they dig in, but you have to act fast. The low-tech flea comb is your best friend after your pup's been on a walk or hike. Comb your pup with this thin-toothed tool to remove ticks before they implant. I keep a separate comb for the kids' hair. (Yes, I flea-comb my kids. Try it before you laugh — it's *effective*.)

THE QUICK SCOOP ON TICK DISEASES

Because ticks feast on blood from birds and other animals on up through the food chain, they often carry diseases. Here are the seven most common diseases:

- **Lyme disease (canine borreliosis):** Lyme disease has spread to more than 47 states. It can affect most mammals (including you) and is transmitted through the common deer tick. (Nearly 50 percent of all adult deer ticks carry the disease.) After the disease gets into your dog's system, it seeks out joints, causing painful inflammation, fever, loss of appetite, and lameness. Left untreated, your dog's kidneys, heart, and neurological processes may be in danger.

- **Rocky Mountain spotted fever:** Ticks carrying this disease are most common in the southeast United States, but they aren't confined to that region. It causes failure of blood-clotting mechanisms, rash, fever, loose and bloody stools, bloody urine, nosebleeds, and respiratory difficulty.

- **Canine anaplasmosis:** This bacterial disease is found the world over and is recognized by its symptoms of fever, lethargy, lack of appetite, joint pain, and lameness. The bacteria is transmitted through the deer tick, western black-legged tick, and brown dog tick.

- **Canine ehrlichiosis:** This nasty condition is transmitted by a brown dog tick (although deer ticks are also in question). Canine ehrlichiosis causes severe anemia, fever, bruises, and bleeding disorders by attacking the white blood cells.

- **Canine babesiosis:** This disease is more common in Europe than in the United States, though the number of cases in the South is growing. It causes severe anemia.

- **Canine hepatozoonosis:** Ambylomma maculatum ticks (say that five times fast) carry hepatozoonosis and can go on to infect many major organs of the dog; however, infection is generally subclinical. (That's doctor talk for a condition that isn't severe enough to present observable symptoms.) Found in the South and Southeast, this disease is identifiable by fever, lack of appetite, weight loss, bloody diarrhea, as well as some bone and muscle issues.

- **Canine bartonellosis:** Like other tick-borne infections, this one is accompanied by fever, vomiting, and diarrhea, in addition to lameness, swelling of the lymph nodes, and inflammation of the nose and eyes (and heart muscles, but you can't see that).

Your veterinarian can run a *titer* test, which measures levels of antibodies or immunity to determine whether your dog has been infected with any of these diseases and needs treatment.

To remove a tick that's already bitten down, follow these steps:

1. **Stun the tick for 30 seconds with a cotton ball soaked in mineral oil.**

2. **With special tick-removing tweezers (available at pet stores), press down on the skin on either side of the tick.**

3. **Squeeze tightly the skin surrounding the tick and grasp the head.**

4. **Lift up and out.**

   WARNING

   This step can be painful for your pup, so you may want to give them a spoonful of peanut butter or some biscuits while you take care of the removal business.

5. **Dispose of the tick.**

   TIP

   It's hard to kill these (blood) suckers. They're drown-proof, squish-proof, and squeeze-proof. I find that the best way to kill ticks is to burn them or drop them into a jar of bleach, rubbing alcohol, or vodka (for lower toxicity). If you have children, keep the jar out of their reach.

6. **Wash your hands when you're done.**

Deterring ticks in the first place

The following tips can help you prevent ticks from feasting on your puppy:

» **Walk your puppy in the open sunshine.** Walking in the sunshine is safer because most ticks prefer to hang out in shaded, woody areas.

» **Clean up your yard.** Ticks lay their eggs, hundreds at a time, in damp, shady environments (like tall grass and leaves). They have several hosts and can pick up bacterial infections from any one of them. Charming.

» **Inspect yourself and your puppy during and after every walk in the woods or a field.** If you're with a human partner, take turns looking each other over from head to toe. If traveling alone, bring a mirror. Ticks can latch on at any level — they fall from trees, attach to the undergrowth, and crawl on the ground. How delightful!

» **Wear protective clothing.** To protect yourself, wear light colors (making the ticks easier to spot), tuck your pant legs into your socks, and wear a cap.

» **Apply a homemade, nontoxic spray.** Spray your puppy with a mixture of eucalyptus, lavender, and tea tree oil.

» **Speak to your veterinarian about recommending a good topical treatment to prevent ticks.** Many products on the market are less toxic and highly effective tick repellants. With topical spot treatments, you put a drop of the product on the puppy's skin; the repellent moves through the pup's oil glands and hair follicles to cover the whole body.

If you prefer a spray repellent to a topical one, remember not to spray repellent around your puppy's eyes. To treat their forehead and ears, place the product on a glove and massage it into those hard-to-reach areas. Don't forget the paws.

Store-bought tick products are toxic; placement is important to prevent your puppy from licking their body after treatment. If they're tempted, occupy them with their favorite game until the product dries.

Ringworm

Funnily enough (I guess), ringworm isn't a worm — it's a fungus. Round and irritating, this parasite feasts on the outermost layer of skin, on nails, and on hair follicles and is prevalent the world over. While most adult dogs develop a natural immunity to ringworm, it isn't uncommon in young puppies. Though not fatal, it's contagious through direct, skin-to-skin contact (dog-to-dog, dog-to-human, dog-to-whatever-living-thing) — and even through contact with objects or surfaces that an infected person or animal has recently touched or rubbed against. Symptoms do not include itching in most pets, but can be recognized by circular, hairless patches or crusty areas of hair loss throughout the body.

Mites and mange

Mites and mange, which live on skin and hair and in blood, are quite content hanging around on or in the skin or coat of your puppy. Before treating for these parasites, make sure you get a diagnosis from your vet to ensure that the treatment is parasite-specific. (Infections can cause some of the same symptoms.) Read on to find out what symptoms may indicate mites or mange.

Ear mites

Ear mites crawl into your puppy's skin to reproduce. These eight-legged buggers nestle in your dog's ear and feed on the outer layer of skin. The first sign of ear mites is your puppy's behavior — they'll scratch their ear intently, shake their head, and walk funny.

You can check for ear mites by examining your dog's ear canal. If the canal is filled with brown wax and is crusty around the edge, take your pup to the vet. Your veterinarian can determine whether mites (or another sort of infection) are the problem and can quickly get your pup on the road to recovery. After your puppy gets a professional flushing from their doctor, you need to follow up with drops and cleaning procedures.

Mange mites

Mange mites are nasty little creatures that are related to ear mites. However, they're more free-ranging than ear mites and often localize along the spine, legs, head, or underside of your puppy's body. Here are the three different types of mange mites (talk to your vet for a diagnosis and treatment):

>> **Cheyletiella, or *walking dandruff*:** These critters hang out along your puppy's spine and create a lot of flaking as they munch on their skin. The surest sign is intense scratching and nibble-biting along the spine.

>> **Demodectic mange:** Demodex mites, which are noncontagious, are usually transferred from a mother dog to their pups during nursing. Under normal conditions, these mites coexist at a harmonious level with dogs. However, if a puppy gets stressed or is malnourished, they can multiply and create either a localized infection (the infected area loses hair and becomes itchy, red, and bald) or a widespread infection (creating large, inflamed, bald patches).

>> **Sarcoptic mange:** Otherwise known as *scabies,* these contagious crab-shaped bugs burrow into your puppy's skin to lay eggs and sip blood. Their favorite spots are the head, legs, and underside. The surest sign is a puppy who literally can't stop itching all over.

REMEMBER

As much as you may want to control your pup's itch with anti-inflammatories, don't. Anti-inflammatory drugs, such as cortisone, lower an already weakened immune system.

Getting Below the Surface: Internal Parasites

Internal parasites are much more of a health hazard to dogs than external parasites are. Internal parasites are especially dangerous to puppies because they can really mess with the pup's developing systems and can deplete the necessary balance of nutrients.

Heartworms

The nasty heartworm is transmitted by mosquitoes (and therefore is more prevalent in warmer climates) and lives in the chambers of the heart and in the lungs.

Left untreated, heartworm disease is fatal. Preventing this disease with medication is much better than curing it after your puppy is affected.

Look into once-a-month prevention pills. These medications are prescribed according to weight. If you have a pup, be sure to ask your veterinarian how to accommodate for their growth. Though these pills are more expensive than daily pills, busy people often prefer them. They have the added advantage of preventing and treating many common intestinal parasites.

REMEMBER

Follow your veterinarian's prescription. If they tell you to use the heartworm prevention year-round, you should do so. Also, your puppy must still have an annual heartworm test because prevention doesn't work 100 percent of the time.

Other internal critters

This section lists other nasty but fairly common internal parasites (see your vet for the diagnosis and treatment options):

» **Coccidia:** These parasites lay their eggs in stools, and dogs become infected by eating other dogs' stools. Intestines playing hotel to these creatures become inflamed, which leads to loose, watery stools, bloating, vomiting, weight loss, and strained elimination. Diagnosis and treatment are easy when the puppy is mildly affected and the stool that's checked shows coccidian eggs; however, this isn't always the case. You may need to have their stool checked more than once because the adult parasite isn't recognizable under the microscope. If the puppy has an extreme case, the procedure to eliminate the invader can be detailed and costly.

» **Giardia:** These water-loving creatures are found in most outdoor water sources, especially in warm climates. After being ingested, they feast on the inner lining of the small intestine, creating inflammation, which leads to loose, mucus-coated stools. vomiting, bloating, and weight loss. Left untreated, it can cause anemia and dry skin. These parasites are easy to detect, but early prognosis is the key, so get your pup to the vet if you notice symptoms.

» **Hookworms:** Hookworms come by their name naturally: they literally hook onto your dog's intestinal lining where they feast on your puppy's blood, causing anemia that can be fatal if left untended. Puppies either pick up hookworms by eating an infected animal's feces, or by nursing on their infected mom, or coming in contact with worms that creep through their tender skin. Symptoms include bloating, excessive gas, loose and smelly stools, weight loss with a failure to gain weight despite a large appetite, bloody stools, a dry and brittle coat, and even severe anemia and death.

- » **Roundworms:** This type of parasite floats inside a dog's body — in the liver, through the heart, and in the lungs. In their final stage, roundworms settle in the small intestine, where they feast on what's left of your dog's dinner. Many dogs who have a case of roundworms are plagued with an insatiable appetite or no appetite and vomiting, smelly diarrhea, gas, and bloating. Often, dogs with roundworms have a potbellied appearance. Make an appointment with your vet if you suspect your dog has roundworms.

TECHNICAL STUFF

  Puppies can be infected with roundworms *in utero* or from nursing on an infected mom. Older dogs can become infected by ingesting roundworm eggs, which are shed in another dog's stool and contaminate the environment, often surviving for years. Lovely.

- » **Tapeworms:** These critters leave evidence when they inhabit your pooch. I remember once asking my brother why a piece of rice was crawling out my dog's rear end. Turns out it was a tapeworm. Yuck. Truth is, most people discover that their dog is infected with tapeworms by using the white rice diagnosis. Other subtle signs include an increased appetite accompanied by weight loss, rectal itching, abdominal pain, and indigestion. Dogs pick up this parasite by eating fleas, which serve as the tapeworms' intermediate hosts. See your vet if you, too, find "rice" in your puppy's bedding or around their potty spot.

- » **Whipworms:** Whipworms live and reproduce in a dog's large intestine, causing inflammation and the following symptoms: bloating and cramps, vomiting, bloody or mucus-coated stools, a dry and brittle coat, smelly diarrhea, and a diminished appetite. Puppies become infected with whipworms by eating worm-ridden stools (an especially popular activity among pups!) or by stepping in feces and licking their paws.

WARNING

Hookworms and roundworms aren't strangers to humans. Children can fall victim to these parasites if their play area is frequented by free-ranging pets (cats as well as dogs). To prevent these problems, clean up after your puppy, wash your hands after cleaning, and check your child's play area twice a day.

IN THIS CHAPTER

» **Preventing accidents before they happen**

» **Staying cool in case of an emergency**

» **Creating a first aid kit**

» **Learning CPR and artificial respiration for dogs**

» **Dealing with catastrophes**

Chapter **19**

Preventing Accidents and Knowing What to Do in an Emergency

want to do everything I can to spare you the trauma of an injured puppy: No one wants to see their baby hit, scraped, burned, poisoned, or suffering in the heat. But accidents happen, so this chapter will help you both prevent and prepare for the worst.

You can take a lot of proactive steps to avoid mishaps, from off-leash training and fencing to learning what environmental and household dangers to avoid. In the emergency sections in this chapter, I cover everything from creating a first aid kit to administering canine CPR, as well as provide emergency-care tips you can use while transporting your puppy to a veterinarian or an emergency hospital. Knowing how to handle situations from cuts and burns to skeletal injuries can save your pup's life!

Accidents Happen: Preventing and Preparing Before They Do

You can do a lot to prevent accidents from happening to your puppy. Thinking out a few steps ahead and knowing your puppy's personality and passions can stop a lot of incidents before they happen. Is your puppy a wire chewer? Tape them up or coat them with a distasteful spray such as bitter apple or oregano oil. Do you have a runner? Having a dog that likes to venture out into the world beyond can be scary for those left behind. First step: Get your puppy fixed — if procreation is on their mind, away they will roam. (For more on spaying and neutering, see Chapter 18.) You'll also need to invest in off-leash training, trips to the dog park, or a fence. (See the later section "Fences Help" for enclosure options.) Is your puppy intent on ingesting interesting items — food items and otherwise? Keeping your house tidy can help, but having a first aid kit on hand and the poison control hotline in your contacts list is a must.

Puppy first aid kit

Plan and collect items you may need in an emergency. Though none takes the place of veterinarian care, you may need to begin lifesaving measures immediately to prevent your puppy from going into shock or losing blood.

Should an incident strike, stay very calm. Your puppy will be dealing with a lot of pain, which may result in lashing out aggressively, especially with well-intentioned strangers and hospital staff. If possible, muzzle-train your puppy ahead of time to allow quick usage.

WARNING

Do not give human medicines or pain relievers to a dog of any age: You may do much more harm than you intend.

Keep your veterinarian's number on speed-dial, and phone them immediately after an accident. Even if your dog seems okay, I recommend speaking with your veterinarian to discuss the issue and possible preventive tips. Additionally, have a backup plan if your veterinarian is out of the office or on vacation. Ask them to recommend a respected clinic for emergencies.

TIP

You can call the 24-hour National Animal Poison Control Center if your puppy has swallowed something poisonous: (888) 426-4435. (You may be charged a $65 fee; however, the immediate and professional assistance they offer is worth a pot of gold when your puppy is in distress.) Keep the label of the ingested matter on hand or describe what was swallowed; the operator is trained to talk you through the incident, translate symptoms, and tell you exactly how to handle each incident.

FIRST AID KIT FOR DOGS AND PUPPIES

Diluted dishwashing soap	Ice pack
Towels and blankets	Disposable gloves
Bright flashlight	Scissors with rounded, blunt end
Muzzle	Tweezers
Pen and paper	Antibiotic ointment
Poison control and veterinarian numbers	Oral syringe or turkey baster
Non-adhesive gauze pads	Styptic powder
Adhesive tape	Saline eye solution
Cotton balls or swabs	

Playing puppy doctor

After you have put a first aid kit together (see the nearby sidebar, "First aid kit for dogs and puppies"), condition your puppy to emergency handling. Practice when your puppy is naturally calm, and use high-value treats and stuffed toys to keep your puppy occupied and happy. Here are four moves that will condition your puppy to not only tolerate veterinary visits, but also enjoy them!

>> **Muzzle on, muzzle off:** Conditioning your puppy to wearing a muzzle is an absolute must. Make it a game and play just before feeding so that you can use their meals and high-value treats as motivation. Memorize the phrase "You look marvelous!" and say it to your puppy in a silly, happy tone each time they slip into their garment. Sure, it looks hideous to you, but wearing a muzzle at some point in their lives may be a necessary option., and a willingness to wear one may help them get the medical care they need. (Refer to my YouTube channel for visual tips!)

>> **Gauze and hold:** Pretend your puppy is bleeding. Just like with people, you need to apply continuous pressure on the wound. Practice holding gauze on an imaginary wound as you talk in a calming voice. Hold the pad on for three seconds, release, and then offer a treat. Continue to increase the holding time, and always reward your dog after you let go in order to reward their cooperation.

>> **Pretend eye applications:** When dogs feel uncomfortable, they squirm. To get yours used to having their face and eyes managed, have a friend lure your puppy with a treat or chew. Touch the dropper to your puppy's cheek, at least 2″ from their eye. Reward your dog after you pull the dropper away. Gradually increase the time and move closer to the eye itself, using a soft voice and touch, and provide tasty lures until your puppy is comfortable with the interaction.

>> **Tweezers, flashlights, and plastic gloves, oh my!** The same rules apply for these objects: Condition your puppy to the feel, smell, and sight of these strange objects before using them in an emergency.

Fences Help

A hundred years ago, the United States had only 8,000 cars and only 150 miles of paved road. These days, roads crisscross just about every path your dog might choose to explore. Though I hate to say it, because fences create a zoo-like vibe, having one is a necessary evil. When choosing a fence, however, you have a few options.

Evaluating fence types

If you're able to fence your yard, do it! Fenced enclosures allow your dog to have freedom versus constantly keeping them leashed or putting them on a tie-out. Both restrict your dog unnaturally and may cause injury or death if affixed to their tender neck. If possible, include your home, also known as your dog's den, within the fenced area, versus placing the pen in a distant portion of the yard — all dogs prefer to be close to the den when resting or eating.

REMEMBER

Your puppy is a social creature and may not want to stay outside alone until they're older and more confident. Be creative when decorating your dog's play yard. Use jumps and tunnels, swinging objects, toys, bones, and puzzle feeders to direct your puppy's attention when you play together.

You can choose from these two types of fences:

>> **Physical barriers:** These above-ground fences are considered by most (including myself) to be the most humane because they don't require that your dog wear a battery-operated collar that shocks your dog when they cross the flagged barrier.

The variety of physical fences includes picket, chain-link, and split rail.

One drawback to physical fences is that gates may be left ajar and your dog may wander. Be careful, especially when visitors come and go.

>> **Underground electric wires:** If a physical fence is out of the question, consider going below the surface. Working with an electric fence company, you'll determine the parameters and have the fence installed. After the wiring is in place, you'll place flags in the ground to let the dog know the location of the fence border. You then take your dog to these flags with the electric collar to demonstrate how the shock works.

Some dogs can habituate to the shock, even on the highest setting, so be mindful of selecting this as your fencing type if your dog is large and bold enough to burst through the shock.

Many people attest that electrical collars are traumatizing and cruel. They are, however, a less expensive option and have caught on around the globe. Though I'm not one for strapping a pronged shocking-collar on my dogs, I respect anyone's personal decision to do so.

Training your puppy to concentrate their attention

When I hear about a puppy breaking away from their person and tragically getting hit by a car, I want to cry. I always think — could training have helped? After all, teaching your puppy the meaning of words like Come and Stay is so that you're able to use them in a pinch to keep them safe around distractions. Off-leash control can be easily shaped during your puppy's late adolescence; flip to Chapter 13 for tips. Until that time, use long lines, dog parks, or enclosures to keep them safe.

When Accidents Happen

If your puppy has an accident, stay cool. If you lose it, they'll get nervous and go to pieces. Be a rock of confidence. Be mentally tough. Organize. Think. If necessary, get them to the hospital as quickly and efficiently as possible. If you've prepared with the following information, you'll be fine.

Restraining a hurt pup

Even the most beloved pet may bite when they're experiencing pain or confusion. All first aid kits should have a muzzle: See the tips in the "Playing puppy doctor" section, earlier in this chapter, about "muzzle on, muzzle off," or watch my YouTube video on how to positively condition your puppy to wear a muzzle.

If you're caught unprepared, though, you can get by using a belt, rope, or bandana to prevent biting. Here's how it would work with a bandana:

1. **Fold a bandana into a long band.**

2. **Drape the center of the band across the top of your dog's nose.**

3. **Cross the two ends underneath your dog's chin.**

4. **Tie the ends securely behind your dog's ears.**

5. **Check the crossing point underneath.**

    If the crossing point is too loose, your dog may paw it off; if it's too tight, you may choke them.

Transporting a hurt pup

Transporting a dog who has internal injuries is a tricky business. They'll be restless and want to move. Your job is to make sure they don't. If you suspect a broken bone, spinal injury, or internal bleeding, transport your puppy on a firm surface, such as a sled, an oversized plastic lid, or a piece of plywood. Otherwise, placing your puppy on a sheet or towel is acceptable. Don't cover their face, or they may panic.

Be ready for an emergency anytime by having a dog-size board in your home or garage.

Puppies can't articulate pain. They can't intellectualize it, meditate on it, or separate themselves from it. To them, it's just pain — an intense feeling and a state of being. Pain puts dogs in a vulnerable state. It confuses their thought process and their physical organization. Their only drive is to protect themselves and alleviate their distress. Add that state of mind to your puppy's natural temperament and what you get is a fairly unpredictable reaction. Though dogs experience pain in the same way, they deal with it differently.

Helping a choking pup

Choking usually occurs when your puppy is chewing or playing with a toy and is suddenly challenged or startled or takes a deep breath. If you're not around or you don't react quickly, choking can be fatal. One way to prevent choking in the first place is to think smart: Don't give your puppy toys that are smaller than the width of their muzzle, and remove any bones once they can fit inside your puppy's mouth.

If your puppy chokes on something, stay calm and focused while following these steps:

1. **If you have a small dog, lay them on their side; if possible, bring your medium- or large-size dog to a standing position.**

2. **Open their jaw to inspect their mouth carefully. If you can see an obstruction, remove it, unless a bone is jammed into their throat; let your veterinarian team know, because these kinds of objects require more careful removal.**

   Be careful: You can jam the object farther in or get bitten if your dog is panicking.

WARNING

3. **If you can't dislodge the object, try a modified version of the Heimlich maneuver.**

   If your puppy can stand, clasp your hands together around their abdomen and pull up into their stomach just behind the sternum. (Identify this point ahead of time.) Repeat this action five times vigorously.

   If they're unable to stand or they're wiggling, place your hand under their lowest rib and thrust up forcefully from the rib base to their spine.

4. **If all else fails, take your dog to the veterinarian immediately.**

Performing artificial respiration (mouth-to-nose resuscitation) and CPR

As horrible as it is to see your puppy lying there after a fire or a car accident or after choking, ingesting poison, or being electrocuted, it may not be too late to save them. Be quick, stay calm, and think clearly when performing the following steps for performing artificial respiration:

1. **Check for a heartbeat and breathing.**

   If your pup's heart is beating but they aren't breathing, proceed to the next step. If you also don't feel a pulse, see the step list after this one for administering CPR.

2. **Check for any obstructions in the mouth, and clear the mouth of any blood or mucus.**

3. **Pull their tongue out to make sure the airway is clear.**

4. **Shut their mouth gently.**

5. **Pull their lips over their mouth and secure them by wrapping one hand under their chin.**

6. **Create an airtight funnel to their nose with your free hand.**

7. **Inhale, and then exhale air smoothly into your puppy's nose.**

8. **Repeat every five to six seconds.**

If you can't feel your puppy's heartbeat, you must pump their heart for them by performing CPR (cardiopulmonary resuscitation), which means doing chest compressions in addition to the artificial breathing method just described.(Be sure to start chest compressions as soon as your puppy seems unresponsive — don't bother with a pulse check; chest compressions are initially more important than rescue breaths.)

To give CPR, follow these steps:

1. **If you have a large puppy (over 15 kg), lay them on their right side and place your hand over the widest part of their chest. If you have a small pup (under 15 kg), place your hand over the apex of the heart.**

2. **Compress the heart area of the chest in short bursts, one compression per second.**

3. **Give one breath every six seconds.**

   You'll know when you've saved your dog because they'll come back to life.

4. **Get your dog to an emergency veterinary clinic as soon as possible.**

   If they are sick enough to need CPR, they will require post-resuscitation support and close monitoring.

Stopping your pup's bleeding

If your puppy is hurt and starts bleeding, you want to stop it immediately. Bleeding comes in three forms:

» **The everyday cut or scrape:** This injury is no big deal. Twice a day, wipe the area with hydrogen peroxide to keep it safe from infection, and it should heal just fine.

» **A continuous or oozing stream:** This type of bleeding requires medical attention immediately. Raise the body part above the heart, if possible, and apply bandages, one on top of the other, to soak up the blood as you press down on the area to slow the flow.

» **A gushing spurt-and-flow:** This type of bleeding is serious — very serious. Your puppy can go into shock quickly and die if they lose too much blood. Place bandage on top of bandage, elevate the limb (if possible), and put constant pressure on their wound. Drive to the nearest animal hospital.

If you suspect internal bleeding, get your puppy to a hospital immediately. Internal bleeding is a life-threatening situation. White gums, a distended abdomen, a bloody cough, or vomiting spells indicate internal bleeding.

Find your puppy's pressure points. While they're sleeping, feel for the pulse near the hip and elbow joints. These arteries regulate blood flow and, in an emergency, you can press them to slow it down. You can also use ice packs to slow the flow of blood from oozing cuts and scrapes.

Treating bug bites and stings

Most bug bites are no more of an annoyance for a dog than they are for humans. A bump or scratch or a bit of swelling won't alter the day too dramatically. However, if a dog is allergic to the bite or sting, the reaction can be severe or even life-threatening. Symptoms of an allergy include facial swelling, hives, fever, joint pain, muscle ache, swelling, vomiting, and diarrhea. If your puppy has this reaction, seek medical attention immediately.

A severely allergic dog goes into respiratory failure, which can be fatal within minutes. This reaction, *anaphylaxis*, requires immediate veterinary attention. If you know that your puppy is sensitive to insect bites, ask your veterinarian to prescribe a bee-sting kit that can counteract the reaction in an emergency.

Treating snakebites

Although most snakes issue pressure bites when they feel threatened, most bites aren't poisonous. How can you tell? Poisonous snakes have fangs that make holes in the skin. Here are some other general guidelines for telling whether a snake is dangerous:

>> Most native North American snakes that are solid colored or have stripes running the length of the body are nonvenomous.

>> Be careful of snakes with diamondback patterns, stripes running around the body, or those with blotch patterns. In North America, poisonous snakes include rattlesnakes, water moccasins, cottonmouths, coral snakes, and copperheads.

If your puppy is bitten by a poisonous snake, get them to their veterinarian immediately, phoning enroute so they know what to expect.

Treating burns

Burns can result when a puppy's curiosity strikes again and their mouth gets mixed up with chemicals or live wires. They can also be caused, of course, by contact with fire.

Stay calm if your puppy gets burned and get them to their veterinarian immediately. Call the vet's office in advance. Do whatever the veterinarian may suggest, such as pouring cool water over the area before you arrive.

TIP

If your puppy gets burned by chewing on electrical cords and is in pain, apply ice to the burns and give them ice water. Then take them to their veterinarian, who may prescribe an oral antibiotic gel to prevent infection and may recommend a dietary change until their mouth returns to normal.

Treating and preventing heatstroke

Because dogs don't have pores, they can't sweat. The only way they can release heat is through the pads in their feet and by panting. Dogs can suffer from heatstroke if left in poorly ventilated areas, such as a car or kennel, or if tired out or over-exercised on a humid day. If you notice that your puppy has shallow breathing, a rapid heart rate, and a high temperature, cool your puppy gradually with wet towels, a cool bath, or ice around their neck, head, and groin. Take them to the veterinarian if signs persist or worsen.

REMEMBER

Heatstroke is preventable. Never leave your puppy in a poorly ventilated environment, and make sure water is always available on warm days. If an emergency necessitates leaving your puppy in the car, contain them in a kennel or seat-belt harness and leave the car running with the air conditioning on and doors locked. For cases like these, keep an extra set of keys in the glove compartment to take with you so that you can get back into your locked car.

The best solution is never to take your puppy with you on hot days. A car, even with all the windows down, can overheat within an hour — what a horrible way for a dog to die — locked in a hot automobile, just wanting, and waiting for, their caretaker to return.

Hunting for household dangers

Walk (or, better yet, crawl) around your house and look at it from your puppy's perspective. What looks tempting? You can use duct tape to secure wires, and you can clean off coffee tables and clear bookshelves. I know that you don't want to rearrange your living space, but remember that puppies are like babies: They get into everything for the sheer fun of discovering something new.

Hanging there like a snake, an electrical cord or a telephone wire can be quite tempting to attack and chew. The damage can range from a sharp to lethal shock or a mild to third-degree burn. If you notice a severed cord, check your puppy's mouth for burns (and then see "Treating burns," earlier in this chapter).

TIP

For a list of all household dangers as well as poisonous plants and environmental concerns, you can search on line or download and print a free list from my website (Sarahsayspets.com).

Taking care of small indigestibles

Some puppies love to swallow what they chew — especially if you're trying to take the object away from them forcefully. The problem is that not all items can pass through a puppy's intestines. Some get stuck inside, initially causing vomiting, gagging, dry heaves, or coughing, which can go on for days. If that's not cause enough for alarm, the puppy's loss of appetite *is*. If the intestine is blocked and nothing is done to remove the obstruction, the intestine ruptures, which can be fatal.

Treatment depends on how soon you get your puppy to the vet, because you often don't know whether the object is sharp or could break (thereby rupturing the intestines), whether it's small and likely to pass, or whether it's large enough to block digestion. Unless your veterinarian can induce your puppy to vomit up the object (which they may or may not be willing to do to guard your dog's safety), an X-ray is needed to identify what was swallowed. To remove the foreign object, the doctor may order surgery.

6

The Part of Tens

Chapter **20**

Ten (Or So) Fun Games

Puppies love to play and, like children, can learn most of their life lessons by playing games and having fun. Think back to your childhood: What are some of your fondest memories? Most everyone learns their most important life lessons — like how to share, use patience, and speak respectfully — in preschool or by playing sports and games with friends and family. Your puppy can learn patience and self-control through play, starting as young as eight weeks old.

In this chapter, you'll find ten-plus games that are as fun to play as they are educational. Watch as your puppy's self-control and focus develop right in front of your eyes. Using directions like Wait, Sit, Down, and Come, you'll play/train quick responses before your puppy has even lost their baby teeth.

JUST FOR FUN

Puppies love to play Chase, but you'll notice a theme in the games I describe in this chapter: Always encourage your puppy to chase you, not the other way around. Teaching your puppy to follow you and to drop an item they're holding for the toy or treat you're holding is an important habit to instill in a young puppy. Consider the opposite: a puppy who runs when you need them to come or who races off with a forbidden treasure, like your cellphone or one of the kids' toys. Let me help you avoid that habit. Embedded in my description of the games in this chapter is the term "Can't catch me," which is a fun way to alert your puppy when you need to get their attention.

Find It

The Find It game is my dogs' favorite activity. Anyone can play it (even strangers) to help your puppy's mood, no matter what's going on around them. Although I mention this game throughout the book, you can start teaching it anytime.

Overall goal: To teach your puppy to look down to find a reward (treat, toy, bone)

Use it: Use Find It to give your puppy some mental foraging fun with mealtimes, to distract an overstimulated puppy during greetings, play, or introductions to new people or dogs on a leash, or when spotting a squirrel, car, or bike. If you have an anxious puppy, Find It can infuse stressful situations with a fistful of fun!

Directions: Pair Find It with Come, Follow, or Give to teach a quick, happy response and to reward quick responses to other directions, like Sit and On Your Mat.

To play: Begin by tossing one treat or kibble on the floor by your puppy's toes as you say "Find it!" After your puppy catches on, toss the kibble by your own toes. Got that? Now take gradually bigger steps away from your puppy as you say "Find it — Follow." Eventually, Follow will help your puppy keep up with you and stay close by your feet. When your puppy has the gist of it, you can expand the game, by tossing kibbles on the ground for them to forage or by using this game to distract your puppy during greetings and other distractions. For more ideas, flip to the index: You'll find Find It there, for sure.

JUST FOR FUN

Foraging mats are now marketed for dogs, designed to hide away a puppy's entire meal in the cracks and crevices of a durable rug that your puppy can root about in yet cannot destroy. The mat is a great diversion for an active puppy, and you can build in the direction Find It, too. My kids and I love the mats: We spread out a good portion of our dogs' meals and say "Find it" when we put down their individualized meal. Be sure to check them out.

Tug

Overall goal: Tug-of-war is a favorite puppy game that is simple to play, and it just happens to be the best way to teach your puppy to "Give" up an object on cue. Notice as you read how the principles of tug-of-war are used to reward puppies for playing a game they love and how treats can be used to teach your puppy the meaning of the word "Give."

Use it: Since your puppy will love to tug on anything, with anyone, teach them to Tug only on their toys and only on cue. Through this simple and fun activity, you will build up your puppy's self-esteem (I guarantee they'll get this one right) and you'll have a handy new way to redirect their excitement and frustration. Remember this one rule however, especially when just starting out: Pocket and position treats strategically around your home so that each time you play "Tug" you can also teach your puppy to let go on cue.

Directions: This game has two parts—the Tug and the Give. (See the next section.) Teach them the words independently of one another for 2 days, then pair them together!

To play: It's easy to pair the word "Tug" with the action. Take any of your puppy's fabric or rope toys, wiggle it until your puppy grabs hold, then say "Tug" as you apply resistance. That's it. Over time, put a little more umpf into your Tug. Initially, just use a second toy or high value food treat to encourage your puppy's release. After two days of practicing the Tug and Give separately (as described below) pair them together as instructed.

Give (Or Drop)

Overall goal: You want to get an automatic "spit out" reaction whenever you say the word "Give." The goal is to spit out whatever they're mouthing, though not necessarily putting it in your hand.

Direction: Give

Use it: Aside from being a handy playing skill, "Give" has safety features that can't be argued against. If your puppy has something you value in their mouths or an object that may endanger them, "Give" covers all bases. After you make "Give" less of a demand and more of a direction, your puppy will be eager to share their treasures.

Players: "Give" can be taught to puppies early on, so puppies of all ages can play this game.

To play: When your puppy is chewing something, whether appropriate or not, approach them with a treat cup or a handheld treat. Hold the treat near their nose, saying "Give" the moment they release the object. If the object is their toy, however, do not take it — let them keep it. If it's something they (in your opinion) shouldn't have, reward them with a jackpot of treats as you remove the object calmly.

TIP

If your puppy runs off with excitement when you approach them, you can practice in a small bathroom to keep them confined. Or, leave a leash on them around the house to enable a calm catch.

WARNING

Rules: If your puppy is growling or clamping the object too tightly, call a professional. Aggression is no joke.

Tug Tug Give

Overall goal: When playing tug-of-war with your puppy remember this: it's important to let your puppy win at least 2/3rds of the rounds to start. Some people would insist that you're being weak, but let's be real. Your puppy is a lot like a 2-year-old child, science says so, and kids feel happier living in a world where play is interactive not domineering.

Directions: Tug and Give.

Use it: Use Tug Tug Give for general play and to redirect your pup's excitement or frustration, especially during greetings or when aggravated by passersby or out of reach animals during walks.

To Play: Go into a quiet room with your puppy's favorite toy. Initially play in the morning or evening when your puppy's energy level is high. Tell your puppy to Tug as you offer their toy, then pull on it for 3-5 seconds. Place a high value treat or another toy by their nose and say "Give" as they release the toy. Reward them with the treat or instruct them to tug the toy. As your puppy becomes familiar with the game, begin to say "Give" moments before offering the treats, gradually increasing the time until your puppy no longer needs treats to give. Flip back to Chapter 12 for more hints on perfecting the "Give!"

Wiggle Giggle Freeze

Overall goal: To teach your puppy not to nip or jump when excited and how to stop quickly and look at you when you say "Wait."

Use it: This game is a great energy release and a way to involve kids in teaching a puppy self-control. Supervision is a must.

Directions: Wait.

To Play: Start with two adult persons and one puppy, adding more players as your puppy learns the rules. Eventually, up to five people can play — but assign only one person the role of Leader — the one who gives the puppy and the rest of the players directions.

Go into an open area with your puppy and have the leader tell the players when they can start to wiggle and dance! If your puppy begins to get excited, instruct "Wait." Repeat "Wait" in a strong voice as you stop abruptly. Toss a toy for your puppy to reward their self-control!

Two-Toy Toss

Overall goal: To teach early fetching skills and remind your puppy that people are the ones to watch.

Use it: Play this game anywhere, anytime, indoors or out.

Directions: Fetch, Go Get It, Bring and Give

To play: Gather two or more toys or balls. Toss one toy, saying "Fetch" or "Go Get It!" and cheering your puppy on as they race towards their toy. If they turn to you with the ball, say "Good puppy," but then produce and play with another similar or identical toy as you race away in the opposite direction, saying "Can't catch me." If your puppy chases you with the toy, say "Bring," but don't demand that they drop the toy at your feet. Puppies, like kids, have to learn to share. If your puppy ends up at your feet with the toy in their mouth, just ignore them as you play with your object. When and if they spit out their toy, say "Give," requiring that your puppy hold still on all four paws before you toss the toy you're holding. Now pick up the first toy and start the game over from the top. Play three to five times, and then quit before your puppy loses interest.

Avoid chasing your puppy for the toy (or any object, for that matter), because they will see your insistence as confrontational play and prize envy. If you don't have two toys, use a treat to encourage them to share, but the same rules apply: Four on the floor and calm before you reward your puppy or toss a toy.

Your puppy's ability to track motion and focus doesn't kick in until about 16 weeks of age, so use short tosses to build their success rate — and don't lose hope if your puppy loses interest. The chasing impulse develops later.

Fishing for Fido

Overall goal: Here's another great predatory and impulse-control game! The goal here is to redirect predatory impulses and encourage following fun!

Use it: This game is a great way to teach your puppy important leash skills while having fun and burning off some energy.

Directions: Go Get Your Toy, Give. Follow

To play: Buy a commercial puppy play pole or make one yourself by tying your puppy's favorite toy to a pole or stick. Bounce the toy along as you say to your puppy, "Go get your toy!" If your puppy loves to tug, teach them to release on the word *Give* by periodically waving a smelly treat in front of their nose and rewarding them as they release the toy.

If your puppy wants to keep playing even when you don't, find a strong object or tree to attach the pole to so that they can play when the mood strikes.

When using this game on walks, pair the play with "Follow" to encourage your puppy's cooperation.

Swing Toss — Can't Catch Me

Overall goal: To release energy and to teach your puppy to run with kids and people without physically jumping or grabbing at them

Directions: Can't Catch Me, Follow, Wait

To play: Tie a favorite toy or an empty soda bottle (cap and label removed) or non-destructible plastic toy (something your puppy cannot easily clamp down on) to a 10-foot rope; if there is an opening, such as with a bottle, spice up the game by slathering some peanut butter around the mouth of the bottle. In a yard or field, say "Can't catch me" and run off in an unpredictable direction. As you come to a stop, say "Wait" and let your puppy play or lick the opening. If the yard or field has tall grass, use it as cover to spice up the game.

Toy Along, Tag Along (also known as The Squeak-Toy Shuffle)

Overall goal: To release energy and teach your puppy to follow along without jumping or nipping at anyone's ankles.

Use it: Toy Along, Tag Along encourages following skills and can be played indoors or out. This game is a great diversion for ankle-happy nippers.

To play: Tie a squeak or rope toy to a 4-foot leash or line, and attach the other end of the line to your shoelace or ankle. Walk around, doing whatever you do. Puppies love to wrestle moving objects: Better the toy than your ankle.

WARNING

Don't move too quickly or snap the object out of your puppy's mouth. If they start to tug assertively, either ignore it or remove the toy from your ankle and clip it to an immovable piece of furniture.

Hide-and-Seek

Overall goal: Hide-and-Seek can be played with people and objects. With people, it teaches your puppy to listen and find you even when they can't see you; with toys, Hide-and-Seek works on impulse control and nose tracking skills.

Directions: Stay, Come, Find *<a toy or person by name>*

To play with toys: Until your puppy learns a strong Stay, as outlined in Chapter 11, have one person hold the puppy as you wave and say, for example, "Here's Piggy." (The choice of toy is up to you.) At first, just hide Piggy behind your back for three to five seconds, and then bring Piggy back into view as you say, "Where's Piggy?" and reward your puppy the moment they nose the toy. Soon your puppy will note Piggy's whereabouts — now you're ready to play the game. Have someone hold your puppy, or leave them in a short Stay. Stand back ten feet, again hide Piggy behind your back, and say, "Where's Piggy?" Reward your puppy the moment they find Piggy. Now hide Piggy somewhere else nearby, and when your puppy runs over, point to wherever Piggy is hiding out. Gradually hide Piggy in more challenging places, and show your puppy how to sniff for the toy if they ever get confused by getting down to their level and pretending to sniff about.

To play with people: If you're alone, you can hide from your puppy and call them by name. Make the hiding spots easy at first, around a nearby tree or piece of furniture so that your puppy wins every time. If your puppy is playing with multiple people, use treat cups to encourage a positive association with leaving one person and racing to another. The player whose name is spoken should kneel down and shake the treat cup as they call out the puppy's name and say "Come"; other players should stand silently and ignore the puppy. (See Figure 20-1 for an illustration.)

FIGURE 20-1:
Play hide-and-seek to encourage your dog's coming skills.

JUST FOR FUN

As your puppy gets better at seeking, increase your distance, eventually hiding in increasingly more concealed spots. When they catch on, you can play outdoors on a long line or in a fenced enclosure. Avoid correcting your puppy if they lose interest—limiting game time ensures fun. Don't forget to call to your puppy as you shake the cup; doing so helps them find you.

Superball Soccer

Overall goal: To release energy and teach puppy to chase toys instead of people.

Use it: Play indoors or out, using similar balls or durable plastic bottles.

Directions: Go Get It

Players: Any number can play. Play with one more ball or plastic recyclable bottle than there are people playing so that no one challenges or accidentally kicks the puppy in the face.

To play: Go into an open room or field with your puppy, placing multiple balls or bottles on the ground. After your puppy sniffs the objects, nudge one with your toe. Once your puppy engages with that object, move on to another, gradually increasing the engagement until your puppy is fully into the game. Now's the time to add other people to the play field. Just make sure everyone knows the rules — always kick a different ball than the one your puppy is playing with.

WARNING

Soccer involves only your feet. Keep your hands out this game and remind your kids, too — lest the puppy think that jumping on them is more fun.

Chapter **21**

Ten (or So) Crowd-Pleasing Tricks

Who says training has to be all work and no fun? Tricks are like dog training recess — super-creative and rewarding for everyone involved. After your puppy learns their ABCs — Sit, Down, and Stand — spice up your routine with a fun trick or two. Whether the trick is super-simple (like Wag Your Tail) or complex, follow the steps in this chapter to teach your puppy new moves in no time flat, and get ready to dazzle your family and friends. Cute and clever tricks make everyone happy — most of all, your puppy.

This chapter outlines ten-plus popular tricks, but you don't have to stop here. In my book, *Agility and Dog Tricks For Dummies* (Wiley), I outline over a hundred cool moves. Take it slow and steady, remembering that your puppy's love of learning will last a lifetime and that it's never too late to choreograph a fun new routine.

If You're Happy and You Know It, Wag Your Tail

Here's one of my favorite moves — it is not only super-simple but also puts everyone in a good mood. Here's how it goes:

1. Find a happy tone of voice that lifts everyone's spirit.

2. Pick a phrase, like the one I use: "If you're happy and you know it, wag your tail!"

3. Say the phrase, or any other you choose, in your happy voice and — voilà! — a doggie who wags their tail to answer your question.

Give a Kiss

The Give a Kiss trick has lots of benefits. Use it to teach your puppy how to use their mouth for an activity other than biting, and then spread the love by teaching your puppy to give a kiss — anywhere, anytime.

1. Swipe the back of your hand with a frozen stick of butter.

2. Point to the spot as you say "Give a kiss!"

3. Repeat Step 1 on the opposite hand.

   Say "Good puppy" when your puppy licks you — they will be happy to cooperate!

4. After practicing this trick three times, try pointing to your hand without buttering it.

5. Praise your puppy's cooperation.

Now try asking your puppy to give a kiss to a friend or family member:

1. Swipe *someone else's* hand with a frozen stick of butter.

2. Hold their hand in yours and point to the spot as you say "Give a kiss!"

3. Continue to use the butter trick on the next five volunteers, then test it without the butter!.

Now your dog can brighten anyone's day!

Stylish Greeting Tricks

Nearly everyone who contacts me to help them with their puppy has this universal complaint: their puppy's sub-par greeting manners. The fancy term is *transitional stress,* but it all boils down to a den issue. Anyone who comes through your door (including you) is entering your puppy's den — and no matter the personality or breed of your puppy, that's a big deal! Trouble can start here if anyone gets excited while trying to calm a puppy, but it doesn't have to go this way. Instead, you can teach your puppy alternative (and more appropriate) ways to share their enthusiasm. The following sections describe three of my favorite moves — and, yes, they're also great tricks that you can and should use throughout the day.

Go Get Your Toy

Place a basket of your puppy's favorite toys or chew bones by their resting area and by your door. Each time you greet and play with your puppy, say "Go get your toy," and then wait to give them attention until they get hold of it.

If your puppy is overexcited at the door, stage pretend visits with a close friend or family member, or simply ring the bell as you prompt your puppy to get their toy. Play tug-of-war or pick up another toy and toss it — make a big fuss.

When people come in the door for real, have a light freedom line or leash dragging so that you can calmly interfere with any shenanigans by stepping on or redirecting your puppy with Go Get Your Toy in their basket. (See Chapter 15 for other tips on jumping.)

Belly Up

The best thing about the Belly Up greeting move is that dogs can't jump when they're sunny-side up. If your puppy loves to roll up for a belly scratch, start to say "Belly up" each time they do. Soon, belly-up will become their new "happy pose." When greeting your puppy, wait until they've calmed down enough to listen to you before kneeling down and encouraging them with Belly Up. Try it with adoring friends and family, before asking your puppy to belly-up to a total stranger.

Spin

If your dog is energetic by nature, their enthusiasm likely spills over to *all* greetings. One classy move is Spin. To teach your puppy to spin, break up ten treats and, starting at your puppy's nose, draw the treat back toward their tail. Initially reward any attempt to turn around, and then reward half a spin, and then progressively (over four 5-minute lessons) encourage your dog to give you a full circle. After your dog catches on to your vision, you can ask for more than one spin. Now you're ready to incorporate the move into greeting family and close friends, and then eventually to anyone who comes into your home.

JUST FOR FUN

You can easily shape Spin into Wipe Your Paws, which you can use on any given day — especially if it's wet and rainy. It's basically the same move as Spin, so after directing your puppy to the given mat, say "Wipe your paws —spin," using treats initially to finesse the connection and rewarding your puppy's cooperation.

Paw

Teaching your puppy the Paw instruction is easy and fun: Start with your puppy in a Sit or Down position — whichever one makes them most comfortable. Then follow these steps:

1. Show your puppy that you have a treat, and then close the treat into your fist and tap the ground in front of your puppy's paws.

2. Wait until your puppy touches your tapping treat hand to flip the hand open and reward them.

3. When this paw-touching move happens quickly, hold the treat in the opposite hand as you tap the floor as you did in Step 1.

4. When your puppy hits the now treat-less hand, open your palm to hold the paw gently as you reward your puppy from the other hand. (See Figure 21-1.)

5. Now try to ask for the paw in different locations and from a Sit or Down position.

TIP

A puppy can learn many tricks from a single action. With pawing, for example, you can teach your puppy to shake your hand, give you a pumping bump, or give you a high-five.

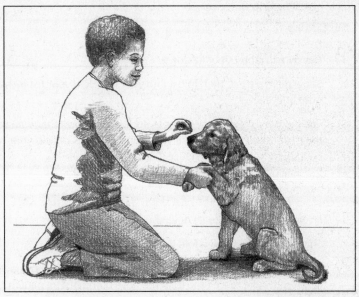

FIGURE 21-1:
"Paw" is always a
crowd pleaser.

Illustration by Barbara Frake

High-Five

Now your puppy's going to learn to high-five. Make sure you've perfected Paw from the earlier section "Paw." Follow these steps:

1. Do two Paw exercises.

   Be enthusiastic!

2. Hold out your hand as though you were prompting a paw, but the moment your puppy lifts a paw, shift your hand so that your fingers point upward. Say "High-five paw!"

3. Lower your hand if your puppy makes an attempt.

   Soon, they'll be raising that paw with gusto!

Bump It

My kids make sure that all our dogs have mastered the Bump. It's the rage with my clients, too — no matter their age or how many legs they walk on. Your puppy can bump your first with their noise or paw. This lesson is easy and fun!

Nose Bump

1. Have your puppy sit or lie down.

2. Show them a treat, then fold it into your fist. Hold your fist inches from their nose at eye level.

3. The moment your puppy bumps your fist, open your hand and say "Find it" as the treat drops to the floor. If your puppy mouths or licks your hand lift your hand quickly, then reintroduce it 3 seconds later.

Paw bump

1. Have your puppy sit or lie down.

2. Show them a treat, then fold it into your fist.

3. Extend your hand on the ground. The moment your puppy paws your fist open it: this may take more time than the nose bump but be patient.

    Alternatively, if your puppy has mastered Paw, you can extend your fist, fingers to the sky and say Paw, Bump. Gradually, flip your fingers down so that your puppy is swatting at your fist rather than your fingers. Each time they slap your fist, say "Find it" as the treat drops to the floor.

TIP

Don't let your puppy become treat dependent. As they catch on to bump, phase out rewarding them each time, offering a toy or praise instead.

Take a Bow

Does your puppy love a good stretch? Betcha didn't know you could turn this one into a trick. Just follow these steps:

1. As your puppy's stretching, bow toward them and say "Bow!"

2. Praise your puppy like they just invented the puppy biscuit.

3. Initially, you can prompt this move (or ask the kids to) by pretending to be a dog and bow like they do — in fancy circles, this is called *mirroring the behavior.*

Repeat these steps each time they stretch. Soon you'll have them bowing on cue.

Go to Sleep, or Time for Bed

I've always thought that the trick Play Dead was a little depressing. It's clever, though, so I suggest switching the direction to something more creative, like Go to Sleep or Time for Bed, depending on the situation. This trick's easy if you have a calm puppy, and it's good practice for high-energy pups. Follow these steps:

1. Give your puppy the Down direction along with a treat. (See Chapter 11 for training.)

2. Draw a treat under your dog's chin and under their ear, to encourage your puppy to rest on one side.

3. Kneel next to, but not in front of, your pup.

WARNING

Avoid staring at your puppy. Staring makes puppies feel nervous or playful. Lure your puppy's head down or pet your puppy's cheek soothingly until it's resting on the ground.

4. Pet them calmly to encourage them to rest their head on the floor.

5. Keep their head in place by stroking it gently while saying "Go to Sleep — Stay" or whatever term you've chosen.

After your pup cooperates, take your hand off their head slowly. Eventually, stand up. Make sure you do everything gradually, and remind them "Go to Sleep — Stay" as needed. Soon, you'll be able to drop the Stay instruction.

Roll Over

Everybody loves the Roll Over routine. Some puppies are into it, but others would rather hibernate in Alaska than roll over. Before you force the issue, ask yourself: Does my puppy roll over on their own? Do they shift from side to side with ease? If you answered yes to either of these questions, your pup will likely be excited about this trick. Follow these steps:

1. **Get a handful of treats and encourage your puppy into the Down position. (See Chapter 11 for Down training.)**

   Using the building block method (see Chapter 10), praise each of the following steps until your puppy does them willingly.

2. **Lure your puppy onto one side by scratching their belly or by circling a treat under their nose and beneath their chin, and then around their ear and over the back of their neck. (See Figure 21-2a.)**

3. **Say "Roll over" as you circle the treat around their nose toward the opposite side of the floor. (See Figure 21-2 b.)**

Imagine a string tied from the treat to your puppy's nose. Basically, you're trying to pull their body over.

4. **If they seem to lean into it, praise them and flip their paws over.**

5. **When they've rolled over, treat and praise them (see Figure 21-2c) and encourage them to jump up.**

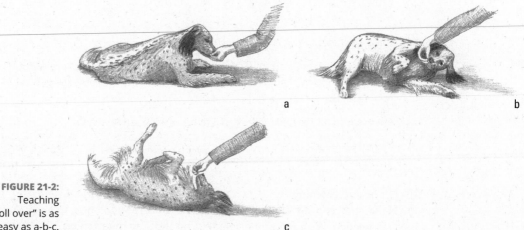

a

b

FIGURE 21-2: Teaching "Roll over" is as easy as a-b-c.

c

Illustration by Barbara Frake

Ask Nicely

REMEMBER

Good balance is a requirement for the Ask Nicely trick. You're asking your puppy to tilt back from a sitting position and balance on their hind paws, like the old begging routine. (Unless your puppy is a natural, wait until your puppy is nine months old before you teach this routine. You don't want to put undue pressure on developing muscles and tissues.) Follow these steps:

1. **Break up five to ten of your pup's favorite treats.**

2. **Find a carpeted surface for traction in a private room to practice initially. With your pup in a sitting position, place a treat a few centimeters above their nose.**

3. **Direct "Ask Nicely" as you bring the treat back toward their ears.**

If they tilt back for a split second, treat and praise them. Encourage the slightest effort initially, and then slowly increase your expectations.

If your puppy is trying but can't seem to balance themselves, stand behind them with your heels together near their tail. Draw the treat back and catch their chest, letting them lean their spine against your legs. Repeat the direction, teaching them how to balance as you hold and treat them. Don't forget to praise and reward when your puppy is in position.

For challenging moves like sitting vertically with their front paws in the air, always release the treat when your puppy is in the pose with two paws off the floor — you don't want to mistake the moment and praise your pup for giving up. If you're having trouble capturing the moment, use a clicker — more on how to use a clicker to shape a behavior in Chapter 5.

Over

All dogs love to jump — over obstacles, up on rocks, onto visitors, and so on. The trick is to teach them what's okay to jump on and what isn't. Before you can quash their people-jumping, though, it's only fair that you give them a good outlet for all their enthusiasm.

Create the first jump out of a broom laid on top of two rolls of toilet paper. A low jump builds your pup's confidence and looks less scary.

Puppies younger than a year should not jump at heights above their elbows — too much development is going on under the skin. Forcing high jumps can cause serious developmental damage.

Follow these steps to teach your pup how to jump:

1. **Place your puppy on-lead for control.**

2. **Let them sniff the jump, and show them a couple of times how you jump the obstacle.**

   Discourage any chewing with a leash tug.

3. **Give your puppy at least five strides of runway space and say "Over" as you trot toward the jump. Jump ahead of your puppy and cheer them for following you.**

   If your puppy refuses to jump, stay calm. Don't pull them over. Walk over the jump several times while your puppy watches. Then try to walk over it together. Although it may take a few tries, your puppy will soon overcome their fear and be more excited for succeeding.

4. **After your puppy takes the jump with pride, put them on a short lead. Drop the lead just before the jump to let your puppy take it alone.**

   Bravo. Enthusiastically praise your pooch.

5. **Slowly fade out your approaching run, but keep saying "Over" as you point to the jump.**

Over can also be a game for the kids. Jumps placed in thresholds encourage jumping to fetch toys and balls. The kids can set up a course, indoors or out, and jump with the puppy.

Through the Hoop

Purchase a hula hoop at a local variety store and then follow these steps:

1. **Practice Over (in the preceding section) with a jumping pole across a threshold or between two pieces of furniture until your puppy is familiar with the routine.**

2. **Put your puppy on a short lead, and let them sniff a hoop as you position it in the center of the jumping area. (See Figure 21-3a.)**

3. **Ask someone to hold the hoop or prop it up securely. Instruct your puppy Over as you run toward the hoop, letting go of the lead as you get close.** When your puppy starts cooperating, combine the Through and Over directions as you start for the jump, like this: "Through — over."

4. **Hold the hoop so that it's even with the height of the original jumping pole and say "Through — over" as they approach.**

   Your puppy may hesitate because the hoop looks, well, like a hoop, not like a level jump. If they hesitate, walk over to the hoop slowly and allow them to walk through it a couple of times. Use food to encourage them.

5. **Prop the hoop at floor level, encourage "Through" as you trot toward the hoop, and allow your puppy to go through alone.**

   Praise them and encourage them back through the hoop by running backward as you cheer.

6. **Gradually raise the level of the hoop and encourage them to jump through alone by saying "Through." (See Figure 21-3b.)**

FIGURE 21-3:
Have your puppy
jump through
hoops for you
for a change!

a

b

Illustration by Barbara Frake

TIP

If you want to be clever (and you have a puppy who won't grow too big), you can practice Through with your encircled arms. Repeat the preceding steps with the assistance of a close friend, this time using your arms in place of the hoop.

Index

chewing, 78, 140–141, 262–268
  being proactive toward, 263
  corrections backfiring, 263–264
  destructive, 16
  puppies older than six months, 266–268
  puppies younger than six months, 265–266
  strategies to prevent, 264–265
  toys for, 164
Cheyletiella (walking dandruff), 347
Chihuahua, 46
children
  calming down around puppies, 123–124
  involving in planning, 124
  jealousy from, 137
  modeling actions for, 123–124
  positive interactions with puppies, 136–139
  socializing puppies with, 165–166
  taking puppies away from, 124
  tasks, assigning, 124
  testing puppies with, 65
Chiweenies, 10, 40
choke collars, 89
choking puppies, 356–357
chronic skin conditions, 41
cleaning stations, 140
clickers, 91
  off-lead training with, 228, 234
  teaching Follow direction with, 216
  for timid puppies, 234
clippers, 321
coats, 24
Coccidia, 348
Cocker Spaniel, 43
cognitive abilities, 99–100
collars
  battery-operated barking, 293
  buckle, 82–83
  chain, 283
  check chain, 89
  compassion wear harnesses, 277
    for protective aggression, 284
    for territorial aggression, 283
  electronic, 1, 262, 355
  head collars, 87–89, 159, 283

light-up, 94
  martingale, 89
  teaching Follow direction and, 217
  tracking, 93
Collies, 44
come, teaching to, 179–180
Come direction, 15, 219, 221
Come-Sit-Lean-In sequence, 199
comfort mats, 211
comfort stations, 78, 159
commands. *See* directions
communication styles
  ears, 107
  eyes, 105–106
  fur, 110
  mouth, 108
  overview, 103
  posture, 103–105
  tail talk, 106–107
  vocalizing, 108–110
compacted anal glands, 341
compassion wear (walking restraint), 86–89, 159
conditioning, defined, 261
conditioning harnesses, 216
conditioning puppies, 162
  barking, 290
  to be touched, 184
  erratic handling, 167
  good habits, developing, 188
  jumping, counter-conditioning, 270–271
  during puberty, 208–210
  travel carriers or kennels, 169
  treat dispensers, using for, 93
  to wear muzzles, 353
  weather events, 162
  to withstand noises, 149
confidence
  introducing puppy to people, 241
  during off-lead training, 225–226
confrontational games, 166
conjunctivitis, 324
constipation, 339
contracts, obtaining copies of, 54–55
core vaccines, 334–335

twitching tails, 107

Twitter, 58

two-person households, 29–30

two-puppy households, 127

Two-Toy Toss game, 234, 369

two-way camera, 93

U

Under direction, 239–240

underground electrical wire fence, 355

unexpressed glands, 341

upward mobility, limiting, 161

urinary tract infections, 252

V

vaccinations, 326, 334–337

vegetable-matter pulp bones, 82

venomous snakes, 359

veterinarians, 55, 142–143

American Animal Hospital Association (AAHA), 327

Dr. Marty Becker's Fear Free organization, 327

finding, 326–327

getting regular checkups at, 326–327

talking about puppy aggression with, 240

training how to act at, 244

vibrating sensation, 92

video chats, 92

visiting procedures, 59

vitamins, 314–315

vomeronasal organ, 101

vomiting, 339–340

W

wagging, 106, 376

Wait direction, 195–196

training during puberty, 218–219

using retractable leashes and, 230

using while teaching Follow direction, 215

walkabouts, 201, 256, 265

walkers, 143

walking dandruff (Cheyletiella), 347

walking restraint (compassion wear), 86–89, 159

walking skills, practicing, 90, 149

water, restricting, 113

water fountain, automatic, 93

water station, 117

weather, cross-training and, 249

weather events, 162

welcome circles, forming, 123

welcoming curve, 158

West Highland white terrier, 41

Western Union, 49

wet (canned) food, 309

whale-eye, 106

whimpering, 108

whining, as signal to potty, 254

Whipworms, 349

Wiggle Giggle Freeze game, 368–369

wolves, domesticated, 98–99

words

associating to everyday routines, 181

choosing carefully, 157–159, 166

Working breeds, 11, 44

wrestling, 128

Y

yapping, 108

yawning, 108

yelling, 110

Z

Zuchon, 40

About the Author

Dog and puppy behavior expert **Sarah Hodgson** is the author of 13 best-selling books on dog training. Her trademark training techniques help dogs become well-behaved members of the family. With more than 32 years of professional experience, Sarah offers her followers a loving alternative to the faddish alpha dog approach pitched by some. A certified member of the IAABC (International Association of Animal Behavior Consultants and a Fear Free™ board member, her message to dog lovers and future puppy raisers — *you don't need to treat your dog wrong to get them to behave right* — is more relevant than ever.

As an influencer, Sarah has a robust following on various social media channels, is a blogger for the *Huffington Post,* and a routine contributor for *Parenthood, Prevention, Martha Stewart Living* and *Country Living* magazines, as well as for *The New York Times.* She's also appears as a guest expert on a number of television networks, including NBC, CNN, CNBC, ABC, FOX, CBS, Animal Planet, and the DIY Network.

Connect with Sarah online at SarahSaysPets.com!

Dedication

For my friends and family — both the ones who walk on two legs and the ones who navigate on four! Thanks for sharing your humor and affection, day in and day out. I love this life we share.

Author's Acknowledgments

My excitement at being at the end of a project is so palpable that I feel like running out and hugging all the people who have been there for me, in numerous ways, throughout its writing. From my friends and family whose reassurance keeps me sane, to my helpers who keep the wheels of my life turning, I could not have pulled this project off without you.

A special thanks to my agent of 31 years, Deborah Schneider. You are my guiding light! I feel your confidence each time my pen hits the paper. In each edition of *Puppies For Dummies* I have been blessed with a great editorial staff — and this edition is no exception. I owe all of you an immense gratitude! Your insightful tweaks and comments raise the quality and comprehension of this book to a height I could never reach alone.

Of course, none of my knowledge would have been formed without the lessons I've learned at the side of each and every dog. Your spirits have been my guide. What a life it's been! I'm grateful for the opportunity to know you and be your teacher.

Publisher's Acknowledgments

Acquisitions Editor: Katie Mohr

Senior Project Editor: Paul Levesque

Copy Editor: Becky Whitney

Editorial Assistant: Matthew Lowe

Sr. Editorial Assistant: Cherie Case

Production Editor: Mohammed Zafar Ali

Cover Image: © BIGANDT.COM/Shutterstock

Leverage the power

Dummies is the global leader in the reference category and one of the most trusted and highly regarded brands in the world. No longer just focused on books, customers now have access to the dummies content they need in the format they want. Together we'll craft a solution that engages your customers, stands out from the competition, and helps you meet your goals.

Advertising & Sponsorships

Connect with an engaged audience on a powerful multimedia site, and position your message alongside expert how-to content. Dummies.com is a one-stop shop for free, online information and know-how curated by a team of experts.

- Targeted ads
- Video
- Email Marketing
- Microsites
- Sweepstakes sponsorship

20 MILLION PAGE VIEWS EVERY SINGLE MONTH

15 MILLION UNIQUE VISITORS PER MONTH

43% OF ALL VISITORS ACCESS THE SITE VIA THEIR MOBILE DEVICES

700,000 NEWSLETTER SUBSCRIPTIONS TO THE INBOXES OF

300,000 UNIQUE INDIVIDUALS EVERY WEEK

# of dummies

Custom Publishing

Reach a global audience in any language by creating a solution that will differentiate you from competitors, amplify your message, and encourage customers to make a buying decision.

- Apps
- Books
- eBooks
- Video
- Audio
- Webinars

Brand Licensing & Content

Leverage the strength of the world's most popular reference brand to reach new audiences and channels of distribution.

For more information, visit **dummies.com/biz**

PERSONAL ENRICHMENT

Staying Sharp
9781119187790
USA $26.00
CAN $31.99
UK £19.99

Facebook
Carolyn Abram
9781119179030
USA $21.99
CAN $25.99
UK £16.99

Guitar
Mark Phillips
Jon Chappell
9781119293354
USA $24.99
CAN $29.99
UK £17.99

Investing
Eric Tyson, MBA
9781119293347
USA $22.99
CAN $27.99
UK £16.99

Beekeeping
Howland Blackiston
9781119310068
USA $22.99
CAN $27.99
UK £16.99

Digital Photography
Julie Adair King
9781119235606
USA $24.99
CAN $29.99
UK £17.99

Meditation
Stephan Bodian
9781119251163
USA $24.99
CAN $29.99
UK £17.99

Pregnancy
6 Books
9781119235491
USA $26.99
CAN $31.99
UK £19.99

Samsung Galaxy S 7
Bill Hughes
9781119279952
USA $24.99
CAN $29.99
UK £17.99

iPhone
Edward C. Baig
Bob "Dr. Mac" LeVitus
9781119283133
USA $24.99
CAN $29.99
UK £17.99

Crocheting
Karen Manthey
Susan Brittain
9781119287117
USA $24.99
CAN $29.99
UK £16.99

Nutrition
Carol Ann Rinzler
9781119130246
USA $22.99
CAN $27.99
UK £16.99

PROFESSIONAL DEVELOPMENT

Windows 10
Andy Rathbone
9781119311041
USA $24.99
CAN $29.99
UK £17.99

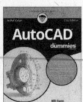
AutoCAD
Bill Fane
9781119255796
USA $39.99
CAN $47.99
UK £27.99

Excel 2016
Greg Harvey, PhD
9781119293439
USA $26.99
CAN $31.99
UK £19.99

QuickBooks 2017
Stephen L. Nelson, MBA, CPA, MS in Taxation
9781119281467
USA $26.99
CAN $31.99
UK £19.99

macOS Sierra
Bob "Dr. Mac" LeVitus
9781119280651
USA $29.99
CAN $35.99
UK £21.99

LinkedIn
Joel Elad, MBAs
9781119251132
USA $24.99
CAN $29.99
UK £17.99

Windows 10
10 Books
Woody Leonhard
9781119310563
USA $34.00
CAN $41.99
UK £24.99

SharePoint 2016
Rosemarie Withee
Ken Withee
9781119181705
USA $29.99
CAN $35.99
UK £21.99

Fundamental Analysis
Matt Krantz
9781119263593
USA $26.99
CAN $31.99
UK £19.99

Networking
Doug Lowe
9781119257769
USA $29.99
CAN $35.99
UK £21.99

Office 2016
Wallace Wang
9781119293477
USA $26.99
CAN $31.99
UK £19.99

Office 365
Rosemarie Withee
Ken Withee
Jennifer Reed
9781119265313
USA $24.99
CAN $29.99
UK £17.99

Salesforce.com
Liz Kao
Jon Paz
9781119239314
USA $29.99
CAN $35.99
UK £21.99

Coding
Nikhil Abraham
9781119293323
USA $29.99
CAN $35.99
UK £21.99

dummies.com

dummies®
A Wiley Brand

Learning Made Easy

ACADEMIC

9781119293576
USA $19.99
CAN $23.99
UK £15.99

9781119293637
USA $19.99
CAN $23.99
UK £15.99

9781119293491
USA $19.99
CAN $23.99
UK £15.99

9781119293460
USA $19.99
CAN $23.99
UK £15.99

9781119293590
USA $19.99
CAN $23.99
UK £15.99

9781119215844
USA $26.99
CAN $31.99
UK £19.99

9781119293378
USA $22.99
CAN $27.99
UK £16.99

9781119293521
USA $19.99
CAN $23.99
UK £15.99

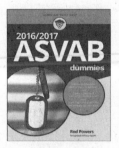

9781119239178
USA $18.99
CAN $22.99
UK £14.99

9781119263883
USA $26.99
CAN $31.99
UK £19.99

Available Everywhere Books Are Sold

dummies.com

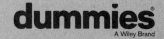

Small books for big imaginations

9781119177173
USA $9.99
CAN $9.99
UK £8.99

9781119177272
USA $9.99
CAN $9.99
UK £8.99

9781119177241
USA $9.99
CAN $9.99
UK £8.99

9781119177210
USA $9.99
CAN $9.99
UK £8.99

9781119262657
USA $9.99
CAN $9.99
UK £6.99

9781119291336
USA $9.99
CAN $9.99
UK £6.99

9781119233527
USA $9.99
CAN $9.99
UK £6.99

9781119291220
USA $9.99
CAN $9.99
UK £6.99

9781119177302
USA $9.99
CAN $9.99
UK £8.99

Unleash Their Creativity

dummies.com

dummies
A Wiley Brand